THE MEN'S FASHION BOOK

The Regency era dandy Beau Brummell was so sartorially splendid he became an eponym that, even to this day, signifies ne plus ultra in men's style and fashion. But that didn't impress Virginia Woolf—she hated "the Beau," as she called him.

"Hovering on the verge of insolence, skimming the edge of nonsense . . . the French revolution had passed over his head without disordering a single hair. An empire had risen and fallen while he experimented with the crease of a neck-cloth and criticized the cut of a coat," Woolf wrote in 1925.

Like so many intellectuals past and present, Woolf was ambivalent about fashion. She understood its ability to reflect character, at least superficially, on and off the page. Clothes, as the twentieth-century fashion historian James Laver once observed, "are nothing less than the furniture of the mind made visible." But Woolf mistrusted fashion's allure and especially the people throughout history, such as Brummell, who placed too much importance on dressing.

After Brummell's age of dandyism and then the Industrial Revolution and Victorianism, men's fashion became exceedingly conformist as more and more people entered an urban workplace, rigid with standards and beliefs about masculinity. Black, brown, blue, and, ultimately, gray flannel suits. An idealized masculine world order and etiquette were perpetuated through suiting, while women's fashion—within its own set of social constraints— was allowed to express more creativity, particularly as seen in fashion magazines. Whether it was what was worn to work or off duty, the acceptable thinking for men's clothing owed more to the idea of a man in uniform than to a means of self-expression.

"For decades in fashion magazines, men were accessories. They were props," says *Vogue* legend Grace Coddington. "If one turned up in a photo shoot, we usually cropped his head off. Women's fashion was about dreams and fantasy; men's fashion was to create this heightened ideal of the masculine, to make sure men never seemed feminized or gay. In the 1960s you saw some eccentricity and flamboyance with rock and roll, but then it retreated. Now there's a full revolution. Men are free to dress however they like—masculine, feminine, gender nonnormative, conservative, eccentric, dandy, it's all good."

This revolution in men's fashion, and the cultural rethinking of notions of masculinity that it reflects, is what made us want to create this book now. There are many books about men's *style*—dressing for success, effortless street style, how to pull off the latest trends—and monographs about designers or icons. But none of the books are actually an integrated, encyclopedic overview of men's *fashion*: the brands, designers, icons, retailers, tailors, editors, influencers, stylists, and photographers. Who made the shoes, the raincoats, the neckties, the swimming trunks, the hats, and even the underwear that make up the canon of men's fashion? When fashion insiders talk about men's fashion, who and what do they talk about?

The list of five hundred entries included in this book was created by Phaidon editors in collaboration with Jacob Gallagher, the men's fashion editor for the *Wall Street Journal*, and a selection of trusted advisors connected to the fashion industry. We considered a range of criteria for inclusion in the book: a subject's relevance at the time they were active and if the work was groundbreaking; individuals and brands with lasting influence on fashion today; key players who sparked a trend or movement, altering the way men dressed; figures who are referenced by designers or have inspired remarkable collections; cultural icons who have influenced men's fashion through their personal style; and finally, current practitioners and brands that will continue to have relevance and impact in the future.

What we hope you find here is a book that both celebrates the rich history of men's fashion and foretells the many stylish, transcendent innovations still to come.

INTRODUCTION

Consider the history of men's fashion as an everlasting lump of clay. The raw matter is the merciful notion that we must cloak our bodies in clothes at all. (Have no fear—this book does not attempt to recreate the thoughts of early man.) From there, at various intervals, men and women, brands and subcultures, and weighty iconoclasts and accidental arbiters of good taste have all pushed upon that lump of clay to reshape it. Their imprint on the form might be fleeting, like that of Willi Smith, a visionary 1980s designer who splashed around with primary-colored prepwear but died all too young (see p.427). Or the teddy boys in 1950s and '60s London, who fancied themselves neo-Edwardians but were swallowed up by punk in short order.

In other cases, these change agents have a seismic impact, as Brooks Brothers did when it packaged the button-down shirt as an off-the-rack commodity (see p.97). Or as Sean Connery achieved during his stint as James Bond, imparting to generations of men the utopian ideal of poise (see p.135). Or, to fall back on the most oft-cited example of a paradigm shifter in men's fashion, as society staple Beau Brummell did in the late 1800s by popularizing the modern men's suit (see p.100)—and, for that matter, transmuting dandyism into an advantage, not some foppish indulgence.

Oh, Beau. I have as much reverence for fair Mr. Brummell as anyone, but I would caution against giving him too much credit for revolutionizing men's attire. This is not to downplay his feats but to make room for the recognition of others. History—and that's history broadly, not just the history of men's fashion—is rife with sartorial rebels. The mind wanders back all the way to around the 1500s and the Landsknechte, roughneck German mercenaries who slashed their sleeves and burrowed mismatched fabrics into their clothes.

This ostentatious manner of dress united the Landsknechte (and for good measure made them look all the more deranged on the battlefield), but was it also in their blood? Is there something fundamental to human nature that invites a sort of sartorial curiosity? I'd wager there is, but sometimes we all just need a little push. Each individual Landsknecht influenced the next to compile this distressed dress code. Notably, some centuries later, the Landsknechte's frayed regalia was still reverberating. You could still see traces of its tattered clothes in the style of the Sex Pistols and in the work of Vivienne Westwood during her pinned-together Seditionaries period (see p.496). Westwood's wares then inspired a faction of young punks throughout London in the 1970s.

This is to say that nothing in men's fashion exists in a vacuum, nor are ideas ever truly lost. Men's fashion is very much alive, bounding forward with ingenuity and then receding back onto timeworn styles again and again. By the time this book is published, there will be yet more new concepts for what to wear brewing up around the world. What this text aims to do is herald the catalysts that took those sartorial swings that have kept fashion in perpetual motion since time immemorial.

A catalyst can take many forms. Through the five hundred entries in this book, we tip our hat to grand garmentos, image makers, corporate behemoths, and men who simply wore clothes really, really well.

In shaping this list of five hundred iconic figures, we looked at both ideas and influence in equal measure. In the fashion world, there have been countless—now largely forgotten—idiosyncratic rakes and dandies who dressed in stunning fashion, but did so largely in isolation, without truly influencing those around them. On the other side, the fashion industry has been stacked with canny businessmen capable of marketing and selling clothes without ever really leaving their mark on the design world creatively. It is also no secret that fashion history has long been discussed from a Western perspective. We have attempted to broaden that scope by including names and stories that have often been unacknowledged and those from oft-overlooked regions of the world. Yet the fact remains that the majority of the figures cataloged here are from North America and Europe, which itself reflects the regrettable manner in which those stories have been prioritized over time. What unites all the disparate characters in this book is that they provided an ingenious spark that spread and affected fashion overall.

The first spark cataloged chronologically in this book is, yes, Brummell, because the flame he provided—a tantalizing, tailored style coupled with his open embrace of intricate self-adornment—can still be perceived in the clothes we wear today.

Brummell, as his once-robust finances allowed, clad himself in bespoke fineries. For Londoners in his social stratosphere, Savile Row became a well-trod destination for such custom costumes. The courtly bespoke ateliers lining this historic street date back to the late 1700s, placing them among some of the oldest continuously operating clothing makers in the world. Much writing has been done about how little has changed on the Row over the centuries. To be sure, the process of ordering a suit remains comfortingly traditional. Clients are measured by hand, after which a tailor uses a pattern reflecting their particular build to fabricate a just-for-them suit. Surely Savile Row institutions would take umbrage at such a simplistic summary. Like sprinters, whose races are determined by a matter of milliseconds, these houses are distinguished by the finest of details.

The London Cut, Anderson & Sheppard's house style, boasts a high armhole and roomy upper sleeve (see p.34). Huntsman cuts jackets in a slight hourglass figure, nodding to its sporting heritage (see p.242). Chittleborough & Morgan—a relative newcomer on the Row, having opened its doors in 1981—cuts a supremely structured suit with a high roped shoulder. Even on a single road known for a single garment, the differences can be as wide as a gulf. Men are particular creatures, and in their wardrobes something as minute as the elevation of a sleeve head can be an earth-stopping consideration. For a dedicated client, an Anderson suit is no match for a Huntsman number, and vice versa. Situated along this fierce little piece of real estate, it's no wonder these houses crow about their highest of high clients. Anderson & Sheppard clad Cary Grant (see p.212) and Gary Cooper. Steve McQueen wore Chester Barrie in his films (see p.327). The Beatles donned Tommy Nutter designs (see pp.65, 350). Dege & Skinner recently fabricated frock coats for princes William and Harry.

Lest you believe that fashion fastidiousness is purely an Anglo concern, let's hop here over to Italy, where after the turn of the twentieth century a clique of tailors emerged pushing a more liberated tailoring style. Much of this mellow suiting was bubbling up out of Naples, a seaside locale where life sashayed at a leisurely pace. Firms such as Cesare Attolini, Rubinacci, and later Isaia and Kiton advocated a sloping, unstructured look in which suit jackets sat as tenderly as dress shirts (see pp.401, 245, 282). This soft style became integral to the Italian look—not merely in Naples but around the country. Its labels abhorred rigidity and its style icons were men who oozed a certain in-the-pocket cool. Take famed actor Marcello Mastroianni, who in Federico Fellini's *8½* (1963) made the simplest outfit—a slate dark suit, pressed white shirt, and solid tie—look like the airy armor of a man in absolute control (see p.320). Off-screen, this élan was typified by Gianni Agnelli (see p.25). An Italian industrialist who had his suits cut at Milan's A. Caraceni as early as the 1940s, Agnelli was the walking spokesman for sprezzatura, the belief that you toss your clothes on in the morning and never, ever consider them again through the day.

But I am getting ahead of myself. Well before Agnelli and his nonchalant league emerged, over in the United States in 1818 Henry Sands Brooks established a dry goods shop in lower Manhattan. Soon after, Brooks's business was inherited by his quartet of sons, who renamed the firm Brooks Brothers, focusing on sartorial fineries for New York's urbane clientele. What Brooks mastered as early as 1849 was ready-to-wear. Whereas previously garments were made to a specific client's specifications and shape, Brooks revolutionized the industry by providing ready-made shirts, suits, and trousers that customers snatched off the shelves. In this way Brooks ignited a new era in menswear: the era of clothing as a commodity.

This isn't to say Brooks Brothers's wares weren't high quality or compelling. Brooks was responsible for outfitting persnickety politicians and economic titans in smart sack suits and pearly white dress shirts throughout the nineteenth and twentieth centuries. Brooks, as the oldest American clothier, came to dress nearly every president and—as a cotton-heavy business—benefited from, and by some accounts stoked, the country's slave trade. Here, the more unforgivable and unforgettable parts of the United States's clothing history cannot be ignored. Yet it is without question that the firm bestowed upon men a bounty of neoteric threads as it coursed through the 1900s, such as stately polo coats, roomy Bermuda shorts, and zesty patchwork shirts.

In Brooks's mold, over the next few decades, global brands bubbled up, slinging specialized ready-to-wear garments to a dedicated clientele. Most of these companies leaned toward casualwear—as in, simply, not suiting—and often placed function to the fore. In the American West starting around 1860, Levi Strauss peddled his hardy jeans to money-manic gold rushers (see p.300). In time Levi's jeans became the alpha of American style, worn by flashbulb-baiting starlets and muck-coated cowboys alike. In England Thomas Burberry struck gold of a different form in 1879 by developing waterproof gabardine (see p.103). Burberry's debonair trench was among the first outerwear to blend technical utility with cutting style. After all, Humphrey Bogart didn't wear a raffish Burberry raincoat in *Casablanca* (1942) simply because it kept his suit dry. Back in the States, just after the turn of the nineteenth century, weathered Maine outdoorsman Leon Leonwood Bean began selling rubber-soled duck boots and pocket-plastered field jackets (see p.304). These burly pieces became the definitive gear for rural toilers around the northeast.

It was clear by the early 1900s that clothing was not merely a single commodity but was becoming a highly segmented one, with specific companies catering to specific needs. These needs, more often than not, were determined by one's given occupation. The world, to be all too elemental about it, had become much larger, and the burgeoning global economy was a diverse one. Field-workers out in Michigan leaned on their trusty Carhartt work coats as diligently as a banker in England clung to his high-twist Charvet dress shirts (see pp.110, 123). The world was ever ballooning, and with it, the clothing market was as well. It must have been nice for Levi's to have been the only denim game in town once upon a time, but how that changed in just a few short decades. Suddenly the company was competing with Wrangler and other blue-jean upstarts encroaching on its market share (see p.507).

And so, through the 1900s marketing became an absolutely fundamental component of the garment trade. It was simply not enough to make a shirt or a suit or a pair of shoes; you had to convince the world that your pure product edged out any competitor. Around this period print media, radio, and, eventually, television were all on the ascent, opening up crucial real estate in which alluring clothing advertisements could be placed.

If early ads were clinical classifieds espousing the merits of a garment in dry terms, by the Mad Men midcentury, American clothing companies such as Haspel, Jantzen, and Penguin had found their appetite for excitement (see pp.226, 253, 371). None did it better than the New England shirtmaker Hathaway (see p.119). In 1951, with an assist from David Ogilvy, it produced "the man in the Hathaway shirt" ads portraying a dignified, slightly salt-and-pepper-haired man in a white shirt. And he had an eyepatch. Why exactly was his right eye cloaked like a pirate? The ads never said. But they worked—drawing customers in and elevating the brand's image.

What these Hathaway ads grasped (with all due respect to the company's surely lovely shirts) was that the clothes were beside the point. The pitch was all about *who you could be* in the clothes. Though sartorial pedants are an undying breed, it became quaint to consider a time in which most men conversed openly with their tailor about shaving an inch off their pant rise or elongating the skirt of their sport coat by a few fingertips. The look itself, not the details that go into it, was the main concern for many men.

In this period fashion itself was scaling up and becoming mass-produced. Men—or at least many men—weren't visiting their tailor to custom-make their suits or shirts anymore; they were often acquiring their clothes like a commodity in a department store. They didn't have the interest, or patience, to consider the actual technical specifications of a dress shirt; they just wanted to know how they would "feel" in it. The ads gave them that.

This is a territory where men's fashion and women's fashion interestingly operated in a similar manner. Though their direct tone may have differed—women's fashion ads back in the postwar period were notorious for driving home the need to appease one's husband—ads for men's and women's clothing both made aspirational pitches that were designed to fill readers' heads with visions of the better person they could be in those clothes. (Over the decades, an advertisement's fantastical relationship to the clothes it shows has grown even thinner. Look at an ad in *GQ* or *Vogue* today, and it's clear for some of them at least that the actual clothes are secondary to the idealized models wearing them.)

It's no coincidence that in the early to mid-twentieth century, this concept of an esteemed style icon got pulled into its sharpest focus yet. Charming sartorial wits such as Frank Sinatra, Cary Grant, and Sammy Davis Jr. were placed on the pedestal and lauded for being paragons of rakish style (see p.151, 157). These men favored fine clothes—Grant was a frequent visitor to Savile Row tailor Kilgour, French & Stanbury—and surely influenced the business attire and eveningwear of certain urbane denizens. Perhaps more striking was the direct impact of James Dean, whose steely style of jeans and a T-shirt was aped by teen boys across the United States (see p.152). They revered his look and recast themselves in his mold. Dean's image was no doubt aided by the Hollywood rags of the time that trumpeted him as a swoopy-haired heartthrob. This period's pushy press set the stage for the onslaught of manicured, well-managed idols who fill pop publications to this day.

It should be noted, though, that Dean's getup was an uncluttered, casual package that could be copied with aplomb. In a similar manner, the loose postwar period reoriented men's fashion. As GIs ventured home they brought back wool trench coats, surplus trousers, and other field-issue garb. (This intermixing of militaria into the contemporary male wardrobe happened again in more forceful terms during the Vietnam War, as the flak jacket was co-opted as an antiwar statement.) Further, during World War II, American soldiers introduced blue jeans into parts of Europe that had not encountered them previously. This isn't to say that overnight men the world over discarded their proper daily clothes for olive-drab garb and denim, but rather that the wars expanded the male wardrobe. It is indisputable, looking back on the long history of men's fashion, that garments birthed in the armed forces—pea coats, cargo trousers, certain forms of field shirt—have been seized and secured as faithful staples in broader men's fashion.

Stepping back to ritzier territory: In the 1950s, as advertising itself grew more competitive, brands found new ways to elevate their image. Italy's Brioni became the first men's fashion label to put on a runway show, in 1952, at the Palazzo Pitti in Florence (see p.96). Suave models in fluid suits and sparkling dinner jackets trotted down a runway perched in the center of a chandelier-filled room. It was the essence of orchestrated glamour.

Attention grabs from brands often leveraged a celebrity's beaming star power. In 1951 Levi's made a peculiar denim tuxedo for crooner Bing Crosby to wear on tour. Nashville tailor Bernard Lansky hitched his wagon to Elvis Presley (see p.380), compelling the King of Rock 'n' Roll to try out splashy cropped trousers and two-tone shoes. Around this period Nudie Cohn, a Jewish Eastern European immigrant, was out in Hollywood concocting extravagant rhinestone-embroidered "Nudie suits" for raconteurs such as Roy Rogers, Tex Williams, and, again, Elvis (see p.132). Cohn mentored Manuel Cuevas, Mexico's most laudable tailor, who carried on his work with can't-miss clients, including Johnny Cash, Marty Stuart, and George Jones (see p.146).

Choice tailors were also called upon to fabricate costumes for movies through the 1950s and '60s. No maker benefited more than English tailor Anthony Sinclair, the hand behind Sean Connery's suits as James Bond (see p.423). His hourglass-shaped Conduit Cut suits solidified Bond's cinematic suavity.

Yet this corner of the fashion world was often still quite reticent. James Bond's suits are incomparably handsome, but they are just suits. There's a compelling case that the staid marketing and pop-culture machinations up until the 1960s kept fashion a bit fenced in. Fortunately, in the next few decades, rambunctious characters emerged and did away with all that predictability.

The 1960s sprawled with subcultures. Communal cliques were hardly a new phenomenon. A decade or so earlier, greasers with their shiny, slicked-back hair and cuffed blue jeans were acting tough in small towns across the heartland. In England teddy boys were united by their zoot-suity drape jackets and "duck's arse" haircuts. The Beatles even sampled this rockabilly style in their early days. (Ever influential yet also quite nimble in their style changes, a few years later the Beatles helped popularize Nehru suit jackets, which were styled on the traditional full-bottom long coats worn by India's first prime minister, Jawaharlal Nehru [see p.343].)

For a far earlier sartorial subculture, you could go back to Les Incroyables in France in the late 1700s, who wore sizable trousers, sizable ties, and sizable earrings that scandalized passersby but branded the wearers as one of the tribe.

This yearning to be part of a clique grew in potency through the 1960s. Clothing was no longer always directly tethered to your occupation. It could be an indulgence that shaped one's self-image. Young folks, free of the concerns of World War II, rejected the rat-race lifestyle of their parents' generation and cared deeply about where they hung out, what music they listened to, what drugs they took (yet another accelerating phenomenon), and, of course, what they wore.

In the States, the first embers of hippiedom began to glow out in San Francisco. Long-haired teens and twenty-somethings (men and women alike) ambled around the Haight in shrunken T-shirts, chopped jean shorts, and denim truckers. The propulsive music of bands such as the Grateful Dead and Jefferson Airplane may have drawn these wayward souls in, but the counterculture look itself became equally urgent. It was clear, from even a quick glance at these ragged, Rapunzel-locked kids, that they were not going in for *The Man in the Gray Flannel Suit* lifestyle of their fathers. Their divergent style became weightier as the Vietnam War marched on, and hippies became a forceful wing of the American protest movement.

Such subcultures are, of course, not strictly an American phenomenon. In the late 1960s in Congo, the musician Papa Wemba helped resurrect the Sapeur style, also known as La Sape (see p.364). This style movement had roots going back as far as the 1920s, when Congolese men co-opted the opulent dress of French and Belgian colonialists and made it their own. Building on this legacy, Wemba and his peers molded themselves into a community of extreme dandies clad in primary-colored suits, tilted bowlers, and meticulously polished dress shoes. These men, who often sauntered through town with walking canes for added drama, were unabashedly proud of their attire. More than fifty years later, this celebratory style movement endures.

In Jamaica right around the 1960s as well, a wave coalesced around a singular item: Clarks shoes (see p.129). Manufactured in England and popularized by Steve McQueen in the 1968 film *Bullitt*, Clarks's crepe-soled chukkas caught on with the American beatnik crowd, mods in the UK, and as the must-have shoe in Jamaica, where DJs wore them on the covers of their albums and singers wrote ballads to the lithe lace-ups.

Clarks's chukkas were particularly enticing to rude boys, a subculture that savored ska music and the sharp, slim suits of the sort that American jazz musicians wore. The modish style of rude boys would have a profound impact on British style in the years to come as Jamaicans emigrated to England. As captured in films such as 1980's *Babylon*, along with the booming dancehall music, the Jamaican diaspora helped popularize smart knit sweaters, striped tracksuits, and trilby hats.

Over in Tokyo in 1964, young men embraced a distinctive Ivy League–inspired style through natty sack suits, cropped trousers, madras jackets, and wavy knit ties. Known as the Miyuki-zoku for their chosen loitering spot in the Ginza shopping district, this penny-loafered pack didn't last long. Less than a year into their loose formation, the police—apparently riled by their Western attire—swept them off the street. The preppy Miyuki-zoku received some sort of vindication just one year later when a group of Japanese photographers published *Take Ivy*, a renowned photo book cataloging the style of baby-faced Ivy Leaguers along the US East Coast. This book elevated the Ivy League look in Japan and the United States alike, turning everyday attire into something to be ogled, inspected, and duplicated. These pieces have become effective staples of any man's wardrobe, the garb of Ivy underclassmen—their white socks, pinched khakis, and athletic hoodies—but they were once subversive in their own right.

It didn't take very long for that sort of neo-preppy look to be co-opted by the commercial fashion industry. In 1967 Ralph Lauren (né Ralph Lifshitz), a boy from the Bronx, began selling ties from a compact filing cabinet in the Empire State Building (see p.294). Lauren rose fast. With the crucial endorsement of Bloomingdale's Marvin Traub, Lauren packaged the best of American style: flannel suits, madras splashes, flecked sweaters. The Lauren look was both inviting and aspirational. Lauren was also an expert image maker. Ralph Lauren ads showed cowboys cavorting in the Southwest, dashing couples out on the town in Rat Pack eveningwear, and Hallmark-card families in cushy cable-knits on a summer jaunt. They were as transportive as Spielberg films, and everyone wanted in.

Well, not everyone. For in the early 1970s, there was a rising class of highly influential fashion figures that cut against all stock norms of men's style. In 1971 David Bowie, a slender British singer, arrived in the United States to promote his album *The Man Who Sold the World* wearing a man's dress by deliriously dandy British designer Michael Fish (see pp.94, 184). The smirking Stateside press didn't quite know what to make of this lanky man dressed in an ethereal frock, but their confusion around Bowie's garb proved its purpose. Bowie and many other stars of this period, such as Mick Jagger (see p.251), Freddie Mercury, and Sly Stone (see p.438), recognized the power that esoteric, envelope-pushing, and often gender-bending outfits had in carving out their image. It's no wonder that their fans would try—and often fail—to ape their beguiling outfits.

What was so notable about Bowie, though, was that he was working in tandem—or at least in conversation with—fashion designers. Menswear and runway fashion were inching closer than ever. Fish's feminine fashions caused a minor splash, but Bowie's most productive industry partner was Kansai Yamamoto, a Technicolor-loving Japanese designer who Bowie linked up with in 1972 as he blossomed into Ziggy Stardust (see p.508). A year earlier Yamamoto had shown his collections on the Paris runway, a landmark move that set the stage for a later mass migration of Japanese designers westward. For Bowie, Yamamoto fabricated skin-tight creations dripping in curious characters and Japanese typography.

A few years later, in 1971, Malcolm McLaren—an industrious Brit (see p.325)—and his then-girlfriend Vivienne Westwood ventured to the United States to promote their London boutique and clothing line Let It Rock. There McLaren met glam-rock titans the New York Dolls, who he began to manage in 1975 with a heavy say in their style (he conceptualized their red patent-leather stage outfits). The Dolls broke up not long after and the partnership fizzled out, but McLaren's finest work was just around the corner.

Feeling the pulse of punk quickening in London, McLaren and Westwood rebranded their shop as SEX, an S&M-infused pleasure pit with tattered trousers and safety-pinned shirts. After spotting some of the band's future members in the store, McLaren helped form the Sex Pistols, outfitting the band in SEX's deliberately destroyed attire. The Pistols were, by a less than kind interpretation, a really great marketing scheme for McLaren and Westwood's burgeoning clothing empire. Of course, punk—in all its bondage-pant, leather-jacket glory—would indeed become an undeniable global sensation and one of the twentieth century's most dynamic clothing movements.

The 1980s arrived, and with them perhaps the most diffuse and discursive period in fashion history, with a veritable buffet of blossoming style movements and brand births. It was, in short, a buyer's market.

One of the decade's earth-shattering events happened just a year in, when Japanese designers Rei Kawakubo and Yohji Yamamoto made their sensational Paris runway debuts—Kawakubo under Comme des Garçons, Yamamoto under his name (see pp.274, 509). No matter that the brands were both specializing in womenswear at the time; their shadowy, cocooning creations set the stage for a new brooding, anti-body-hugging moment in fashion. In time, male obsessives of both brands began cloaking themselves in their voluminous pleated trousers, stretched shirts, and off-the-body tailoring. This is an oversimplification—each designer stands on their own. Kawakubo in particular is impossible to pin down. With each idiosyncratic collection, she presents creations that can be as enchanting as they are enigmatic. What Yamamoto and Kawakubo both offered, though, was easy-wearing drama, and that was a compelling sell to artful types the world over.

The pair also helped open the lane for more Japanese designers to jump out globally. Issey Miyake's playful pleated garb was not merely a technical wonder but offered a quite futuristic and uncomplicated way to dress (see p.333). It placed him in a league with French designer Pierre Cardin, the godfather of radical fashions such as zippered Cosmocorps suits that pushed clothing into a not-yet-arrived future (see p.109). Kenzo Takada, a Japanese designer living in France, introduced menswear in 1984, offering his extravagant, patterned collage clothes to men (see p.448).

Two years later, in 1986, the Belgian collective known as the Antwerp Six reshuffled the deck yet again by showing in London at the British Designer Show. It would be wrong to say that this sextet of graduates from Antwerp's Royal Academy of Fine Arts—Walter Van Beirendonck, Dirk Bikkembergs, Ann Demeulemeester, Dries Van Noten, Dirk Van Saene, and Marina Yee—was aligned aesthetically (see pp.71, 80, 155, 475). Some, such as Demeulemeester, tipped toward a cerebral and often quite romantic minimalism. (Martin Margiela, another graduate of the school, favored not exactly minimalism but deconstruction and disassembly, spawning ingenuity from nothing at all [see p.315].) Others, such as Van Beirendonck, were raucous and toyed with manic colors. But the Antwerp Six's left-field country of origin and unified avant-garde air placed Belgium on the map and proved that great fashion did not merely come from predictable "fashion capitals."

But, of course, it did often come from those predictable locales. In the 1980s Gianni Versace's sizzling, sexed-up clothes caught fire with the disco-fueled, club-loving crowd (see p.478). With his renaissance silk shirts, revealing skin-tight white jeans, and bare-chested models, Versace epitomized the "leave nothing to the imagination" moment.

This is not the entire Italian story. Romeo Gigli was fabricating lush suits and sweaters in inviting earthy tones (see p.206). And then there was Giorgio Armani, who had founded his label in 1972 but was soaring ever higher after creating costumes for Richard Gere's character in the 1980 film *American Gigolo* (see p.42). The accommodating pleated trousers, gleaming white shirts, taut knit sweaters, and massive camel-hair polo coat that Gere wore on-screen captured everything that Armani stood for. It was studied and sculpted, yet magnetic. Armani did not offer boring corporate wear or feather-ruffling avant-garde gimmicks; it was a new form of luxury dressing.

He was surely not the only one aiming for a modern, luxe look. In the States, Kenneth Cole and Calvin Klein were selling modish, minimalist tailoring and slick dress shirts (see pp.133, 283). These clothes were "designed," yet you couldn't tell as much—you could not feel the designer's hand in them, which many splurging daily commuters and big-pocketed businessmen preferred. Klein's biggest legacy in menswear is perhaps his sensationalist underwear ads shot by Bruce Weber (see p.491).

At that moment fashion in the United States was splitting. Big-ticket tailors such as Alan Flusser—who forged costumes for the 1987 film *Wall Street*—molded the braggadocious style of finance guys through contrast-collared shirts, spangled suspenders, and can't-miss pinstripes (see p.187). At Merona Sport designer Jeffrey Banks was marketing primary-colored poppy knits and chinos to the masses (see p.56). It was a cheery yet uncontroversial look that many conventional Reagan-era consumers were looking for.

Convention busters had plenty to choose from too, however. Helmut Lang emerged from Austria in 1987, showing his clothes on the New York runway (see p.291). A kindred spirit to Margiela, with a similar appetite for deconstruction, Lang blended revamped military garb with streamlined tailoring, designer jeans, and just a dash of avant-garde expressionism. It was minimalism, sure, but it had a whole lot of thought behind it.

What was certainly not minimalism was the snowballing street fashion that got its start in the 1980s. In 1985 Michael Jordan and Nike unveiled the basketball star's first signature sneaker model (see pp.268, 349), the Air Jordan 1. It was the spark that ignited a sneaker-collecting mania that would become a mutant, industry-swallowing force in the aughts. The explosion of hip-hop and rap (and the subsequent airing of such music videos on MTV) validated a maximalist mode of dressing. Dapper Dan of Harlem minted screaming-loud "knocked-up" coats and tracksuits with Louis Vuitton and Gucci logos all over them for the likes of LL Cool J and Eric B. & Rakim (see p.149).

Notorious B.I.G.'s drippy color-soaked Coogi sweater became iconic (see p.137), as did Karl Kani's logo hoodies and sweats (see p.273). Often rappers would wear forms of athletic garb in their videos. Snoop Dogg posed in a Pittsburgh Penguins jersey in the video for "Gin and Juice." Eazy-E of N.W.A. wore baseball caps and coaches jackets. These moments lifted authentic sportswear into lust-worthy artifacts of style.

In the 1990s luxury houses began to assert themselves as the key players in the fashion space. Gucci, Louis Vuitton, and Prada: these titanic firms were once accessories specialists (see pp.216, 309, 379), but in the final decade of the twentieth century they stole all the stitches-and-seams spotlight. Miuccia Prada brought forth graceful suits and trusty underpinnings, melding them with technical nylon accessories and outerwear. Prada was confident, cutting, and just a smidge cold—in a way that you definitely wanted to be. Though Tom Ford's Gucci is now best remembered for its sexualized womenswear, its menswear was equally alluring with slick tailoring, moody silk shirting, and luxurious exotic leather jackets (see p.188). Louis Vuitton was the latecomer of the bunch, not introducing menswear until 1997—and it took some time to find its legs. Indeed it wasn't until 2011 with the entrance of Brit Kim Jones—who put on show after show of plush sweaters, heart-stopping scaly trench coats, and gotta-have-it go bags—that Vuitton's menswear really began to shine on its own (see p.265).

The 1990s also gave us the debut of Hedi Slimane at Yves Saint Laurent (see pp.405, 424). The taciturn wunderkind poured forth a reverent 1970s French style with flared trousers, wide-lapeled suiting, and glossy leather outerwear. Other debuts of this period included California native and gothic, drop-crotch specialist Rick Owens and the graphic-heavy, proportion-questioning clothes of Belgium's Raf Simons (see pp.359, 421).

The trends that manifested in the 1990s were surely not all orchestrated from on high in the Paris fashion runways. Musicians such as Kurt Cobain of Nirvana and Eddie Vedder of Pearl Jam in the US Pacific Northwest ushered in grunge with its frugal, catch-as-catch-can style cobbled together through flannel shirts, dingy sneakers, and ratty jeans (see p.131). The distress of it all was compelling and became a bona fide fashion trend to the point that Marc Jacobs co-opted it, polished it, and attempted to sell it (at a much higher price point) at Perry Ellis (see pp.170, 249).

More enduring is the birth of Supreme and the streetwear scene (see p.443). Following in the mold of Stüssy, the Los Angeles surf-rooted label where he once clocked time (see p.439), Brit James Jebbia started Supreme in downtown New York in 1994. What began as a minute skatewear label blossomed into the most influential clothing brand of this chapter in American style. Supreme releases its covetable "box logo" hoodies, workwear-inspired chinos, wool chesterfield coats, and collaborations with everyone from Comme des Garçons to Nike and Damien Hirst in small-batch "drops" that stoke hype. Yet one shop does not make a scene, and so the burgeoning streetwear subculture was rounded out by labels such as Nigo's A Bathing Ape (see p.348), Fuct, and X-Large. Supreme rose above the others, though, by eventually collaborating with Louis Vuitton for a Paris runway show and in 2020 selling to VF Corp for $2 billion.

In the new millennium, ideas sprouted like daisies. Starting in 2001 Hedi Slimane was at Dior Homme in Paris, and Thom Browne kick-started his eponymous label in the United States (see p.99), which helped usher in a new shrunken men's silhouette. Perhaps the world was sick of the sloppiness of grunge. Perhaps people just wanted to show off how fit they were. Whatever the reason, this skin-tight style took off.

And it spread. Slimane brought the look to the runway with calf-squeezing rock-star jeans. Browne was in his downtown New York atelier making nipped suits for particularly progressive businessmen. But soon every self-respecting label had its own iteration of the slim suit. By the mid-2000s it had hit mall stores such as J.Crew—the former mail-order label had kept pace with trends and was finding itself at the center of a heritage-y, Americana-y wave that swept the country (see p.255).

Young men were falling back on reliable, analog clothes. There were many forces animating this desire. Don Draper on *Mad Men* suddenly made the suit sexy again. But also there was a cultural swell around hipsterdom and looking like a lumberjack—even if you lived in a Brooklyn loft. The rise of the internet had a hand too. With men increasingly working and living their intangible lives in front of a computer screen, they sought to convey a sort of traditional credibility through their clothes.

The more burly types were shopping at L.L.Bean and Orvis. Those whose tastes angled more prep were buying from André 3000's Benjamin Bixby, Band of Outsiders, and Gant Rugger (see pp.36, 435). And those who wanted to think a little but get a lot were styling themselves in the image of the mannequins at J.Crew.

This heritage surge, like all waves, crashed and broke apart eventually. It could be said that it was the last dominant trend to reign over men. We are now in a far wilder "choose your own adventure" period in menswear. And there is much to choose.

Streetwear continues to swell. Supreme is larger than ever, partnering with everyone from Hanes and Loro Piana to Oreo (see pp.222, 308), and the hype around streetwear has contributed to the now-massive secondary fashion resale market that flourishes on websites including Grailed, the Real Real, and Depop. For many consumers, men's fashion is in its "older is better" moment, as so-called archival designer pieces from the 1980s, 1990s, and 2000s are eclipsing new designs in perceived value. In recent years elite auction houses such as Sotheby's and Christie's have hosted big-ticket auctions for rare Nike Dunks, Supreme hoodies, and past Prada designs.

In other ways "new" trends aren't entirely new. New York–based creative Emily Adams Bode works with antique quilts, tablecloths, and other aged fabrics to create upcycled jackets, trousers, and shirts (see p.89). Bode is working in the realm of sustainability, a much-talked-about term in the industry. The existential threat that clothing production poses on the planet has led brands to cut back on waste and pollution by reusing textiles or altering production processes to use less water and dye. Yet this is an area where the industry continues to falter. For every niche brand like Bode, there is a mammoth fast-fashion label still burning excess merchandise or manufacturing in a carbon-spewing factory. Though there have lately been valuable innovations—for example, Zegna making runway apparel from discarded scraps of old designs and Patagonia using recycled fleece (see pp.172, 367)—the industry has very far to go.

The COVID-19 pandemic has also shifted consumer behavior, driving folks back toward reliable, functional pieces and predictably away from suits at a time when many were not clocking in at the office. Athleisure, a trend many predicted would die out years ago, has lingered as men and women idled at home in Entireworld sweats (see p.435) and Nike workout gear.

Simultaneously, as many escaped on hikes or took up rock climbing to shake off isolation boredom, outdoor brands experienced a boom. This trend—known as "gorpcore"—had been in the air for a few years, with decades-old REI-style clothes by mountaineering labels such as Marmot, Salomon, and Arc'teryx recontextualized as "cool" (see p.41). Frank Ocean wore them, Japanese collectors hoarded them, and Instagram accounts posted lusty photos of these brands' Gore-Tex puffers and waterproof pants, which nimbly fused high design and high function.

The past several years were also a memorable period for true runway fashion. England delivered a bounty of box-breaking yet shrewdly commercial runway designers, particularly from the creative-director factory that is Central Saint Martins. Grace Wales Bonner's tender collections inspired by notions such as the Jamaican diaspora and the 1970s Lovers Rock scene teem with smart, sporty trousers, delectable patchwork suiting, and intricate dress shirts (see p.483). Jonathan Anderson, at both his own label and Loewe, has proved to be a punchy ideasman with barrel-cut sailor jeans and crafty knitwear, particularly a patchwork cardigan that became a TikTok sensation when pop princeling Harry Styles wore it (see pp.33, 440). And on the runway, Craig Green is constructing larger-than-life human sculptures that he magically pares down into versatile workwear for the sales floor (see p.214).

In Italy no designer has had a greater recent impact than Alessandro Michele, who spins vintage-inspired granny wear for a new generation of young artistes (see p.331). His pussy-bow blouses, tapestry suits, and babushka scarves—all for men—have helped ring in an era of gender-fluid style that has allowed for welcome reappraisals of past barrier breakers such as Quentin Crisp (see p.143) and the disco singer Sylvester.

Equally welcome is the fact that the fashion industry is finally waking up to its all-too-long overlooking of Black designers. In New York Telfar Clemens and Shayne Oliver of Hood by Air are creating mesmerizing, deconstructed, and challenging clothes that allude to masters such as Margiela and Yohji Yamamoto—and they are reaping the press they deserve for it (see pp.130, 355). On a more traditional stage, Virgil Abloh was appointed to lead Louis Vuitton's menswear, joining Olivier Rousteing at Balmain as one of the few Black designers to steer a global label (see pp.18, 399). British designer Ozwald Boateng led the way: in 2003 he was appointed creative director for menswear at Givenchy, becoming the first Black designer to helm a luxury fashion house (see p.88). Hopefully more such appointments are to come.

In recent years the monopoly of rote fashion capitals has also begun to slack. South Korea has emerged as a force in menswear thanks in large part to sensational (and carefully styled) K-pop acts such as BTS and G-Dragon (see pp.102, 200). And African-born designers including Thebe Magugu, Kenneth Ize (see p.247), and Niyi Okuboyejo have come into the spotlight.

For hundreds of years men's fashion has been guided and reshaped by people who are no doubt inventive but who arrived largely from predictable Western regions or with anticipated pedigrees. It's a welcome change that the next catalyst in menswear is likely to emerge from somewhere entirely unexpected.

Jacob Gallagher
Men's Fashion Editor at *Off Duty*
in the *Wall Street Journal*

A-COLD-WALL*

A-Cold-Wall* burst onto the luxe-streetwear scene in late 2015 when founder and designer Samuel Ross was just twenty-five years old. It was as quick-fire an ascent as a new label could hope for; in just a few short years, the brand was named the British Emerging Menswear Designer at the Fashion Awards and a finalist for both the LVMH Prize and ANDAM Award. Ross grew up in a middle-class neighborhood in London and went on to study graphic design and illustration, but his natural talent for fashion was unmissable. He eventually caught the eye of the influential creative director Virgil Abloh,

who offered up gigs at both his Off-White label and at Kanye West's Yeezy. Ross then launched A-Cold-Wall*, with his earliest collections made up of utilitarian T-shirts and sweatshirts that referenced both British public housing and Bauhaus design. The label inched toward high fashion with each passing season: asymmetrical topcoats and sharp shirting replacing graphic tees and hoodies. Today Ross continues to push his genre-blurring vision at A-Cold-Wall* —inventive streetwear motifs laced with studious points of reference—to new and unexpected heights.

Designer Brand

A-Cold-Wall*
est London (UK), 2015.

A-Cold-Wall* Fall/Winter 2020 men's campaign.

Photograph by Rob Rusling.

↳ ABLOH, GREEN, NIKE, WANG

A$AP ROCKY

Since practically the birth of the genre, rappers have lyrically relayed an interest in fashion by referencing household labels, such as Louis Vuitton and Gucci. When it comes to fashion obsession, though, A$AP Rocky stands in a league of his own. In songs the Harlem-bred rapper, who began bounding up the charts in the mid-2010s, has made an art of name-checking cult labels, including Ann Demeulemeester, Rick Owens, Damir Doma, and Jean Paul Gaultier. The musician has even dedicated an entire song to Belgian designer Raf Simons. Such lyrical allusions reflect Rocky's roving fashion sense—which has happily been a mix of Japanese streetwear brands, such as A Bathing Ape, and European fashion labels. The chameleonlike rapper has sported everything from a citrus-orange Balenciaga puffer vest and a slouchy pink peaked-lapel Loewe tuxedo to a slender Gucci suit with a florid scarf tied around his head like a babushka. Rocky has also tried his hand at design. In 2017 he collaborated with Guess on a run of dual-logoed shirts and jackets. And more recently he has created collections with designer Jonathan Anderson and Japanese brand Needles through his creative agency AWGE.

Icon

A$AP Rocky (Rakim Mayers).
b New York (USA), 1988.

A$AP Rocky outside the Gucci Fall/Winter 2017 show at Milan Fashion Week.

Photograph by Melodie Jeng.

↳ ANDERSON, VAN ASSCHE, MICHELE, NIGO, OWENS, SIMONS, STONE

A. SAUVAGE

Adrien Sauvage, a London-born, Los Angeles–based tailor, specializes in shapely, hourglass-silhouetted blazers and tuxedos that give off—to use one of the designer's favorite words—a "louche" look. Sauvage (who moonlights as a filmmaker and photographer for publications such as *GQ*) started his men's tailoring business, A. Sauvage, in 2010 as an offshoot of a fashion venture consulting moneyed European women on how to dress. He came to realize that these socialites' husbands were often inadequately dressed. With this cosmopolitan man in mind, he created his first line,

This Is Not a Suit, which was picked up swiftly by Harrods and Matches Fashion. Sauvage's clothes are often drawn from African subcultures—his ancestral homeland is Ghana—resulting in kente-cloth tuxedos and shoes and raffish, flare-trouser suits. Today Sauvage caters to stars, including Robert Downey Jr. and John Legend, and lank basketball players, such as Dwyane Wade. Still, the regal tailor is often his brand's greatest model, posing on his Instagram in creations such as a velvety smoking jacket, an ivory double-breasted suit, and an immaculate white pajama set.

Designer Brand

A. Sauvage.
est London (UK), 2010.

Fernando Cabral for A. Sauvage
Non-Seasonal 000—1.000—17
collection, 2017.

Photograph by Adrien Sauvage.

↳ BOSWELL, M. DAVIS,
   SIDIBÉ, WADE

JOSEPH ABBOUD

As a teenager, Joseph Abboud, an American of Lebanese descent, got an early start in the clothing industry when he was hired at Louis Boston, a historic East Coast boutique that introduced chic New Englanders to names such as Giorgio Armani and Brioni. In 1981 Abboud arrived at another institution: Ralph Lauren. He worked his way up, eventually becoming the associate director of menswear design before departing in 1986 to start his own label. His clothes reflected a louche confidence that was more commonly seen from Italian labels of the time. His suits showcased Scottish tweeds with an easy drape across the body. Abboud also demonstrated a superb color sense, not just in his swirling paisley ties (which were all the rage in the 1990s) but in his rich autumnal knits and inky black eveningwear. The first designer to win the Council of Fashion Designers of America (CFDA) Menswear Designer of the Year award two years in a row, Abboud has dressed everyone from news anchor Tom Brokaw to jazz musician Wynton Marsalis and has created red-carpet looks for Jeremy Renner and Tracy Morgan, finding recognition in the fashion industry and pop culture alike.

Designer

Joseph Abboud.
b Boston (USA), 1950.

Joseph Abboud Fall/Winter 2019 collection at New York Fashion Week.

Photograph by Laurie Schechter.

↳ ARMANI, BRIONI, LAUREN

CHITOSE ABE

With admirers who have included Karl Lagerfeld and Jean Paul Gaultier, Chitose Abe may be your favorite fashion designer's favorite fashion designer. A creative who sidesteps the limelight, Abe has methodically scaled up Sacai, the label she founded in 1999. In 2009 she launched menswear and hosted the line's first runway show. Today Sacai is carried in more than ninety stores worldwide, and Abe has imparted her signature mélange aesthetic onto some of the most coveted, high-value Nikes in recent memory. Abe is a masterful patternmaker

who clocked time working for Junya Watanabe, and her collections teem with arresting, almost sculptural patchwork parkas, sweaters, and shirts. Military green is a frequent presence in Sacai collections, as are eclectic patterns, such as bandanna prints and Pendleton blanket motifs. Pendleton was one of a number of recent collaborations with companies large (Beats headphones) and small (Bar Italia, a homey London bar) as Abe stretches Sacai's reach into new realms.

Designer

Chitose Abe.
b Gifu (JAP), 1965.

Sacai Spring/Summer 2018 menswear collection at Paris Fashion Week, 2017.

Photograph by Peter White.

↳ KAWAKUBO, NIKE,
   PENDLETON, WATANABE

ABERCROMBIE & FITCH

Though it has been best known as a trendy retail chain since the 1990s, Abercrombie & Fitch's roots lie in burly pursuits like hunting, fishing, and camping. The company was founded in 1892 by David Abercrombie, who was later joined by Ezra Fitch. The firm introduced a mail-order catalog for outdoor goods in 1909, generating enough sales to open a twelve-story store on Manhattan's Madison Avenue and dubbing itself the Greatest Sporting Goods Store in the World. Despite dressing notable names, including Teddy Roosevelt and Ernest Hemingway in the mid-1900s, the company declined and went bankrupt in 1976 before being revived by Limited Brands in 1988 to sell mid-price casualwear to a much younger clientele. Stores opened throughout the United States, and later in Europe and Japan, selling preppy clothes largely for the teenage market. In the early 2000s the company was known as much for its racy campaigns—conceived by the creative director Sam Shahid and photographed by Bruce Weber— attractive staff, and bare-chested male greeters as for its clothes. A decline in sales led the company to a rebrand in 2017, when it dropped its well-known aesthetic and overt sexuality.

Retailer

Abercrombie & Fitch.
est New York (USA), 1892.

Abercrombie & Fitch Quarterly
Christmas Issue, 1999.

Photograph by Bruce Weber.

↳ DIESEL, GAP, J.CREW,
L.L.BEAN, WEBER

VIRGIL ABLOH

A creative director/DJ/artist/lecturer/furniture designer/ Instagram influencer, Virgil Abloh has redefined the once narrow parameters of his primary job of designing clothes. A trained architect who worked closely with Kanye West in his younger years, Abloh's first foray into clothing design came in 2012 when he screenprinted onto existing Ralph Lauren Rugby shirts and marketed them under the name Pyrex Vision. The shirts were polarizing—Were they a stunt? Were they even design?—but sold swiftly and, perhaps more importantly, made headlines. A year later

Abloh founded Off-White, a Milan-based fashion house, stretching his reach into Armani-esque camel coats and deconstructed workwear that nodded heavily to Margiela. In 2017 Abloh collaborated with Nike on the Ten, a run of immensely popular reimagined sneakers. Abloh has since worked with everyone from Perrier and Ikea to Mercedes-Benz. In 2018 Louis Vuitton appointed him head of mens-wear design, and Abloh has since inched further away from streetwear with collections punctuated by straightforward suits and luxe leather outerwear.

Designer

Virgil Abloh.
b Rockford, IL (USA), 1980.

Virgil Abloh walks the runway during the finale of the Off-White Fall/Winter 2019 show at Paris Fashion Week.

Photograph by Peter White.

↳ LOUIS VUITTON, MARGIELA, NIKE, ANDRE WALKER, WEST

HAIDER ACKERMANN

In 2019 Hollywood wunderkind Timothée Chalamet waltzed down the red carpet in a shimmering Haider Ackermann satin suit, a confident getup befitting the ascending actor. Although Chalamet's career took off rapidly, Ackermann's built as a slow simmer. Adopted by a French Alsatian family before his first birthday, Ackermann spent his teen years in the Netherlands. He enrolled at Antwerp's Royal Academy of Fine Arts but fell into the city's nightlife scene and left school early. After an internship with John Galliano, Ackermann worked in the studio for avant-garde-leaning labels, such as

Bernhard Willhelm and Patrick Van Ommeslaeghe. Striking out on his own, Ackermann established a womenswear line in 2002. Menswear arrived nearly a decade later as Ackermann riffed on the slinky, sexy look of rock stars, such as Jimi Hendrix and Mick Jagger, with plenty of skin-tight trousers, velvet, and shapely suits to go around. In 2016 Berluti tapped him to lead its creative direction, and Ackermann met the mandate with languid, jewel-toned suits and luxurious leather coats. The partnership lasted just three seasons, but Ackermann continues to design for his namesake brand.

Designer

Haider Ackermann.
b Bogotá (COL), 1971.

Timothée Chalamet wearing Haider Ackermann at the Venice Film Festival, 2019.

Photograph by Vittorio Zunino Celotto.

↳ BERLUTI, DEMEULEMEESTER, HENDRIX, JAGGER, WILLHELM

ACNE STUDIOS

Stockholm-based Acne Studios (an acronym for Ambition to Create Novel Expression) was cofounded in 1996 by Jonny Johansson, the brand's creative director, as part of a fashion collective. Using a multidisciplinary approach that marries function and form—coupled with disparate inspirations from art, architecture, and the culture at large—the Swedish powerhouse has become a go-to for cool, streamlined designs, offering smart tailoring, textural layers, and an honest, minimalist aesthetic. Originally a denim line (Johansson first created one hundred pairs of jeans with red stitching, which he gifted to friends), Acne transformed into a hip global brand known for its elevated normcore essentials—largely proportioned oxfords, the consummate white T-shirt, an oversized shearling-lined wool bomber jacket, or slim and tapered light-wash jeans. Uninterested in fleeting trends, Acne maximizes minimalism for optimal comfort in an accessible, everyday format. The studio's focus on eclectic menswear has far-reaching loyalists from Paris Fashion Week to the streets of Seoul and has attracted names such as Russell Westbrook, who collaborated on a collection with the brand.

Designer Brand

Acne Studios.
est Stockholm (SWE), 1996.

Models backstage at the Acne Studios Fall/Winter 2017 menswear presentation at Paris Fashion Week.

Photograph by Jason Lloyd-Evans.

↳ OUR LEGACY, RAG & BONE, TOUITOU, TROUBLÉ, WESTBROOK

ACRONYM

Established in 1994 by Errolson Hugh and Michaela Sachenbacher as a Berlin-based design agency, Acronym, as was Hugh's wont, blossomed into a techwear brand offering some of the most mesmerizingly complex garments on the market. Acronym's pants and jackets are cut from materials that evoke science fiction—Schoeller Dryskin and HD Nylon, which make for clothes that are supremely waterproof and insulating, respectively. Hugh sculpts garments like a sartorial Michelangelo, crafting articulated trousers and jackets that bend at the joints so the fabric never bunches. More than being technically impressive, Acronym's designs are striking to behold. In austere color schemes and sharp silhouettes, Acronym makes wearers look as though they stepped right out of a futuristic video game (in fact, Hugh designed clothes for the game *Death Stranding* in 2019). Whether for their function or their "goth-ninja" aesthetic, Hugh's designs have fostered a rabid cult around the brand, with a fan base that includes John Mayer, sci-fi author William Gibson, and artist Ai Weiwei.

Designer Brand

Acronym.
est Berlin (GER), 1994.

Acronym Fall/Winter 2019 editorial for the streetwear retailer Bodega.

Photograph by Brian Valdizno.

↳ ARC'TERYX, CANADA GOOSE, MONCLER, NIKE, OSTI

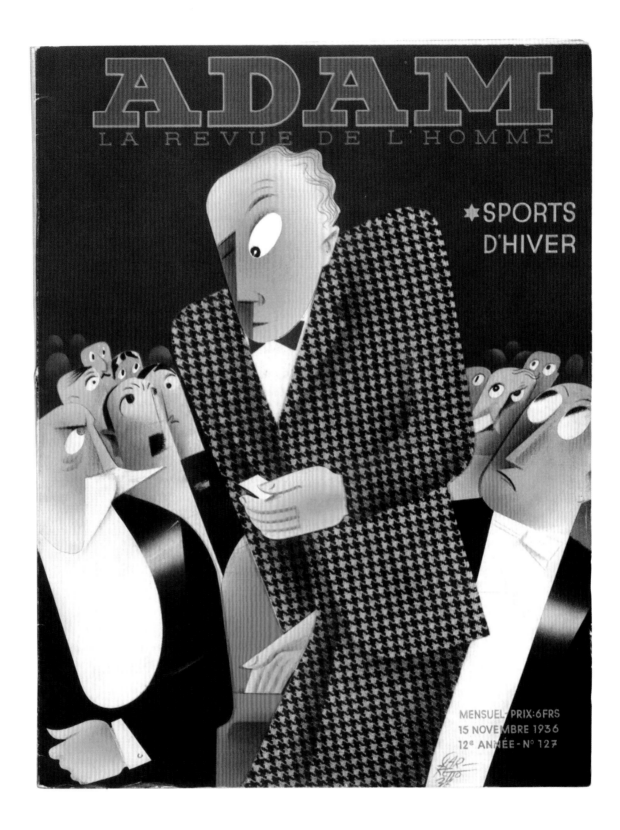

ADAM

Adam: La Revue de l'Homme was a French bimonthly magazine that combined fashion with society news, reflecting the interests of its well-heeled readers. While the fashion pages resembled a trade magazine—with advertisements from woolen mills and reports on the rising popularity of "feminine" colors and lightweight fabrics—the society pages were devoted to theater, motoring, winter sports, and life on the Cote d'Azur. Founded in 1925 by Edmond Dubois, the magazine soon established itself as an arbiter of taste for the refined male, assisted in the 1930s by the columns of Dubois's close friend André de Fouquières, considered to be "the French Beau Brummell," who habitually pondered fashion dilemmas such as "Suit or tuxedo?" *Adam* was a vociferous supporter of the French fashion industry, especially in the face of the primacy of London tailoring, and in the years before and after World War II, the publication posited that dressing well would help maintain national morale. The magazine, which had a fruitful collaborative relationship with the renowned fashion illustrator René Grau in the 1950s, shuttered in 1973.

Publication

Adam.
est Paris (FR), 1925.

Cover of the November 15, 1936 issue of *Adam*.

Illustration by Paolo Garretto.

↳ BACHELOR, ESQUIRE, GENTRY, L. WARD

CAMPBELL ADDY

London-born photographer and filmmaker Campbell Addy uses his work to push for change in the fashion space. Following his graduation from Central Saint Martins College of Art and Design in 2016, he launched *Nii Journal*, a biannual publication examining sexuality, style, art, race, and faith, which was swiftly followed by Nii Agency, a casting and model agency focused on diversity. In the ensuing years, Addy's still and moving images have celebrated eclectic men's style, beauty, and physicality, acknowledging communities and individuals often underrepresented in the wider fashion landscape. In his photographs, tender close-ups of faces and youthful bodies entwined or in motion contrast vulnerability and empowerment. Addy has converged portraiture and fashion editorials across numerous magazines, such as *Dazed*, *Time*, *i-D*, *Love*, and *Garage*, creating stunning images of notable faces, including Edward Enninful, Tyler the Creator, and Paul Smith, among other global style leaders. His work has been exhibited in galleries internationally, and his first book, *Unlocking Seoul*, was published in 2017. In 2018 and 2019 Addy received the British Fashion Award for New Wave Creatives.

Photographer

Campbell Addy.
b London (UK), 1993.

Model Cheikh Tall photographed for "And the Heat Goes On x Fendi Special," *i-D*, June 2018.

Photograph by Campbell Addy.

↳ AGYEMANG, ENNINFUL, i-D, P. SMITH

ADIDAS

The story of Adidas officially began in 1949 when German cobbler Adolf "Adi" Dassler registered "Adi Dassler adidas Sportschuhfabrik" alongside a landmark shoe with "3-Stripes." Dassler launched his business with a vision to provide the best-performing sportswear for world-class athletes, and he did just that. Years before, US track star Jesse Owens famously wore Adidas at the 1936 Berlin Olympics, and in 1954 the German national soccer team wore them during the World Cup. Soon the company moved into clothing, launching a tracksuit in 1967 with footballer Franz Beckenbauer in its signature striping. The brand extended beyond sports, and in 1986 hip-hop's Run-DMC released a hit song called "My Adidas," the video for which popularized the M45k Best bomber and Superstar shoes. Recognizing their appeal, Adidas signed Run-DMC to an unprecedented million-dollar-endorsement deal—and the first with hip-hop stars. Since then, Adidas's Samba training shoes and Stan Smith tennis shoes have reached cult status, along with styles designed in partnership with Yohji Yamamoto's Y-3 and Kanye West's sought-after Yeezy line.

Brand

Adidas.
est Herzogenaurach (GER), 1949.

Barack Obama wearing Adidas Stan Smith tennis shoes at an Obama Foundation event, Kuala Lumpur, Malaysia, 2019.

Photograph by Mohd Rasfan.

↳ ALI, BECKHAM, WALES BONNER, WEST, Y. YAMAMOTO

GIANNI AGNELLI

Once dubbed "the best-dressed man in the history of the world" by *Esquire* magazine, the industrialist Giovanni Agnelli—commonly known as Gianni or L'Avvocato (the Lawyer)—was a living expression of sprezzatura, or studied casualness, from the 1960s through the '80s, a time when Italian fashion was a byword for glamour. The chairman of the motor company Fiat, Agnelli became a media staple thanks to his good looks, refined taste, international swagger, and, perhaps most distinctively, his personal style. Employing the world's best tailors to make suits in solaro,

a blend of wool and gabardine, Agnelli favored soft grays for daywear and navy for the evening, with an idiosyncratic twist. He would often pair his suits with suede hiking boots, Brooks Brothers shirts with button-down collars, and loosely knotted ties. Agnelli also had the habit of wearing his watches (including an Omega Seamaster Ploprof and a Patek Philippe World Time) over—rather than under—his cuff. For casualwear, he embraced denim jeans and shirts, classic white linen trousers, navy blazers, and long-sleeved linen polo shirts with mother-of-pearl buttons.

Icon

Gianni Agnelli.
b Turin (IT), 1921.
d Turin (IT), 2003.

Gianni Agnelli, 1983.

Photograph by Vezio Sabatini.

↳ BROOKS BROTHERS, ELKANN, OMEGA, PATEK PHILIPPE, TOD'S

WARIS AHLUWALIA

It is a rare feat to be both a chameleon and also instantly recognizable. Whether he's rubbing elbows with Hollywood elite at a film premiere or racing across India in a rickshaw to raise funds for endangered elephants, Waris Ahluwalia's style is unmistakable, a modern-day dandy: Sikh *dastar* turban, full beard, richly hued suit, and some sort of colorful wink, whether it's pink suede Esquivel shoes or a silk pocket square from his native India. Ahluwalia describes himself as a designer and actor, but his long list of gigs and pet projects proves he is much more than that—a true twenty-first-century renaissance man. He has appeared in films made by Spike Lee and Wes Anderson; created both fine jewelry and high-end teas for his eponymous brand House of Waris; collaborated with fashion brands, such as Forevermark, Webster, Pringle of Scotland, Colette, A.P.C., Illesteva, and Gap; written essays on art for the *Paris Review*; walked in runways at New York Fashion Week; and more. It's always a surprise where this multi-hyphenate pops up next, but Ahluwalia's love of soft, luxurious tailoring translates across cultures and industries.

Designer/Icon

Waris Ahluwalia.
b Amritsar (IN), 1974.

Waris Ahluwalia photographed for
L'Uomo Vogue, August 2013.

Photograph by Pierpaolo Ferrari.

↳ ACKERMANN, BRUMMELL,
  PRINGLE OF SCOTLAND,
  TOUITOU, WILDE

ALDEN SHOES

New England was once the epicenter of American shoe manufacturing. Today Alden is the last golden-age company standing. When Charles H. Alden established his factory in 1884, it was able to produce hundreds of dress shoes a day. As time wound on, Alden's specific styles helped the company soar past competitors. These styles (which are still available today) included a casual unlined ankle-high chukka boot in suede and the conservative wing-tipped blucher—often sold in Shell Cordovan, a lustrous leather that Alden sources from the Horween

Leather Company, a Chicago-based tannery. Alden's most iconic style is the Indy Boot, a tall lace-up stomper that Indiana Jones (played by Harrison Ford) wore in the beloved film series. In the 2000s, as an Americana wave swept over the fashion industry, Alden's stout shoes were suddenly in vogue, sparking collaborations with boutiques such as Context in Wisconsin and sprawling chains such as J.Crew.

Footwear

Alden Shoes.
est Middleborough, MA (USA), 1884.

The Alden 990 Plain Toe Blucher in Horween Shell Cordovan.

Photograph by Tom Piyo.

↳ FLORSHEIM SHOES, HERBERT JOHNSON HATTERS, J.CREW

ALFRED DUNHILL

In 1893 Alfred Dunhill inherited his father's leather saddlery business in London and was among the first to create men's leather goods and accessories, such as driving goggles for automobiles. By 1907 Dunhill opened his first store on Duke Street, later expanding to Jermyn Street, where the brand continues to reside. With an eye for innovation, the label has covered an extensive range of luxury products throughout its history, from tailoring and jewelry to lighters and watches. In 1985 the brand purchased the US-based label Dunhill Tailors—solving the ever-present confusion between the

two—which was known for its bespoke suits and tuxedos worn by names including Truman Capote, Paul Newman, and Frank Sinatra. Since merging, Alfred Dunhill has further expanded its clothing business, especially with its ready-to-wear line, which has been spearheaded by creative directors such as Kim Jones and John Ray. Appointed in 2017, creative director Mark Weston has recontextualized the house's tailoring and has reimagined leather icons, such as the men's crossbody Lock Bag with its rectangular silhouette and brass closure.

Designer Brand

Alfred Dunhill.
est London (UK), 1893.

Truman Capote wearing an Alfred Dunhill bespoke tuxedo at his Black and White Ball, New York, 1966.

Photograph by Barton Silverman.

↳ CHARVET, ERMENEGILDO ZEGNA, GUCCI, K. JONES, LEIBOVITZ, NEWMAN

MUHAMMAD ALI

Icon

Self-described as "the Greatest," Muhammad Ali was the world's most celebrated boxer—and the most stylish. As he fought his way from a tough upbringing to become an Olympic and world heavyweight champion, Ali was highly conscious of his appearance, observing "I had to prove you could be a new kind of Black man." Inspired by Malcolm X, the boxer wore classic suits, white shirts, and narrow ties. But he also worked in leather jackets as well as patterned shirts and sport coats to show off his own personal flair. He favored houndstooth jackets and neat polo shirts, often offset by his Ray-Ban Wayfarers—and he occasionally veered toward extravagant styles, such as full-length fur coats. For training, he wore simple white and gray sweatshirts, reserving his more eye-catching robes for wearing to the ring along with his outsize silk boxing shorts. Ali became an icon of Black American pride. As photographer Gordon Parks noted, "He wanted to present himself as the opposite of a thug, and his well-cut suits and the attention to detail in his dress was a crucial element in that image."

Muhammad Ali.
b Louisville, KY (USA), 1942.
d Scottsdale, AZ (USA), 2016.

World heavyweight champion Muhammad Ali walks underneath elevated train tracks, Chicago, 1966.

Photograph by Thomas Hoepker.

↳ BALDWIN, M. DAVIS, FRAZIER, MALCOLM X, PARKS, RAY-BAN

ALPHA INDUSTRIES

Brand

The bomber jacket is a classic—a quintessential men's fashion piece. A military flight jacket originally issued during World War I, it broke free from its utilitarian roots to become a garment that projected just the right amount of attitude— think Steve McQueen in *The Hunter* (1980) or Tom Cruise in *Top Gun* (1986). Alpha Industries led the way in producing and popularizing the bomber jacket, specifically the MA-1 flight jacket, with its impossible-to-miss orange lining and three-bar Flying A logo. Founded in 1959 in Knoxville, Tennessee, Alpha Industries initially produced outerwear for the US military with just a few employees; the Vietnam War changed that. With the changing times, countercultures of rebels and punks (and later grunge kids and early hip-hop artists) appropriated military apparel, including the bomber jacket. More than sixty years later, Alpha Industries continues to provide military-inspired fashion to the world. The company has found fans in celebrities, such as Kanye West, Chance the Rapper, and the Weeknd, and has collaborated with high-end fashion brands including Stüssy, Vetements, Comme des Garçons, and AAPE.

Alpha Industries.
est Knoxville, TN (USA), 1959.

Fear of God designer Jerry Lorenzo wears an Alpha Industries x Vetements flight jacket, Paris, 2017.

Photograph by Christian Vierig.

↳ GVASALIA, KAWAKUBO, LORENZO, McQUEEN, STÜSSY

JUNE AMBROSE

Caribbean-born, Bronx-raised June Ambrose has shaped the way we see music since the 1990s. After leaving a job in finance, Ambrose pursued a career at Uptown/MCA Records, where as an intern she styled emerging hip-hop groups. Soon she went on to dress high-profile clients of her own, including Enrique Iglesias, Will Smith, and Sean Combs. Ambrose first collaborated with Jay-Z, who is perhaps her most important client, in 1999. Ever since, she has styled him for photo shoots, music videos, and tours, pushing him to reinvent his style for more than twenty years. Ambrose is behind many of hip-hop's most iconic music-video fashion moments—including Busta Rhymes and Janet Jackson's metallic looks for "What's It Gonna Be?!" and Combs's colorful tracksuits in "Mo Money Mo Problems." She is credited with pivoting hip-hop artists away from the street-focused trends of the '90s toward high-end designers. Ambrose became one of the first celebrity stylists to transform her expertise into a lifestyle brand in its own right, expanding into clothing and accessory collections for brands such as Target, Selima Optique, and Puma, where she was appointed creative director in 2020.

Stylist

June Ambrose.
b (AG), 1972.

Jay-Z, June Ambrose, and Sean Combs attending the Roc Nation Brunch, Los Angeles, 2020.

Photograph by Kevin Mazur.

↳ COMBS, JAY-Z, REMBERT, WELCH, YANG

SIR HARDY AMIES

Designer/Writer

Sir Hardy Amies.
b London (UK), 1909.
d Langford, Oxfordshire (UK), 2003.

A confident Brit, Sir Hardy Amies quite literally wrote the book on menswear when he published the enduring *ABC of Men's Fashion* in 1964. The book is filled with cracking guidance such as, "Underwear should be as brief as wit and as clean as fun," and for decades Amies's vast wisdom has helped men construct reliable wardrobes and avoid style mishaps. During his lifetime, he also built up a robust clothing label on London's illustrious Savile Row. His men's business, which began in 1959, specialized in tidy tailoring and stalwart essentials. Amies took a fairly conservative approach to dressing men, but he still kept up with the times. In the 1960s he dabbled in modish striped blazers and narrow, barely there ties. And in the 1970s he tiptoed into disco-ish fare with pointy-collared dress shirts and flared suits with frying pan–sized lapels. Amies also left a profound mark through films, having designed costumes for several movies throughout the 1960s, most notably Stanley Kubrick's 1968 opus *2001: A Space Odyssey*. At the start the characters wore Amies's classic tailoring, and then moved into slick, forward-thinking clothes as the film progressed.

Men's tailor Hepworths presents designs by Sir Hardy Amies that were created to represent fashion of the future, 1964.

↳ BEATON, CARDIN, ESQUIRE, NUTTER, SINCLAIR

JONATHAN ANDERSON

Jonathan Anderson was just twenty-four when he launched his men's fashion label in 2008. But the comely Irishman was ready for the limelight. His JW Anderson collections have been among the best reviewed in contemporary fashion, and in 2014 Anderson earned Menswear Designer of the Year followed in 2015 by Menswear Brand of the Year, from the British Fashion Council. Anderson persistently reconsiders the male silhouette, presenting imposing A-line parkas in popping plaids, barrel-legged jeans that flash a generous amount of ankle and taut zip-up sweaters that accentuate the neck. His clothes have a childlike wit to them: shirts button asymmetrically, and crunchy cardigans are done up in a patchwork of vivid colors. The distinctiveness of his designs has made Anderson a favorite of celebrities, such as Harry Styles and A$AP Rocky, and other fashion empires. Anderson has designed for Topshop, Uniqlo, and Versace Versus. His most enduring partnership is with the Spanish luxury label Loewe, where he has been creative director since 2013.

Designer

Jonathan Anderson.
b Magherafelt, Northern Ireland (UK), 1984.

Loewe Spring/Summer 2015 campaign.

Photograph by Jamie Hawkesworth.

↳ A$AP ROCKY, HAWKESWORTH, STYLES, UNIQLO, VERSACE

ANDERSON & SHEPPARD

Founded in 1906, Savile Row tailor Anderson & Sheppard is one of the most esteemed names on that renowned street. Dutchman Frederick Scholte, who was a cutter and master tailor—most famously to the Duke of Windsor—mentored Swede Peter "Per" Gustav Anderson. Scholte pioneered a style known as the English Drape, which Anderson, along with trouser cutter Sydney Horatio Sheppard, evolved. Together Anderson and Sheppard formed their namesake tailor, modernizing men's bespoke suits from a restrictive, Victorian-era silhouette to a more fluid, relaxed form with soft shoulders and added ease. As a radical yet refined departure point, Anderson & Sheppard were regarded as the rebel tailors of Savile Row. Their business began to boom by 1927, and they expanded from 13 Savile Row to a larger corner shop across the street at 30 Savile Row. They have gone on to dress global figures for nearly a century, including Charlie Chaplin, Cole Porter, Cary Grant, Fred Astaire, and the British royal family. In 2011 Anderson & Sheppard opened its ready-to-wear haberdashery, dedicated to the house's classic and contemporary codes.

Tailor

Anderson & Sheppard.
est London (UK), 1906.

Manolo Blahnik wearing Anderson & Sheppard, 2010.

Photograph by Richard Grassie.

↳ ASTAIRE, COWARD, FERRY, C. GRANT, SCHOLTE

ANDOVER SHOP

The Andover Shop, the Massachusetts-based made-to-measure menswear boutique and haberdashery, boasts decades of sartorial tradition rooted in the East Coast. Founded in 1948 by Charlie Davidson, known in the local press as the Baron of Bespoke, and Virgil Marson, the Prince of Tweeds, the store quickly found an audience with students at the surrounding prep schools and Ivy League institutions. The Andover Shop tailored suits, sport coats, and blazers, featuring their natural-shoulder signature cut and made from the finest woolens and textiles. It also offered Ivy style staples, such as gingham dress shirts, Shetland sweaters, and colorful repp-stripe ties. In 1953 the Andover Shop opened its Cambridge store. Located in Harvard Square, it became a mainstay for politicians, such as Senator Ted Kennedy and President George H. W. Bush, and jazz legends, including Miles Davis and Chet Baker. With pieces from Andover, Davis—who married the period's Ivy style with the hip world of jazz—pioneered a new sensational look that redefined cool, taking seersuckers, tweed sport coats, and Oxford button-downs to center stage.

Andover Shop.
est Andover, MA (USA), 1948.

Andover Shop, c. 1950s.

↳ ALDEN SHOES, BROOKS
   BROTHERS, M. DAVIS,
   J. PRESS, PAUL STUART

ANDRÉ 3000

On the cover of 1994's *Southernplayalisticadillacmuzik*, the debut album from Outkast, André "3000" Benjamin—half of this unsinkable rap duo, alongside Big Boi—wore an oddball bowler-style hat that typified his unconventional fashion sense. Through the 1990s he moved from lampshade bucket hats to varsity jackets worn with boxing sneakers to leather trousers and bandanna headbands. In the early aughts, 3000 settled into neo-dandyism with outfits that would make a Crayola crayon box blush. For the 2003 smash "Hey Ya!," he sported an emerald green shirt with an orange tie and tartan

trousers. In 2008, after Outkast went on hiatus, 3000 spun his style into a short-lived prepster label, Benjamin Bixby, offering jockey-inspired polos and tattersall tailoring. While performing again as Outkast, he's taken to wearing jumpsuits with poignant and pointed political messages such as, "Across cultures, darker people suffer most. Why?" More than his own creations, though, 3000's happily freewheeling style has encompassed Americana workwear, radical prep, and actual uniforms, and shattered the cliched "urban" style stereotype lazily ascribed to rappers in the 1990s and 2000s.

Icon

André 3000 (André Benjamin).
b Atlanta (USA), 1975.

André 3000 at the 2003 MTV Europe Music Awards, Edinburgh.

Photograph by John Rogers.

↳ A$AP ROCKY, CONVERSE, LAUREN, LEVI'S

ANTO BEVERLY HILLS

Many clothing companies like to boast that they're a tailor to the stars. For Anto this claim is truer than most. Since 1955 the Los Angeles–based haberdasher has cut custom shirts for marquee names, such as Frank Sinatra, Mick Jagger, and Leonardo DiCaprio. Started by Anto Sepetjian, who immigrated from Beirut, Anto is still run by the family today. To create one of its bespoke patterns for a client, Anto's tailors take as many as eighteen measurements of the client (its vault holds more than ten thousand of these patterns), and each custom shirt is stitched by hand.

At a time when many of the United States's specialized clothiers are withering away, Anto's business is climbing. In recent years it shipped shirts to the set of *Mission: Impossible—Fallout* for Tom Cruise to wear in the film, and its shirts have also appeared in Oscar-nominated films such as *Ford v Ferrari* (2019) and *Once Upon a Time . . . in Hollywood* (2019). Off-screen, Anto has garnered a new generation of star clients, including Post Malone and John David Washington.

Retailer

Anto Beverly Hills.
est Beverly Hills, CA (USA), 1955.

Kobe Bryant wearing an Anto Beverly Hills shirt, photographed for *Los Angeles Confidential*, October 2010.

Photograph by Marc Baptiste.

↳ S. DAVIS, DEVORE, C. GRANT, JAGGER, TURNBULL & ASSER

APPAREL ARTS

Founded by Arnold Gingrich, who also later established *Esquire* magazine, *Apparel Arts* arrived in 1931 and proved to be the father of all men's fashion magazines. Long before mass photography, garment trade shows, and the information overload of the internet, *Apparel Arts* was a quarterly guidebook for industry denizens—those retail store buyers and wholesale middlemen. A flip through the lush illustrations in *Apparel Arts* would reveal what style trends were dominating the moment, telling vendors what they should be selling that season. In orderly infographics, readers could soak up that herringbone gray was in for suits, that tattersall was the shirt pattern of the moment, or that dark suede gloves were about to be an essential. *Apparel Arts* synthesized the style trends from major cities and dispersed them nationwide. Though it was offered solely to industry professionals, the magazine was so popular that purportedly customers stole copies from their local shops. The handy periodical ran until the late 1950s, when it was reshaped into *Gentlemen's Quarterly*, a more public-facing fashion magazine, and eventually *Esquire*'s chief rival in the US and UK.

Publication

Apparel Arts.
est New York (USA), 1931.

"Wool in the Wardrobe," *Apparel Arts*, October/November 1937.

↳ ESQUIRE, GENTRY, GQ

AQUASCUTUM

As with many British heritage brands, Aquascutum's story began during a frenetic period of invention and progress in the mid-nineteenth century. Gentleman's clothier John Emary opened his shop in 1851 and two years later invented and patented the first waterproof wool, which went on to be used for officers' coats during the Crimean War and later for trench coats in both world wars. That same year Emary renamed his brand Aquascutum (Latin for "water shield"). In the 1870s he sold Aquascutum to Scantlebury & Commin, under whose ownership its overcoats became a staple for country pursuits and were worn by King Edward VII and his son the Duke of Windsor, as well as Winston Churchill. The trench coat, introduced in 1914 for military use, is the brand's most iconic design. The coat quickly became a British fashion staple that later was considered more understated and classic than Burberry. It helped too that in its heyday the Aquascutum trench found fans in Hollywood with stars such as Cary Grant and, most famously, Humphrey Bogart, who wore the Kingsway design in the 1941 film *The Maltese Falcon* and 1946's *The Big Sleep*.

Designer Brand

Aquascutum.
est London (UK), 1851.

A man models a checkered raincoat by Aquascutum (left) for the British Menswear Guild reception, London, 1966.

↳ BELSTAFF, BURBERRY,
C. GRANT, MACINTOSH

JEFF AQUILON

Widely considered to be the first male supermodel, Jeff Aquilon was scouted by famed photographer Bruce Weber and *GQ* art director Donald Sterzin at Malibu's Pepperdine University in 1978. The captain of his school's water polo team, Aquilon had a golden-boy look that immediately appealed to Weber and Sterzin. For the next few years, the beefy, blue-eyed Aquilon was a consistent presence in the pages of *GQ*. He could certainly wear a pressed glen-plaid suit and microdot tie, but Aquilon often appeared less clothed, reflecting how Weber and other photographers were tilting men's fashion toward a sexualized, body-worshipping aesthetic. Aquilon had the type of athletic, pretty-boy look that many fashion labels wanted for their advertisements—not just in the United States but abroad as well. Through the 1980s and '90s, you could spot him in ads for labels such as Loewe, Sulka, and even Gap, wearing everything from sandy three-piece suits to paisley dressing gowns or boxer shorts. Aquilon continues to model occasionally, having appeared most recently in editorials for *V* magazine and *Arena Homme +*.

Model

Jeff Aquilon.
b Santa Barbara, CA (USA), c. 1959.

Jeff Aquilon, c. 1980.

Photograph by Bruce Weber.

↳ GQ, LAUREN, SULKA, WEBER

ARC'TERYX

In 1989 Arc'teryx—then known as Rock Solid—was created in Vancouver by a band of local climbers, including Dave Lane and Jeremy Guard, with the goal of designing hypertechnical performance gear for their outdoor pursuits. Inspired by evolutionary design, Guard, in 1991, changed the name to Arc'teryx—a nod to the late Jurassic era's archaeopteryx—which is now depicted in fossilized form as the company's logo. With the Coast Mountains as its natural testing ground, the brand has become a pioneer in premium equipment, such as the Vapor harness, launched in 1993, or the Bora backpack

with heat-laminate technology. Multifunctional and often monochromatic, Arc'teryx designs are made to endure harsh weather. In 2009 the company debuted Veilance, an elevated line of city-inspired casualwear. Coveted by both Alpine enthusiasts and style icons—including Virgil Abloh, Drake, and Frank Ocean, all of whom don the label's bicolor technical outerwear or toasty accessories—Arc'teryx has made its way into the fashion world and begun releasing collaborative products, such as an Ar022 backpack and Mantis 2 side bag with Japanese lifestyle brand Beams.

Brand

Arc'teryx.
est Vancouver (CAN), 1989.

Prince Harry wearing an Arc'teryx jacket during a visit to a Help For Heroes Recovery Centre at Tedworth House, Wiltshire, England, 2017.

Photograph by Ben Birchall.

↳ ABLOH, BEAMS, CANADA GOOSE, MONCLER, OSTI

GIORGIO ARMANI

Devoid of stiff padding, the Armani sport coat flows with an ease that has long defined Italian tailoring. Over an almost fifty-year career, founder Giorgio Armani's comfortable, confident way of styling changed the way men dressed throughout the world and influenced generations of designers, including Calvin Klein, Ralph Lauren, and Donna Karan. After spending time as an assistant at Nino Cerruti, Armani started his label in 1973. His reach exploded in 1980 when he created the costumes for the Richard Gere vehicle *American Gigolo*. The film's shrug-it-on sport coats, cream-colored knit sweaters, and legendary camel-hair polo coat became some of the most well-known clothes ever captured on-screen, and defined the Armani aesthetic. From the lapel down, the ease of it all was infectious. Soon Eric Clapton, Willem Dafoe, Robert De Niro, and elegant men of all flavors were drawn to Armani's lengthy wool coats and finely patterned shirts. Decades later the earth-toned ease that Armani propagated feels both influential and relevant—as *GQ* wrote in 2020, "'90s Armani Looks So Good Now."

Giorgio Armani.
b Piacenza (IT), 1934.

Richard Gere wearing Armani in a publicity still for Paramount Pictures's *American Gigolo*, 1980.

↳ ABBOUD, CERRUTI, C. KLEIN, LAUREN, PRADA, RITTS

ARNYS

Founded by Léon Grimbert in Paris in 1933, Arnys rose to be the preeminent tailoring house of the French capital. It built upon the fashion sense of Left Bank Parisians: very regal and smart yet also a bit hardscrabble—country, even. Arnys's dignified suits came in rich tweeds and cashmere, and the retailer offered ample silk scarves and pocket squares in bursting hues that could instantly liven up a wintry outfit. Arnys customers included French paragons of style, such as Jean Cocteau, Yves Saint Laurent, and Jean-Paul Sartre. Its signature garment, the Forestière

jacket, was commissioned by the famed architect—and steady Arnys client—Le Corbusier. In 1947 Le Corbusier tasked Arnys with fabricating a garment that recreated the pocket-packed body of a gamekeeper's field coat but also featured wide kimono-inspired sleeves to accommodate drawing. With unlined shoulders, this functional, easy-to-wear coat became a hit at Arnys. The Forestière was worn by prime ministers, artists, and professors and remained in the Arnys line until the label closed in 2013.

Retailer

Arnys.
est Paris (FR), 1933.

French writer René Barjavel wearing the Forestière jacket, 1979.

Photograph by Louis Monier.

↳ BERLUTI, GOYARD, HERMÈS, Y. SAINT LAURENT

ARROW

For a period in the 1920s, Arrow, whose shirts were manufactured by Cluett, Peabody & Company, was among the most successful businesses in the United States. Founded in 1851 to produce detachable shirt collars, the company later rose to prominence thanks to a renowned advertising campaign featuring the Arrow Collar Man. This firm-jawed and athletic young man, initially drawn by the commercial artist J. C. Leyendecker, appeared widely in publications between 1905 and 1930. The illustration's reach turned the character into a cultural icon, an enduring shorthand for a particularly "all-American" man. Arrow reached its peak in the 1920s when it manufactured shirts with fixed collars to meet a change in customer preference, using a new manufacturing process that helped avoid collar shrinkage. Cluett, Peabody & Company later developed a full range of men's clothing, but Arrow's popularity declined in the decades after World War II with the rise of commercial competition and the trend toward more informal dressing. In 2004 the Arrow brand was sold and became part of the Phillips-Van Heusen Corporation.

Brand

Arrow.
est Troy, NY (USA), 1851.

Advertisement for Arrow collars and shirts, c. 1920s.

Illustration by J. C. Leyendecker.

↳ C.F. HATHAWAY COMPANY, LEYENDECKER, VAN HEUSEN

覇者の誇り。栄光に輝く『選手』のアフターウエア。

ASICS

The founder of Asics, Japanese designer Kihachiro Onitsuka, was first inspired by octopus tentacles for the designs of his cult running shoes. The unlikely muse led him to create a suction cup sole for his 1951 Onitsuka Tiger basketball shoe with courtside grip. With a belief that sports could rebuild postwar Japan, his designs became a mainstream sensation, even worn by Japan's Olympic basketball team. By 1960 he devised a lightweight running shoe called the Magic Runner for long distances, and in 1966 his signature Tiger stripe was born. In the 1970s the brand designed more sports models, including a baseball shoe with cleats and a breathable mesh volleyball shoe. In 1977 Onitsuka changed his company name to Asics, an acronym for the Latin phrase "Anima sana in corpore sano," meaning "sound mind, sound body." The shoes have been worn by martial arts hero Bruce Lee and actress Uma Thurman in the 2003 film *Kill Bill: Vol. 1*. Asics and its retro Onitsuka Tiger designs have partnered with high-fashion names including Issey Miyake, Kiko Kostadinov, Givenchy, and Valentino.

Brand

Asics.
est Kobe (JAP), 1949.

Catalog published in 1976 by Onitsuka Co., Ltd.

↳ ADIDAS, LEE, MIYAKE, NEW BALANCE, NIKE

KRIS VAN ASSCHE

Designer Kris Van Assche is known for bringing street-wear-inspired style to precision tailoring. After studying at the Royal Academy of Fine Arts in Antwerp under designer Walter Van Beirendonck, he interned with mentor Hedi Slimane at Yves Saint Laurent, later following him to Dior Homme in 2000. Four years later, Van Assche launched his eponymous menswear label, creating runway looks that fused avant-garde suiting with sportswear. In 2007 he made his debut at Dior Homme, where he reimagined house codes, including reinventing Christian Dior's seminal 1947 Bar Jacket for men, blending subcultural references with high design in the form of graphic logos and slim-cut proportions, and working with new ambassadors, such as A$AP Rocky and filmmaker Larry Clark. Van Assche eventually put his own label on pause in 2015, and in 2018 he left Dior Homme for Berluti, where he was artistic director until 2021. His designs lent an edgy sensibility to the storied label through hand-patinaed dress shoes and zesty colorful suits—a direction that was meticulous and mature but also radically Van Assche.

Designer

Kris Van Assche.
b Londerzeel (BEL), 1976.

Dior Homme Fall/Winter 2016 collection at Paris Fashion Week.

Photograph by Jason Lloyd-Evans.

↳ VAN BEIRENDONCK, BERLUTI, SLIMANE

46

FRED ASTAIRE

Fred Astaire was a triple threat—a debonair dancer, talented actor, and unforgettable style icon—starring in Hollywood's most acclaimed musicals. Born in Omaha, Nebraska, Astaire began his formal training in 1905 in New York, where he later, in 1916, met renowned composer George Gershwin. In 1933 Astaire made his silver-screen debut in *Dancing Lady*; outfitted in his signature top hat and tails, these elements would become inseparable from his Hollywood persona. With discerning taste and a deep appreciation for men's fashion, Astaire revamped the image of the romantic on-screen hero, embodying a self-made spirit with a natural, urbane, and effortless charm. His preference for British tailoring (Savile Row's Anderson & Sheppard designed his dress ensembles) coupled with a casual comfort and soft shapes that maximized his movement reinvigorated men's dressing with a newfound attitude and ease. Off-screen he wore preppy Brooks Brothers shirts, straw boater hats with grosgrain bands, tweed jackets, and custom-tailored suits (favoring darker shades of blue, gray, and brown), often adding his own flair whether using a silk handkerchief as a belt or accessorizing with boutonnieres.

Icon

Fred Astaire.
b Omaha, NE (USA), 1899.
d Los Angeles (USA), 1987.

Fred Astaire, 1936.

↳ ANDERSON & SHEPPARD,
BROOKS BROTHERS, GABLE,
C. GRANT, DUKE OF WINDSOR

RICHARD AVEDON

Not many photographers have a world-famous figure as their first sitter, but Richard Avedon was just ten years old when he photographed his family's neighbor, Russian composer Sergei Rachmaninoff. It was the start of a career spanning more than sixty years, during which Avedon redefined fashion and portrait photography working for *Harper's Bazaar*, *Vogue*, and the *New Yorker*. His fashion models moved, laughed, and smiled, while his portraits positioned subjects against a white background, a conscious move on Avedon's part to disconnect them from their environment. Avedon's career in advertising

work was equally as long—he photographed ads for Hart Schaffner Marx in the late 1950s and early '60s, and in the '90s he shot campaigns for Hugo Boss as well as Dior Homme and Versace, whom he continued to work for through the early 2000s. He also made striking images of establishment figures, President Eisenhower and Henry Kissinger, and antiestablishment players, including anti-Vietnam protestors and the Chicago Seven. Avedon himself had a striking sartorial sense and was known for his signature blue jeans or black slacks, button-downs, classic shirts, and horn-rimmed spectacles.

Photographer

Richard Avedon.
b New York (USA), 1923.
d San Antonio, TX (USA), 2004.

Richard Avedon, 1963.

Photograph by Alfred Eisenstaedt.

↳ D. BAILEY, BALDWIN, HART SCHAFFNER MARX, HUGO BOSS, PARKS, VERSACE

BRENDON BABENZIEN

For fourteen years as Supreme's creative director, Brendon Babenzien was the quiet force molding the skatewear brand into a vital, and highly influential, clothing label. In 2015 Babenzien struck out on his own, reviving— with the aid of his wife, Estelle Bailey-Babenzien—Noah, the side project he had first attempted in 2002. Noah's second go-round found purchase with maturing men who fondly recalled their rebellious youth but now also could admire a high-twist cashmere suit. These were folks not unlike Babenzien, who grew up skateboarding, surfing,

and listening to punk music but had become family men with a taste for Belgian Shoes. Noah's seasonal offerings are an enticing mélange—a Trash and Vaudeville–style pink leopard sweater vest sits next to corduroy running shorts and alongside a tattersall flannel shirt. Noah aims to be a "responsible label," highlighting social movements—Abolish ICE and Black Lives Matter—as well as environmental organizations, such as the Feminist Bird Club. In 2021 J.Crew appointed Babenzien as its men's creative director.

Designer

Brendon Babenzien.
b East Islip, NY (USA), 1972.

Noah Fall/Winter 2018.

Photograph by Samuel Bradley.

↳ J.CREW, PALACE, SUPREME

BACHELOR

AUGUST 1937 • **PRICE THIRTY FIVE CENTS**

BACHELOR

The first edition of *Bachelor* magazine described itself as "A visual expression of contemporary thought—mirroring the varied interests of the discerning cosmopolite," but that was not its only true appeal. *Bachelor* took its name from the euphemism "confirmed bachelor" to refer to a gay man, and operated in a gray area of coded subtext at a time when homosexuality was illegal. Founded in 1937 and aiming to be a cut above *Esquire*, the magazine set out to appeal to an emerging sophisticated subculture—covering high society, theater, polo, and lacrosse—that belonged squarely in traditions of dandyism, aestheticism, and athletic young men. The magazine was filled with notable contributors—artists such as Paul Cadmus, Luigi Lucioni, and Charles Baskerville; photographers including Cecil Beaton; and eye candy such as Tyrone Power, Cary Grant, and Larry "Buster" Crabbe—and included articles by leading style commentators, such as Lucius Beebe. Its fashion pages concentrated on dressing the discerning, well-groomed, urbane male. Despite its illustrious contributors, the publication had a short run, only lasting one year.

Publication

Bachelor.
est Philadelphia (USA), 1937.

Cover of the August 1937 issue
of *Bachelor*.

Portrait by Luigi Luccioni.

↳ BEATON, BEEBE, ESQUIRE,
  GENTRY, C. GRANT

CHRISTOPHER BAILEY

Designer

Christopher Bailey.
b Halifax, West Yorkshire, England (UK),
1971.

Model Montell Martin for the Burberry
Fall/Winter 2017 men's campaign.

Photograph by Alasdair McLellan.

↳ BURBERRY, FORD, McLELLAN,
TISCI

Christopher Bailey's radical transformation of Burberry from a timeworn English coatmaker into a highly profitable luxury business saw him initially abandon its iconic checks. A graduate of the Royal College of Art who had worked at Donna Karan and had been Tom Ford's right-hand man for five years at Gucci, Bailey became creative director at Burberry in 2004. Attracted to the unisex quality of the trench coat, Bailey reimagined Burberry's designs for the twenty-first century. He introduced an unflashy, muted palette to the clothes that radiated modernity and sophistication. Known for his unstuffy approach, he embraced digital campaigns and social media. A master of promotion, Bailey regularly worked with leading photographers, such as Mario Testino and Alasdair McLellan, models (Burberry gave Romeo Beckham his first shoot), and actors, including Eddie Redmayne and Josh Whitehouse, to showcase his designs. Bailey became so integral to the brand that for his final three years he headed up both the boardroom and the design studio before stepping down in 2018, when Burberry was valued at $3.8 billion.

DAVID BAILEY

British photographer David Bailey shaped the image of the Swinging Sixties with his iconic photographs of London's most notable personalities of the time—from Mick Jagger and Twiggy to the Beatles and Michael Caine. Bailey was a new breed: a celebrity photographer who was as much part of the London scene as his subjects. He started his career as a studio assistant to photographer John French, and in 1960 he was hired as a staff photographer at British *Vogue*. Inspired by the work of Henri Cartier-Bresson, Bailey's photographs—sharp black-and-white images, closely cropped and brightly lit—reflected an incredibly innovative approach. Famously prolific, he once generated eight hundred pages of editorial in just one year. In 1965 his studio portraits of thirty-six 1960s personalities, including Lord Snowdon and Cecil Beaton, were published in his book *Box of Pin-Ups* (only four were women). More than forty years later, his photographs for Valentino's men's ad campaigns in the 2010s harked back to those portraits. In 2015 Bailey was commissioned by Jaeger to shoot its Fall/Winter campaign, returning to the brand more than five decades after first working with it in the 1950s.

Photographer

David Bailey.
b London (UK), 1938.

Michael Caine, 1965.

Photograph by David Bailey.

↳ AVEDON, THE BEATLES, BEATON, JAGGER, LINDBERGH

JAMES BALDWIN

American novelist, playwright, essayist, poet, and activist James Baldwin was a cultural heavyweight who changed the narrative for Black Americans with his first novel, *Go Tell It on the Mountain* (1953), and for queer Americans with his second novel, *Giovanni's Room* (1956). Known for his dress sense as much as his challenging stare, Baldwin was rarely seen without a scarf around his neck—perhaps silk paisley—his trademark heavy sunglasses, impeccable shirts with three-inch collars, and wide-bottomed ties, often worn with double-breasted jackets. He also excelled at winter layering, favoring shearling coats and fur toque hats. He combined the hipster feel of the contemporary jazz scene with a sense of East Coast cool and a slightly professorial bent, in corduroy suits and button-down shirts. In 1970 despair with civil rights in the United States forced Baldwin to leave for France, where he settled in the south, often wearing lightweight, short-sleeved shirts in vertical stripes. In 2021 one of Baldwin's essays, "Stranger in the Village," a reflection on his life, inspired a Louis Vuitton menswear show designed by Virgil Abloh.

Icon

James Baldwin.
b New York (USA), 1924.
d Saint-Paul-de-Vence (FR), 1987.

James Baldwin, Paris, 1972.

Photograph by Sophie Bassouls.

↪ ABLOH, ALI, AVEDON,
  M. DAVIS, MALCOLM X,
  PARKS

IL VESTITO ANTINEUTRALE

Manifesto futurista

Glorifichiamo la guerra,
sola igiene del mondo.
MARINETTI.
(1° Manifesto del Futurismo - 20 Febbraio 1909)

Viva Asinari di Bernezzo!
MARINETTI.
(1ª Serata futurista - Teatro Lirico, Milano, Febbraio 1910)

L'umanità si vestì sempre di **quiete**, di **paura**, di **cautela** o d'**indecisione**, portò sempre il lutto, o il piviale, o il mantello. Il corpo dell'uomo fu sempre diminuito da sfumature e da tinte **neutre**, avvilito dal nero, soffocato da cinture, imprigionato da panneggiamenti.

Fino ad oggi gli uomini usarono abiti di colori e forme statiche, cioè drappeggiati, solenni, gravi, incomodi e sacerdotali. Erano espressioni di timidezza, di malinconia e di **schiavitù**, negazione della vita muscolare, che soffocava in un passatismo anti-igienico di stoffe troppo pesanti e di mezze tinte tediose, effeminate o decadenti. Tonalità e ritmi di **pace desolante**, funeraria e deprimente.

OGGI vogliamo abolire:

1. — Tutte le tinte **neutre**, « carine », sbiadite, *fantasia*, semioscure e umilianti.

2. — Tutte le tinte e le foggie pedanti, professorali e teutoniche. I disegni a righe, a quadretti, a **puntini diplomatici.**

3. — I vestiti da lutto, nemmeno adatti per i becchini. Le morti eroiche non devono essere compiante, ma ricordate con vestiti rossi.

4. — L'equilibrio **mediocrista**, il cosidetto buon gusto e la cosidetta armonia di tinte e di forme, che frenano gli entusiasmi e rallentano il passo.

5. — La simmetria nel taglio, le linee **statiche**, che stancano, deprimono, contristano, legano i muscoli; l'uniformità di goffi risvolti e tutte le cincischiature. I bottoni inutili. I colletti e i polsini inamidati.

Noi futuristi vogliamo liberare la nostra razza da ogni **neutralità**, dall'indecisione paurosa e quietista, dal pessimismo negatore e dall'inerzia

Vestito bianco - rosso - verde
portato dal parolibero futurista Cangiullo, nelle dimostrazioni dei Futuristi contro i professori tedescofili e neutralisti dell'Università di Roma (11-12 Dicembre 1914).

GIACOMO BALLA

For the Turin-born Italian artist Giacomo Balla, one of the founders of the Futurist art movement, fashion was a weapon in the fight to forge a classless society that matched the rhythms of modern life in the early twentieth century. Balla's designs, which he himself wore, were made by local tailors in Rome or by his two daughters at home in simple asymmetric shapes—his suit jackets lacked both lapels and collars—with diagonal geometrical patterns, mixing triangles, cones, and spirals in myriad vibrant colors. During a visit to Germany, he noted with satisfaction that his outfit created "a real furore." In 1914 Balla issued a manifesto (*Il vestito antineutrale: Manifesto futurista,* or *The Antineutral Clothing: Futurist Manifesto*) in which he explained how the "dynamic joy of clothing will move along the many streets transformed by new Futurist architecture, sparkling like the prismatic splendor of a giant jeweler's window." Ahead of his time in predicting the artistic status of the fashion designer, Balla proved inspirational to later Italian designers, including Missoni and Laura Biagiotti.

Designer

Giacomo Balla.
b Turin (IT), 1871.
d Rome (IT), 1958.

Il vestito antineutrale: Manifesto futurista by Giacomo Balla, 1914.

↳ BASQUIAT, BRUMMELL, FLÜGEL, MISSONI, PICASSO

BALLY

Founded by businessman Carl Franz Bally, Bally started as a small family-run ribbon factory before moving into leather-crafted shoes beginning in 1851 and eventually transforming into a global luxury brand. A purveyor of innovative designs, today's Bally merges Swiss craftsmanship with a contemporary aesthetic, making multifunctional shoes, accessories, and ready-to-wear items. Bally's technical expertise in shoemaking spans more than 170 years—sponsoring Olympians as well as early twentieth-century Swiss expeditions to the Himalayas and Andes Mountains. In 1953

Tenzing Norgay wore Bally's Reindeer-Himalaya boots to the summit of Everest with Sir Edmund Hillary. The brand's formal men's Scribe collection of dressy Derbys or sleek Oxfords with broguing details are handmade in Switzerland and take more than 240 steps to complete; they, along with the more casual red-and-white Bally Stripe series, are iconic bestsellers. Whether worn by Zurich-based bankers or 1980s hip-hop enthusiasts (the latter of whom highly prize the brand's leather sneakers), Bally balances city living with the great outdoors–a decidedly Swiss notion indeed.

Designer Brand

Bally.
est Schönenwerd (SW), 1851.

Bally advertisement, 1959.

Illustration by Donald Brun.

↳ ADIDAS, BERLUTI, BLUNDSTONE, R.M.WILLIAMS, SALVATORE FERRAGAMO

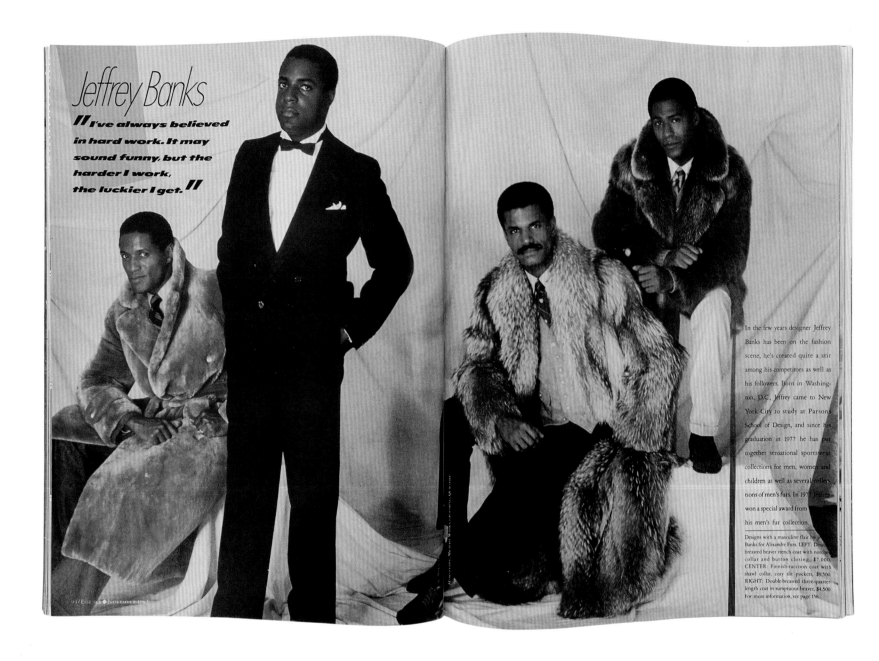

JEFFREY BANKS

Largely considered to be one of the first Black men to become a major mainstream fashion designer, Jeffrey Banks started his career at the very peak of 1970s American style with posts at Ralph Lauren and Calvin Klein. He quickly made a name for himself independently by designing a men's fur collection for Alixandre Furs. That line won Banks—then just twenty-three—a special Coty Award in 1977 and sent his career running. Banks started his own eponymous line but found the greatest success in the 1980s as the design director for Merona Sport. Banks offered an approachable, preppy style with ·

breezy knits ringed in primary-colored stripes and relaxed khakis. At its height, sales of Merona Sport hit $85 million annually, reflecting Banks's commercial savvy. In the 1990s and beyond, the ever-prolific Banks designed collections for Haggar and Bloomingdale's private label brands, and consistently appeared on the Home Shopping Network, selling his line of home decor. Banks is one of the longest-standing members of the CFDA and has written extensively on fashion, including coauthoring 2011's *Preppy: Cultivating Ivy Style* and 2013's *Perry Ellis: An American Original*.

Designer

Jeffrey Banks.
b Washington, DC (USA), 1955.

Jeffrey Banks with models wearing his designs for Alixandre Furs, photographed for *Essence*, November 1982.

Photograph by Anthony Barboza.

↳ ELLIS, C. KLEIN, LAUREN, WHITE

BARACUTA

Baracuta is about as British as they come. The brand was started in Manchester in 1937 by brothers John and Isaac Miller, and its cornerstone jacket—the waist-length G9—features a very Anglo tartan-checked lining. (The *G* in the jacket's name stands for *golf*, as the cropped cut made it easier to swing a club.) Despite its British detailing, the G9's biggest boost came in 1958 when Elvis Presley wore the jacket in *King Creole*. This silver-screen appearance, coupled with the fact that three years prior James Dean had worn a similar jacket in *Rebel Without a Cause* (1955), helped the G9 shed its demure country-club roots and become something truly cool. Through the 1960s the ever-suave Steve McQueen tooled around on motorcycles in the G9. Ryan O'Neal wore such a coat on TV's *Peyton Place*, giving the jacket its Harrington nickname after his character, Rodney Harrington. The versatile Baracuta jacket was a favorite of both Ivy Leaguers on the East Coast and 1970s punks in England, such as Topper Headon of the Clash. Today the G9 can be seen on the likes of Daniel Craig, Bradley Cooper, and Jason Statham, reflecting how this jacket has become an icon on both sides of the pond.

Brand

Baracuta.
est Manchester, England (UK), 1937.

Steve McQueen wearing a Baracuta G9 jacket in a publicity still for United Artists's *The Thomas Crown Affair*, 1968.

↳ DEAN, McQUEEN, PENGUIN, PRESLEY

BARBOUR

Founded by John Barbour in 1894, this family-owned brand built its reputation with waterproof clothing for extreme conditions, including the decks of submarines during World War II. In 1939 Barbour developed the Ursula suit—a four-pocket wax jacket—for the Royal Navy after they were requested by HMS *Ursula*'s Captain George Philips. These durable jackets, an adaptation of an earlier Barbour one-piece oversuit for motorcyclists, have been worn by seamen and sailors and were eventually rediscovered by bikers, including Steve McQueen. Since then Barbour has become synonymous with country pursuits and pastimes, informing the brand's pragmatic all-weather design and imbuing it with an upper-class allure. The jackets were a favorite of the Sloane Rangers—young upper-middle-class Londoners in the 1980s—and have appeared in many films, including *Skyfall* (2012), in which Daniel Craig dons a Barbour in the iconic James Bond role. The jackets have enjoyed a revival among hipsters in the twenty-first century, fueled in part by their popularity at music festivals, where they are often paired with another British mainstay—Hunter Wellington boots.

Designer Brand

Barbour.
est South Shields, England (UK), 1894.

Prince Charles wearing a Barbour jacket, 1978.

Photograph by Tim Graham.

↳ BELSTAFF, BURBERRY, MACINTOSH, McQUEEN

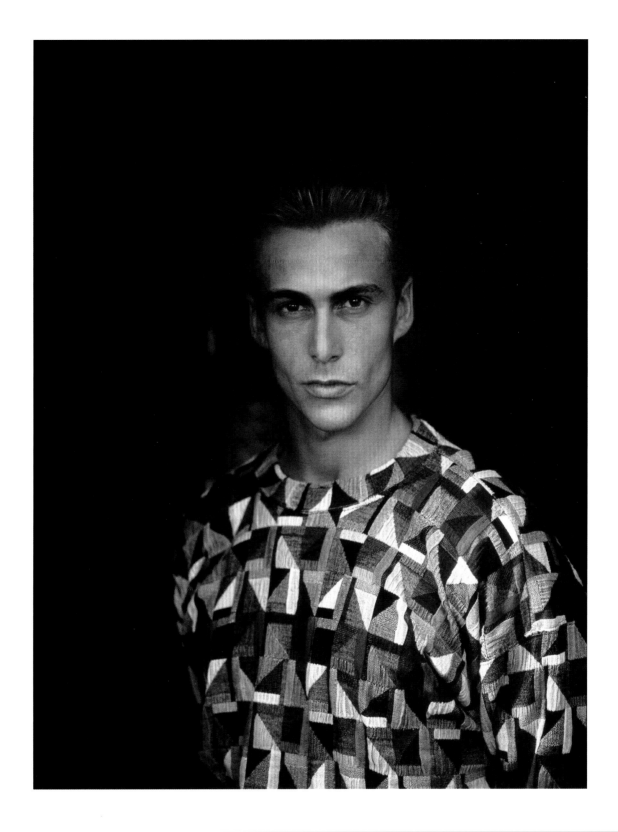

JHANE BARNES

Dubbed a "fashion nerd" by *Wired* magazine in 1996, Jhane Barnes was among the first designers to embrace computer technology in her textile designs. In 1976 Barnes started her label with a single pant design—the trousers notably lacked back pockets to accentuate the male rear end. More unconventional ideas followed, such as jackets featuring mammoth "bag" pockets, a sport coat crossed with a flat-hem blouson, and tuxedos that literally sparkled. Her early customers included rakes such as Elton John, Hall & Oates, and John Lennon, and in 1980, at just twenty-five,

she became the youngest Coty Award winner. Two years later, Barnes designed her first textile using an Atari computer, and soon she was exploring how technology could help her create ever more abstract textiles. In 1998 she developed a jacket from tencel, a wood fiber–based textile—an early example of sustainable fashion. From 1999 to 2007, her idiosyncratic shirts were easy to spot on Tony Soprano. Though Barnes has become increasingly focused on furniture and interior design, she keeps pushing the boundaries of clothing and textiles.

Designer

Jhane Barnes.
b Phoenix, MD (USA), 1954.

A model wearing a Jhane Barnes Checkmate stretch woven sweater from the Spring 1991 collection.

Photograph by Paul Jasmin.

↳ ACRONYM, THE BEATLES, COOGI, MIYAKE

To be more formal about it, we've got an absolutely smashing, positively dashing collection of men's formal wear at Barney's exciting RSVP Shop. Such an extravagance of selection, so many extraordinary brands ...we can be counted upon to rise to any occasion handsomely. Opening night? Formal dinner? We have an infinitude of tuxedos and tails for you to choose from. Special party coming up soon? Luxury cruise? We've got an array of dinner jackets that includes every subtle fashion variation. Spring wedding? Our elegant morning coats and striped trousers will get you to the church on time. Can you picture any other kind of formal attire? Got it? You can be sure we've got it...at the RSVP Shop, one of the six fabulous shops at Barney's, *where you select your clothes, you don't just settle for them.* **BARNEY'S**

BARNEYS NEW YORK

Once the mecca of all things luxury fashion, Barneys New York began its life in 1923 as Barney's, a men's discount clothing store located on Manhattan's West Side. When the baton was passed from Barney Pressman to his son, Fred, in the 1970s, the store became a more upscale destination, focusing on bringing European and obscure new brands to a highly discerning clientele. With its high-concept window displays designed by Simon Doonan and haute-cuisine take on lunch at "Fred's," Barneys pioneered the look and feel of the modern luxury department store. More importantly, the store played pivotal roles in the careers of hundreds of designers: Barneys was the first American retailer of Martin Margiela, Dries Van Noten, Prada, Ann Demeulemeester, Rick Owens, and Giorgio Armani. Although it filed for bankruptcy in 2020, Barneys will be remembered as a taste-making New York institution and a temple for rarefied aesthetes.

Retailer

Barneys New York.
est New York (USA), 1923.

"By George" advertising campaign for Barneys New York, 1965.

↳ ARMANI, MARGIELA, PRADA, UNITED ARROWS

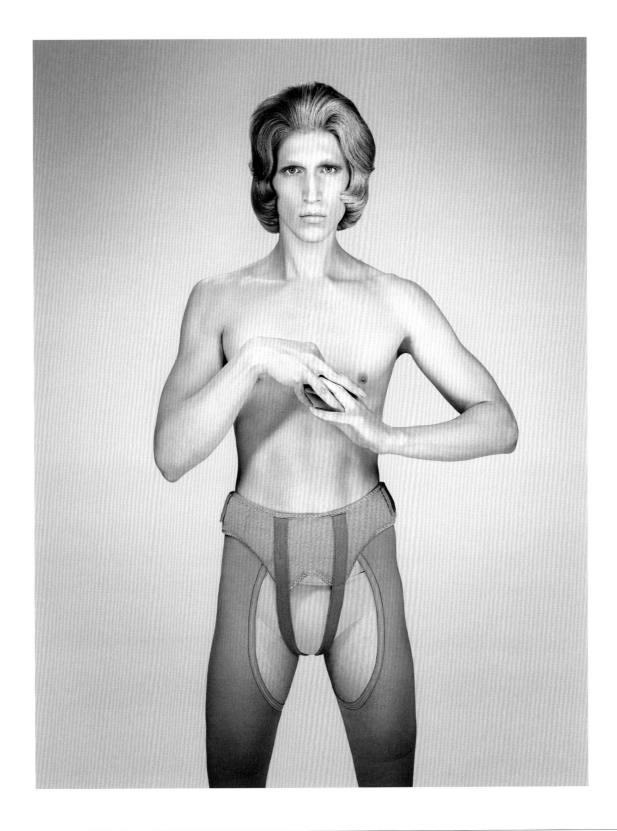

FABIEN BARON

Art Director/Photographer

Fabien Baron is arguably the most influential art director of the late twentieth century, bringing his signature sleek, modern designs and arresting visuals to a slew of magazines—*Vogue Italia*, *Vogue Paris*, *Harper's Bazaar*, and *Interview*, where he became editorial director in 2008. But through his work with brands—he set up his own agency, Baron & Baron, in 1990—he has reached a wider audience and at a prodigious rate. He has worked with Burberry, Armani, Fendi, Givenchy, and, most famously, with Calvin Klein, where he was installed as creative director for twenty years and notably created the branding and bottle design for CK ONE, the first fragrance widely marketed as unisex. Once described by *Vanity Fair* as the most sought-after creative director in the world, Baron has worked across all areas of visual identity, from logos and packaging to filmed commercials, and has photographed a number of iconic campaigns and cover stories, not to mention his own fine-art photography.

Fabien Baron.
b Antony, Hauts-de-Seine (FR), 1959.

Photographed for *Document Journal*, 2014, with hair by Guido.

Photograph by Fabien Baron.

↳ ARMANI, BOTTEGA VENETA, BURBERRY, C. KLEIN, MEISEL

JOHN BARTLETT

On the runway, John Bartlett courted risk. A native of Ohio and a graduate of Harvard University, Bartlett steered into fashion by enrolling at the Fashion Institute of Technology in the late 1980s. Stints at beloved brands WilliWear and Ronaldus Shamask followed, until he started his own eponymous line in 1991. Bartlett's menswear collections simmered with a potent sexuality, offering see-through mesh tanks and barely there speedos. His runway shows were staged for maximum controversy and drama. Early presentations featured blindfolded and caged models and porn stars, and Bartlett later teamed up with famed fashion show producer Alexandre de Betak to bring his runways to new heights. In 1997 Bartlett won both the Swarovski Best Newcomer Award and Best Menswear Designer of the Year from the Council of Fashion Designers of America. His risks did not always lead to financial reward, though, and so in 2005 he relaunched his brand with a focus on classic, iconic American pieces, such as khaki suits and cable-knit sweaters. In 2008 Bartlett was appointed creative director at Claiborne, where he stayed until 2010.

Designer

John Bartlett.
b Cincinnati, OH (USA), 1963.

John Bartlett Spring/Summer 2005 ready-to-wear collection presented at the Harvard Club of New York City.

Photograph by Márcio Madeira.

↳ JACOBS, W. SMITH, WOOSTER

JEAN-MICHEL BASQUIAT

Icon

Neo-Expressionist artist Jean-Michel Basquiat first gained recognition in the late 1970s as one of the names behind SAMO, a graffiti tag appearing around Manhattan. His subsequent rise to fame was confirmed when he showed his work as part of MoMA PS1's 1981 exhibition *New York/New Wave*. Basquiat was central to a dynamic cast of creative people in Lower Manhattan—along with fellow artist and friend Keith Haring and mentor Andy Warhol—where music and nightlife merged with the burgeoning art scene. Preternaturally cool, Basquiat combined the extravagant suits of Giorgio Armani with basic T-shirts and sweats. He wore thrift-store overcoats and paired hip-hop sportswear with preppy blazers. Basquiat created himself as a living work of art and was aware of the power of his image. In 1986 he walked the runway for Comme des Garçons's Spring/Summer 1987 collection in a pale gray double-breasted suit and Mary Janes. Though his life was cut short in 1988, his legacy lives on—in 2017 he became the highest-selling Black artist at auction—and remains an inspiration for designers, including Virgil Abloh, and streetwear brands, such as Supreme.

Jean-Michel Basquiat.
b New York (USA), 1960.
d New York (USA), 1988.

Jean-Michel Basquiat in his studio, photographed for the cover of the *New York Times Magazine*, 1985.

Photograph by Lizzie Himmel.

↳ ABLOH, ARMANI, JAY-Z, KAWAKUBO, SUPREME

BEAMS

Founded in Japan in 1976 the first Beams shop was pioneered by Etsuzo Shitara in Tokyo's Harajuku district. Inspired by American style, the store sold a mix of varsity men's fashion, lifestyle products, and housewares that appealed to Americana enthusiasts. The store was even modeled after a UCLA dorm room. Expanding Beams's reach to include clothes derived from East Coast America, along with European trends, the company launched Beams F and International Gallery Beams by 1981. Beams created more concept stores, and with the help of men's style magazine *Popeye*, the brand built on its unique formula, later adding its own line of products. Today this multilayered empire boasts multiple menswear lines, including the longstanding Beams, inspired by casual Ivy, rock, surf, and skate styles; Beams F, which offers elegant men's suiting inspired by European traditions; and premium line Beams Plus, an exceptional homage to retro Americana with contemporary workwear. At the nexus of so many converging influences, it's no wonder their collaborations have included Arc'teryx, Engineered Garments, Nike, Citizen, Seiko, Yoshida Porter, Fred Perry, Vans, and Champion.

Retailer

Beams.
est Tokyo (JAP), 1976.

Beams Plus garment tag, 2019.

Photograph by Rachel Murray.

↳ ARC'TERYX, CHAMPION, FRED SEGAL, NIKE, SUZUKI, UNITED ARROWS, VANS

THE BEATLES

The Beatles could be considered the most influential band ever both in terms of their music—their global sales exceed 1.6 billion singles—and in their impact on popular culture and fashion. Carefully dressed in the early days by manager Brian Epstein in matching collarless suits and skinny ties, they sparked Beatlemania in 1963 and led the British Invasion of the United States shortly afterward. With mop-top collar-length hair, then considered shockingly long, Chelsea boots, and turtlenecks—a uniform that was widely emulated—the Beatles played a key role in the postwar interest in the idea of male beauty. Later in the decade, their experiments with psychedelia and spirituality made them pioneers of more eclectic and flamboyant hippie fashion, reaching a peak in the colored "ringmaster" uniforms of *Sgt. Pepper's Lonely Hearts Club Band* in 1967. John Lennon in particular was highly revered for his individualistic style—such as the iconic white suit made for him by designer Ted Lapidus and his now-namesake round-frame eyeglasses—well after the band split in 1970.

Icons

John Lennon. b Liverpool, Merseyside (UK), 1940. d New York (USA), 1980; **Ringo Starr (Sir Richard Starkey).** b Liverpool, Merseyside (UK), 1940; **Sir Paul McCartney.** b Liverpool, Merseyside (UK), 1942; **George Harrison.** b Liverpool, Merseyside (UK), 1943. d Los Angeles (USA), 2001.

The Beatles, 1963.

↳ GRANNY TAKES A TRIP, J&J CROMBIE LTD., LAPIDUS, NEHRU, NUTTER

CECIL BEATON

Cecil Beaton received his earliest photographic training from his nanny and was later educated at Harrow School and the University of Cambridge. In 1926 he met Stephen Tennant and began to immortalize the effervescent world of the Bright Young Things. One of them, Osbert Sitwell, backed his first show of photographs and drawings at London's Cooling Gallery. Beaton moved to New York in the late 1920s and worked regularly for Condé Nast. In 1938, after being fired from *Vogue*, he returned to London, where he revived his career recording the Blitz during World War II. Beaton was the society photographer of his era. He took portraits at Queen Elizabeth II's coronation, recorded the Duke of Windsor's wedding, and photographed style icons, including Gary Cooper, Truman Capote, Andy Warhol, David Hockney, and Cristóbal Balenciaga. He was also a style icon in his own right, with clothes that echoed the dressed-up spirit of the Bright Young Things—mixing colorful suits, military jackets, antique textiles, and cravats with extravagant hats. Beaton had a lifelong love of tailoring, so much so that when he died, one of his tailors was among the first to be notified.

Icon/Photographer

Cecil Beaton.
b London (UK), 1904.
d Broad Chalke, England (UK), 1980.

Self-portrait in the Winter Garden, Reddish House, Wiltshire, England, 1961.

Photograph by Cecil Beaton.

↳ D. BAILEY, COWARD, HOCKNEY, DUKE OF WINDSOR

TYSON BECKFORD

Model

Tyson Beckford.
b The Bronx (USA), 1970.

Polo Ralph Lauren Underwear,
Spring/Summer 1998.

↳ COMBS, HARDISON, LAUREN,
RITTS, VANDERLOO, WEBER

Tyson Beckford's exalted status as a supermodel is a far cry from his being teased during childhood for his looks. Born in the Bronx, Beckford was raised in Jamaica before returning to New York when he was seven years old. In 1993 Beckford was scouted by the editor of the hip-hop magazine *The Source*, and the following year he signed with Bethann Hardison's model agency. By 1994 he was the face of Ralph Lauren Polo Sport cologne, and he became the first Black model to sign an exclusive contract with the brand, modeling its fashion through the 1990s. What Lauren hailed as Beckford's "all-American look with a dramatic edge" appealed equally to editors—he appeared in magazines such as *Esquire*, *GQ*, *Attitude*, and *Agenda*, and worked with celebrated photographers, including Herb Ritts and Bruce Weber. In 1995 he was selected as one of the 50 Most Beautiful People in the World by *People* magazine and Man of the Year by VH1. A vocal advocate for greater Black representation in fashion, Beckford once turned down an appearance at Milan Fashion Week in protest because he was the only Black man cast for the show.

DAVID BECKHAM

David Beckham began his football career at seventeen years old, when he joined Manchester United in 1992. Over his twenty-plus-year career, he won six Premier League titles and two FA Cup Finals and was a six-year captain of the England team. After marrying pop star Victoria Adams in 1997, Beckham's style off the pitch made him a regular feature in fashion magazines. The pair famously appeared in matching Gucci black outfits in 1999, and the footballer became known for his growing collection of tattoos and ever-changing hairstyles, which ranged from bleached and shaved looks to a Mohawk, man bun, and cornrows. After Beckham retired in 2013, at thirty-eight, he began a second career as an immaculately dressed style icon, fronting campaigns for Adidas, Armani, Belstaff, Breitling, and H&M. His personal style has matured, playing on British tweeds and tailoring, and he often wears flat caps, cords, and subdued colors of classic country style. In 2018 the British Fashion Council created the role of Ambassadorial President for Beckham, in which he promotes British designers globally.

Icon

David Beckham.
b Leytonstone, England (UK), 1975.

David Beckham leaving Balthazar, New York, 2016.

Photograph by James Devaney.

↳ ADIDAS, ARMANI, BELSTAFF, GUCCI, LOUIS VUITTON

LUCIUS BEEBE

During the Great Depression, author and arbiter Lucius Beebe claimed to brush his teeth with Chablis and *only* spend one hundred dollars a day on food and drink. Such outré statements—and an even more flamboyant style—made Beebe a popular columnist for the *New York Herald Tribune* in the 1930s and 1940s, reporting on the beautiful and fashionable habitués of the city's finest establishments. Known for his eye-catching dress sense and imposing six-foot-four-inch-tall stature, Beebe was dedicated to formal clothing—as a reporter, he once arrived at a house fire wearing a morning coat and top hat—and typically donned bespoke Savile Row suits (he reportedly owned forty) with John Lobb boots, a mink overcoat, and doeskin gloves. Luscious Lucius, a sobriquet coined by fellow columnist Walter Winchell, was formally acknowledged as a style setter—he particularly influenced men to adopt formal evening dress—when he was featured on the cover of *Life* magazine in January 1939. Ahead of his time, Beebe lived openly with his partner, Charles Clegg; they traveled the country in their own railroad car, decorated in the style of the Venetian Renaissance.

Icon

Lucius Beebe.
b Wakefield, MA (USA), 1902.
d San Francisco (USA), 1966.

Lucius Beebe in the Garden Court of the Palace Hotel, San Francisco, c. 1960.

Photograph by Slim Aarons.

↳ BEATON, BRUMMELL, CRISP, JOHN LOBB BOOTMAKER

THE AGGRESSIVELY STRIPED SUIT BY GEOFFREY BEENE

GEOFFREY BEENE

Geoffrey Beene was one of the US's leading designers, hailed by the *New York Times* in 1993 as "an artist who chooses to work in cloth." Born in Louisiana, he studied medicine before training in fashion in New York and Paris, and eventually made a name for himself with the eponymous fashion house he founded in 1963. Although he initially designed womenswear, Beene launched his first men's line in 1969, later making a license agreement with Van Heusen to produce shirts. Beene told *Vogue* in 2004 that he found menswear more difficult to design than womenswear, observing that "womenswear is about creativity, and menswear is more about taste. . . . Menswear does not need trends." Beene's approach to all his clothes was based on cut and line, eschewing decoration almost entirely. His suits, shirts, and shoes were exactly what the contemporary business executive wanted to wear: smart, understated, and comfortable. His design talent and financial savvy—as well as the introduction of his classic men's fragrance, Grey Flannel—made him highly successful. Over his career Beene was honored with eight Coty Awards.

Designer

Geoffrey Beene.
b Haynesville, LA (USA), 1924.
d New York (USA), 2004.

Advertisement for the Aggressively Striped Suit by Geoffrey Beene, c. 1973.

↳ ABBOUD, BLASS, LAUREN, VAN HEUSEN, WEITZ

WALTER VAN BEIRENDONCK

As part of the Antwerp Six, the bold, brilliant, and transgressive Belgium-based fashion designer Walter Van Beirendonck helped place Antwerp on the fashion map. A graduate of the city's Royal Academy of Fine Arts, Van Beirendonck has pushed boundaries with his designs since starting his label in 1983. His collections are a loud and colorful homage to fluidity, queerdom, and kink, born from his early fascination with London nightlife in the 1970s, icons including David Bowie and Iggy Pop, and magazines such as *The Face*. Built upon a skillful, classic technique of exceptional tailoring and the ability to manipulate textiles, his clothes are wearable objets d'art: graphic suiting, BDSM-inspired masks, and phallic-silhouetted hats. He does not shy away from making a psychedelic—or political—statement either, with humor and wit, of course, putting everything from alien anarchists to the AIDS epidemic to the environmental crisis on full display on the runway. Van Beirendonck returned to the Royal Academy of Fine Arts in 2007 as head of the fashion program, and has mentored designers such as Bernhard Willhelm, Craig Green, and Kris Van Assche.

Designer

Walter Van Beirendonck.
b Brecht (BEL), 1957.

Models pose backstage before the Walter Van Beirendonck Fall/Winter 2020 show at Paris Fashion Week.

Photograph by Francois Durand.

↳ VAN ASSCHE, BIKKEMBERGS, DEMEULEMEESTER, GREEN, WILLHELM

BELGIAN SHOES

From a small shop on Manhattan's East 55th Street, Belgian Shoes introduced a new form of ultra-supple loafer. With shoes designed by Henri Bendel, the boutique opened in 1955, the year he retired as president from the eponymous retailer. The firm's soft-soled shoe with its distinctive tiny bows is hand-cut from fine calf leather and hand-sewn inside out by shoemakers in Belgium. As comfortable as house slippers—the soles are padded with a thin layer of "piano hair" (similar to the material used to dampen piano keys)—Bendel's initial Mr. Casual style became a status symbol among wealthy Upper East Siders and the Long Island and Palm Beach set. The shoes remained an insider secret until they were noticed by fashion bloggers in the early 2010s and began showing up during fashion week and fashion fairs. Today the firm has extended its range, introducing leopard print, tartan, and other trendier styles that attract a more creative, younger clientele. Fans of the brand range from the king of Belgium to designer Isaac Mizrahi and Noah founder Brendon Babenzien.

Footwear

Belgian Shoes.
est New York (USA), 1955.

Luca Rubinacci wearing Belgian loafers at Pitti Immagine Uomo 85, Florence, 2014.

Photograph by Jacopo Raule.

↳ COX, ELKANN, G.H. BASS & CO., RUBINACCI, TOD'S

BELSTAFF

Like many British heritage brands, Belstaff was shaped by two world wars and the rise of the golden age of motorcycle sport. In 1924—after years of dealing reclaimed materials and rubber products and providing capes and groundsheets to the military—Eli Belovitch founded the waterproof clothing brand in Staffordshire, England, with his son-in-law Harry Grosberg. The company's reputation was built on sportsmen, such as motorcyclist Joe Wright, and adventurers who wore the brand's rugged outerwear, including T. E. Lawrence, and even the revolutionary Che Guevara. In 1948 the company introduced the Trialmaster—a belted waxed-cotton jacket with four large front pockets and elbow patches—which was later worn by Steve McQueen in *The Great Escape* (1963). McQueen also went on to be the inspiration for Belstaff's sportier Brooklands—or Mojave—jacket, modeled after the one he wore during a race across the Mojave Desert in 1963. In more recent years, Belstaff has been worn by Leonardo DiCaprio in 2004's *The Aviator* and Tom Cruise in 2006's *Mission: Impossible III*, as well as by contemporary sportsmen such as David Beckham.

Designer Brand

Belstaff.
est Staffordshire, England (UK), 1924.

Steve McQueen wearing a Belstaff jacket during a five-hundred-mile motorbike race across the Mojave Desert, 1963.

Photograph by John Dominis.

↳ BARBOUR, BECKHAM, BURBERRY, McQUEEN

UMIT BENAN

Umit Benan was raised in Istanbul, schooled in Switzerland, and early on took design positions in New York. When he launched his eponymous label in 2009, he melded his global influences by offering regal Italian-style suiting, band-collared shirts, and swooping, billowing trousers. Just a year in, he won the Who Is On Next? award at Pitti Uomo, and in 2011 the illustrious Italian house Trussardi hired Benan to lead its design. Two years later Benan left, hinting at creative differences between himself and the stalwart label. He kept his own line running. The shows for Umit Benan were playful and cinematic: a man wakes up and gets dressed, he takes to the tennis court, he reports for military duty. In 2016 the Umit Benan line itself ceased, and after a hiatus, Benan returned with B+—a seriously sleek luxury line produced in part by Italy's Caruso.

Designer

Umit Benan.
b Stuttgart (GER), 1980.

Umit Benan Fall/Winter 2016 collection at Paris Fashion Week.

Photograph by Kay-Paris Fernandes.

↳ JACOBS, LEVI'S, PILATI, PRADA

BEN SHERMAN

Before the British designer Ben Sherman became synonymous with men's shirts, he was born Arthur Benjamin Sugarman in Brighton, England, in 1925. After emigrating to the United States in 1946, and working in the garment industry there, he returned to Brighton inspired and began to craft shirts of his own. In 1963 he launched the first Ben Sherman design, in homage to America's Ivy League style and using only the highest-quality American fabrics. Sherman had a vision beyond the basic work shirt—injecting bold choices that have become rampant, if not expected,

today: a buttoned collar, box pleat, and locker loop on the back of the shirt; a sharp, slim fit; or use of classic American materials and patterns (think gingham, madras check, or candy stripe) in colorful hues. Each Ben Sherman shirt was also individually boxed—a radical notion at the time. Known for well-fitting, slim silhouettes and square hems, Ben Sherman designs sparked the interest of British youth subcultures as the go-to for every generation, and have continued to do so for more than six decades.

Designer Brand

Ben Sherman.
est Brighton, England (UK), 1963.

Ben Sherman advertisement, c. 2010s.

↳ BROOKS BROTHERS,
C.F. HATHAWAY COMPANY,
DR. MARTENS, PENGUIN,
PERRY

PETER BERLIN

In the 1970s Peter Berlin stepped in front of his camera and transformed himself into a gay icon. Born in Poland, he was raised in Berlin but in his twenties fled the German capital. He landed in San Francisco in the early 1970s to find a liberated city with a bustling gay and gender-fluid community. He was a striking presence with a shaggy Dutch-boy haircut and a chiseled six-pack. His mission was to challenge the concept of traditional male sexuality by wearing body-conscious clothing that invited shock; Berlin fabricated his own clothes, such as shrunken, torso-baring button-ups and impossibly tight leather trousers. His penchant for body-hugging white jeans and joggers pioneered their popularity and is referenced to this day. A photographer by trade, Berlin turned his camera on himself, composing portraits that oozed glamour and overt sexuality. By donning leather motorcycle caps and sailor uniforms, Berlin subverted rote masculine stereotypes. Berlin's influence on fashion can be seen in designs by Tom Ford, Thierry Mugler, Hood By Air, and Ludovic de Saint Sernin, as well as in the imagery of David LaChapelle and Tom of Finland.

Peter Berlin.
b Lodz (POL), 1942.

Peter Berlin, *Self Portrait on the Roof of the Ansonia (White Pants)*, c. 1970s.

Photograph by Peter Berlin.

↳ FORD, JACOBS, LaCHAPELLE, OLIVER

BERLUTI

Master shoemaker Alessandro Berluti learned the importance of a well-made wooden last from local craftsmen in his hometown of Senigallia, Italy. He later moved to Paris to hone his expertise in making shoes and founded the French heritage house Berluti in 1895. His debut design, named the Alessandro, was a lace-up dress shoe fabricated from one piece of leather and had no visible stitching; today this signature style, known as the wholecut shoe, endures as a legendary men's staple. Continuing in Berluti's tradition, the atelier excelled in its bespoke precision and savoir faire,

making shoes for international gentlemen, including the Duke of Windsor and artists Jean Cocteau and Andy Warhol. (Berluti's Andy loafer, originally crafted for the artist, remains a house staple.) In the 1980s Olga Berluti evolved the brand's codes, introducing supple Venezia leather and a novel patina that liberated the shoe from blacks and browns. In 1993 Berluti was acquired by LVMH, and in 2011 the brand introduced custom tailoring and ready-to-wear. Its artistic directors have included Alessandro Sartori, auteur Haider Ackermann, and Belgian designer Kris Van Assche.

Designer Brand

Berluti.
est Paris (FR), 1895.

Berluti shoes from the Spring/Summer 2013 collection on display at Paris Fashion Week, 2012.

Photograph by Antonio de Moraes Barros Filho.

↳ ACKERMANN, VAN ASSCHE, SALVATORE FERRAGAMO, DUKE OF WINDSOR

GEORGE BEST

Northern Ireland's George Best was arguably the first footballer known as much for his playboy and fashion-icon status as for his athletic talent, paving the way for others, including David Beckham and Cristiano Ronaldo, to craft careers beyond the pitch. A star athlete for Manchester United, Best was voted sixth in the top one hundred players for the FIFA Player of the Century award. Best was a dedicated follower of fashion, wearing everything from Chelsea boots and tight-fitting cord trousers to collarless woolen shirts and polo sweaters. Not only did

his striking looks embody the style of the Swinging Sixties—he was dubbed El Beatle for his mop-top haircut and legions of young female admirers—he also founded his own fashion boutique, the Edwardia, in March 1967 to cater to "the extrovert male." The store stocked similar styles to those Best wore, including purple corduroys and tweed jackets. Best's soccer career ended in 1974, but his extravagant lifestyle and impeccable style kept him in the public eye for long after.

George Best.
b Belfast, Northern Ireland (UK), 1946.
d London (UK), 2005.

George Best and his fiancée, Eva Haraldsted, outside his clothing boutique, Manchester, UK, 1969.

↳ THE BEATLES, BECKHAM, FRAZIER, WADE, WESTBROOK

BIJAN

Bijan is a store for the one percent of the one percent. Its designs—including $2,350 silk polos, $15,000 deerskin jackets, $580 logo ball caps, and $1,350 knit T-shirts—are far out of reach for most, but this store has never catered to the average shopper. In the mid-1970s Bijan Pakzad, an Iranian immigrant, opened his boutique on Rodeo Drive, offering clothes for discerning, and deep-pocketed, gentlemen. By 1985 Bijan (as he was known) boasted that he had dressed four kings and sixteen presidents. Rounding out that client list were names such as Giorgio Armani and Tom Cruise. To most Rodeo

Drive passersby, Bijan's designs—such as a cornflower blue cashmere cardigan sweater or a sandy silk and linen blouson—wouldn't elicit a raised eyebrow. To the wearer, however, they feel extraordinarily plush and luxe. Bijan's flash has always come more through its marketing. In the 1980s and '90s, Bijan's ads playfully starred the smiling (and ever well-dressed) store owner next to stars such as Michael Jordan. Bijan also made it a habit to park his bright "Bijan yellow" luxury cars outside the shop like a beacon of wealth. Since his death in 2011, his son, Nicolas, has maintained the label's lofty reputation.

Retailer

Bijan.
est Los Angeles (USA), 1976.

Bijan Pakzad, 1983.

Photograph by Douglas Kirkland.

↳ ARMANI, FORD, HERMÈS, JORDAN

DIRK BIKKEMBERGS

Along with other notable alumni of Belgium's Royal Academy of Fine Arts, Belgian designer Dirk Bikkembergs was an integral part of the avant-garde fashion collective known as the Antwerp Six. In 1988—six years following graduation—Bikkembergs launched his own menswear label after creating a series of standout shoes that merged Flemish craftsmanship with heavy-duty work boots. Available in myriad iterations, the shoes experimented with eyelet hooks, metal heels, and wraparound laces. Initially Bikkembergs's own aesthetic in menswear involved functional, streamlined styles with a sensual edge, but in the early aughts, he sought to move away from the niche world of high fashion toward a more mainstream audience, designing collections for athletes, specifically soccer players. In 2005 he staged a fashion show at FC Barcelona's Camp Nou, debuting "sport couture," and later collaborated with Serie A club Inter Milan. A year later he even bought his own Italian soccer club, FC Fossombrone, on whose players (who double as models) he continues to test design garments, producing T-shirts, kits, underwear, and suits—for on and off the pitch.

Designer

Dirk Bikkembergs.
b Cologne (GER), 1959.

Model Brodie Scott for the Bikkembergs Fall/Winter 2018 campaign.

Photograph by Roberto Rapetti.

↪ VAN ASSCHE, VAN BEIRENDONCK, DEMEULEMEESTER, VAN NOTEN

HU BING

Chinese model Hu Bing is one of Asia's most recognizable faces as a top model and actor. Born in Hangzhou, China, in 1971, Bing was a world-class rower who competed with China's 1988 Summer Olympic team. After suffering an injury, he began modeling, earning the title of China's Top Male Model in 1991. Shortly thereafter, he became a transnational talent, walking in global fashion shows for brands such as Louis Vuitton, Dolce & Gabbana, and Valentino. In 1994 he segued into singing and acting, and was propelled into megastardom with the 1999 hit Chinese television drama *Love Talks*. Through the 2000s and 2010s, Bing worked with top fashion brands, including Cartier, Gucci, and Salvatore Ferragamo. Known for his dapper style, Bing was appointed by the British Fashion Council in 2015 to be a London Collections: Men ambassador (along with British model David Gandy), serving as a sartorial liaison and promoting brands, including Savile Row tailor Huntsman.

Model

Hu Bing.
b Hangzhou (CHN), 1971.

Hu Bing photographed for "The Kyoto Affair" fashion editorial, *GQ Japan*, October 2012.

Photograph by Maciej Kucia.

↳ DOLCE & GABBANA, GANDY, HUNTSMAN, LOUIS VUITTON

CASS BIRD

With a portfolio that reads as a who's who of contemporary culture, the artist, photographer, and director Cass Bird has become known for her alternative, authentic view from behind the lens. A native of Los Angeles and graduate of Smith College, Bird moved to New York City in 2001. Her work spans art, fashion, and commercial projects that are notable for their playful, spirited depictions of models, celebrities, and luxury goods. Eschewing a prescriptive ideal of beauty and gender, her approach advocates for new ideals of identity, frequently blurring these distinctions. With her

joy for life and fashion, she captures leading men in unexpected poses: Mahershala Ali clowning around in a fluorescent green suit, Adam Driver hanging off a street sign, or Michael B. Jordan besuited and childlike, playing on a lawn. Her fresh, unfettered style has led to major advertising campaigns and celebrated editorials for *Vogue*, *Dazed and Confused*, *i-D*, and *T: The New York Times Style Magazine*. Working in collaboration with her subjects, her goal is to connect with people, and the relaxed, genuine portraits she captures are testament to this approach.

Photographer

Cass Bird.
b Los Angeles (USA), 1974.

Michael B. Jordan, East Hampton, New York, photographed for *Vanity Fair*, November 2018.

Photograph by Cass Bird.

↳ D. BAILEY, i-D, LUCHFORD, MASON, UNWERTH

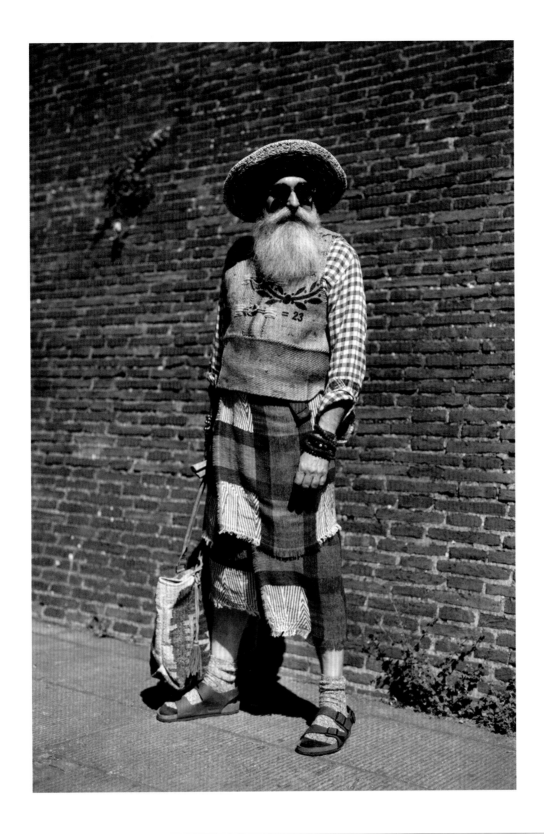

BIRKENSTOCK

Casual, comfortable, and universally appealing, the Birkenstock sandal was created as an orthopedic innovation and unexpectedly became a global go-to. With its distinctive cork sole that molds to the foot, the understated design has found popularity with many subcultures: it was discovered by health-conscious consumers in the 1960s, worn by hippies in the '70s, and then reborn as a grunge must-have in the early '90s when the shoe appeared in Marc Jacobs's 1993 Perry Ellis collection. In 1774 Johann Birkenstock registered his shoemaking business in Langen-Bergheim in eastern Germany. However, it was his great-great-grandson Konrad Birkenstock who developed the first contoured insole in 1896, and then *his* grandson Karl who designed the first Birkenstock sandal in 1964. Karl went on to create the iconic two-strap Arizona sandal in 1973 and built the firm into an international brand, with fans such as Grateful Dead guitarist Bob Weir and actor Jason Momoa. The original counterculture shoe has surged in popularity in the twenty-first century, increasing its cult appeal through collaborations with Rick Owens, Valentino, and Kith.

Footwear

Birkenstock.
est Langen-Bergheim (GER), 1774.

A guest attending Pitti Uomo 94 wearing Birkenstock sandals, Florence, 2018.

Photograph by Matthew Sperzel.

↳ BEAMS, CLARKS, JACOBS, JIL SANDER, OWENS

JUDY BLAME

Icon/Stylist

A punk who frequented Vivienne Westwood's Seditionaries in the late 1970s, Judy Blame was a stylist, designer, and art director whose underground aesthetic defined *i-D* and *The Face* in the 1980s and '90s. As a stylist, Blame worked with musicians, including Duran Duran, Boy George, and Björk, and designers, such as Richard Nicoll, Gareth Pugh, and John Galliano. He also collaborated with stylist Ray Petri, the creative behind Buffalo style, for editorials seen in *i-D* and *The Face*. Blame's influence permeated London's creative world: he was the first to shoot Helmut Lang and Alexander McQueen,

and he took a young Edward Enninful under his wing. Blame was commissioned by Rei Kawakubo of Comme des Garçons in 2005, and his upcycled, fantastical jewelry made from *objets trouvés* found along the banks of the River Thames was sustainable fashion before the concept existed. Blame died in 2018, but his influence continues to be seen on the runway—in 2020 Kim Jones presented his Fall/Winter men's collection partly inspired by the stylist. With Jones's embellished berets, gloves, and earrings and brooches made from an assortment of materials, it was impossible to miss Blame's touch.

Judy Blame (Christopher Barnes).
b Leatherhead, England (UK), 1960.
d London (UK), 2018.

Judy Blame in his Curtain Road studio in Shoreditch, London, 1984.

Photograph by Paul Hartnett.

↳ ENNINFUL, THE FACE, i-D,
   K. JONES, S. JONES, PETRI

TIM BLANKS

"What I do is evocation, not evaluation," says Tim Blanks, one of fashion's foremost authorities. Revered as a longtime editor and writer, his prescient insights tell unique sartorial tales, tying his criticism to a broader cultural layer and lens. Born in Auckland, New Zealand, Blanks's insatiable curiosity led him to amass an encyclopedic knowledge of fashion, inspired by formative exposure to music and style icons, such as David Bowie and Bryan Ferry. In 1989 Blanks became the host of the popular Canadian TV show *Fashion File*; he left nearly two decades later, in 2006, to join Style.com as editor at large.

Initially covering menswear—from Helmut Lang's departure to Craig Green's breakout show—he expanded to include a "Throwback Thursdays" series that highlighted fashion's most memorable moments. Blanks has also written for *Vogue*, *GQ*, the *Financial Times*, *Fantastic Man*, and *Arena Homme +*, and in 2013 he was honored by the CFDA with the Eugenia Sheppard Media Award for his contributions to fashion journalism. In 2015 he joined the Business of Fashion as editor at large, continuing his in-depth reporting on the state of the industry.

Editor/Writer

Tim Blanks.
b Auckland (NZ), 1955.

Tim Blanks attends a runway show during London Fashion Week, 2020.

Photograph by Tristan Fewings.

↳ FANTASTIC MAN, GELLERS, GQ, GREEN, LANG, O'BRIEN

BILL BLASS

In 1967 Bill Blass became the first American high-fashion designer to enter into menswear, earning him the inaugural Coty Award for menswear a year later. Blass, who took up fashion after serving with the US Army in World War II, said he sought to design clothes for men who wanted to look "with it, but not ridiculous," adding, "The man over forty needs help." Taking his cue from earlier fashion icons such as the Duke of Windsor, he designed classic but casual and affordable ready-to-wear menswear. His two-button suits were fitted, and his jackets were cut higher in the armhole to make his customers appear slimmer. A natural salesman, Blass knew he could sell his menswear better than any model, so he appeared in his own advertisements long before Ralph Lauren or Calvin Klein did so. In 1970 he formed Bill Blass Limited to license products from bed linens to chocolates, with eighteen licensees producing menswear alone. Always dressed immaculately, he was included in *Vanity Fair*'s International Best-Dressed Hall of Fame in 1970.

Designer

Bill Blass.
b Fort Wayne, IN (USA), 1922.
d New Preston, CT (USA), 2002.

Bill Blass, c. 1970.

Photograph by Jack Robinson.

↳ BEENE, DE LA RENTA, HALSTON, C. KLEIN, LAUREN, WEITZ, DUKE OF WINDSOR

BLUNDSTONE

The Blundstones were a family of British immigrants that landed in Tasmania in the mid-1800s. At first the family's business was importing boots from their homeland, but in 1870 they began cobbling their own shoes out of local leathers. By the early 1900s, hundreds of shoes were whirring off Blundstone's production lines each week, and the company was tapped to produce footwear for the Australian army in World War I. The Great Depression hit the Blundstone family hard, and they were forced to sell the label to brothers T. J. and Thomas Cuthbertson,

whose descendants still own the brand today. It was not until the 1960s, though, that Blundstone's most iconic style—the elastic-sided pull-on Chelsea #500 boots—arrived. Often known as Blunnies, these burly work boots are ideal for traipsing through the bush or simply tending a backyard garden. More than merely functional, the #500 has dipped into fashion, particularly since the 2010s, as on-the-pulse urbanites in areas such as Brooklyn have co-opted these brawny boots.

Footwear

Blundstone.
est Hobart, Tasmania (ASL), 1870.

Machine operator at the Blundstone boot factory, 1951.

↳ THE BEATLES, RED WING, R.M.WILLIAMS

OZWALD BOATENG

As a teenager, Ozwald Boateng studied computer science. Fortunately for men everywhere, he swapped the keyboard for the sewing machine. In 1991, at just twenty-four, Boateng—a Londoner of Ghanaian descent—opened an atelier on Portobello Road. With venerated tailor Tommy Nutter as a mentor, Boateng daringly presented a collection during Paris Fashion Week in 1994. The spotlight lifted Boateng's burgeoning bespoke firm, and he moved his studio closer to Savile Row, offering slender suits, often in fetching jewel tones. Boateng became an atelier to stars on-screen and off. He fabricated flashy customwear for Spike Lee (an aubergine number for the Oscars) and Idris Elba (emerald green for the Golden Globes) while creating costumes for movies such as *Lock, Stock and Two Smoking Barrels* (1998) and *Black Panther* (2018). Starting in 2003 Boateng briefly served as creative director for Givenchy, and in his later career he has spread his name globally through headline-grabbing runway shows in Accra, Ghana, and at Harlem's Apollo Theater.

Designer/Tailor

Ozwald Boateng.
b London (UK), 1967.

Ozwald Boateng, 2010.

Photograph by Fabrice Dall'Anese.

↳ A. SAUVAGE, BOSWELL, NUTTER

EMILY ADAMS BODE

From a compact studio on New York's Lower East Side in 2016, Emily Adams Bode opened up a new chapter in American fashion. Bode emerged with comely, one-of-a-kind coats and shirts refashioned from salvaged quilt tops, tablecloths, and lace. The brand is at once nostalgic—her wearable canvases pay their respects to the artistry of once-forgotten textiles—and completely forward-looking. Rather than spinning her wheels in the thread-worn territory of American preppiness, Bode carved a novel path lined in colorful mishmashery and unexpected patterns. In a few short years, she made her way to the Paris runway, displaying captivating ready-to-wear pieces produced in New York and India. Narrative lies at the core of her work—often quite literally. One of Bode's most sought-after pieces is the Senior Cords: corduroy pants covered in custom hand-lettering and drawings alluding to the wearer's interests and story. In 2020 Harry Styles wore his specialized Bode cords in the pages of American *Vogue*.

Designer

Emily Adams Bode.
b Atlanta (USA), 1989.

Models backstage at the Bode Fall/Winter 2020 menswear show at Paris Fashion Week.

Photograph by Kay-Paris Fernandes.

↳ JAY-Z, LEVI'S, STYLES, WALES BONNER

BODYMAP

In London during the early 1980s, fashion was rapidly being infused with the eclectic dress-up style—military coats, pirate jackets, pierrot collars, and ruffled shirts—worn at clubs, such as Steve Strange's Blitz. Launched in Covent Garden in 1979, Blitz spawned a generation of creatives. Two of them, David Holah and Stevie Stewart, formed their label BodyMap when they graduated from Middlesex Polytechnic in 1982. Their designs—including their signature bodysuits—were colorful, layered, and often featured graphic prints created by textile designer Hilde Smith. Blitz Kids—including Boy George, pop singer Marilyn, and Leigh Bowery—modeled in BodyMap's spectacular shows, which were choreographed by dancer Michael Clark, and their campaigns were photographed by up-and-coming names such as David LaChapelle and Mario Testino. The aesthetic and creativity of their shows, which blended art, fashion, dance, and music, echoed the gender-blurring spirit of the time. Despite the label closing in the early 1990s, BodyMap's groundbreaking use of layered knits and stretchy materials, including viscose lycra, filtered through into mainstream fashion.

Designer Brand

BodyMap.
est Middlesex, England (UK), 1982.

BodyMap Spring/Summer 1986.

Photograph by Judy Montgomery.

↳ ANDERSON, GAULTIER, C. JEFFREY, LaCHAPELLE, WESTWOOD

GIUSEPPE BORSALINO

The millinery shop founded in northern Italy by Giuseppe Borsalino in 1857 not only gave its name to a movie (1970's *Borsalino*, starring Alain Delon) but also was celebrated nationally, with an Italian postage stamp commemorating its 160th anniversary in 2017. Its felt or beaver fur hats, available in a range of classic styles but always with distinctive dimples in the sides near the front, helped the company make its name in 1900 when it won a prize at the Paris Exposition, the city at the heart of the belle époque. After Borsalino's death that same year, the brand's

popularity spread, helped by eye-catching advertising campaigns illustrated by leading artists, such as Marcello Dudovich and Max Huber. Beginning in the 1930s the brand enjoyed a close link with the film industry— Humphrey Bogart and Ingrid Bergman both wore Borsalino hats at the end of *Casablanca* (1942) and Marcello Mastroianni wore a style in Fellini's *8½* (1963), as did John Belushi in *The Blues Brothers* (1980). The golden logo stitched into the hatband remains a byword for luxury design.

Milliner

Giuseppe Borsalino.
b Pecetto di Valenza (IT), 1834.
d Alessandria (IT), 1900.

Jean-Paul Belmondo and Alain Delon in a publicity still for Paramount Pictures's *Borsalino*, 1970.

↳ DELON, HERBERT JOHNSON HATTERS, LOCK & CO. HATTERS, MASTROIANNI

WARAIRE BOSWELL

If not for his towering height, Waraire Boswell might not have ended up becoming a fashion designer at all. While working at talent agencies in his twenties, Boswell struggled to find suits that fit his six-foot-seven-inch build. Spotting an opportunity, Boswell changed careers, and in 2002 he launched his eponymous tailoring label. His client list soon looked like an NBA roster, boasting similarly statuesque stars such as LeBron James, Kobe Bryant, and Blake Griffin. Some celebrity clients favored Boswell's close-to-the-body suits in reticent colors, but others allowed him to dabble in brow-raising textiles. The rapper YG has worn a double-breasted cherry red Boswell suit, while the singer Raphael Saadiq has sported a leopard-print Boswell number. Jolting customwear may hog the spotlight, but Boswell's widest-reaching project may be his most egalitarian: in 2017 he designed uniforms for McDonald's fourteen thousand locations. Boswell's collection today is a mix of inventive formalwear, such as kimono-esque blazers, and casual styles, including joggers and T-shirts bearing slogans such as "Black Awareness," a reference to Boswell's work raising the visibility of Black creatives in fashion.

Designer

Waraire Boswell.
b Altadena, CA (USA), 1975.

Waraire Boswell 2019–20.

Photograph by Colin Jacob.

↳ A. SAUVAGE, JAY-Z, LORENZO

BOTTEGA VENETA

Since its founding in 1966 by Michele Taddei and Renzo Zengiaro, the Kering-owned Italian luxury house Bottega Veneta has been synonymous with sophisticated elegance. Popular with jet-setters, such as Jacqueline Kennedy Onassis, and art-world stars, including Andy Warhol, Bottega Veneta is best known for its braided *intrecciato* leather goods, an instantly recognizable trademark that continues to define the house's craft-focused approach to design. In 2001 the brand installed Tomas Maier as creative director, who guided the house's revered designs until 2018 when Daniel Lee took the helm. A former disciple of Celine designer Phoebe Philo, Lee has continued Bottega's architectural minimalism and low-key opulence, offering a welcome breath of fresh air amid the clutter of logo-mania. Standout pieces include the iconic leather Pouch bag, pointy woven-leather loafers, chunky rubber rain boots, and oversized eyewear, all of which have achieved cultlike status among celebrities, such as Donald Glover and the rapper Future.

Designer Brand

Bottega Veneta.
est Vicenza (IT), 1966.

Bottega Veneta Fall/Winter 2010 campaign.

Photograph by Robert Longo.

↳ GUCCI, LANG, PRADA, SALVATORE FERRAGAMO

DAVID BOWIE

Though he was more of a cookie-cutter, mop-topped raconteur at the onset of his career, by the early 1970s David Bowie had found his footing as a gender-bending provocateur, enticing and often confounding onlookers. When he arrived in Los Angeles to promote *Hunky Dory* in 1971 wearing a frilly dress, *Rolling Stone* remarked that he appeared "almost disconcertingly reminiscent of Lauren Bacall." As glam-rock alter ego Ziggy Stardust, Bowie performed in Technicolor body-accentuating getups by Japanese designer Kansai Yamamoto.

Always striving to be one step ahead, by the middle of the 1970s, Bowie shifted into his Thin White Duke period with sleek tailoring and suave slicked-back hair. In the 1980s he shepherded the New Romantic movement while wearing soft-toned tailoring and glimmering white shoes. Though his eccentricity tempered in time, in the '90s and beyond, Bowie was still performing in costumes by Alexander McQueen and remained a striking fashion fixture with his wife, the model Iman, by his side.

Icon

David Bowie.
b London (UK), 1947.
d New York (USA), 2016.

David Bowie at RCA Studios, New York, 1973.

Photograph by David Gahr.

↳ FISH, HUDSON, P. SMITH, K. YAMAMOTO

KWAME BRATHWAITE

"Black is Beautiful," a slogan common to contemporary ears, was revolutionary during the 1950s and '60s when photographer Kwame Brathwaite helped popularize the phrase through his work. In his photographs the Black models he depicted celebrated their natural beauty—something unprecedented in the fashion world at the time. Growing up in Harlem Brathwaite was surrounded by jazz, which not only led him to photography but also defined the very rhythm and style of how he visualized the world. In 1956 Brathwaite, with his brother, cofounded the African Jazz-Art Society & Studios (a collective of artists, playwrights, designers, and dancers), and six years later he started Grandassa Models, a modeling agency for Black women. Throughout the 1960s and '70s, Brathwaite regularly contributed to Black publications, such as the *Amsterdam News* and *City Sun*, and helped guide the way for the Black arts and Black power movement. His images of top Black performers—including greats such as Stevie Wonder, Bob Marley, James Brown, and Sly Stone—as well as icons, such as Muhammad Ali, portrayed uplifted and empowered men who also kept a keen eye on the way they dressed.

Photographer

Kwame Brathwaite.
b Brooklyn (USA), 1938.

Jimmy Abu, Kwame Brathwaite, and Elombe Brath, Jacob Riis Park, Queens, NY, c. 1963.

Photograph by Kwame Brathwaite.

↳ ALI, BROWN, MARLEY, PARKS, SIDIBÉ, STONE

BRIONI

In 1945 master tailor Nazareno Fonticoli and his business partner Gaetano Savini founded Brioni. Opening its first store on Via Barberini 79 in Rome, Brioni (named after the Brionian Islands) became an international sensation, defining a distinct, Italian way of formal dress for men. Providing sharp, sartorial cuts for the global jet set, Brioni hosted its inaugural men's fashion show in 1952 at Florence's Palazzo Pitti. Merging forward-thinking shapes with traditional British codes, Brioni created a new Roman style with a subtly freeing, body-conscious shape, best highlighted by actor Marcello Mastroianni in Federico Fellini's 1960 film *La Dolce Vita*. In 1959 Brioni opened its innovative factory in Penne, Abruzzo, and introduced "prêt-a-couture," a more accessible made-to-order line. The company later established the tailoring school Scuola di Alta Sartoria in 1985 to safeguard its unique traditions. To date, each Brioni suit undergoes its generations-old house method, incorporating 220 artisanal steps and more than 7,000 meticulous stitches. Its star-studded clientele includes Sting, Drake, Samuel L. Jackson, Brad Pitt, and Usain Bolt.

Designer Brand

Brioni.
est Rome (IT), 1945.

Prince Raimondo Orsini d'Aragona stands in the ancient Roman forum wearing a suit by Brioni, c. 1982.

Photograph by Slim Aarons.

↳ CANALI, CORNELIANI, ERMENEGILDO ZEGNA, MASTROIANNI

BROOKS BROTHERS

American men owe a tremendous deal to Henry Sands Brooks and his four sons. It was the family's Brooks Brothers firm that, in the mid-1800s, repackaged the suit as an off-the-rack commodity. Their soft-shouldered, three-button Sack Suit was for decades the armor of Wall Street raiders, DC wonks, and budding moguls. Brooks's influences touched all points of a man's wardrobe. Brooks Brothers brought the curvaceous button-down collar of English polo players stateside and introduced India's electric madras cloths to the American masses. Through the twentieth century, the brand engrained camel-hair polo coats, swinging Bermuda shorts, and fuzzy Anglo Shetland sweaters in the annals of American fashion. The Brooks Brothers style is indelibly imprinted on the history of the United States—they have dressed at least forty presidents. Though the label has changed hands frequently as its conservative designs struggled to keep pace with modern tastes, Brooks's many gifts to American fashion can never be overlooked.

Retailer

Brooks Brothers.
est New York (USA), 1818.

Jon Hamm, as Don Draper, wearing Brooks Brothers in a publicity still for AMC's television series *Mad Men*, 2007.

↳ ALDEN SHOES, ANDOVER SHOP, BROWNE, J. PRESS, PAUL STUART

JAMES BROWN

Known as "the hardest-working man in show business," James Brown defined the flashy look of soul and funk music with unequaled flamboyance over his forty-year career. Brown burst onto the scene as a young man in the 1950s. With his signature processed coif, sharply cut suit with a short jacket, holy-roller bow tie, and a backing band dressed to the nines in matching tuxedos (and later dashikis), Brown quickly established that his appearance was an essential component of his concert experience. By the late 1960s, during the era of his hit songs "Sex Machine" and "Sing It Loud—I'm Black and I'm Proud," Brown's costumes became wilder, with big lapels, flared pants, and low-cut jumpsuits embellished with rhinestone initials. His outrageous appearance was an influence on subsequent stars' costumes—from David Bowie to Harry Styles. Toward the end of his sets, Brown would sink to his knees while singing "Please, Please, Please." Danny Ray, Brown's longtime cape man, emcee, and valet, would drape a glittering cape over the singer's back and lead him offstage, only for the Godfather of Soul to rush back from the wings moments later, ready to lay down the grooves again.

Icon

James Brown.
b Barnwell, SC (USA), 1933.
d Atlanta (USA), 2006.

James Brown, Los Angeles International Airport, 1969.

Photograph by Julian Wasser.

↳ BOWIE, M. DAVIS, LITTLE RICHARD, PRINCE, STONE, STYLES

THOM BROWNE

Thom Browne wanted to be an actor. Instead he became a landmark fashion designer. In 1997 Browne left his Hollywood hopes behind, taking a salesman's gig at Giorgio Armani in New York. His talent for conceiving fashion became evident, and soon enough he was leading design at Club Monaco. In 2001 Browne started his label with just five of his now-iconic, ankle-baring, super-sucked-in suits. Detractors likened them to Pee-wee Herman's suit, but as men's fashion shook off the grungy 1990s, Browne's razor-sharp suits became a market-shaking smash. In 2007 Brooks Brothers tapped him to start Black Fleece, an uber-luxe sublabel. On the runways, Browne's collections are often more art than attire, meditating on athleticism, fantasy, and gender. But his suits—and now his posh sweatpants—remain in demand with brand fans such as LeBron James, Eddie Redmayne, and Lil Uzi Vert. In 2018 Browne became the official outfitter of FC Barcelona. That same year, Ermenegildo Zegna bought an 85 percent stake in Thom Browne, valuing it at $500 million.

Designer

Thom Browne.
b Allentown, PA (USA), 1965.

LeBron James arrives for Game 1 of the 2018 NBA Finals in Oakland, CA wearing Thom Browne.

Photograph by Lachlan Cunningham.

↳ BROOKS BROTHERS,
ERMENEGILDO ZEGNA,
S. JONES, SLIMANE

BEAU BRUMMELL

At the beginning of the nineteenth century, Beau Brummell became a style leader to a new world order that was shrugging off the extravagance and frivolity of the aristocracy and adopting an updated masculine dress code that was luxurious but understated. Brummell, a commoner, was educated at Eton College and Oriel College, Oxford, before joining the regiment of the Prince of Wales. Brummell befriended the future King George IV, and in 1798, when he left the army as a captain, he established himself in Mayfair, London, and quickly became an arbiter of men's fashion and the father of dandyism. Brummell understood that the social mobility of the new age required a dress code to match, and he popularized a modern uniform for men: a tailored dark blue wool coat, buff full-length trousers, a linen shirt, and a white linen cravat, which was the precursor to the ties men wear today. Brummell's grooming habits, including a daily bath, were also hugely influential to his peers. However, his influence waned when he fell out with the king and had to leave England with mounting debts in 1816.

Icon

Beau Brummell
(George Bryan Brummell).
b London (UK), 1778.
d Caen (FR), 1840.

Portrait of Beau Brummell, 1805.

Lithograph by Robert Dighton.

↳ AHLUWALIA, BEATON,
   CRISP, WILDE

BRYANBOY

In 2004 Bryan Grey Yambao began blogging under the name Bryanboy from his family's home in Manila and quickly built an audience drawn to his humorous, incisive takes on the fashion industry. By 2009 he had taken the fashion world by storm, becoming a regular front-row fixture at fashion weeks around the world. From the beginning Bryanboy has reviewed—and worn—both men's and women's collections, always preferring ebullience above all else: punchy colors, clashing patterns, statement coats, piles of fur, schoolboy shorts, and over-the-top accessories.

He often collaborates with major brands, including Prada, Dolce & Gabbana, Hermès, and Marc Jacobs. Bryanboy is considered a pioneer among fashion bloggers and influencers, having grown his following from a niche audience in his native Philippines into a global brand in its own right. Fashion, per the way Bryanboy approaches it, is the ultimate self-expression and should be an exuberant, genderless endeavor. While he no longer maintains a traditional blog, his candor and more-is-more aesthetic continue to engage and delight his fans on social media.

Bryanboy (Bryan Grey Yambao).
b Manila (PH), 1981.

Bryanboy during Paris Fashion Week, 2018.

Photograph by Christian Vierig.

↳ DOLCE & GABBANA, HERMÈS, JACOBS, KAYE, PRADA, SABBAT, WOOSTER

BTS

Who are RM, Jin, Suga, J-Hope, Jimin, V, and Jungkook? Only the world's most popular record-shattering K-pop supergroup, known as BTS. These seven stars, who were discovered in 2010, released their debut album *2 COOL 4 SKOOL* in 2013. Their music, which focuses on themes of authenticity and acceptance, also references their identity as Korean artists. "The Beatles of the Twenty-first Century," BTS topped Billboard charts with their 2020 hit "Dynamite," among other infectious tunes. Building upon Korean pop's meteoric rise around the world, the singers are standout ambassadors (and front-row fashion fixtures)—exporting a subculture verging on megaculture. Their viral fan base chronicles the group's dynamic individual style, which pairs exuberant streetwear with high-end looks. Favorite BTS brands include Berluti, Gucci, Saint Laurent, Bottega Veneta, Visvim, and Dior, and designs worn by BTS often sell out immediately, as with a color-blocked Prada gabardine jacket photographed on youngest member Jungkook. In 2021 Louis Vuitton men's artistic director Virgil Abloh announced that BTS would become global ambassadors for the brand.

Icons

BTS. J-Hope (Jung Ho-seok). b Gwangju (KOR), 1994. Jimin (Park Ji-min). b Busan (KOR), 1995. Jin (Kim Seok-jin). b Gwacheon (KOR), 1992. Jungkook (Jeon Jung-kook). b Busan (KOR), 1997. RM (Kim Nam-joon). b Seoul (KOR), 1994. Suga (Min Yoon-gi). b Daegu (KOR), 1993. V (Kim Tae-hyung). b Daegu (KOR), 1995.

BTS on the red carpet for the Grammy Awards, Los Angeles, 2020.

Photograph by Emma McIntyre

↳ ABLOH, THE BEATLES, G-DRAGON

BURBERRY

Thomas Burberry struck sartorial gold in 1879 by developing gabardine, a taut, waterproof cotton textile. The invention shot the humble country clothier to grand heights—soon he had hundreds of employees and a shop in London. In the early 1900s Burberry scored another smash with the trench coat. Developed under a commission from the British military during World War I, the oversized Burberry trench eventually became iconic in pop culture: Humphrey Bogart wore one in *Casablanca* (1942), as did Audrey Hepburn in *Breakfast at Tiffany's* (1961). Yet it was the tan-based check pattern lining the trenches that would dictate the brand's more recent history. Through licensing deals, that plaid exploded—particularly in Japan through the 1980s—appearing on clothes but also golf bags, strollers, and umbrellas. In the 2000s British soccer youth flocked to the brand's checkered wares. Around that time, though, in an effort to class up the classic label, renowned retail executive Rose Marie Bravo hired designer Christopher Bailey to take the helm and Burberry entered the runway realm. Today Riccardo Tisci is the brand's creative director.

Designer Brand

Burberry.
est Basingstoke, Hampshire (UK), 1856.

Humphrey Bogart wearing a Burberry trench coat in a publicity still for Warner Bros.'s *Casablanca*, 1942.

↳ AQUASCUTUM, C. BAILEY, KNIGHT, McLELLAN, TISCI, WESTWOOD

SARAH BURTON

In 2010, when Sarah Burton stepped into the head position at Alexander McQueen following the untimely passing of the brand's beloved founder, she had mammoth shoes to fill. A graduate of London's Central Saint Martins College of Art and Design, Burton has spent her whole career at the house that McQueen himself built, and under Burton's tutelage, it has become a force within men's fashion. Her collections brim with a baroque dandyism, exemplified by inky-black officers' coats, crimson red suiting, museum-quality brocade sport coats, and paint-splattered trench coats that allude to Jackson Pollock. These extravagant designs implore men to view fashion in its purest form: as the ornamentation of self. Though many of her creations are lofty and luxe (Burton is also a favorite couturier of the British royal family), her tenure at McQueen has had some brilliant commercial successes, such as the blocky, platform-soled trainers that debuted in 2014, years before the bulbous "dad sneaker" became a must-have trend.

Designer

Sarah Burton.
b Macclesfield, Cheshire (UK), 1974.

Alexander McQueen Fall/Winter 2016 collection at London Men's Fashion Week.

↳ ANDERSON, BOWIE, WESTWOOD, WILDE

CAB CALLOWAY

Cab Calloway was an American jazz singer and bandleader as renowned for his sartorial magnificence as for his scatting and swinging band. A resident musician at Harlem's famed Cotton Club, Calloway was famous for hits such as "Minnie the Moocher," and for starring in George Gershwin's groundbreaking opera *Porgy and Bess* (1953). Onstage and about town, he frequently appeared in splendid and billowing zoot suits, best captured in the 1943 film *Stormy Weather*. During a musical number, Calloway slinks onstage in all-white attire—a jacket with ultrawide shoulders and extra drape in the chest paired with parachute pants and accessorized with a long chain drooping from his pocket. Amid the austerity of the Great Depression and World War II, these exuberant looks were sometimes frowned upon, especially by establishment critics who saw the youthful style as dangerous and unpatriotic. However, in his 1939 book *Cab Calloway's Cat-ologue: A "Hepster's" Dictionary*, Calloway sets the record straight on his signature zoot suit, defining it as "the ultimate in clothes" and "totally and truly American."

Icon

Cab Calloway.
b Rochester, NY (USA), 1907.
d Hockessin, DE (USA), 1994.

Cab Calloway in a publicity still for Twentieth Century Fox's *Stormy Weather*, 1943.

↳ BROWN, M. DAVIS, S. DAVIS, ELLINGTON, TIN TAN

CANADA GOOSE

Made in the "Great White North," Canada Goose was first launched by Sam Tick in Toronto in 1957 as Metro Sportswear Ltd., offering technical performance wear for cold weather. In the 1970s Tick's son-in-law David Reiss joined the company, eventually creating the Snow Goose line, which used new technology for volume-based down and produced custom uniform jackets for specialized professions, including the Canadian Rangers. The line evolved to become Canada Goose in the early 1990s. The label's iconic Snow Mantra expedition parka—nicknamed

Big Red—was developed in the 1980s for scientists to brave extreme temperatures at Antarctica's McMurdo Station and is touted as the "warmest coat on Earth." Subsequent styles, endorsed by names such as polar explorer Ben Saunders and mountaineer Laurie Skreslet—the first Canadian to summit Everest—are unique in their hand-stitched precision and made from Hutterite goose down. The brand has been worn on the silver screen by actors from Daniel Radcliffe to Daniel Craig (the latter in 2015's James Bond film *Spectre*) and spotted on celebrities such as David Beckham and Drake.

Brand

Canada Goose.
est Toronto (CAN), 1957.

Jackets in the showroom of the Canada Goose factory in Toronto, 2018.

Photograph by Mark Blinch.

↳ ARC'TERYX, BECKHAM,
   MONCLER, OSTI, PARACHUTE,
   WOOLRICH

CANALI

Italian menswear brand Canali embodies "Made in Italy" with its careful craftwork and studied designs. A family-run company, the label originated from Giacomo Canali's 1908 tailoring workshop in Triuggio, Brianza, a textile town near Milan. In 1934 Giacomo and his brother Giovanni expanded the business, establishing the roots of today's Canali brand. Coinciding with the rise of sartorial suits and a clean, modern look, Canali gained prominence with its fine craft tradition. Its tailor-made Su Misura service is an intimate and intensive process, allowing you to choose from more than five hundred fabrics or personalize a button detail. In the late 1970s Canali introduced its high-quality suits and signature tailoring to the global market, entering the United States and the UK. Three decades later, in the 2000s, Canali launched a sportswear line and its now bestselling Kei jacket, an ultra-elegant, unstructured, lightweight blazer. A sophisticated choice, Canali is worn by—among many others—actors Chris Pine, Michael Fassbender, Michael Douglas, and George Clooney, who wore the label in 2007's *Michael Clayton*.

Designer Brand

Canali.
est Triuggio (IT), 1934.

Canali Spring/Summer 2017 collection at Milan Fashion Week.

↳ BRIONI, CORNELIANI, ERMENEGILDO ZEGNA, KITON

KODAK 125PX

41

ENNIO CAPASA

As creative director at Costume National, the Milan-based company he founded in 1986 with his brother Carlo, Ennio Capasa brought a fresh minimalism to Italian ready-to-wear in the 1990s. He was largely inspired by the precise tailoring and modernist aesthetic he had absorbed from his two years as an assistant to Yohji Yamamoto following his studies. In 1993 Capasa launched Costume National Homme and sent men's and women's collections down the catwalk together, an innovation that highlighted the continuity of thought between his menswear and womenswear. The cool minimalist designs, with an edgy urban feel characterized by leather and a palette of blacks, caught the spirit of the decade, drawing on inspirations as varied as rockabilly music and Ducati motorcycles. The fashions were beloved in particular by downtown New Yorkers, whose favored dress code at the time was black and minimal. Costume National opened boutiques around the world, but it failed to endure as the popularity of its aesthetic faded and sales fell; its ownership eventually passed to the Japanese group Sequedge, and the Capasas left the company in 2016.

Designer

Ennio Capasa.
b Lecce (IT), 1960.

Vincent Hoogland for the Costume National Fall 2006 campaign.

Photograph by Sofia Sanchez & Mauro Mongiello.

↳ LANG, MARGIELA,
  Y. YAMAMOTO

PIERRE CARDIN

Pierre Cardin did not fear the future; he made a career out of it. He arrived in Paris at age twenty-three and swiftly began working for Paquin, Schiaparelli, and Dior. But his eyes were always looking ahead. In 1950 he started his own label and had his first smash product in the form of shapely bubble dresses. He started a menswear line in 1960, presenting his first collection on 250 students from the University of Paris. Soon thereafter he dressed the Beatles in sharp suits that buttoned to the neckline, like his own version of the Nehru jacket. As the world became fixated on the Space Race, Cardin responded with futuristic clothes, such as zippered Cosmocorps suits and jackets with Pagoda shoulders. In 1972 he launched his first men's fragrance and soon became a licensing maven, placing his name on pens, kitchenware, and cars. In 2019 the Brooklyn Museum hosted a seven-decade retrospective exhibition of Cardin's career.

Designer

Pierre Cardin.
b Sant'Andrea di Barbarana (IT), 1932.
d Neuilly-sur-Seine (FR), 2020.

Daily Mirror journalist Christopher Ward wearing a revolutionary new Cardin space-age suit, 1966.

Photograph by Doreen Spooner.

↳ ACRONYM, AMIES,
   THE BEATLES, NEHRU,
   Y. SAINT LAURENT

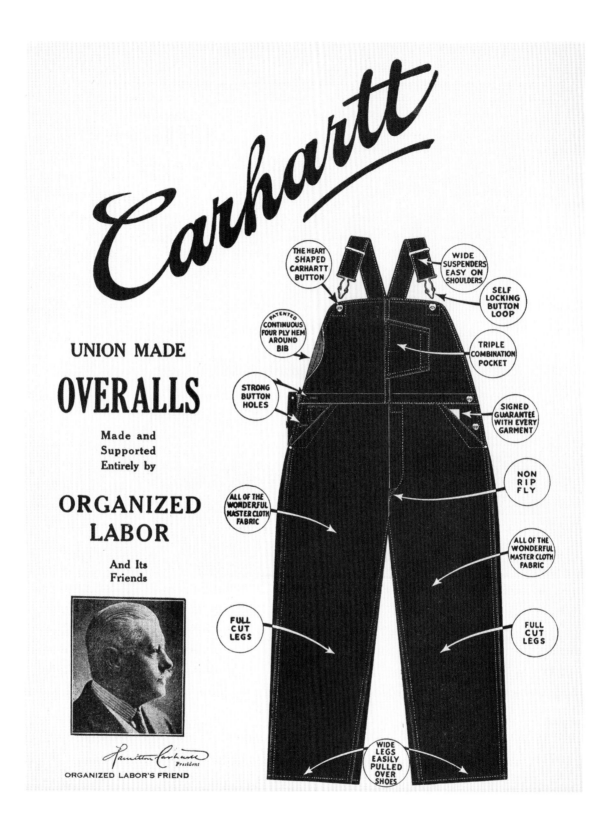

Carhartt

UNION MADE

OVERALLS

Made and
Supported
Entirely by

ORGANIZED
LABOR

And Its
Friends

ORGANIZED LABOR'S FRIEND

THE HEART SHAPED CARHARTT BUTTON

WIDE SUSPENDERS EASY ON SHOULDERS

SELF LOCKING BUTTON LOOP

PATENTED CONTINUOUS FOUR PLY HEM AROUND BIB

TRIPLE COMBINATION POCKET

STRONG BUTTON HOLES

SIGNED GUARANTEE WITH EVERY GARMENT

NON RIP FLY

ALL OF THE WONDERFUL MASTER CLOTH FABRIC

ALL OF THE WONDERFUL MASTER CLOTH FABRIC

FULL CUT LEGS

FULL CUT LEGS

WIDE LEGS EASILY PULLED OVER SHOES

CARHARTT

In the late 1800s, heeding the needs of local railroad workers, Hamilton Carhartt developed a set of hardy bib overalls in his small lofted factory in Detroit, Michigan. Only a few decades later, Carhartt's business was whirring, with locations in Paris, Ontario, and Atlanta. In 1907 Carhartt introduced the highly functional four-pocket duck-canvas chore coat, further enticing the brand's core audience of blue-collar workers. Like many American clothiers, Carhartt's business dipped during the Great Depression but surged back starting in the mid-twentieth century. In 1975 the hooded Active Jac arrived;

it has been a worksite staple since. Carhartt Work in Progress, a style-forward sublabel, arrived in 1989, the same year the oversized jacket was worn by Albee Ragusa, an employee of hip-hop's first major artist label Tommy Boy Records. The style soon took off on both the east and west coast, spotted on rappers such as Nas, Tupac, Easy E, and Naughty By Nature. In the 2000s, as young men with blissfully uncalloused hands turned to reliable, heritage pieces over ever-changing trends, Carhartt's workwear came into vogue, appearing on the likes of Daniel Day-Lewis, Jonah Hill, and Jake Gyllenhaal.

Brand

Carhartt.
est Detroit, MI (USA), 1889.

Carhartt Overalls advertisement, c. 1925.

↳ DICKIES, LEVI'S, RED WING, SHAKUR, WEST

FRANCESCO CARROZZINI

Multihyphenate Francesco Carrozzini has had a remarkable career as a photographer, filmmaker, creative director, and sunglasses designer (for the brand Children of Ra). Carrozzini's work spans genres—he has crafted fashion photographs and portraits of actors, such as Eddie Redmayne, Robert De Niro, and Tim Roth, as well as music videos for artists including Jay-Z and A$AP Rocky. His work in fashion has led him to photograph campaigns for brands such as Ermenegildo Zegna, Roberto Cavalli, Salvatore Ferragamo, and Tommy Hilfiger and editorials for magazines, including *L'Uomo Vogue* and *Vanity Fair*. Carrozzini studied film at the University of California at Los Angeles and later served as a studio assistant to Bruce Weber and Peter Lindbergh, whose influences are evident in Carrozzini's own distinctive black-and-white photographs and cinematic portraits. In 2016 he made a full-length feature film about his late mother, *Franca: Chaos and Creation*, and in 2017 he debuted *X-Ray Fashion* at the Venice Biennale, a virtual-reality experience that shines a light on the fashion industry's impact on the environment.

Photographer

Francesco Carrozzini.
b Monza (IT), 1982.

Pedro Pascal photographed for *L'Uomo Vogue*, September 2015.

Photograph by Francesco Carrozzini.

↳ ERMENEGILDO ZEGNA,
LINDBERGH, L'UOMO VOGUE,
SALVATORE FERRAGAMO,
WEBER

MICAIAH CARTER

Seamlessly blending youth culture, fine art, and street style with a distinct visual and political sophistication, Micaiah Carter is a welcome presence in contemporary fashion. A graduate of Parsons School of Design, Carter splits his time between Brooklyn and Los Angeles, shooting a mixture of fashion editorials, advertising campaigns, and personal work that puts the Black experience front and center while playing with traditional codes of masculinity. With a distinct vision of what it means to appear masculine and an impeccable eye for detail, Carter has become a frequent collaborator with brands, such as Thom Browne and the uber-cool Pyer Moss. Carter's magazine covers include Michael B. Jordan for *Highsnobiety*, Playboi Carti for *Fader*, and Pharrell Williams in his eye-catching full-length Moncler puffer coat for *GQ*. Carter's work was also exhibited at the Brooklyn Museum's *Black History, Black Future* show in 2018, and in 2020 he launched the See in Black initiative, a collective of creatives who mentor and foster Black talent in photography.

Photographer

Micaiah Carter.
b Apple Valley, CA (USA), 1995.

LaKeith Stanfield photographed for *Esquire*, September/October 2019 issue.

Photograph by Micaiah Carter.

↳ BROWNE, ESQUIRE, GQ, JEAN-RAYMOND, P. WILLIAMS

CAZAL

Oversized and impossible to ignore, Cazal frames skyrocketed the brand to success in the 1980s and positioned its wearers as fashion leaders rather than followers. Founded in 1975, Cazal's name comes from the first letters of the first and last name of its founder, Cari Zalloni, an Austrian-Greek born in Athens, who moved to Vienna for school before landing in Germany. After working for the eyewear firm Carrera Optyl, Zalloni launched Cazal and began to design frames so large in size that they dominated the wearer's face. With styles featuring decorated or asymmetrical frames, Cazals soon established a following in Europe, but the style really took off once they became associated with hip-hop and streetwear in the 1980s: Darryl McDaniels of Run-DMC wore 607s, MC Hammer wore 858s, and filmmaker Spike Lee wore outsize 616s. The distinctive frames were a major style statement, and it wasn't uncommon to see people sporting Cazals with the lenses taken out. Cazal revived its classic Legends in 2011, one year before Zalloni's death, and since has continued to pioneer bold frames, attracting today's biggest stars, from Jay-Z to Brad Pitt, and influencing designers from Virgil Abloh to Rihanna.

Cazal.
est (GER), 1975.

Rolling Partners, Downtown Brooklyn, NYC, 1982.

Photograph by Jamel Shabazz.

↳ ADIDAS, S. DAVIS, JAY-Z, NEW ERA, OAKLEY, PERSOL, RAY-BAN

CERRUTI

Having taken over his family's woolen firm in 1950 after the death of his father, the Italian-born Nino Cerruti used his knowledge of textiles to found a ready-to-wear menswear company, Hitman, in 1957. The brand worked with a long series of designers, including most prominently Giorgio Armani, who joined in 1965. Cerruti and Armani combined the traditions of Italian tailoring with a new kind of casual elegance to create a deconstructed men's jacket with wide shoulders, made from unlined fabrics to soften the outline. *L'Uomo Vogue* observed that Cerruti created clothes with an

"elegant simplicity that doesn't smack too much of fashion." In 1967 Cerruti launched Cerruti 1881 in Paris (1881 is the year his grandfather opened his first wool mill in Italy). Other brands followed, including Cerruti 1881 Sport and Cerruti Jeans, as well as a highly successful fragrance line, Cerruti Pour Homme. In the 1980s Cerruti dressed a series of Hollywood A-listers, from Robert Redford to Harrison Ford, in casual chic attire. Cerruti sold the company in 2000, but the label continues to produce the suits that made Cerruti a trusted name in design.

Designer Brand

Cerruti.
est Paris (FR), 1967.

Nino Cerruti examining fabric samples with John Cooper, owner of the British textile company John Cooper & Son, and Dino Hafele, the export director of the company Cerruti 1881, London, 1967.

Photograph by Sergio Del Grande.

↳ ARMANI, CORNELIANI, HUGO
  BOSS, LAPIDUS

C.F. HATHAWAY COMPANY

Why is that man wearing an eyepatch? That was the question asked by so many Americans throughout the 1950s when they came upon Hathaway Shirts advertisements. Founded in Maine by Charles Foster Hathaway in the mid-1800s (the exact date is unclear), the C.F. Hathaway Company, during its first century, made shirts that everyday men—including thousands of Union soldiers—wore. By 1951 the American clothing market was quite crowded, and Hathaway was looking for an edge. With the help of famed advertising agent David Ogilvy (later of Ogilvy & Mather), the company launched "The Man in the Hathaway Shirt" campaign, showing an elegant man in a pressed white shirt with a mysterious patch over his eye. They never answered why he had the patch on, but they did prove that a clothing company could sell products based on the mystique around the item more than the item itself. Hathaway closed its business in 2002, by which point it was one of the last American shirtmakers still standing.

Brand

C.F. Hathaway Company.
est Waterville, ME (USA), c. 1850s.

"The Man in the Hathaway Shirt" campaign, 1951.

↳ ANDOVER SHOP, ARROW, BROOKS BROTHERS, VAN HEUSEN

CHAMPION

For more than a century, Champion has been known for its quality sportswear. From the 1970s to the '90s the brand was the official outfitter to the National Football League, and later the National Basketball Association. But perhaps more significantly, Champion pioneered two of the biggest sportswear innovations of the twentieth century: the sweatshirt and the hoodie. Founded by brothers Abe and Bill Feinbloom in 1919, the Knickerbocker Knitting Company (renamed Champion in the 1930s) introduced sweatshirts in the 1920s as undergarments for outdoor workers, but they also proved popular for physical exercise because the loose-fitting cotton jersey absorbed sweat. In the early 1930s the hoodie was introduced, again as workwear, but it became a staple of streetwear after its use by basketball teams in the 1970s. Champion enjoyed a revival in the 2010s thanks to its smart promotion of retro fashion and has been worn by celebrities, including Kendrick Lamar, Chance the Rapper, Justin Bieber, Robert Pattinson, and Odell Beckham Jr. Now a key streetwear brand, Champion has collaborated with Rick Owens, Supreme, Off-White, and Vetements.

Brand

Champion.
est Rochester, NY (USA), 1919.

Champion advertisement, c. 1954.

↳ ABLOH, GVASALIA, HANES, NEW ERA, OWENS, SUPREME

ASCOT CHANG

In 1953 Ascot Chang was established in Hong Kong, rising to become the epitome of the city's bespoke tailoring tradition and distinctive flair. Its namesake founder, Ascot Chang, was born in Fenghua, Ningbo, in 1923 and moved to Shanghai at fourteen to study under a master tailor. In 1949 Chang left for Hong Kong to go door-to-door selling custom-made shirts to Shanghainese businessmen. By 1953 he set up his first shop at 34 Kimberley Road, later opening a second storefront in Hong Kong's iconic Peninsula Hotel. Chang gained recognition as a prominent suit and shirt maker with a hybridized

Shanghai, or "Red Gang," style unique to his training. In 1967 he traveled to the United States for a global trunk show, continuing to build a steady roster of clientele, including high-profile names such as Sammy Davis Jr., Marlon Brando, Steve McQueen, Kirk Douglas, and former US presidents George H. W. Bush and Richard Nixon. In 1986 the company opened its New York storefront. Today's Ascot Chang continues to court discerning gentlemen with artisanal separates such as classic twill shirts, polos, reversible cashmere jackets, and formal blazers.

Tailor

Ascot Chang.
est Hong Kong (CHN), 1953.

Inside an Ascot Chang store,
Hong Kong, China, 2013.

Photograph by Lam Yik Fei.

↳ CHARVET, S. DAVIS, McQUEEN,
   TURNBULL & ASSER

CHARIVARI
On the edge

Yohji Yamamoto Pour Homme

CHARIVARI

In its day Charivari was the most fashionable, fun, and forward-thinking family-run clothing business in New York. Started by Selma Weiser in 1967 as a women's dress shop on Manhattan's Upper West Side, Charivari expanded to a handful of stores over the next few decades as Weiser's children, Jon and Barbara, joined the business. In 1976, the very year Charivari opened its men's shop, it was named one of the eight best stores in America by *Esquire* magazine. Rightfully so. This was the store that introduced Yohji Yamamoto to the United States; it was where you could find the newest shirts, suits, and ties from Armani and Versace. It also championed avant-garde Belgian greats, such as Dries Van Noten and Martin Margiela. The multifloor shops played the best new music all day long and courted star shoppers, including Elton John and John Lennon. (Marc Jacobs was also an early employee.) In the 1980s Charivari's cheeky ads—such as "Keep New York City Clean," featuring a row of models wearing all white next to a graffitied wall—filled magazines. In 1998 the party came to a close as Charivari shuttered its last store.

Retailer

Charivari.
est New York (USA), 1967.

Charivari "On the Edge" advertisement for Yohji Yamamoto Pour Homme, 1989.

Photograph by James Porto.

↳ ARMANI, MARGIELA, VAN NOTEN, VERSACE, Y. YAMAMOTO

122

CHARVET

French shirtmaker Charvet is among the world's most legendary luxury institutions, with a history dating back to 1838. Since 1877 it has been based in a stunning mansion in Paris's Place Vendôme. Founded by Joseph-Christophe Charvet—whose father, Jean-Pierre, was Napoleon Bonaparte's wardrobe curator—Charvet's first storefront was established on Rue de Richelieu as a shopping destination for men, predating London's Savile Row as the epicenter of tailoring. Charvet became known for its bespoke shirts with classic high collars, mother-of-pearl buttons, and French cuffs,

as well as for its seven-fold ties of patterned silk jacquard, all carefully handcrafted. The heritage house has dressed formidable men throughout history, including Impressionist Édouard Manet, King Edward VII of Britain, Alfonso XII of Spain, Winston Churchill, John F. Kennedy, Charles de Gaulle, Yves Saint Laurent, and Barack Obama. With more than five thousand fabrics to choose from, its signature shirt is still classic white. In 1964 the Colban family purchased Charvet from its founding family, and it is now run by brother and sister Jean-Claude and Anne-Marie Colban.

Tailor

Charvet.
est Paris (FR), 1838.

Fashion plate published in *Le Follet*, Paris, 1839.

↳ COWARD, FERRY, GOYARD, HERMÈS, KENNEDY, Y. SAINT LAURENT, WILDE

WILLY CHAVARRIA

The power of Mexican American designer Willy Chavarria's work hits full force, weaving together identity and sociopolitics. He draws inspiration from Chicano culture, both in the silhouettes and styling of his clothing. Originally from Fresno, California, Chavarria studied at the Academy of Art University in San Francisco in the 1980s and later worked as a menswear designer for Ralph Lauren, Dickies Construct, and Yeezy. In 2015 he launched his eponymous label. Over the years Chavarria has designed playful collections, such as referencing the aesthetics of lowrider culture and the gay leather bar scene. In 2021 he was hired as senior vice president of men's design for Calvin Klein, and his namesake label was selected as a finalist for the CFDA/Vogue Fashion Fund. There is a unique undercurrent present in Chavarria's work—a forward-looking masculine strength with a quiet sensitivity. In the ever-evolving world of men's fashion—one that is chasing a new version of masculinity—that vision has put the designer in high demand.

Willy Chavarria.
b Fresno, CA (USA), 1967.

Model Alexis Chaparro wearing Willy Chavarria Fall/Winter 2020, photographed for *Le Mile* magazine, September 2020.

Photograph by Brent Chua.

↳ DICKIES, C. KLEIN, LAUREN, WEST

ZIGGY CHEN

Shanghai-based menswear designer Ziggy Chen launched his namesake label in 2012. Debuting at Shanghai Fashion Week, Chen's minimalist designs combine his Chinese heritage—including nods to Imperial China's Song and Qing dynasties and the country's more modern era—with contemporary construction and innovative techniques. Using deconstructed garments (Comme des Garçons's Rei Kawakubo is among his inspirations) in relaxed and refined materials, his unisex styles are multilayered, with languid, utilitarian silhouettes in earth tones or all black. His collections, now shown at Paris Fashion Week, include graphic-print T-shirts, slouchy, drop-crotch trousers, and loose-fitting linen blazers. Chen's mastery of textiles should come as no surprise. After studying fashion design at Shanghai's Donghua University, he was a lecturer in textile design and amassed a collection of ancient historical fabrics, which he now uses regularly as references. In 2015 Hong Kong–based high-fashion retailer Lane Crawford selected Chen for its "Created in China" platform and two years later, in 2017, collaborated with him on a sustainable capsule collection.

Designer

Ziggy Chen.
b Shanghai (CHN), (Active 2000s—).

Ziggy Chen Fall/Winter 2020 menswear collection.

Photograph by Gio Staiano.

↳ KAWAKUBO, Y. YAMAMOTO

CHROME HEARTS

Edgy and irreverent, Chrome Hearts is a legendary jewelry house known for its limited-edition designs and high-octane collaborations. The brand was founded in 1988 by the husband-and-wife duo Richard and Laurie Lynn Stark, whose empire was built by merging rock 'n' roll and craftsmanship. Started in Los Angeles, the family-run label is most known for its gothic motifs—graphic skulls, hearts, and crosses—whether diamond-encrusted in sterling silver or 22-karat gold. Their distinct shapes and hefty style are ever present in cuff links, bracelets, dagger pendants, necklaces, and rings, with men's clothing including cross-laden denim, T-shirts, and zip-up hoodies. Chrome Hearts has collaborated with the Rolling Stones and the Robert Mapplethorpe Foundation, as well as with fashion's Rick Owens (their 2010 high-top sneakers are highly coveted on the resale market), Comme des Garçons, and Virgil Abloh. The accessories have been worn by hip-hop phenoms—including Travis Scott, Offset, and Drake—and icons such as Elton John, Iggy Pop, Lenny Kravitz, and the late Karl Lagerfeld.

Accessory Design

Chrome Hearts.
est Los Angeles (USA), 1988.

Chrome Hearts jewelry, 2004.

Photograph by Ricky Chung.

↳ ABLOH, KAWAKUBO, LAGERFELD, OWENS

ELLERY CHUN

In 1936 Yale economics graduate Ellery Chun tried to drum up business for his family's Honolulu-based Chinese dry goods store, King-Smith Clothiers, by registering a trademark for what he termed the Aloha shirt—the now-ubiquitous style of shirt with short sleeves and a square bottom made from patterned Japanese yukata cotton. Hawaiian business owners, including Chun, had started printing these shirts to meet demand from the US tourist cruise ships that began arriving in the 1920s, but Chun was the first clothier to mass-produce them. His early designs

were bright and graphic, featuring patterns of palm trees, pineapples, and local dancers. The Aloha shirt became popular with local surfers and singers and soon attracted Hollywood stars, such as Bing Crosby, Frank Sinatra, and Elvis Presley, who introduced the style to the West Coast. Chun's more modest designs were soon rivaled by brighter, gaudier versions produced by imitators. After closing the business in 1945, Chun spent his last decades working in banking; in 1991 he was honored by the Hawaii Senate for his contribution to the state.

Designer

Ellery Chun.
b Honolulu (USA), 1909.
d Honolulu (USA), 2000.

Aloha shirt designed by Ellery Chun, c. late 1930s.

Photograph by Dale Hope.

↳ NAKAMURA, PENDLETON, PRESLEY

CHURCH'S

In 1873 Thomas Church established a small factory in Northampton and began producing quintessentially British shoes. The shoes were made by individual craftsmen, and the company innovated by introducing half sizes and creating models in various materials and widths. In the 1920s Church's opened boutiques in both London and New York. Each pair of its signature shoes—such as the Shanghai (launched in 1929), with its weathered look and silver buckle or brogue details—takes approximately five hundred different steps to make. Church's slip-on leather loafer, popularized by King George VI in the 1930s, appealed to American businessmen in the 1960s. The company's Westbury monk straps have also made a sartorial statement with a streamlined shape, as have the polished binder Grafton brogues, known for their chunky sole. Church's iconic Consul shoe—introduced in 1945 with a sleek silhouette and rounded toe—speaks to the brand's tradition of formal English elegance. Today actors, including Pierce Brosnan and Tom Hiddleston, and politicians, such as Tony Blair, wear Church's heritage soles, and the brand has stayed fresh through collaborations with Adidas and Vetements.

Footwear

Church's.
est Northampton, England (UK), 1873.

Church's Fall/Winter 2019 campaign.

Photograph by Laura Jane Coulson.

↳ ADIDAS, ALDEN SHOES, GVASALIA, J.M. WESTON, JOHN LOBB BOOTMAKER, PRADA

CLARKS

Founded in Somerset, England, in 1825 by Cyrus Clark, Clarks began with the premise of making sheepskin rugs but soon started to create slippers from offcuts produced in the manufacturing process. Over the next century, the brand experienced ups and downs with their footwear business. In 1950, however, the British shoemaker launched a crepe rubber–soled ankle boot—the Desert Boot—that remains a cult classic more than seventy years later. Inspired by the suede boots that were made in Cairo and adopted by British soldiers, Nathan Clark (great-grandson of the company's founder) designed the Desert Boot following his stint as an officer in the British Army. In the late 1950s, the shoes were adopted as part of the mod uniform in London and took off with the Jamaican rude boys of the '60s. In 1967 Clarks created another suede shoe, the Wallabee, which also became a subcultural hit, particularly within hip-hop. Rapper Slick Rick wore them throughout the 1980s, and in the 1990s the Wu-Tang Clan and MF DOOM also became avid wearers. Today the brand has 1,400 stores worldwide, sells 46 million shoes each year, and still maintains its headquarters in Somerset.

Footwear

Clarks.
est Somerset, England (UK), 1825.

Junior Reid wearing Clarks Wallabees in King Jammy's yard, Kingston, Jamaica, 1985.

Photograph by Beth Lesser.

↳ BECKHAM, MARLEY, McQUEEN, STYLES

TELFAR CLEMENS

No designer better demonstrates the twenty-first century's cultural shifts than Telfar Clemens. In less than two decades, he has gone from being a DJ and a business student at New York's Pace University to launching Telfar in 2005 and turning it into a globally successful label with inclusivity and community at its heart. Menswear is an outdated notion for Clemens, who creates designs that are intentionally gender-less and that combine comfort with conceptual twists. One-shoulder crop tops, thigh-high boots, cutaway track pants, and multipocket gilets punctuate his collections,

attracting fans that include actor Ashton Sanders and rappers A$AP Ferg and Swae Lee. The embossed T-inside-a-C logo adorning his vegan leather bags helped make them a unisex must-have for celebrities and budget-conscious Gen Zers alike. Clemens has democratized fashion in other ways, such as staging mobile pop-up shows and selling clothing directly to customers during New York Fashion Week in 2011 and designing fashionable unisex uniforms for White Castle in 2021. The winner of multiple CFDA awards, Clemens has sealed his reputation as a new-era fashion titan.

Designer

Telfar Clemens.
b Queens, NY (USA), 1985.

Backstage at the Spring/Summer 2019 show at New York Fashion Week, 2018.

Photograph by Sam Penn.

↳ BODE, DAPPER DAN, JEAN-RAYMOND, OLIVER

KURT COBAIN

The powerful rock music emanating from America's Pacific Northwest in the 1990s via bands such as Alice in Chains, Pearl Jam, and Nirvana sparked a grunge revolution. At the fore was Nirvana's long-haired front man, Kurt Cobain, who, to his own surprise and sometimes dismay, became a '90s heartthrob. Purveyors of grunge wore clothes that were thrifty and often literally bought at thrift shops: droopy flannel shirts, washed-out jeans, and shredded sneakers. Cobain fostered sartorial idiosyncrasies. He favored fuzzy mohair sweaters (the mossy cardigan he wore on *MTV Unplugged* sold at auction for $334,000 in 2019) and would often sport dresses and paint his nails as a sort of antihomophobic provocation and alternative music's long-playing challenges to anything gender normative. As with so many homegrown and street fashion trends, grunge was eventually co-opted by the commercial fashion industry, by Marc Jacobs at Perry Ellis and later by Japanese label Number (N)ine, which designed a Cobain-themed collection in 2003.

Icon

Kurt Cobain.
b Aberdeen, WA (USA), 1967.
d Seattle (USA), 1994.

Kurt Cobain, New York, c. 1990.

Photograph by Kevin Mazur.

↳ CONVERSE, JACOBS, MARNI, MIYASHITA

NUDIE COHN

Nudie Cohn lived the American dream. A Jewish Eastern European immigrant, Cohn arrived in New York City in the thick of the Great Depression. Like many immigrants, he and his wife migrated westward to California in the 1940s. There, Cohn started sewing clothes in his garage, and soon thereafter he began crafting costumes for Tex Williams, a rising country star. Cohn's reputation for western wear expanded, and he soon opened Nudie's of Hollywood. Spangled, embroidered suits were Cohn's specialty, and he made them for stars of all stripes,

including Roy Rogers, John Lennon, and Ronald Reagan. Among his most famous creations were a drug-themed getup for Gram Parsons, which he wore on his band's album cover for *The Gilded Palace of Sin*, and a gold lamé suit for Elvis Presley, who also sported it for his 1959 compilation album cover. Cohn died in 1984, but his legacy carries on today as designers such as Alessandro Michele, and upstart tailors continue to make so-called Nudie suits for stars such as Diplo and Lil Nas X.

Designer

Nudie Cohn.
b Kiev (RUS), 1902.
d Burbank, CA (USA), 1984.

Nudie Cohn in one of his designs, 1973.

Photograph by Mike Salisbury.

↳ CUEVAS, MICHELE, PRESLEY

KENNETH COLE

Before stepping out on his own, American businessman and designer Kenneth Cole helped manage his father's women's shoe factory in Brooklyn. Nearly six years later, in 1982, Cole launched Kenneth Cole Productions—moonlighting as a film production company to circumvent permitting and the high cost of venues during New York Market Week. While Cole was shooting his fake film *The Birth of a Shoe Company*, he sold forty thousand pairs of shoes in one week. In 1984 Cole introduced men's shoes, such as slip-on loafers, leather dress shoes, and sneakers, setting the foundation for his fashion empire. The company also took an activist stance early on with its 1985 advertising campaign focused on the American Foundation of AIDS Research (amfAR). In 1997 menswear was introduced, and the following year it was shown at an inaugural show at the New York Public Library. Cole's collections featured everyday city separates in neutral tones, including utilitarian jackets and coats paired with denim and khaki trousers. Cole's behemoth business is a testament to American fashion, covering a wide array of accessible products and diffusion lines in fragrances, watches, and eyewear.

Designer

Kenneth Cole.
b Brooklyn (USA), 1954.

Kenneth Cole advertisement, 2007.

↳ FLORSHEIM SHOES,
   G.H. BASS & CO., C. KLEIN

SEAN COMBS

By 1998 Sean Combs had already built Bad Boy Records into a colossus. This was the mogul who signed the Notorious B.I.G. and Faith Evans and had his own booming solo career, with multiple number-one hits and a Grammy. Then, with Sean John, Combs conquered the fashion world. Sean John's collection brimmed with highly wearable denim and pullover turtlenecks, as well as more tantalizing concepts, such as swinging shearling coats and black leather tracksuits, nodding to the impresario's own boisterous style. By 2002 Sean John was sold in more than

1,200 stores and pulled in $200 million in annual revenue the previous year. Two years later, in 2004, Combs nabbed the CFDA Menswear Designer of the Year award and for Fall 2008 staged his most pivotal collection, "If I Were a King," featuring all Black models. Having conquered the New York runway with splashy million-dollar shows (Channing Tatum walked for Sean John before he was Magic Mike), Combs tilted toward the mainstream, inking a distribution deal with Macy's in 2010 that sealed his legacy as one of America's greatest fashion businessmen.

Designer/Icon

Sean Combs.
b New York (USA), 1969.

Sean Combs wearing Sean John.

Photograph by Antonio Guilez.

↳ BECKFORD, FUBU, JACOB & CO., C. KLEIN, LAUREN

SEAN CONNERY

"The name's Bond. James Bond." When Scottish actor Sean Connery played the famous spy in seven films, he also established himself as one of the world's most stylish men. Born into a working-class family, Connery left school at thirteen years old, served in the Royal Navy, and did some modeling to help pay the rent, before becoming an actor in the 1950s. In 1962 he won the coveted role of Bond in *Dr. No*. As the character, Connery wore suits, often in classic gray, made by tailor Anthony Sinclair that emphasized his height—he was six feet two inches tall—and broad shoulders. But his athletic frame was equally suited to preppy slacks and polos (typically by John Smedley), pastel-colored terry cloth beachwear (1964's *Goldfinger*), and impeccable eveningwear, with crisp white shirts and black bow ties. Connery's own effortless air of detached elegance made him as much of a style icon as his fictional alter ego, whether he was sporting a kilt—as a loyal Scotsman—dressing for the red carpet in signature tuxedos, or teeing off on the golf course in a roll-neck sweater and checked pants.

Icon

Sean Connery.
b Edinburgh (UK), 1930.
d Lyford Cay (BHS), 2020.

Sean Connery setting off for a game of golf, 1962.

Photograph by Chris Ware.

↳ JOHN SMEDLEY, McQUEEN, PARKS, SINCLAIR, VINCE MAN'S SHOP

CONVERSE

No single shoe has exemplified a sport as much as Converse, which began making the All Star basketball shoe in 1917, combining a nonslip vulcanized rubber sole with ankle-high canvas uppers. In 1921 semiprofessional basketball player Chuck Taylor joined the company as a salesman. He helped redesign the shoe, and in 1932 his name was added to it. Four years later the US basketball team won Olympic gold wearing All Star high-tops. In the succeeding decades the shoe—including the iconic black-and-white iteration released in 1949 (the originals were brown with black accents)—rose to account for 80 percent of the US sneaker market. In the late 1970s, the growth of brands such as Nike and Adidas left Converse flat-footed, but its decline on the court was mirrored by its growing popularity on the street after being worn notably by the Ramones and, later, Kurt Cobain. Converse went bankrupt in 2001 before being brought back by its competitor, Nike, two years later. In addition to its classic styles, Converse produces sneakers customized with the work of artists, including Keith Haring, and in collaboration with labels such as Comme des Garçons and Todd Snyder.

Footwear

Converse.
est Malden, MA (USA), 1908.

Journalist Hunter S. Thompson wearing Converse sneakers at Owl Farm in Woody Creek, CO, c. 1976.

↳ ADIDAS, CLARKS, COBAIN, DEAN, DR. MARTENS, NIKE, TIMBERLAND, VANS

COOGI

Striking, colorful knitted sweaters made with intricate textures are the immediate calling card of Coogi. Established in 1969 as Cuggi by Jacky Taranto in Toorak, Australia, the knits were originally conceived as upscale tourist souvenirs for Europeans and Americans—Taranto's idea was to capture the vibrant topography of Australia's dramatic desert landscapes in wearable form. Its association with wealthy tourists was eclipsed when Bill Cosby adopted the Coogi sweater as a staple of his outfits in the hit comedy *The Cosby Show*. The prismatic knits became

known as "Cosby sweaters" and gained popularity with the 1990s hip-hop scene. High-profile devotees included musicians Walt G and the Notorious B.I.G., who rapped about the brand and were often captured wearing Coogi pieces. Coogi's twenty-first-century revival continues with fans including Drake, Snoop Dogg, A$AP Rocky, and Action Bronson, as well as collaborations with brands such as Rag & Bone. The asymmetrical, vivid knits are recognized as an iconic design and are held in the collection of the Cooper-Hewitt, Smithsonian Design Museum.

Designer Brand

Coogi.
est Toorak, Victoria (ASL), 1969.

Notorious B.I.G., Brooklyn, photographed for the *Los Angeles Times*, 1995.

Photograph by Iris Schneider.

↳ BARNES, CROSS COLOURS, FUBU, MISSONI, RAG & BONE

CORDINGS

Originating in London's Strand in 1839, Cordings was founded by John Charles Cording and quickly established itself as an in-demand outfitter known for exceptional waterproofing techniques. By 1843 Cordings began to manufacture Mackintosh coats, which had evolved from simply being hunting and driving wear to everyday attire. In 1909 the company received its first Royal Warrant as waterproofers to King George V, and later created the innovative Newmarket boots, made of canvas and leather, for the Duke of Windsor. In the 1920s the company expanded from its waterproofing service and bootmaking to offer a broader country collection, with signatures including its iconic covert coat. Made from covert cloth by heritage mill Fox Brothers & Co, in West England, this durable outerwear style has become a British menswear staple. Cordings also offers tweed jackets, corduroy trousers, plus fours, and tattersall and needlecord shirts. In 2003 one of Cordings's top customers, Grammy Award–winning English rocker Eric Clapton, helped revive the brand. As its co-owner, he has modernized Cordings and launched a full women's range.

Designer Brand

Cordings.
est London (UK), 1839.

Cordings of Piccadilly advertisement, *Illustrated Sporting & Dramatic News*, 1910.

↳ AQUASCUTUM, FOX BROTHERS & CO, MACINTOSH, DUKE OF WINDSOR

CORNELIANI

A family business from the historic city of Mantua in northern Italy, Corneliani has become a byword for high-quality Italian menswear. Originally making raincoats and overcoats when it was founded by Alfredo Corneliani in 1930, the company went on a long hiatus during and after World War II, until Alfredo's sons, Claudio and Carlalberto, reopened the firm in 1959. They insisted on using only Italian materials and manufacturing for their rainwear while also adding men's suits to their repertoire. Concentrating on sharp styling and unusual fabric, color, and pattern combinations, Corneliani reinterpreted the traditional suit. In the 1980s a third generation of the family, Sergio, established Corneliani USA for an American market eager to buy into Italian elegance and achieved considerable commercial success. In 2005 Corneliani released its revolutionary ID jacket. Designed as a cross between a formal jacket and outerwear, the relaxed single-breasted blazer with a detachable internal chest piece—making it suitable for all climates—continues to be a brand staple. The company still employs six hundred workers at its Mantua factory, but the family sold its controlling stake in 2016.

Designer Brand

Corneliani.
est Mantua (IT), 1930.

Corneliani Fall/Winter 2012 menswear collection at Milan Fashion Week.

Photograph by Antonio de Moraes Barros Filho.

↳ BRIONI, CANALI, CERRUTI, ERMENEGILDO ZEGNA, ETRO

GEORGE CORTINA

With a career in fashion spanning more than thirty years, George Cortina has become one of the industry's most prolific image makers. Cortina pioneered the idea that a top stylist can work seamlessly across editorial, advertising campaigns, runway, and celebrity dressing. Cortina's aesthetic is rooted in classical menswear references, but his subjects always appear effortless and modern, never dusty or contrived. He has styled numerous shoots for publications, such as the *WSJ.*, *Interview*, *W*, *GQ*, and *V* magazines as well as multiple international editions of *Vogue*, and also for campaigns for the likes of Calvin Klein, Giorgio Armani, and Hugo Boss. Alexander Skarsgård, Brad Pitt, and Jared Leto have been among his celebrity clientele, and he has styled runway shows for brands from New York to Milan. Beyond his substantial résumé, Cortina's impeccable taste is on display nowhere more clearly than on himself. A presence at fashion weeks and in street-style photography, Cortina's aesthetic is instantly recognizable: cosmopolitan, sleek, and impossibly cool.

Stylist

George Cortina.
b Miami (USA), (Active 1990s—).

Actor Ashton Sanders, styled by George Cortina, for the *Last Magazine*, November 2018.

Photograph by Lachlan Bailey.

↳ ARMANI, GQ, C. KLEIN, L'UOMO VOGUE, RABENSTEINER

NOËL COWARD

Despite Noël Coward's long list of accomplishments—playwright, actor, composer, and entertainer—he was celebrated as much for his appearance as his talents. After his first hit play, *The Vortex*, in 1924, photographer Cecil Beaton noted, "All sorts of men suddenly wanted to look like Coward—sleek and satiny, clipped and well-groomed." Coward's glamorous, dapper aesthetic captured the mood of London between the wars. He perfected his flamboyant style onstage and off, be it wearing striped pajamas in *Private Lives* (1930), a silk dressing gown in *Present*

Laughter (1939), or the white shoes and polka-dot silk bow ties with which he graced London's social scene. Arch and slightly camp, Coward was the first writer since Oscar Wilde whose appearance was as important and influential as his writing. Men who admired Coward's wit wanted to look like him; even Cary Grant, no style slouch himself, claimed to base his look on a combination of Coward and Scottish actor Jack Buchanan.

Icon

Noël Coward.
b London (UK), 1899.
d Oracabessa (JAM), 1973.

Noël Coward, Las Vegas, 1955.

Photograph by Loomis Dean.

↳ ANDERSON & SHEPPARD, BEATON, CHARVET, C. GRANT, SULKA, WILDE

PATRICK COX

Not many men cite Pee-wee Herman as a fashion inspiration. Yet Patrick Cox is not like many men. The Wannabe—a lithe square-toed, moccasin-stitched loafer with a stacked heel that shot Cox's career into the stratosphere when it debuted in 1993—was, in fact, inspired by Herman's own block-heeled white loafers. The design, which came in everything from rainbow stripes and snakeskin to the iconic Union Jack motif, became a vital part of the 1990s rave-scene look. By the time the Wannabe hit his stores, Cox had already seen his earlier shoe designs saunter down the London runways. With connections to Vivienne Westwood, John Galliano, and Richard James, he produced shoes for their collections. Into the 2000s Cox continued to work with a number of designers on their runway collections and produce more trend-driven styles. In 2008 he left his label and has since produced lines for Charles Jourdan and Geox.

Footwear Designer

Patrick Cox.
b Edmonton, Alberta (CAN), 1963.

Patrick Cox wearing Wannabe loafers in one of his boutiques, 1993.

Photograph by Kin Ho.

↳ BABENZIEN, G.H. BASS & CO., JAMES, WESTWOOD

QUENTIN CRISP

"Fashion is what you adopt when you don't know who you are," said British queer icon Quentin Crisp—born Denis Charles Pratt—whose flamboyant and dandyish appearance underlined the fact that he knew precisely who *he* was. Raised in suburban London, Crisp decided in his early twenties to dedicate his life to making people aware of his homosexuality, then illegal. It was an enterprise he wholly embraced: dressing in women's clothes in London in the 1930s, he was met with widespread abuse. Undeterred, Crisp painted his nails, plucked his eyebrows, and wore makeup. When he moved to New York City at the age of seventy-two, Crisp felt he had finally come home. The success of his 1968 account of his life in London, *The Naked Civil Servant*, made him a celebrity in the 1970s, and he became a familiar figure on the New York social scene, notable for his pithy wit but also for his look: white hair upswept under a trademark fedora, and wearing rouge and mascara. By then his uniform was invariably a suit—be it white linen or green velvet—set off by a loosely tied silk scarf and an open-necked shirt.

Icon

Quentin Crisp (Denis Charles Pratt).
b Sutton, England (UK), 1908.
d Manchester, England (UK), 1999.

Quentin Crisp, New York, 1993.

Photograph by Steve Pyke.

↳ BEATON, BRUMMELL, COWARD, JACOBS, WILDE

143

CROSS COLOURS

During the 1990s, Will Smith (as the Fresh Prince of Bel-Air), Mark Wahlberg (as Marky Mark), Tupac Shakur, and the entire cast of *In Living Color*—along with nearly every rap, hip-hop, and R&B artist of the time—wore the impossible-to-miss designs of Cross Colours. The streetwear label made baseball caps, baggy T-shirts, jackets, jeans, and more—often in bright colorways of yellow, green, red, and blue. Launched in 1989 by Carl Jones and Thomas "TJ" Walker, Cross Colours was created with a unifying vision for Black communities: its slogan "Clothes without Prejudice" appears on every one of their designs and upholds the company's philosophy of spreading its political and social messages ("Stop D Violence" and "Educate 2 Elevate" being two of the early slogans). Cross Colours was one of the first brands to popularize street fashion for young men and women, taking inspiration from the popularity of hip-hop and its style. Cross Colours closed in the mid-1990s due to the influx of competition, but it relaunched in 2014.

Designer Brand

Cross Colours.
est Los Angeles (USA), 1989.

Billy Brown for Cross Colours, c. 1991.

Photograph by Michael Segal.

↳ COMBS, FUBU, HOUNSOU, KANI, ROCAWEAR, SHAKUR, APRIL WALKER

DAPPER DAN

As a teenager growing up in Harlem, Daniel Day—known as Dapper Dan—turned to gambling to scrape by. A trip to Africa sponsored by Columbia University in the 1970s sparked an interest in fashion, and in 1982 he opened Dapper Dan's Boutique on 125th Street. Day's specialty was "knock-ups," which appropriated logos from luxury houses, such as Gucci, Louis Vuitton, and Fendi. Any self-respecting '80s star, from LL Cool J to Mike Tyson, owned a custom Dap jacket or ensemble. Day also catered to clandestine characters such as kingpin Alpo Martinez, who requested bulletproof coats and hats. In 1992 the luxury houses began to take legal action against Day, largely shutting down his operations and forcing his designs underground. But at its 2017 runway show, Gucci presented a puffy-sleeved bomber jacket that nearly matched one Day made in 1989 for Olympic gold medalist Diane Dixon. The knock-upper had been knocked off, and people noticed. Gucci made things right, tapping Day to create a cobranded collection and restart his Harlem atelier. His name back at center stage, Day was dubbed one of *Time* magazine's 100 Most Influential People of 2020.

Designer

Dapper Dan (Daniel Day).
b New York (USA), 1944.

Dapper Dan at a shoot for MTV, 1989.

Photograph by Wyatt Counts.

↳ GUCCI, LOUIS VUITTON, MICHELE, APRIL WALKER

MILES DAVIS

One of the fathers of cool jazz, hard bop, and jazz fusion, Miles Davis reinvented his appearance as often as he reinvented his music. Coming up under Charlie Parker and making his first solo records in the 1950s, Davis epitomized the sharply tailored jazzman, embracing Brooks Brothers sack suits, tab collar shirts, skinny ties, seersucker blazers, and other emblems of Ivy Style. This preppy style—crafted with clothing Davis largely purchased at the Ivy League hot spot Andover Shop—was novel, forever solidifying the relationship between jazz artists and this distinct look.

The 1969 Newport Jazz Festival marked a turning point for Davis, during which he debuted his new abstract trumpet sound of *Bitches Brew* and appeared onstage in a three-piece denim ensemble and wraparound shades. This psychedelic jazz fusion period was defined by leather jackets, African tribal prints, and groovy looks designed by Stephen Burrows. After a five-year hiatus, Davis reemerged in the 1980s with a new pop electronic sound, wearing Japanese designers, such as Koshin Satoh and Issey Miyake, whose avant-garde constructions defined his late style.

Icon

Miles Davis.
b Alton, IL (USA), 1926.
d Santa Monica, CA (USA), 1991.

Miles Davis at the Newport Jazz Festival, Rhode Island, July 1969.

Photograph by David Redfern.

↳ ANDOVER SHOP, BROOKS
   BROTHERS, ELLINGTON,
   G.H. BASS & CO., MIYAKE

THE FASHION MAGAZINE FOR MEN   SEPTEMBER 1967   ONE DOLLAR

GQ

GENTLEMEN'S
QUARTERLY

Sammy Davis, JR.
something else!

SAMMY DAVIS JR.

Arguably the most stylish member of the Rat Pack (sorry, Frank Sinatra and Dean Martin), Sammy Davis Jr. was a pioneering, multitalented entertainer who broke racial barriers throughout his career. Trained as a comedian, singer, and dancer, Davis got his big break during a performance at a nightclub packed with stars coming back from the 1951 Oscars. Known for his trademark pencil mustache and slick Vegas fashion sense, Davis frequently wore mohair and sharkskin suits cut by bespoke tailor Sy Devore. To enhance his slight stature (Davis was five feet five inches tall) and show off his dance moves, he preferred narrow lapels and straight pants with a high waist and no break at the cuff. Davis's talent and good looks helped him become one of the first Black stars to cross over into a mainstream American culture that was dominated by white film stars. He is credited with having the first interracial kiss on Broadway, in 1960, and being the first Black cover star of *GQ*, in 1967—all the while using his celebrity to raise money and awareness for civil rights.

Icon

Sammy Davis Jr.
b New York (USA), 1925.
d Beverly Hills, CA (USA), 1990.

Sammy Davis Jr. wearing a double-breasted plaid suit by Sy Devore, photographed for *GQ*, September 1967.

Photograph by Milton Greene.

↳ CAZAL, DEVORE, GQ

JAMES DEAN

Icon

Despite having starred in only three films before his death, James Dean remains one of Hollywood's most widely imitated fashion icons. When Dean appeared on-screen as the troubled teenager Jim Stark in 1955's *Rebel Without a Cause*, he wore a white T-shirt, Lee 101Z Rider jeans, and a red Harrington jacket—and a cigarette often hanging nonchalantly from his pursed lips. His appearance was considered subversive at a time when most movie stars wore suits; but, both on-screen and off, his wardrobe simply echoed what he had worn growing up in rural Indiana: a Stetson, a leather biker jacket with a fur collar (an homage to Marlon Brando's clothes in 1953's *The Wild One*), and engineer boots. Anything Dean wore—whether Breton striped shirts, plain sweaters, open-necked shirts worn sans tie, penny loafers, or Converse sneakers— reflected a casual confidence that remains inspirational more than sixty-five years after his death. Dean's effort- lessly androgynous look and his ambiguous sexuality set the tone for youthful rebellion and cool defiance that still rings out today.

James Dean.
b Marion, IN (USA), 1931.
d Cholame, CA (USA), 1955.

James Dean, New York, 1955.

Photograph by Dennis Stock.

↳ BARACUTA, CONVERSE,
G.H. BASS & CO., HANES,
LEE JEANS, LEVI'S, STETSON

OSCAR DE LA RENTA

Elegant is the adjective used most widely to describe the late, celebrated fashion designer Oscar de la Renta. Though he is more closely associated with the rise of exuberant, glamorous womenswear in the United States, the New York–based native of the Dominican Republic did enter into menswear in the 1980s and '90s, having had a measurable influence on the way men wanted to dress. His early apprenticeships at Balenciaga and Lanvin honed an eye for detail, proportion, and cut that was evident in his ladies' fashion, particularly in his tenure designing couture at

Balmain from 1993 to 2002. De la Renta's own style became an extension of this sophisticated sensibility. Smart, well-cut suits were the cornerstone of his dapper appearance, whether of fine wool weave or loose, light linen. Paired with a silk tie; a delicate, floppy pocket square; and his handsome looks, he introduced a debonair presence to his adopted US home. Rarely seen without his dazzling smile, the Oscar aesthetic was both charming and proper—and offered a refined contrast to the nation's classic aesthetic of rugged, all-American charm.

Designer/Icon

Oscar de la Renta
b Santo Domingo (DOM), 1932.
d Kent, CT (USA), 2014.

Oscar de la Renta in the living room of his apartment, Casa de Madera, in the resort of Casa de Campo, Dominican Republic, 1985.

Photograph by Slim Aarons.

↳ FORD, HALSTON, KAISERMAN

ALAIN DELON

There's suave and then there's Alain Delon. The icy-blue-eyed French actor was an inescapable force in films throughout the 1960s and '70s. Born in an upscale Parisian suburb, Delon was scouted at the Cannes Film Festival during the late '50s. In his breakout role as Tom Ripley in the 1960 film *Plein Soleil*, he smoldered in barely buttoned dress shirts, a preppy striped rowing blazer, and skimpy swim trunks. A sort of raffish French Riviera style became the Delon look—both on-screen and off. He favored uncomplicated white shirts worn breezily and polo-collared or V-neck sweaters. As his

career progressed, he dressed more in conservative, almost imposing tailoring, such as the impressive pinstripe double-breasted suit with mammoth lapels that he donned in the 1970 film *Borsalino*. Three years before that, in 1967, Delon wore perhaps his most iconic outfit ever in *Le Samouraï*: a black suit with a slick Burberry trench coat over the top. In the broad beige trench he was the very picture of a poised Lothario. Into the 1980s, '90s, and beyond, Delon kept his style sharp, appearing in public in orderly shawl-collar sweaters, straightforward dark sport coats, and sporty polos.

Icon

Alain Delon.
b Sceaux (FR), 1935.

Alain Delon, Buenos Aires, 1969.

Photograph by Jean-Pierre Bonnotte.

↳ ARNYS, BORSALINO, BURBERRY, CHARVET, GUCCI

ANN DEMEULEMEESTER

Designer

A sartorial standout of the avant-garde Antwerp Six, Ann Demeulemeester launched her eponymous brand in 1985—just four years after graduation—alongside husband Patrick Robyn. Her early creations of monochromatic suiting and ensembles in languid silhouettes set the tone for her signature androgynous aesthetic, which lifted fashion from prescribed gender norms and offered an understated way of dressing free from trends. In 1991 she presented her first show in Paris, later introducing menswear in 1996. Inspired by brooding music (she has worked with longtime collaborator and friend Patti Smith throughout her career), her collections conveyed a moody air that was perfect for romantic punks. Her penchant for elegantly tailored gothic menswear sprinkled with bohemian flourishes resulted in fluid designs, including tattered waistcoats, shirts printed in graphic florals, lengthy robe coats, and commanding leather combat boots. In 2013 Demeulemeester stepped down from the brand, announcing her sudden departure from fashion; she has since launched a successful housewares collection. However, her fashion label lives on under the ownership of Claudio Antonioli.

Ann Demeulemeester.
b Waregem (BEL), 1959.

Models backstage before the Ann Demeulemeester Spring/Summer 2018 show at Paris Fashion Week, 2017.

Photograph by Julien de Rosa.

↳ VAN BEIRENDONCK,
   BIKKEMBERGS, VAN NOTEN

APRIL 1985

$2

BILLY IDOL TALKS TO TERENCE STAMP
ABOUT ROCK 'N' ROLES

IN FASHION: HIPPIES, RAINWEAR, PATTI HANSEN, IN BRIEF

DETAILS

Conceived by editor and publisher Annie Flanders in 1982, *Details* was an avant-garde magazine that covered downtown Manhattan's innovative and alternative fashion, music, night-life, and arts scene. Its impact—and success—was immediate. Its pages featured early photographs by Bruce Weber, along with columns by man-about-town Stephen Saban. From 1982 to 1990, street-style photographer Bill Cunningham produced elaborate fashion spreads, chronicling notable style moments such as John Galliano's fluid men's designs and the all-black-clad army surrounding Yohji Yamamoto and Rei Kawakubo's

Paris Fashion Week shows. In 1988 the magazine was bought by Condé Nast and shifted focus to cover men's lifestyle. In 2000 it relaunched under editor Dan Peres, pushing bound-aries with a new energetic voice that included contributions from writers Augusten Burroughs, Michael Chabon, and Pete Wells, as well as photographers Steven Klein and Norman Jean Roy. With ideas that were often polarizing in their hypermasculinity, *Details* coincided with a time when the mainstream concept of manhood was changing. In 2015 the magazine published its last issue.

Publication

Details.
est New York (USA), 1982.

Cover of the April 1985 issue of *Details*, featuring Billy Idol and Terence Stamp.

Cover photograph by Stephan Lupino.

↳ BASQUIAT, CUNNINGHAM, THE FACE, S. KLEIN, WEBER

SY DEVORE

In the mid-twentieth century, Sy Devore reigned as Hollywood's hottest tailor. A Brooklyn native who ventured west to establish his own haberdashery in 1943, Devore was soon schmoozing with and cutting suits for idols such as John Wayne, Desi Arnaz, and Rock Hudson. Devore's most faithful clientele were the members of the Rat Pack, whom he outfitted in crisp sharkskin suits, punchy plaid sport coats, and narrow ties. Devore's creations appeared in films such as *Ocean's 11* (1960) and *The Nutty Professor* (1963). At around $285 for a custom suit and $200 for a blazer, his clothes weren't cheap for that time. But for the stars who wore them, they were worth it. Sammy Davis Jr. once spent thirty thousand dollars on a palette of eighty-four suits. Elvis Presley (one of Devore's most committed customers) would come in and buy fifteen suits in his 42 regular size. And it was said that Jerry Lewis spent seventy-five thousand dollars a year at Devore's. Though Devore died in the mid-1960s, his suave and slender clothes defined Hollywood's postwar period.

Tailor

Sy Devore.
b Brooklyn (USA), 1907.
d Los Angeles (USA), 1966.

Publicity still of the stars of Warner Bros.'s *Ocean's 11*—Frank Sinatra, Dean Martin, Sammy Davis Jr., Peter Lawford, and Joey Bishop—wearing Sy Devore suits, 1960.

↳ ANTO BEVERLY HILLS, COHN, S. DAVIS, PRESLEY

DICKIES

Men's fashion has always been closely associated with workwear, and for much of the twentieth century, Texas-based Dickies was the leading manufacturer of work clothes in the United States. Established in 1918 by C. N. Williamson and E. E. "Colonel" Dickie as the US Overall Company, the brand would officially change its name in 1922, but its purpose remained the same—to make denim bib overalls. Dickies sold work clothes throughout the 1920s and the Great Depression before shifting to military uniforms during World War II. In the 1950s oil workers from Texas popularized the brand's chinos and Eisenhower jackets around the world. The 65 percent polyester and 35 percent cotton blend used by Dickies was considered by many to be indestructible. In 1967 Dickies introduced the iconic 874 work pant, whose popularity spread throughout Southern California with its adoption by skateboarders and as part of cholo fashion in the 1980s. While Dickies maintained its dominance of the workwear market in the face of foreign imports, hip-hop artists made Dickies clothes—with their recognizable Ox Collar logo—a staple of '90s streetwear.

Brand

Dickies.
est Fort Worth, TX (USA), 1922.

Dickies "Men of Production" advertisement, 1949.

↳ CARHARTT, CHAVARRIA, FILSON, LEVI'S, RED WING

DIESEL

It's all about denim and disruption for Diesel's founder Renzo Rosso, who began fashioning jeans with his mother's sewing machine at just fifteen years old. Since launching in 1978 the duality of material and rebellion have been recurring themes for the company. With a focus on transforming denim with new, alternative styles, Diesel was one of the first brands to design distressed denim, which reached peak popularity in the 1990s. Diesel's edgy, worn-in look featured heavy whiskering, faded seams, and ripped knees on classic straight-leg jeans. The brand's bold, provocative advertisements also helped promote the company's mantra, "For Successful Living." In 2008 Diesel launched its Diesel Black Gold ready-to-wear line during New York Fashion Week. With more than two thousand innovative washes, Diesel continues to make premium denim fashionable and distinct, boasting collaborative capsule collections with Shayne Oliver and Samuel Ross's A-Cold-Wall*. Drawing inspiration from a wide range of sources—New York City, motocross, ravers in Berlin—Diesel's youthful energy and spirit are embodied by brand ambassadors such as DJ Steve Aoki and Brazilian soccer star Neymar.

Brand

Diesel.
est Molvena (IT), 1978.

Model Sang Woo Kim for the Diesel Fall/Winter 2015 campaign.

Photograph by Richard Burbridge.

↳ A-COLD-WALL*, FIORUCCI, LaCHAPELLE, MARGIELA, MARNI, OLIVER

159

PIERO DIMITRI

To describe Piero Dimitri as just a master tailor is to do an injustice to his remarkable rise from being a tailor's apprentice in Palermo, Italy, to a business owner on Manhattan's Fifth Avenue. Known as the Maestro by his contemporaries, many of whom he helped train, Dimitri opened his first shop in Milan at just nineteen years old. In the late 1960s Dimitri moved to the United States, where he soon became a leader in the American menswear designer movement of the early 1970s. He designed suits in woolens and worsteds made from subtle multicolored threads, with ventless jackets featuring natural shoulders, tapered waists, and full trousers, and he was quickly recognized for his craftsmanship. He won three consecutive Coty Awards, in 1973, 1974, and 1975, and became the first menswear designer elected to the Coty Hall of Fame in 1975. Hugely admired by his peers—Ralph Lauren and Bill Blass were fans—he perfected a suit that managed to look both traditional and fashionable. In the 1990s he divided his time between his stores in New York and Hollywood, and the perfection of his clothes attracted customers from Wall Street and Hollywood.

Designer

Piero Dimitri.
b Monreale (IT), c. 1933.
d Milazzo (IT), 2019.

Piero Dimitri wool plaid suit for "The Good Life," *Ebony*, April 1973.

Photograph by Moneta Sleet Jr.

↳ BLASS, DEVORE, FLUSSER, KAISERMAN, LAUREN

DNR

In the very late 1800s, Edmund Fairchild took the fortune he had made in soap and acquired the *Chicago Herald Gazette*. It may sound alien now, but the *Gazette*'s entire stock in trade was the men's garment industry. Fairchild and his brother Louis distributed the paper at the 1893 Chicago World's Fair and soon after renamed it the *Daily News Record*. The clinical name masked all the intrigue that would fill its pages, as over the next century-plus the *DNR* (as it became known) covered all the mergers, bankruptcies, and fashion-show flash that captivated the industry. It was not a publication for passing fashion fans. It was a true garment industry delight, where you could read about how men's pleated bottoms were selling that year or what Ralph Lauren's earnings would look like this quarter or what trends were emerging out of the Las Vegas trade shows. In 1910 *Women's Wear Daily* (*WWD*) was born as an insert in *DNR*, and ninety-eight years later, in 2008, Fairchild Publications (as the media firm became known) folded *DNR*'s men's coverage into *WWD*.

Publication

DNR.
est Chicago (USA), 1892.

"Off the Drawing Board," *DNR*, January 1992.

Illustrations by Robert Melendez.

↳ APPAREL ARTS, ESQUIRE, GENTRY, GQ, MELENDEZ

DOCKERS

The definitive label for khaki pants, Dockers was created in 1986 by Levi Strauss & Co. Dating back to the 1840s khakis originated as military uniforms with the Corps of Guides, a regiment of the British Indian Army. The dress was eventually adopted by all regiments, preferring a more breathable pant in linen or cotton to blend in and adapt to the terrain. Later finding their way stateside, khakis were popularized by beatnik Jack Kerouac and US President John F. Kennedy. In the late 1980s Dockers contributed to the evolution of this men's sartorial staple with a style inspired by British longshoremen. (Its logo even features two wings and a nautical-themed anchor.) As "America's favorite khaki," Dockers became part of the prevailing aesthetic and prep-school style of the 1990s and helped spur smart casual dressing in the workplace, begetting "casual Fridays," a day men could be free from the constraints of suits. Today the label designs its signature pants in contemporary and classic fits and also makes chinos, shorts, and everyday workwear. In 2019 celebrity stylist Karla Welch collaborated with the brand on a unisex basics collection.

Brand

Dockers.
est San Francisco (USA), 1986.

Illustration on the Dockers Launch Collection hang tag, 1986.

↳ DICKIES, KENNEDY, LEVI'S, WELCH

DOLCE & GABBANA

Since their runway debut at Milan Fashion Week in 1985, the duo Domenico Dolce and Stefano Gabbana has created one of Italy's greatest fashion brands. Shaking off conservative strictures of the 1980s, the label allowed Dolce's Sicilian roots and tailoring expertise to blend with Gabbana's artistic Milanese heritage, and the innovative complementary fusion proved intoxicating. Marrying the heat and lust of the south with the history and craftsmanship of the north, the result was a sensual vision of male beauty. Their preppy, sexy style was epitomized by pieces such as pleated wool trousers, glossy loafers, and smart polo necks or crisply cut cashmere coats wreathed by chunky knitted scarfs. Equally, Dolce & Gabbana came to mean coveted underwear: ribbed cotton trunks on ripped male models, such as Tony Ward and Antonio Beis. Shot in black and white by Steven Meisel, these iconic campaigns created fashion history. Along with their diffusion line D&G, the brand led '90s men's ready-to-wear, offering an extravagant, sharp alternative to the traditional Italian look.

Designer Brand

Dolce & Gabbana.
est Legnano (IT), 1985.

Dolce & Gabbana Spring/Summer 2018 at Milan Men's Fashion Week, 2017.

Photograph by Victor Boyko.

↳ GANDY, S. KLEIN, MEISEL, VERSACE, T. WARD

DRAKE'S

Established by Michael Drake in London's East End, Drake's roots began in high-end haberdashery. Since 1977 the fashion house has created artisanal men's scarves, shawls, plaids, and, most famously, handmade ties and handkerchiefs with a relaxed elegance and charm. Traditionally made of ancient madder silk from English mills, Drake's ties boast a bevy of styles—knitted, patterned, bow, or solid plain. In 2010 Michael Drake's decades-long lead designer Michael Hill (who learned the craft from his father, Charles Hill, a renowned artisanal tie maker) took over as creative director. Together with Mark Cho, the cofounder of Hong Kong haberdasher The Armoury, Hill has modernized Drake's, marrying the best of English design and detail with a contemporary aesthetic, reflected in ties with surfer prints or classic woven silk grenadine from Florence. In 2013 the company acquired the Rayner & Sturges shirt factory in Somerset, allowing them to produce bespoke and ready-to-wear shirts. Drake's latest collections also include selvedge denim and a Perennials line of everyday sartorial pieces. They have recently collaborated with Aimé Leon Dore, J.Crew, and Fred Perry.

Accessory Design

Drake's.
est London (UK), 1977.

Newly tailored floral-patterned ties
on display at Drake's, London, 2015.

Photograph by Matthew Lloyd.

↳ BROOKS BROTHERS, HERMÈS,
J.CREW, LAUREN, PERRY

DR. MARTENS

The durable and timeless Dr. Martens boot is the ultimate subversive footwear. Adopted by subcultures from mods and punks in the 1970s to grunge kids in the '90s, the boots have since transcended specific groups to become an enduring symbol of rebellious youth and countercultural style. Designed by German soldier Dr. Klaus Maertens following a skiing accident in 1945, the boots featured a unique air-padded sole that made them both comfortable and hard-wearing. By 1952 the demand for the boots had grown so much that a factory was opened in Munich. Seven years later the British company R. Griggs Group Ltd. bought the patent and decided to refine the heel and add the distinctive yellow stitching, rebranding the boots as Dr. Martens AirWair in 1960. The pragmatic boots became a working-class staple but were also adopted by musicians such as the Who's Pete Townshend and later by bands including the Clash, the Stranglers, and Madness. On film, the boots made appearances in the rock opera *Tommy* (1975), which featured Elton John wearing a supersize version, and in 1979's mod classic *Quadrophenia*, as well as many others.

Footwear

Dr. Martens.
est Northamptonshire, England (UK), 1960.

Punks wearing Dr. Martens outside BOY on King's Road, London, 1979.

Photograph by Janette Beckman.

↳ BLUNDSTONE, McLAREN, TIMBERLAND, WESTWOOD

DSQUARED2

Founded by Canadian-born twin brothers Dean and Dan Caten, Dsquared2 captured the exuberance of the 2000s with over-the-top runway shows, bold sexuality, and an outré sensibility. After a brief stint at Parsons School of Design and years working at Versace and Diesel, the Caten brothers launched their own brand in Milan in 1995. Dsquared2 quickly made a name for itself as an envelope-pushing house that wasn't afraid of overtly sexualizing the male body with revealing cuts or offending classic tastes with over-the-top graphics, becoming popular with celebs, such as Lenny Kravitz, Nick Jonas, and Justin Timberlake. Dsquared2 has managed to maintain its relevance by capitalizing on a particular niche market—the brand's tight leather pants, revealing underwear, and even scantier swimwear are especially popular with customers who want to showcase their natural assets. To capture the brand's distinctive edge, Dsquared2 has partnered with top photographers on its advertising campaigns, including Steven Klein, Steven Meisel, and Mert & Marcus.

Designer Brand

Dsquared2.
est Milan (IT), 1995.

Dsquared2 Spring/Summer 2008 menswear collection at Milan Fashion Week, 2007.

Photograph by Filippo Monteforte.

↳ DIESEL, S. KLEIN, MEISEL, MERT & MARCUS, VERSACE

EBONY

Since its first appearance in 1945, *Ebony* has celebrated the Black experience, showcasing Black culture and lifestyle as well as celebrities, sports figures, activists, and entrepreneurs. Legendary figures such as Jay-Z, Prince, Samuel L. Jackson, Marvin Gaye, Muhammad Ali, and Billy Dee Williams have graced its covers and pages. Modeled on *Life* magazine, *Ebony* was founded by businessman John Harold Johnson, who also launched *Jet* magazine in 1951. In its more than seventy-five years, *Ebony*'s focus, like the world of fashion, has shifted with changing times—political activism and civil rights in the 1960s and '70s, luxury and opulence in the '80s and '90s, and controversial issues in the aughts and 2010s—while remaining at the forefront of representing Black life. In addition to featuring and lauding Black models and designers on the magazine's pages, Johnson's wife, Eunice, established the Ebony Fashion Fair in 1958. The fair was an annual event that for five decades traveled to dozens of cities, bringing couture to Black men and women across North America. In 2019 the magazine suspended its print edition; it relaunched as a digital publication in 2021.

Publication

Ebony.
est Chicago (USA), 1945.

Models photographed for "The Good Life," *Ebony*, April 1973.

Photograph by Moneta Sleet Jr.

↪ ALI, ESQUIRE, GQ, KELLY, PARKS, W. SMITH, WHITE

LAPO ELKANN

Born into Italian business royalty, Lapo Elkann has a style often likened to that of his grandfather, the late Fiat CEO, Gianni Agnelli. Yet where Agnelli's tastes tilted toward the conservative—think pinstripe double-breasted tailoring, pressed fair blue shirts, and steady ties—his grandson's clothes are far less conventional, even when they are in fact the grandfather's suits that he has inherited and refashioned. Elkann has sported suits in marinara-sauce red, pumpkin-pie brown, and flamingo pink; he wears Rubinacci and Gucci sport coats with massive dinner plate–sized peak lapels, shirt collars spread wide enough to flap in the wind, and sprightly suede loafers, often from Belgian Shoes. Such conspicuous clothes have not always aided Elkann—a persistent tabloid fixture in Italy—in dodging the paparazzi, but they have burnished his image independent of his grandfather. In 2007 he founded Italia Independent. The Turin-based brand is best known for its blocky carbon-fiber sunglasses with pastel-tinted frames that reflect Elkann's kaleidoscopic fashion sense.

Icon

Lapo Elkann.
b New York (USA), 1977.

Lapo Elkann, Florence.

Photograph by Scott Schuman.

↳ AGNELLI, BELGIAN SHOES, GUCCI, RUBINACCI, TOD'S

DUKE ELLINGTON

Icon

Duke Ellington.
b Washington, DC (USA), 1899.
d New York (USA), 1974.

Pianist, jazz composer, bandleader, and debonair gentleman Duke Ellington codified the elegance of the big-band era. Raised in Washington, DC, Ellington moved to New York in the early 1920s and rose to fame as a piano player. Over the course of a fifty-year career, Ellington toured the world while crafting and recording hundreds of tunes that have become essential parts of the Great American Songbook, such as "It Don't Mean a Thing (If It Ain't Got That Swing)" and "Take the 'A' Train." As a young man Ellington sharpened his musical chops and his style playing at Harlem's Cotton Club, where he developed his image as a suave dandy, wearing immaculate tuxedos or white double-breasted dinner jackets with top hats or, later, wide-brim fedoras. Off-duty Ellington was known for bold printed button-down shirts and large houndstooth jackets (which he is often credited with popularizing), and while relaxing at home, he favored the ultimate dandy look: a leopard-print smoking jacket with black satin facing.

Duke Ellington writing on music scores.

↳ ASTAIRE, CALLOWAY,
   M. DAVIS, PRESLEY

PERRY ELLIS

Perry Ellis was a maverick who redefined American sportswear. Born in Portsmouth, Virginia, in 1940, he created his namesake line in 1976, later introducing menswear in 1980. Pioneering a new sartorial formality, Ellis lifted fashion from its rigidity while crafting elegant clothes that looked simple and sublime for everyday wear. He modernized men's fashion with subtle twists on quintessential classics, whether immaculate khakis, languid roll-neck sweaters, or the perfect trench. His aesthetic played with pattern and proportions,

developing new shapes and experimental details such as the "dimple" sleeve, to transformative effect. In addition to receiving nine Coty Awards beginning in 1979, he received the CFDA Designer of the Year award in 1982 and became president of the CFDA in 1984. Largely lauded as part of America's triumvirate of fashion, he joins Calvin Klein and Ralph Lauren as design doyens. In 1986 Perry Ellis tragically died from AIDS-related complications. His contributions to American fashion continue to influence generations of designers.

Designer

Perry Ellis.
b Portsmouth, VA (USA), 1940.
d New York (USA), 1986.

Perry Ellis, 1981.

Photograph by Eve Arnold.

↳ BANKS, HILFIGER, C. KLEIN, LAUREN, W. SMITH

EDWARD ENNINFUL

After being discovered by men's stylist Simon Foxton during the late 1980s, a young Edward Enninful alternated between modeling for *i-D* and assisting Foxton. Then, at eighteen years old, the Ghanaian-born, London-based prodigy became the fashion editor at the magazine—a meteoric and unprecedented rise. Even more groundbreaking was his appointment in 2017 as editor in chief of British *Vogue*, becoming the first man and the first person of color ever to hold the revered title. In the years between his teenage modeling debut and his arrival at British *Vogue*, Enninful was a contributing editor to *Vogue*

and *Vogue Italia*, and from 2011 to 2017 he was the creative style director at *W*. His menswear editorials, particularly during his time at *i-D*, conveyed a keen awareness of diversity in model casting (which is evident today in his approach at British *Vogue*) and an instinctive flair for channeling inspirations found within London's vibrant nightclub culture of the 1990s. He seamlessly fused sportswear with high-fashion brands at a time when the two worlds still rarely collided. In 2020 Enninful took on an additional role at Condé Nast as *Vogue*'s first European editorial director.

Edward Enninful.
b (GHA), 1972.

Edward Enninful at London Fashion Week, 2019.

Photograph by Wayne Tippetts.

↳ THE FACE, FOXTON, HARDISON, i-D, L'UOMO VOGUE, MEISEL, SIMS, TALLEY

ERMENEGILDO ZEGNA

Ermenegildo Zegna's humble vision was to create "the best fabrics in the world." In 1910 Zegna established the Lanificio Zegna wool mill in his hometown of Trivero, at the foot of the Italian Alps. The company blossomed as Zegna pulled in wool, cashmere, and mohair from Mongolia, Australia, and South Africa. In the 1930s Zegna braved a two-week boat trek to New York City, where he convinced American tailors to buy his cloth—the start of his global exporting business. While the label became known for its fine featherweight fabrics, Zegna himself set a standard of philanthropy and eco-consciousness. He erected a Modernist swimming pool, school, and hospital for Zegna employees and planted more than five hundred thousand conifer trees around Trivero. After Zegna's death in 1966, his sons, Aldo and Angelo, took over, expanding into ready-to-wear and custom clothing. Today, under the guidance of Gildo Zegna, the founder's grandson, the third-generation family business is expansive, with a runway collection, a flourishing textile business, and stakes in labels such as Thom Browne and Agnona.

Designer Brand

Ermenegildo Zegna.
est Trivero (IT), 1910.

Mahershala Ali for Ermenegildo Zegna's #WhatMakesaMan Fall/Winter 2019 campaign.

Photograph by Josh Olins.

↳ BROWNE, CANALI, CORNELIANI, CUCINELLI, PILATI

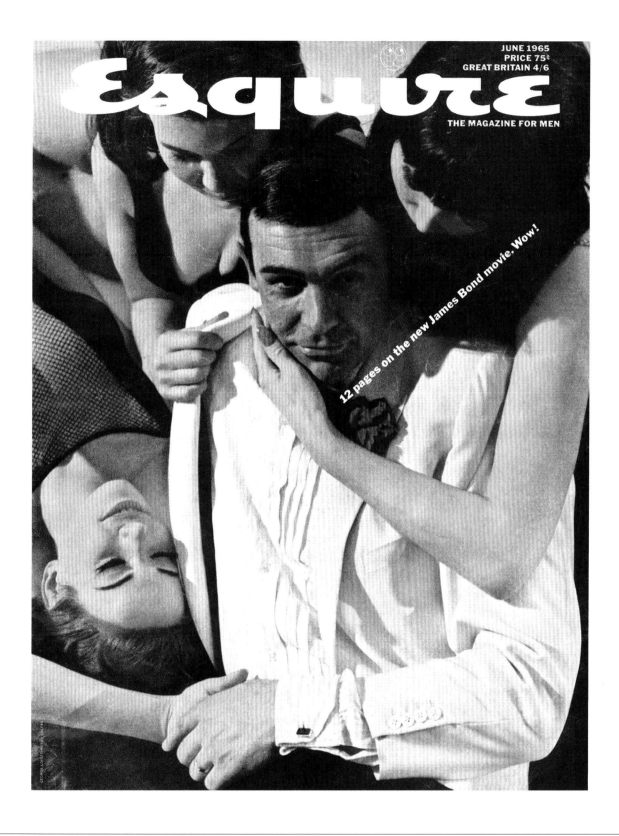

JUNE 1965
PRICE 75¢
GREAT BRITAIN 4/6

Esquire

THE MAGAZINE FOR MEN

12 pages on the new James Bond movie. Wow!

ESQUIRE

When *Esquire* was founded by Chicago publisher David Smart and editor Arnold Gingrich in 1933, it set out to tell men "what to eat, what to drink, what to wear, how to play, and what to read." Gone was the dreary office worker; in his place came men who enjoyed their leisure pursuits, shopping, and sex. In its early days the large-format magazine was mainly taken up with fashion illustrations but also included long-form articles by high-profile authors, including F. Scott Fitzgerald and Ernest Hemingway. By the late 1950s the pages were dedicated more and more to photography, including images by Art Kane,

Diane Arbus, and Richard Avedon, which were accompanied by writings from pioneers of New Journalism in the 1960s, such as Norman Mailer and Tom Wolfe. Between 1962 and 1972 George Lois's arresting covers—including Muhammad Ali as Saint Sebastian—changed the face not just of *Esquire* but of all magazines. As trends changed around the 2000s, *Esquire* shifted its focus, covering a mix of celebrity, politics, and culture. Remaining unchanged, however, are the editorials shot by leading photographers, now including names such as Mark Seliger, Alexi Lubomirski, and Max Vadukul.

Publication

Esquire.
est Chicago (USA), 1933.

Cover of the June 1965 issue of *Esquire* magazine, art directed by George Lois, featuring Sean Connery as James Bond.

Photograph by Timothy Galfas.

↪ ALI, APPAREL ARTS, CONNERY, EBONY, GQ, LAURENCE, SELIGER

JACQUES ESTEREL

Despite describing himself as simply a "craftsman of dresses and songs," French couturier and performer Jacques Esterel pioneered a radical approach to fashion in the 1960s. After training as an engineer, Esterel opened his couture house in 1953, becoming known as much for gestures—such as building lights into umbrellas—as for bespoke sartorial accomplishments, including designing Brigitte Bardot's wedding dress in 1959. During the 1960s and '70s Esterel—joined for a year by the young Jean Paul Gaultier—experimented with menswear and mod street fashion, creating a plaid suit with a kilt, a salmon pink Nehru jacket, and trousers with zippers at the front and back. In the late 1960s he launched his celebrated Casual Snob line of clothing, which saw him push the boundaries of unisex clothing, an approach also investigated by designers such as Rudi Gernreich and Ted Lapidus, dressing men and women in the same pantsuits, coats, and tops, all made from jersey cloth. Soon after, in 1970, Esterel released a similar collection but with men and women outfitted in long dresses.

Designer

Jacques Esterel.
b Bourg-Argental, Loire (FR), 1917.
d Saint-Cloud (FR), 1974.

Jacques Esterel's "Elle et Lui" Spring/ Summer 1970 collection.

↳ CARDIN, GAULTIER, GERNREICH, LAPIDUS, NEHRU

ETRO

Etro is intrinsically tied to paisley prints and haute bohe-mian fashions. Founded by Gerolamo "Gimmo" Etro in 1968, the Milan-based, family-run house first sold high-quality textiles to ready-to-wear labels. Developing saturated hues and opulent motifs, Etro was inspired by the distant Mughal Empire and vintage shawls collected by his wife, Roberta, an antiques dealer. Coupled with an emerging countercultural current, Gimmo applied his signature style and irreverent flair to textiles, printing striking paisleys on sumptuous silks and wool. Paving the way for the company's next generation

(children Jacopo, Kean, Ippolito, and Veronica all work in the family business), Gimmo expanded into eclectic home wares and accessories in the 1980s. In the 1990s the company expanded into menswear, led by Kean, and introduced sophisticated suiting with geometric or pinstripe patterns, as well as signature cotton shirts with floral motifs and unexpected undercollars. Today the independent spirit of the brand persists, with a commitment to craft, care, and a curious whimsy that is evident in a dizzying array of designs, including quilted coats and jacquard ponchos.

Designer Brand

Etro.
est Milan (IT), 1968.

Models backstage at the Etro Fall/Winter 2020 show at Milan Fashion Week.

Photograph by Acielle/Style du Monde.

↳ GRANNY TAKES A TRIP, MARNI, MISSONI, PRADA, P. SMITH

THE FACE

ROCKS FINAL FRONTIER   No 8
DECEMBER 1980   MONTHLY   65p

JOHN LYDON
AT LARGE

IAN DURY
THE SLITS
POLYSTYRENE
Paul Weller colour   TV cops
Manchester Bowie scene
Gossip mags   Music Movies Style

John Lydon by Sheila Rock

THE FACE

Launched in London in 1980 by former *NME* editor Nick Logan, *The Face* was a style bible and magazine that covered the nexus of music, film, fashion, and popular culture. The publication became the voice of a generation, documenting underground subcultures such as the New Romantics and putting names such as Boy George, Alexander McQueen, and Kurt Cobain on its covers. *The Face* recruited the best talent of the day, with articles penned by Robert Elms, Nick Kent, Tony Parsons, Jon Savage, and Julie Burchill and fashion editorials photographed by Corinne Day,

Juergen Teller, David Sims, Glen Luchford, Nick Knight, and Jamie Morgan, who captured the Buffalo style with stylist Ray Petri. Stylists Joe McKenna, Karl Templer, and Melanie Ward also worked with the publication throughout the 1980s and '90s. The magazine highlighted new narratives and alternative expressions of an emerging British creative class that mixed high-low styling, graphic tees, and punk inspirations. In 2004 *The Face* came to an end, but it was reborn in 2019 under the editorship of Stuart Brumfitt, a former fanboy.

Publication

The Face.
est London (UK), 1980.

Cover of the December 1980 issue
of *The Face*, featuring John Lydon.

Photograph by Sheila Rock.

↳ KNIGHT, LUCHFORD,
McKENNA, PETRI, SIMS,
TELLER, TEMPLER, M. WARD

1. MASCULINITY

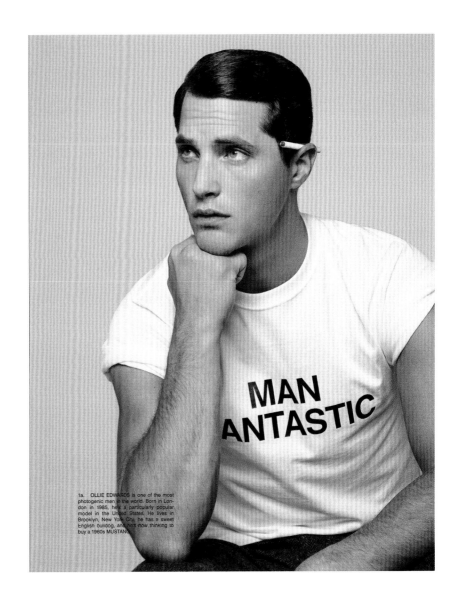

1a. OLLIE EDWARDS is one of the most photogenic men in the world. Born in London in 1985, he's a particularly popular model in the United States. He lives in Brooklyn, New York City, he has a sweet English bulldog, and he's now thinking to buy a 1960s MUSTANG.

– 232 –

FANTASTIC MAN

For many fashion devotees the launch of *Fantastic Man* in 2005 posed a challenge. Not only were the founders, Gert Jonkers and Jop van Bennekom, fashion outsiders from Amsterdam, but the biannual magazine contained far more words than most men's fashion publications. Prior to *Fantastic Man*, Jonkers and van Bennekom worked together on lifestyle magazine *Boulevard*, and in 2001 they launched the gay culture magazine *Butt*. Sticking resolutely to print in a digital age, *Fantastic Man* has subtly changed the male fashion dynamic, concentrating on what it calls men in clothes rather

than models in fashion, with long profiles of men from a range of fields—including Raf Simons, Rem Koolhaas, Bryan Ferry, Helmut Lang, and Bret Easton Ellis—and photography by names such as Juergen Teller, Wolfgang Tillmans, Collier Schorr, and Inez & Vinoodh. Its aim is to reflect personal style in whatever form it takes: thrift-store clothes, upcycled, designer, or perfectly on-trend. With its distinct vision present in both the features and fashion editorials, *Fantastic Man* celebrates male individuality and men's capacity to question and challenge today's world, even the very patriarchy itself.

Publication

Fantastic Man.
est Amsterdam (NL), 2005.

Ollie Edwards photographed for "Workshop," *Fantastic Man*, Fall/Winter 2013.

Photograph by Collier Schorr.

↳ FERRY, LANG, SCHORR, SIMONS, TELLER, TILLMANS, VRIENS

LAURENCE FELLOWS

In the decades before widespread photography, Laurence Fellows's painterly sketches offered men a guide to the day's style trends. After training at the Pennsylvania Academy of the Fine Arts and working briefly in advertising, Fellows, in the early 1930s, began penning illustrations for *Vogue*, *Cosmopolitan*, *Apparel Arts*, and *Esquire*. Those last two publications, which were hitting newsstands for the first time, were where the bulk of Fellows's jaunty gents appeared. Unlike the youth-focused magazine spreads of today, the men Fellows depicted were his generational peers, with the occasional wrinkle or gray hair. These illustrated icons wore high-rise pleated trousers, emerald green three-piece suits, box-checked raglan-sleeve over-coats, and striped ties knotted to perfection. Through his drawings, one could track the whims of men's fashion during the 1930s and '40s as lapel widths expanded and contracted, new patterns came into vogue, and suit colors fizzled out. Posthumously, in 2009, Fellows was inducted into the Society of Illustrators Hall of Fame.

Illustrator

Laurence Fellows.
b Ardmore, PA (USA), 1885.
d East Hampton, CT (USA), 1964.

Illustration from "North and South Fashions," *Apparel Arts*, December 1940.

Illustration by Laurence Fellows.

↳ APPAREL ARTS, ESQUIRE, LEYENDECKER

GIANFRANCO FERRÉ

The Italian designer Gianfranco Ferré trained as an architect and brought his architectural approach to fashion, saying, "It's basic geometry; you take a flat form and revolve it in space." In 1978 he launched his ready-to-wear label in Milan before releasing his first menswear collection four years later. He was inspired by classic British tailoring but modernized it with more relaxed, elegant shapes. While working as artistic director at Christian Dior, from 1989 to 1997, Ferré released his own highly successful line of men's jeans in 1996; they were available in two colors, black or white, and three styles, including basic, athletic, or beach. Over his illustrious career Ferré won the Occhio d'Oro Award for Best Italian Designer six times. His global business, licensing agreements (including the unisex perfume Gieffeffe and golfwear for Japan), and luxurious lifestyle—he commuted between Milan and Paris in a private jet—confirmed his status as one of Italy's most successful ready-to-wear designers.

Designer

Gianfranco Ferré.
b Legnano (IT), 1944.
d Milan (IT), 2007.

Hoyt Richards for Gianfranco Ferré Spring/Summer 1991.

Photograph by Gian Paolo Barbieri.

↳ ARMANI, DIMITRI

BRYAN FERRY

As the lead singer of the 1970s English rock band Roxy Music, Bryan Ferry reveled in a combination of fashion, art, and music, creating a new, glamorous approach to everything from stage outfits to album covers. Working with designer Antony Price, the band's attire combined a 1950s elegance with military style and a sense of futurism, which translated into glossy satins, shiny sequins, and camera-friendly colors. Ferry also launched a solo career, through which he channeled his passion for both the Hollywood glamour of stars such as Humphrey Bogart and his personal love of tailoring (he worked in a tailoring shop as a teen in northern England). He embraced sartorial flourishes, including embroidered cowboy jackets, wide-lapeled suiting, Ivy League–style striped ties, and white tuxedos. Nowadays the singer also favors the handmade, wearing bespoke shirts from Charvet in Paris and Sean O'Flynn in London, his clothes impeccably tailored by Anderson & Sheppard. Ferry's sharp look has not only earned him plaudits on countless best-dressed lists but also turned him into a fashion icon; in 2007 Belgian designer Dries Van Noten based an entire collection on Ferry's singular style.

Bryan Ferry.
b Washington, England (UK), 1945.

Bryan Ferry at his home in Notting Hill Gate, London, 1975.

Photograph by Mick Rock.

↳ ANDERSON & SHEPPARD, CHARVET, VAN NOTEN

180

FILA

Swedish tennis star Björn Borg's technique shook up the game, but on court it was his chic FILA sportswear that stole the show. Dressed head to toe in FILA with his trademark pinstripe polo shirt, red Settanta track jacket, and red-white-and-blue sweatband, Borg and the brand became an unbeatable team. FILA was originally established by Italian brothers Ettore and Giansevero Fila in 1911 as an underwear manufacturer, but by the 1970s it had reinvented itself as a sportswear label, hiring designer Pierluigi Ronaldo to lead the charge. Under his direction the "F-box" logo was born, alongside bright, quality sporting separates that reinvented traditional all-white tennis ensembles. Its collaboration with Borg—and his raft of global admirers—had fans clamoring to copy the look. Its sporty style was revived in the 1980s and '90s when hip-hop artists adopted the look—a young LL Cool J onstage in FILA or the Notorious B.I.G. in its tees—turning the brand into a streetwear staple. Today new editions of old favorites continue to win fans, and it's even expanded its offerings through collaborations with Fendi and Brooks Brothers.

Brand

FILA.
est Biella (IT), 1911.

LL Cool J wearing a FILA track jacket, New York, 1986.

Photograph by Janette Beckman.

↳ ADIDAS, ASICS, BROOKS BROTHERS, LACOSTE, UMBRO

FILSON WOOLEN CRUISING COATS

*These Coats Are of
Filson Super Quality
Mackinaw!*

The Filson Woolen Cruising Coats are of finest grade mackinaw, in a quality especially manu-factured for us. We are informed by our weavers that we use the finest quality mackinaws that can be made; and **such as is used by no other manufacturers.**

In soft, warm colors. These coats afford unbelieveable protection against cold and rain and for all-'round outdoor use are unsurpassed.

Plenty of pockets; the whole back is a big, roomy pocket, with flaps and fasteners.

In plain red mackinaw; 24-oz. virgin wool, in the following plaids: red and black, green and black, gray and black, and in 20-oz. gray flannel.

All at $15.00 the garment.

Order one inch larger than white collar size.

Also in Forestry Cloth at $16.00.

Forestry Cloth is the beautiful forest green woolen material, which is cravenetted and will shed unbelieve-able quantities of water. This is one of our finest gar-ments and we recommend it for every use.

At a popular price we offer Red and Black Plaid or Green and Black Plaid Filson All Wool Mackinaw Cruising Coats...**$10.00**

FILSON

In the late 1800s gold rushers trekking to the Yukon would make a vital pit stop at Clinton C. Filson's Pioneer Alaska Clothing and Blanket Manufacturers to scoop up burly clothes for braving the bitter northwestern winters. When these fortune seekers faded away as the gold rush ended, Filson—and after he died, his family—pivoted to making practical clothes for hunters and loggers, such as the multipocketed Mackinaw Wool Cruiser jackets and the water-resistant Tin Cloth Field Jacket. In the decades that followed these pieces would gain recognition for being functional outside the forest and even fashionable. Filson saw its greatest surge starting in the early 2000s as young, city-dwelling men—drawn in by the line's consistent quality and Americana backstory—flocked to the brand. Suddenly lumberjack-looking men were clutching the company's recognizable tan briefcases and wearing its red-and-black plaid coats into offices around the nation. More than a century after its founding, Filson was once again outfitting bright-eyed fortune seekers.

Brand

Filson.
est Seattle (USA), 1897.

Page from a Filson catalogue, 1926.

↳ ALDEN SHOES, L.L.BEAN,
PATAGONIA, PENDLETON,
RED WING, WOOLRICH

ELIO FIORUCCI

Elio Fiorucci was a manic fashion merchant from an early age. A trip to London as a teenager during the Swinging Sixties inspired him to open up his own modish Carnaby Street–style shop back in Milan. Fiorucci really found his footing in 1970, when he founded his eponymous label. At age thirty-five he was older than his target audience—teens and twenty-somethings craving fun fashions such as poppy Lurex boots and navel-flashing cropped tees. His jeans stole the show, though. Before Calvin Klein and Gloria Vanderbilt made their fortunes on designer denim,

Fiorucci offered his painted-on Buffalo 70 jeans. They largely appealed to women, but liberated men, such as Rod Stewart, wore them as well. In 1976 Fiorucci opened his landmark shop on New York's 59th Street. The store became a destination. Designed by Ettore Sottsass of the Memphis art movement, it featured the work of Keith Haring and Kenny Scharf, and it was where the Studio 54 fixtures would shop before clubbing, picking up animal-printed or Day-Glo-colored clothes that would command the spotlight all night long.

Designer

Elio Fiorucci.
b Milan (IT), 1935.
d Milan (IT), 2015.

British singer and songwriter Rod Stewart wearing a Fiorucci shirt, c. 1975.

Photograph by David Montgomery.

↳ DIESEL, FISH, JORDACHE, C. KLEIN

MICHAEL FISH

Prior to the 1960s British men's fashion was a bit buttoned-up. Then Michael Fish splashed onto the scene. A working-class kid-turned-unapologetic dandy who honed his skills at Turnbull & Asser, Fish began producing palm-sized, punchy-patterned kipper ties in 1965. A year later he opened his store, Mr. Fish, where he offered flamboyant ruffled shirts, velvet coats, and flower-printed caps. The most impactful Fish designs were the boundary-breaking flowy dresses worn by Mick Jagger in concert and David Bowie on the cover

of *The Man Who Sold the World* (1970). Fish specialized in opulent fabrics, such as silk and brocade, but the priciness of these materials spurred his demise. Unable to keep the shop viable, he closed Mr. Fish in the 1970s and went to work for New York's Sulka. Though the label was short-lived, Fish's influential gender-fluid foppishness can be sensed today in the work of Jonathan Anderson and Gucci's Alessandro Michele.

Designer

Michael Fish.
b London (UK), 1940.

A man wearing a Mr. Fish tweed dress, London, 1970.

Photograph by Jack Garofalo.

↳ ANDERSON, BOWIE, JAGGER, MICHELE, SULKA, TURNBULL & ASSER

The FLORSHEIM Shoe

Most Styles $10

The Man Who Wears Florsheims —

does not think of them as *shoes*, but as *friendly companions* on his walk through life. You should wear FLORSHEIMS.

THEY will give you pleasure in their appearance and will satisfy you with their loyal, comforting service.

See your Spring FLORSHEIMS at the local agency—new smart styles for the young man—refined styles for the more conservative—all quality built—and *Skeleton Lined* for coolness

Booklet STYLES OF THE TIMES *on Request*

THE FLORSHEIM SHOE COMPANY · MANUFACTURERS · CHICAGO

FLORSHEIM SHOES

Early in the 1974 film *Chinatown*, Jake Gittes (played by Jack Nicholson) stumbles and scuffs his precious shoes. "Goddamn Florsheim shoe," he declares. In the 1930s when the film was set, those lace-up leather dress shoes were a cherished commodity that showed Gittes's refined taste. Founded in Chicago in the late 1800s by Milton Florsheim, the label was early in understanding the importance of branding—in 1896 it added a pull tab to the back of its wing tips and bluchers so customers could be certain they were acquiring a "genuine Florsheim" product. Florsheim was again ahead of the curve in introducing boxy, square-toed shoes in 1926, pioneering a shift in style trends. In the decades to come, Florsheim established its own shops, where its cap toes and loafers were conveniently out on the sales floor, and by 1966 a Florsheim shoe was reported to be sold every four seconds. In the 1980s some of Michael Jackson's moonwalking "magic shoes" were Florsheim loafers with a heel tacked on. And in the 2010s the company moved into higher fashion through partnerships with designers Duckie Brown and George Esquivel.

Footwear

Florsheim Shoes.
est Chicago (USA), 1892.

Florsheim Shoes advertisement, 1926.

↳ ALDEN SHOES, ANDOVER SHOP, BROOKS BROTHERS, CHURCH'S

of any physical excellencies on the part of the wearer. If, in contemplating this picture, we try to carry out Carlyle's instruction 'to look fixedly on clothes, or even with armed eyesight, till they become transparent', how poor and puny does the royal figure become when deprived of his luxuriant trappings. Indeed, this whole style of dress, in which clothes are everything and the body is little more than a means of suspension, depends upon the assumption, so well stated recently by R. H. Mottram, 'that civilisation is an artificial thing and that man is not beautiful or remarkable but must be made to appear so'.[1]

Between these two extremes (which have been emphasised in order to make clear the principle) there is of course a whole series of continuous gradations, on which fashion rings the changes. During the period of artificiality that distinguished the eighteenth century, the body itself fell relatively into the background; its purpose was largely to serve as a support for gorgeous clothes. With the naturalism that followed the French Revolution, the body once more came into its own rights, and the purpose of clothes became the relatively secondary one of throwing into relief the beauties of the body. Clothing became extremely simple and exiguous (much more so than in recent years), underclothing being almost dispensed with. A fashionable lady's costume had to pass two tests: it must not weigh more than $\frac{1}{2}$ lb. in all (as against 2 lb. or more at the present day) and her dress must be of such thinness and flexibility that it could be passed through her wedding-ring. Not content with this, she damped her dress before putting it on, so that it should cling closer to the figure. The Victorian period was again one of comparative artificiality, in which little attention was paid to the natural form of the body, and in which the quantity, if not the beauty, of the clothes enormously increased. Of late years we have, of course, again laid the accent on the body and indulged in a drastic simplification of dress.

[1] *Daily Mirror*, July 4, 1928.

Fig.19. Louis XVI, by Callet. An elaborate costume, the effect of which is independent of bodily form

(By permission of Messrs. Levy and Neurdein)

JOHN CARL FLÜGEL

Academic/Writer

The analysis of dress carried out by English psychologist John Carl Flügel in the 1920s continues to shape how we understand fashion. In particular, he explored the Great Masculine Renunciation, a term coined for the period in the late 1700s and early 1800s when men gave up the brightly colored and patterned clothes they had traditionally worn and instead began to dress in tailored suits in sober browns, grays, and blacks. Flügel's work addressed two main questions: why humans wear clothes at all and why clothes vary so much, particularly between men and women.

As explained in the seminal *The Psychology of Clothes* (1930), Flügel predicted clothing might ultimately become obsolete as humans moved beyond the requirements of modesty, adornment, and physical protection—the functions of all clothing. Flügel was also a member of the Men's Dress Reform Party, founded in 1929, which argued that men's clothes should be more emancipating in the same way as contemporary women's dress. Clothes, he ultimately believed, should reflect a man's reconciliation between the competing demands of his body and his psyche.

John Carl Flügel.
b London (UK), 1884.
d London (UK), 1955.

Interior spread from *The Psychology of Clothes*, 1930.

↳ BALLA, BRUMMELL, WILDE

ALAN FLUSSER

Tailor/Writer

In 1980s New York, the stock market was up, the lunches were long, and the suits were powerful. The tailor du jour for many boom-time corporate raiders was Alan Flusser, a New Jersey native who established a bustling Midtown Manhattan atelier in 1985. Two years later, Flusser was tapped to fashion suits for Gordon Gekko (played by Michael Douglas) in Oliver Stone's economic epic *Wall Street*. Gekko's attire cemented the look of this money-hungry moment: slick contrast-collar dress shirts, imposing peak-lapel suits, and natty suspenders holding it all together. In 2000 Flusser presented a slightly sleeker take on corporate wear by designing cutting clothes for Patrick Bateman (played by Christian Bale) in the C-suite thriller *American Psycho*. Flusser's atelier still whirs along, gingerly keeping pace with the changing tastes of the city's business class. Over the past four decades, Flusser has also written authoritative texts on men's style, including most recently a biography of Ralph Lauren.

Alan Flusser.
b West Orange, NJ (USA), 1945.

Michael Douglas, as Gordon Gekko, wearing a shirt tailored by Alan Flusser in a publicity still for Twentieth Century Fox's *Wall Street*, 1987.

↳ ANDERSON & SHEPPARD, DEVORE, LAUREN, NUTTER

TOM FORD

With his dashing good looks and fanatical attention to detail, Tom Ford has become as well-known for his own image as for his wide-ranging career. For more than three decades, Ford has championed the disco-era glamour that he grew up with, repackaging it for a new generation. Ford's career began in the early 1980s as a student at Parsons School of Design, during which time he also interned at Chloé in Paris. Following graduation in 1986 he got a job with sportswear designer Cathy Hardwick, and two years later he was designing for Perry Ellis

America. In 1990 Ford was hired by Gucci, where he presided over the brand's renaissance (under his tenure as creative director, Gucci went from near bankruptcy to a four-billion-dollar valuation in 1999). His menswear played on Studio 54 glamour; it was sexually charged and sumptuous, with louche velvet suits, printed silk shirts, and rich colors. When Ford left the company in 2004, he set up his own highly covetable eponymous brand, initially with a focus on the most luxurious bespoke tailoring, and quickly found fans in Daniel Craig, Ryan Gosling, and Jay-Z.

Designer

Tom Ford.
b Austin, TX (USA), 1961.

Tom Ford walks the runway at his Fall/Winter 2020 ready-to-wear show, Los Angeles.

Photograph by Frazer Harrison.

↳ GUCCI, JAY-Z, MICHELE, Y. SAINT LAURENT

FOX BROTHERS & CO

For the classic British suit, the only material is flannel; and for classic British flannel, the only maker is Fox Brothers, a woolen mill in the small west England town of Wellington. The first mill opened on the site before 1620, and in 1772 Thomas Fox became a partner in the firm, producing wool and flannel with a workforce that grew to five thousand people in the 1800s. A pioneer of mechanization, the company had a global market, importing cloth from Australia and New Zealand and exporting it to India and China. At home it has clothed the top tier of Englishmen, from Regency dandies to the businessmen of modern Savile Row, creating a wide variety of cloths in traditional colors and different weights, from a lightweight fabric to the classic—and heavier— West of England cloth. Winston Churchill wore suits made from the West of England chalk stripe, while Cary Grant sported the gray chalk stripe; Ralph Fiennes donned a navy suit in this pattern in 2012's *Skyfall*, proving that it never goes out of style.

Textile Designer

Fox Brothers & Co.
est Wellington, Somerset, England (UK), 1772.

Winston Churchill wearing a Henry Poole & Co. suit made in Fox Brothers chalk-stripe flannel, 1951.

↳ ANDERSON & SHEPPARD, GIEVES & HAWKES, C. GRANT, HENRY POOLE & CO., LORO PIANA

we haven't stopped dancing yet

positive!
by Simon Foxton

SIMON FOXTON

In the early 1980s British stylist Simon Foxton pioneered street casting: taking edgy London blokes, often Black or biracial—he discovered Edward Enninful on a train—into the studio to pose in a combination of sportswear, classic tailoring, and fetishwear that appealed to contemporary publications such as *i-D* and *The Face*. Only styling men, Foxton focuses more on creating an impactful image than reflecting the latest fashion trends, using clothes as tools rather than the primary subject. Having studied fashion at Central Saint Martins College of Art and Design, Foxton formed a fashion label in 1983 before *i-D* founder Terry Jones encouraged him to start styling editorials for the photographer Nick Knight, beginning an enduring creative partnership. Foxton's work has appeared in all major men's magazines, including *V*, *Arena Homme +*, *Vogue Hommes*, *Details*, and *GQ Style*, and he has also advised companies such as Levi's and Stone Island through his consultancy &Son. In 2005 Foxton was invited to guest-edit *i-D* for its twenty-fifth anniversary, and four years later, in 2009, his work was collected in the exhibition *When You're a Boy* at the Photographers' Gallery in London.

Stylist

Simon Foxton.
b Berwick-upon-Tweed, England (UK), 1961.

Spread from *i-D*'s The Positive Issue, January 1992. Styling by Simon Foxton.

Photograph by Simon Foxton.

↳ ENNINFUL, THE FACE, i-D, KNIGHT, McKIMM

WALT "CLYDE" FRAZIER

Long before NBA stars such as Dwyane Wade and Russell Westbrook were being hailed as style icons, Walt "Clyde" Frazier paved the way as the league's most extravagantly dressed juggernaut. Drafted to the New York Knicks in 1967, Frazier blossomed into a two-time NBA champion on the hardwood and a peacock off. A natty fixture of Manhattan's nightlife scene, he navigated between hot spots in black turtlenecks, plaid suits, and towering fedoras, earning the nickname Clyde, a reference to the wide-brimmed hats Warren Beatty wore in *Bonnie and Clyde*. At six foot four,

and often wearing glittering gold medallions and black capes, the suave Frazier wasn't someone you could easily miss. In 1973 he signed a contract with Puma, becoming one of the first NBA names to have a signature sneaker. That model— a graceful suede low-top known as the Puma Clyde—is still sold today. In his later years Frazier has become an in-game commentator for the MSG Network, with his riotous 1970s-infused fashion sense still intact. The website Clyde So Fly documents Frazier's ostentatious on-screen suits, in patterns such as leopard print, sprawling paisley, and lumberjack plaid.

Icon

Walt "Clyde" Frazier.
b Atlanta (USA), 1945.

Walt "Clyde" Frazier gets fitted for a new pair of pants, New York, 1970.

Photograph by Walter Iooss Jr.

↳ ALI, BEST, JORDAN, WADE, WESTBROOK

FRED SEGAL

Few fashion insiders can take as much credit for creating the California look as Fred Segal and his namesake stores. What began as a three-hundred-square-foot jeans shop on Santa Monica Boulevard in 1961 quickly turned into a twenty-nine-thousand-square-foot shopping destination, led by Segal's visionary approach to fashion retail. The space included specialty shops, one owned by his nephew Ron Herman, and another by former employee Ron Robinson. Segal is credited with kicking off the designer-jeans concept, creating the first denim bar, and selling embellished and lowrider jeans as early as the mid-1960s, attracting customers such as the Beatles, Elvis Presley, and Bob Dylan. When the store moved to Melrose Avenue and expanded, Segal developed the idea of the store within a store, allowing brands—from Beams to the streetwear platform Stadium Goods—to create their own environments within his space for maximum contrast and buzz. Fred Segal has been featured in fashion-obsessed films and books, such as Bret Easton Ellis's *Less Than Zero* (1987), and is popular with local celebs, including David Beckham, Jason Statham, and John Legend.

Retailer

Fred Segal.
est Los Angeles (USA), 1961.

The Fred Segal 2020 Collection.

↳ BEAMS, THE BEATLES, GAP, JEFFREY, MAXFIELD, PRESLEY

FRUITS

More of an affordable monthly photo book than a true magazine, *Fruits*'s issues were dedicated almost entirely to individual page-by-page photographs of people out on the street in Tokyo. Founder Shoichi Aoki had previously published *Streets* magazine, but *Fruits* arrived in 1997 with a specific aim: to capture the beguiling and entirely fresh style of the denizens of Harajuku. What Aoki perceived was that at this moment young people in Japan were mastering—truly, for the first time ever—how to mix traditional Japanese garments, such as the kimono and tabi shoes,

with Western clothing. They also were experimenting with color like never before. If Japanese fashion of the previous years was defined by the brooding black fabrications of Comme des Garçons and Yohji Yamamoto, *Fruits* was capturing a new flamboyantly futuristic generation traveling around in enormous rave-ready boots, pink hair (on men and women alike), and plastic outerwear. What *Fruits* put to paper was a fashion scene unlike any other in the world. In 2017 Aoki abruptly shuttered *Fruits*, declaring, "There are no more cool kids to photograph."

Publication

Fruits.
est Tokyo (JAP), 1997.

Tokyo streetstyle photographed for *Fruits*, June 1998.

Photograph by Shoichi Aoki.

↳ CUNNINGHAM, GENTRY, RUBINSTEIN, SCHUMAN

FUBU

Founded in 1992 in Queens, New York, by childhood friends Daymond John, J. Alexander Martin, Keith Perrin, and Carlton Brown, FUBU—For Us, By Us—rose to become one of the world's mightiest street-fashion brands. In 1997 red-hot rapper LL Cool J appeared in a Gap commercial wearing a hat not by Gap but by FUBU. LL Cool J's Trojan horse FUBU endorsement—which somehow went unnoticed by Gap's execs—helped take FUBU to new heights. At its peak from 1999 to 2002, the brand was grossing $500 million a year. Its oversized

logo hoodies, hats, and jackets were inescapable across music videos on MTV and in the pages of vital hip-hop magazines, such as *The Source*. FUBU's ubiquity was bolstered by a robust licensing business: there were FUBU home goods, FUBU kidswear, even FUBU rental tuxedos. The brand fizzled in the 2000s as fashion trends leaned away from logo-mania, but more recently FUBU has been enjoying a nostalgia-based surge as customers young and old embrace the label's signature swaggering style once again.

Designer Brand

FUBU.
est Queens, NY (USA), 1992.

J. Alexander Martin, Carlton Brown, Keith Perrin, and Daymond John wearing FUBU at the Essence Awards, Los Angeles, 1999.

Photograph by Robin Platzer.

↳ COMBS, CROSS COLOURS, KANI, ROCAWEAR, APRIL WALKER

HIROSHI FUJIWARA

Hiroshi Fujiwara, Japan's "godfather of streetwear," is a multihyphenate extraordinaire. After moving to Tokyo in the 1980s at the age of eighteen, he embedded himself in the Harajuku scene, bringing punk and hip-hop inspirations from London and New York to his clothing. In 1990 he launched the original streetwear label Goodenough, pioneering the now commonplace use of scarcity and hype as selling tools. Three years later he helped designers Nigo and Jun Takahashi open the store NOWHERE. Featuring American clothing and memorabilia, the two also stocked the shelves with products of their own. Their boutique became a platform for emerging brands that defined Japanese cool, including Nigo's A Bathing Ape, WTAPS, and Neighborhood. In 2003 Fujiwara launched his agency Fragment Design, producing collaborative, limited editions, such as "Hi & Lo" sneakers with Takashi Murakami, Moncler puffer coats, Levi's premium jeans, and more with brands such as Louis Vuitton and Carhartt. (Nike is also a longtime collaborator.) His pop-up concept stores are equally hyped—from the POOL aoyama to THE CONVENI—and he is celebrated by fans such as Kim Jones and Pharrell Williams.

Designer

Hiroshi Fujiwara.
b Ise (JAP), 1964.

7 Moncler Fragment Hiroshi Fujiwara Spring/Summer 2019 collection at Milan Fashion Week.

↳ K. JONES, MURAKAMI, NIGO, NIKE, TAKAHASHI

CLARK GABLE

With Clark Gable, one must look past the mustache. Yes, his reedy stripe of facial hair proved to be Gable's signature throughout his career, but beyond his attention-grabbing upper lip, Gable's fashion sense is worth celebrating. Even at the onset of his film career in the 1930s, the brawny Gable had a taste for urbane fashions. In 1935 *Screenland* magazine dubbed him "a lumberjack in evening clothes." In Hollywood's early golden age, actors often wore their own clothes on-screen, and Gable's were primarily made by Eddie Schmidt, a famed tailor of the era. Schmidt's elegant style was epitomized by "drape-cut" suits with wide, confident lapels and a broad chest. Gable often favored plaid patterns for his suits, and ties in dramatic geometric patterns. His most significant contribution to trends, though, was through the most ordinary of garments. In 1934's *It Happened One Night*, Gable removed his sweater and dress shirt to reveal that he was not wearing an undershirt. Legend has it that this startling omission caused undershirt sales to drop 40 percent nationwide almost immediately. Such was the influence of an icon like Gable.

Icon

Clark Gable.
b Cadiz, OH (USA), 1901.
d Los Angeles (USA), 1960.

Clark Gable, dressed in a pinstripe suit, at his home in Los Angeles, 1946.

Photograph by Bob Landry.

↳ ANTO BEVERLY HILLS, DEVORE, C. GRANT, ROLEX, SCHOLTE, TIN TAN

DAVID GANDY

David Gandy—Britain's most famous male model—came onto the scene in 2001 when he competed in a modeling competition on ITV's *This Morning*. He won the title of Male Face of 2001, and his career took off with him modeling for brands including Hugo Boss, Gant, H&M, and Carolina Herrera. Perhaps his most notable brand partnership has been with Dolce & Gabbana, a relationship that started in 2006 when he starred in their Light Blue fragrance campaign, shot by Mario Testino. Shortly after, he became the globally renowned face of the Italian house, appearing in their campaigns and fashion shows, and was ranked among the world's highest-paid male models. With an athletic build, Gandy's look was in contrast to the trendy, slimmed-down physique of the early aughts, and he was in high demand, appearing on sixteen magazine covers in 2012. He is regularly shortlisted on *British GQ*'s list of Best Dressed Men, and in 2012 he walked with supermodels Kate Moss and Naomi Campbell at the London Olympics closing ceremony. A British *Vogue* columnist and charity ambassador, Gandy also serves as an official liaison for London Collections: Men.

Model

David Gandy.
b Billericay, England (UK), 1980.

David Gandy photographed for *GQ México*, October 2016.

Photograph by Richard Ramos.

↳ BECKHAM, DOLCE & GABBANA, HUGO BOSS

Hemingway wore khakis.

GAP
KHAKIS

GAP

The quintessential purveyor of casual American style, Gap has been bringing jeans and khakis to the masses since 1969 and is now the world's third-largest clothing retailer. What began as a humble San Francisco jeans shop, founded by Donald and Doris Fisher, evolved into a fashion juggernaut under the leadership of former CEO Mickey Drexler, who brought the brand's accessible but aspirational spirit to malls around the world. During Gap's 1990s and early 2000s heyday, the brand's iconic white serif font against a navy background was ubiquitous on sweatshirts and T-shirts, helped along by massive ad campaigns. From LL Cool J dressed in a tucked white tee and easy-fit jeans rapping that "Any other brand is childish" to the swirling choreography of dozens of dancers swinging in the Gap's khakis, the brand's ads were synonymous with pop culture. Now, with a fresh ten-year deal with Kanye West's Yeezy label, spearheaded by Mowalola Ogunlesi, the Gap is set to find a new generation of customers to connect with their classic, all-American look.

Retailer

Gap.
est San Francisco (USA), 1969.

Gap "Who Wore Khakis" campaign featuring Ernest Hemingway, 1993.

Photograph by Hans Malmberg.

↳ ABERCROMBIE & FITCH, DOCKERS, J.CREW, LEVI'S, OGUNLESI, UNIQLO, WEST

JEAN PAUL GAULTIER

Jean Paul Gaultier's impact on men's fashion is immense, particularly his provocative collections from the 1980s. Beginning as a studio assistant to Pierre Cardin at eighteen years old, he introduced his first collection in 1976. After launching his eponymous line in 1982—notably unveiling his first man skirt in 1984—he founded his couture house in 1997 and also designed for Hermès as artistic director from 2003 to 2010. His inspirations ranged from London punks to sci-fi, and tattoos and hunky sailors to fetishwear and Tom of Finland he-men. Gaultier was an early pioneer of diversity on the runway, casting a multiracial mix of old and young, transgender, plus-sized, and street-cast and professional models. Memorable collections featured everything from backless striped nautical-inspired T-shirts and sailor hats to reworked MA-1–style bomber jackets and sleek bodycon leggings. Gaultier's fans included high-profile names such as Boy George and Leslie Cheung. Gaultier's own uniform during the 1980s and '90s felt as iconoclastic as his collections, consisting of a tartan kilt teamed with a classic Breton striped T-shirt and biker boots: witty, subversive, totally JPG.

Designer

Jean Paul Gaultier.
b Arcueil (FR), 1952.

Jean Paul Gaultier, 1993.

Photograph by Ron Galella.

↳ ABE, BODYMAP, CARDIN,
  ESTEREL, HERMÈS, WESTWOOD

G-DRAGON

G-Dragon is K-pop's undisputed king and one of Asia's biggest megastars. Both onstage and off, he has established himself as an international style icon. The Korean artist came on the scene in 2006 as part of the boy band Big Bang, and launched his solo career in 2009. G-Dragon's breakout celebrity is credited to his eclectic punk aesthetic, with a personal style that blurs genres. Espousing a fluid, gender-bending look, he's equal parts high fashion and street, comfortable in slender sequined suits, color-crazed ensembles, or head-to-toe denim. He moves through sartorial eras and personas, influencing tens of millions of fans. Future-forward and sleek, his distinct edge is further reflected in his genre-defying performances—moving between EDM, hip-hop, and pop. With an elusive mystique, G-Dragon has become a big "get" at fashion shows, and he is admired by designers such as the late Karl Lagerfeld (G-Dragon is one of Chanel's global ambassadors), Hedi Slimane, and Jeremy Scott. He also oversees his own fashion line, Peaceminusone, with Big Bang stylist Gee Eun, and has collaborated with Nike, Hiroshi Fujiwara's Fragment Design, and Ambush.

Icon

G-Dragon (Kwon Ji-yong).
b Seoul (KOR), 1988.

G-Dragon at the Chanel Spring/Summer 2015 haute-couture show, Paris.

Photograph by François Guillot.

↳ BTS, FUJIWARA, LAGERFELD, NIKE, SCOTT, SLIMANE

BIG & TALL

Where Have All the Young Men Gone?

There's a growing demand for young men's B&T resources, but are the numbers there to justify the start-up costs of entering this highly specific market?

By STAN GELLERS

The Big & Tall market is a "Catch-22" situation for young men's sportswear manufacturers currently doing a successful job in this very specialized business — or those eager to jump into it.

B&T executives admit that they look at the burgeoning young men's portion market with mixed feelings. On one hand, they say there's a void in specialty manufacturers able to satisfy the growing demand for young fashions. But as good as the potentials sound, the executives point to the business side and a serious question that has to be answered.

Is there really enough young men's B&T business to support the expense of starting out from square one — developing new sets of patterns and then going through the period of earning the respect and trust of B&T retailers?

Veteran manufacturers insist that one serious mistake can be fatal in this very demanding market. And even without fumbling the ball, they confide that the business has built-in risks that can be expensive.

Everybody agrees that the population numbers are certainly there, in terms of young men who are either big or tall — or both.

The latest survey of this segment of the male population from 1976 to 1980 by the U.S. Department of Health, Education and Welfare (see DNR, Feb. 2, 1988, Sec. 3, Page 19) revealed that more than half the men over 6 feet 2 inches and weighing 230 pounds were between 18 and 24. This group, alone, numbers close to 200,000 — a total that hints at big potential.

> "The young guy wants to wear the pleated pants and the pocket treatments on shirts. He wants to look like his counterpart who wears regular sizes. Most Big & Tall stores show basic sportswear and solid sweaters. Young men want the jacquard sweaters and then some."
>
> — Harvey Turell
> President, Zeppelin

Equally impressive is the fact that during the same period there was a gain of more than 30 percent in the number of all men at least 6 feet 3 inches in height. Significantly, this is hardly reflected in the percentage of tall merchandise reportedly sold in special-size stores.

Certainly, at this point, the arguments for breaking into the young end of the B&T business are all there. For example, the B&T buyer for a major group of department stores reports, "We see a tremendous number of new resources coming into the Big & Tall market each season. But the problem is that there still aren't enough young lines to shop."

This problem is compounded, claims a B&T manufacturer, by the Daube group, a membership association of B&T stores, which admittedly focuses on 45-and-older customers. This, of course, leaves the door wide-open for young men's manufacturers to become an important part of the Big & Tall Men's Apparel Needs Show, which draws buyers representing 2,500 stores. And the next show, to be held at the Miami Convention Center Feb. 12 to 15, has an exhibitor list that includes many new young men's, as well as young contemporary, lines.

Even with the risks, companies that successfully invaded this market sector agree that it can be a money-maker. Harvey Turell, president, Zeppelin, says enthusiastically, "There is such a void in young men's fashions, and the retail reception of the right goods is unbelievable. At times, it sounds as if stores are selling merchandise right out of the cartons.

"What's missing with most of the regular Big & Tall companies is the look. The young guy wants to wear the pleated pants and the pocket treatments on shirts. He wants to look like his counterpart who wears regular sizes. Most Big & Tall stores show basic sportswear and solid sweaters. Young men want the jacquard sweaters and then some."

The challenge, he confides, is to find the magic number of styles to satisfy this market. "We're very aggressive about this market," he says, "and we've learned how to get it

Continued on Page 49

J.J. COCHRAN

DAMON

Velour is Back

DAMON: crewneck in cotton/polyester with triple-tone vertical stripes in an end-on-end effect. J.J. COCHRAN: classic pullover shirt with broad horizontal stripes accented with twill pattern.

STAN GELLERS

With a career spanning more than fifty years, veteran journalist Stan Gellers was the preeminent authority on tailored men's clothing. Based in New York, Gellers started writing about men's fashion in 1952 for *DNR*, a weekly trade publication considered to be "the bible of the menswear industry," and *Menswear* magazine. As a writer he chronicled the sartorial shifts in the industry. Whether it was commenting on the ubiquitous use of new stretch lycra in men's clothing by Nautica, Kenneth Cole, or Van Heusen in the early aughts ("It was a gimmick; now it's a given—from a young, cutting-edge customer to the mainstream," he wrote) or hailing designers, including Michael Bastian, as the future of American fashion with "just the right combination of Ralph Lauren, Thom Browne, and eighties-era Perry Ellis," he imparted his encyclopedic knowledge of men's fashion in a quippy, conversational style. He enthusiastically observed changing trends, like the narrowing width of a tie (from four inches to three and a half) to the slimming silhouette of suits.

Writer

Stan Gellers.
b New York (USA), 1925.
d Southampton, NY (USA), 2009.

"Where Have All the Young Men Gone?," written by Stan Gellers, *DNR*, February 1989.

Illustration by Robert Melendez.

↳ BLANKS, DNR, FLUSSER, MELENDEZ, O'BRIEN

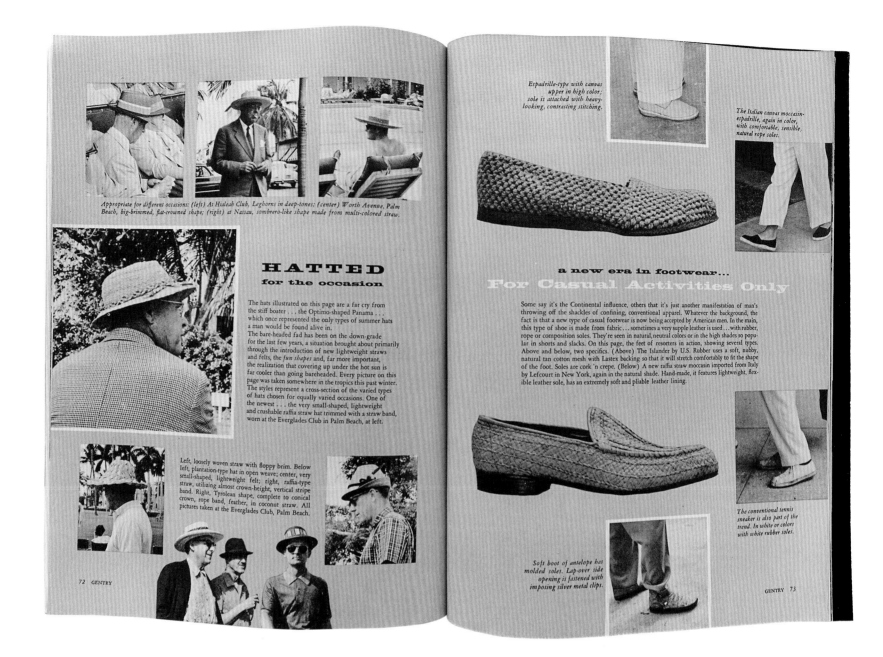

HATTED
for the occasion

The hats illustrated on this page are a far cry from the stiff boater . . . the Optimo-shaped Panama . . . which once represented the only types of summer hats a man would be found alive in.

The bare-headed fad has been on the down-grade for the last few years, a situation brought about primarily through the introduction of new lightweight straws and felts, the *fun shapes* and, far more important, the realization that covering up under the hot sun is far cooler than going bareheaded. Every picture on this page was taken somewhere in the tropics this past winter. The styles represent a cross-section of the varied types of hats chosen for equally varied occasions. One of the newest . . . the very small-shaped, lightweight and crushable raffia straw hat trimmed with a straw band, worn at the Everglades Club in Palm Beach, at left.

Appropriate for different occasions: (left) At Hialeah Club, Leghorns in deep-tones; (center) Worth Avenue, Palm Beach, big-brimmed, flat-crowned shape; (right) at Nassau, sombrero-like shape made from multi-colored straw.

Left, loosely woven straw with floppy brim. Below left, plantation-type hat in open weave; center, very small-shaped, lightweight felt; right, raffia-type straw, utilizing almost crown-height, vertical stripe band. Right, Tyrolean shape, complete to conical crown, rope band, feather, in coconut straw. All pictures taken at the Everglades Club, Palm Beach.

72 GENTRY

a new era in footwear...
For Casual Activities Only

Some say it's the Continental influence, others that it's just another manifestation of man's throwing off the shackles of confining, conventional apparel. Whatever the background, the fact is that a new type of casual footwear is now being accepted by American men. In the main, this type of shoe is made from fabric . . . sometimes a very supple leather is used . . . with rubber, rope or composition soles. They're seen in natural, neutral colors or in the high shades so popular in shorts and slacks. On this page, the feet of resorters in action, showing several types. Above and below, two specifics. (Above) The Islander by U.S. Rubber uses a soft, nubby, natural tan cotton mesh with Lastex backing so that it will stretch comfortably to fit the shape of the foot. Soles are cork 'n crepe. (Below) A new raffia straw moccasin imported from Italy by Lefcourt in New York, again in the natural shade. Hand-made, it features lightweight, flexible leather sole, has an extremely soft and pliable leather lining.

Espadrille-type with canvas upper in high color; sole is attached with heavy-looking, contrasting stitching.

The Italian canvas moccasin-espadrille, again in color, with comfortable, sensible, natural rope soles.

The conventional tennis sneaker is also part of the trend. In white or colors with white rubber soles.

Soft boot of antelope has molded soles. Lap-over side opening is fastened with imposing silver metal clips.

GENTRY 73

GENTRY

Gentry is likely the most influential men's magazine that you may never have heard of. Established by William C. Segal, a Georgia native, in 1951, *Gentry* broke convention by being not an insider trade rag in the mold of *Apparel Arts* and *American Fabrics* but a weighty lifestyle booklet aimed at a very sophisticated consumer. In its all too brief twenty-two-issue run, *Gentry*'s pages brimmed with high cultural diversions, including an excerpt from Hermann Hesse's *Siddhartha* (1922), a multipage rumination on what it means to be a man, and an essay on the paintings of Hieronymus Bosch. The latter half of each issue was unabashedly dedicated to fashion, presenting photographs of real men cavorting at soirees and on vacation (street style long before Bill Cunningham), dissections into seasonal tweeds complete with tangible fabric inserts, and fanciful explorations on ski clothing. Though its uncompromising packaging meant *Gentry* did not succeed financially, it set the standard for later lifestyle publications.

Publication

Gentry.
est New York (USA), 1951.

Gentry magazine feature, Summer 1955.

↪ APPAREL ARTS, CUNNINGHAM, DETAILS, ESQUIRE, GQ

RUDI GERNREICH

Some may consider Rudi Gernreich's most notorious contributions to fashion to be the monokini, a topless women's bathing suit, introduced in 1964 and the male and female thong in 1974, but he was a far more vital and contemplative designer than those cheeky garments suggest. Gernreich's swimwear reflected a view that men's and women's fashion should be interchangeable—a political provocativeness that was further reflected in his cofounding of one of the earliest gay organizations in the United States, the Mattachine Society. Gernreich believed that as women dressed with more freedom, men's clothes should reclaim some of the decorative qualities they had lost in the 1800s. In his 1970 Unisex Project, a man and woman shaved their body hair before dressing identically, both in bikinis, then topless in miniskirts. Gernreich also designed interchangeable kaftans and bell-bottom trousers, worn with a crop top by both men and women. Constantly experimenting with new materials, such as white vinyl, Gernreich argued that clothing should be "an anonymous type of uniform with an indefinite revolutionary cast."

Designer

Rudi Gernreich.
b Vienna (AUS), 1922.
d Los Angeles (USA), 1985.

Rudi Gernreich (foreground), Vidal Sassoon (far right), and models wearing Gernreich's thong bathing suits, 1974.

Photograph by William Claxton.

↳ ESTEREL, GAULTIER, LAPIDUS, SPEEDO

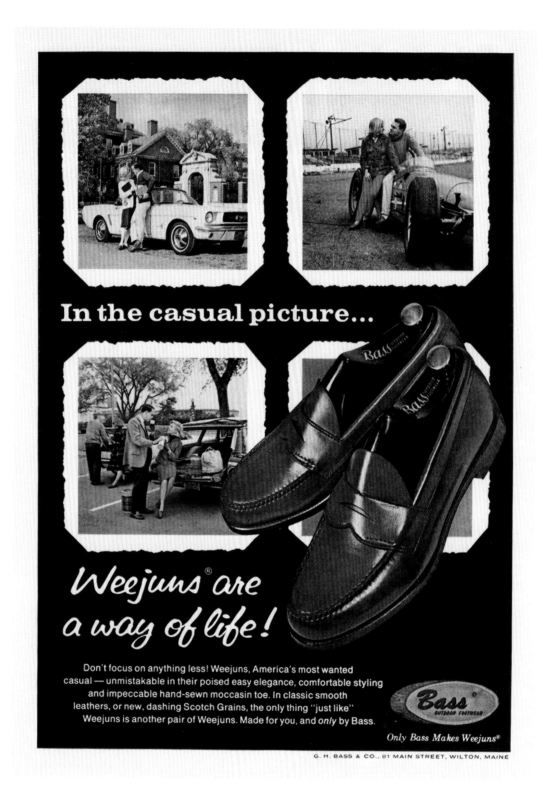

In the casual picture...

Weejuns® are a way of life!

Don't focus on anything less! Weejuns, America's most wanted casual — unmistakable in their poised easy elegance, comfortable styling and impeccable hand-sewn moccasin toe. In classic smooth leathers, or new, dashing Scotch Grains, the only thing "just like" Weejuns is another pair of Weejuns. Made for you, and *only* by Bass.

Only Bass Makes Weejuns®

G. H. BASS & CO., 81 MAIN STREET, WILTON, MAINE

G.H. BASS & CO.

George Henry Bass set out in the late 1800s to fabricate functional, purpose-driven shoes. And for a time, that's what his label specialized in. In its early decades, Bass produced tread-soled moccasins for outdoorsmen, bulky boots for American fighter pilots, and calf-high boots to protect farmers. Yet in 1936 Bass introduced the Weejun, a flexible loafer inspired by Norwegian mocs that were made for "loafing in the field." That slip-on became Bass's signature style and was beloved for its look, not just its durability. Reflecting a clean-cut American style,

Weejuns were worn by James Dean, John F. Kennedy, Paul Newman, and Miles Davis. They were also readily co-opted by a number of global subcultures. British rude boys sported them with cropped trousers in the 1960s, as did *paninari* in Italy in the 1980s with their white socks flashing. Bass's penny loafer remains perennially popular, and the label has recently collaborated with Tommy Hilfiger and Engineered Garments on some fashion-forward, face-lifted Weejuns.

GIEVES & HAWKES

Housed at No. 1 Savile Row, London, Gieves & Hawkes is the paragon of that famous street, with roots in British military and court tailoring. It was born of two companies: Gieves was founded in 1785 by James Watson Gieves, the appointed tailor for the British Royal Navy, while Hawkes was established in 1771 by Thomas Hawkes, who supplied uniforms to the British Army. In 1974 the prestigious tailors merged, espousing a house style derived from its combined military tradition, favoring high armholes and roped shoulders. Gieves & Hawkes has had notable names walk through its doors. From 1984 to 1988, Alexander McQueen served as an apprentice there, gaining formative skills that helped shape his eponymous label. In 1988 Michael Jackson wore a custom military-inspired suit for his Bad tour. Icons such as Winston Churchill, Charlie Chaplin, and Ian Fleming also wore their suiting. Whether in its bespoke, made-to-measure, or ready-to-wear men's clothing, Gieves & Hawkes focuses on precision, producing individualized, timeless garments with excellence and craft at every stage.

Tailor

Gieves & Hawkes.
est London (UK), 1974.

Display of uniforms at Gieves & Hawkes, London, 2017.

Photograph by Horst Friedrichs.

↳ ANDERSON & SHEPPARD,
HENRY POOLE & CO.

ROMEO GIGLI

Romeo Gigli was orphaned in his late teens. Feeling lost, he trekked around the globe, picking up an expansive mishmash of ideas and references that would later inspire his romantic clothes. During a stint in New York in the 1970s, designer Piero Dimitri was so taken by Gigli's own style that he hired him. Back in Milan, Gigli founded his own label in 1983 with the aid of Carla Sozzani. Toying happily with color and texture, he created cable-knit sweaters in autumnal hues, blazers in Anglo check patterns, and brash shirts in collaged motifs. By the late 1980s he was leading the charge for other Italian labels, such as Giorgio Armani and Gianni Versace, briefly assisted in 1989 by Alexander McQueen. But shortly after relocating to the grand fashion stage of Paris, in the early 1990s, Gigli lost control of his brand—Sozzani's renowned concept shop 10 Corso Como now sits where Gigli's flagship store once was. Since then Gigli has designed for companies such as Callaghan by Zamasport, Joyce, Barneys New York, Louis Vuitton, and Donghia, and from 1993 to 1997 he was the creative director of C.P. Company.

Designer

Romeo Gigli.
b Castel Bolognese (IT), 1949.

Romeo Gigli Fall/Winter 2001
ready-to-wear collection
at Milan Fashion Week.

Photograph by Mario Laporta.

↳ ARMANI, BARNEYS NEW YORK,
DIMITRI, MATSUDA, OSTI,
VERSACE

GLOVERALL

Rarely has a clothing company been associated with a single garment as closely as the British clothier Gloverall is with the duffle coat. The company's history began in 1951, when brothers Harold and Freda Morris, who were London-based glove and overall suppliers, acquired a large supply of World War II military-surplus duffle coats. When the coats sold out in 1953, the Morrises formed Gloverall and began producing their own. Harold redesigned the coat with leather straps rather than string ties and added an Italian check lining. Known

as the Monty after Field Marshal Bernard Montgomery, who often wore the original coat, Gloverall's duffles had a lighter cloth and a slimmer cut. During the 1960s and '70s, the coat was worn by everyone from David Bowie to Paddington Bear, and became associated with freethinking liberals and social rebels, including beatniks, philosophers, and students from Paris to Los Angeles. In 1987 Gloverall became the first winner of the British Apparel Export Award.

Brand

Gloverall.
est London (UK), 1951.

Jack Nicholson and Art Garfunkel wearing duffle coats in a publicity still for AVCO Embassy Pictures's *Carnal Knowledge*, 1971.

↳ BARBOUR, BOWIE, BURBERRY, HACKETT, J&J CROMBIE LTD., MACINTOSH

GOLDEN BEAR

A century ago, when Golden Bear was founded, fashion was not the company's aim. Perched off the coast of the Pacific in San Francisco, Golden Bear set out to produce brick-thick coats for the city's population of weathered dock workers and longshoremen. Within just two decades, Golden Bear was more openly courting fashion-minded consumers, producing bomber jackets for civilians and fringed trucker jackets for high-fashion hippies, though Golden Bear would find its greatest success with varsity jackets. As far back as 1952, the brand was fabricating collegiate letterman jackets for nearby schools. What distinguished a Golden Bear varsity—and helped the jacket transcend the schoolyard—was its taut woven ribbing along the jacket's border, as well as its application of fine European wools and imported leathers for the jacket body and sleeves, respectively. In the twenty-first century, the Golden Bear varsity crossed into even more elite territory: celebrities such as Dwayne "the Rock" Johnson and LeBron James have worn the jackets, while Golden Bear has also created punchy custom pieces in collaboration with streetwear labels such as Kith, Stüssy, and Noah.

Brand

Golden Bear.
est San Francisco (USA), 1922.

Ben Simmons, wearing a Golden Bear jacket, arrives for Game 2 of the Eastern Conference Semifinals of the 2019 NBA Playoffs in Toronto.

Photograph by Jesse D. Garrabrant.

↳ BABENZIEN, CARHARTT, STÜSSY

E. GOYARD AINÉ

LE "PORTE-HABITS"

GOYARD

In the second half of the nineteenth century, trunk makers began to proliferate, focused on serving increasingly mobile populations. In 1845 seventeen-year-old François Goyard arrived at the trunk maker Maison Morel in Paris as an apprentice; when Louis-Henri Morel died in 1853, Goyard took over the firm and changed the name to Goyard. Under his son Edmond, who succeeded François in 1885, Goyard became increasingly international, taking part in many of the world expositions in the early twentieth century. The trunks were instantly recognizable with their Goyardine, a chevron canvas introduced in 1892 that was the first to include the trunk maker's name. Since then, the intricate design has adorned cases, trunks, bags, and portfolios, as well as special orders that are entirely made by hand with the brand's signature painted monograms. The company remained in family hands, serving clients such as the Duke of Windsor, Pablo Picasso, and Sir Arthur Conan Doyle, until it was bought by Jean-Michel Signoles in 1998. Signoles transformed Goyard into a global luxury brand that crossed over into pop culture—even appearing in Kanye West's 2007 hit song "The Glory."

Accessory Design

Goyard.
est Paris (FR), 1853.

Goyard advertisement for Valise "Porte-Habits."

↳ LOUIS VUITTON, PICASSO, WEST, DUKE OF WINDSOR

NOVEMBER 1958

ONE DOLLAR

THE FASHION MAGAZINE FOR MEN

GQ
GENTLEMEN'S QUARTERLY

GQ

Founded in 1931 as *Apparel Arts*, *GQ* has evolved from a trade publication marketed to clothing retailers to one of the world's most successful men's magazines. In 1957 it became available to the wider public for the first time, and the following year it was renamed *Gentleman's Quarterly*. For nearly three decades, the magazine covered clothing almost exclusively—Bruce Weber and Rico Puhlmann photographed editorials that created a new version of masculinity that was more athletic and frankly sexualized. It was bought by Condé Nast in 1983 and rebranded with a shortened title: *GQ*. Under longstanding editor Art Cooper, *GQ* took on a broader scope, with sophisticated articles on subjects ranging from politics and technology to sports and culture. In the 1990s the magazine was widely noted for fueling the phenomenon of metrosexuality, and in 1996 the publication introduced its influential Men of the Year Awards. Today the magazine continues to attract the top stars and fashion-industry talent: recently Micaiah Carter photographed Pharrell Williams, Tyler Mitchell snapped Kanye West, and Renell Medrano shot Timothée Chalamet.

Publication

GQ.
est New York (USA), 1931.

Cover of the November 1958 issue of *GQ*.

Photograph by Emme Gene Hall.

↳ APPAREL ARTS, CARTER, EBONY, ESQUIRE, WEBER, WHITE

GRANNY TAKES A TRIP

Shaping the look of Swinging Sixties London, the boutique Granny Takes a Trip opened in 1966 at the "wrong" end of London's King's Road—appropriately named World's End. Founded by Nigel Waymouth, Sheila Cohen, and the former Savile Row tailor John Pearse, the store was designed to appeal, as its name suggested, to the contemporary psychedelic culture with romantic and exotic clothes. The boutique was filled with clothing made of velvet, sequins, and fur; paisley-printed button-downs and jackets were plentiful in purples and bold stripes, looking not unlike the era's extravagant wallpapers. In Waymouth's words, "We were coming out with ideas that we as young people wanted to wear, not what we were told was fashionable." Granny Takes a Trip became a popular destination—it was decorated with a real car crashing out of its shopfront—and attracted celebrities, such as Andy Warhol, the Beatles, Pink Floyd, and Jimi Hendrix. Within a couple of years, the founders feared the shop had become too mainstream and sold it; the new owners offered more dandified clothes to ever-aging hippies until the shop moved in 1974 and closed in 1979.

Retailer

Granny Takes a Trip.
est London (UK), 1966.

Nigel Waymouth wearing Granny Takes a Trip, with models Jess Down, Rufus Potts Dawson, and Amanda Lear, 1967.

Photograph by Colin Jones.

↳ THE BEATLES, HENDRIX, I WAS
LORD KITCHENER'S VALET,
JAGGER, STEPHEN, STONE

CARY GRANT

Hollywood superstar Cary Grant—born Archibald Alec Leach—was celebrated for his good looks, debonair style, and effortless glamour but was in fact down-to-earth in his approach to his appearance. Fashion, he believed, was about simplicity: clothes should last; they should be practical and a good value. After an unhappy early life in England, Grant reinvented himself when he sailed to New York. Spotting Douglas Fairbanks Sr. on the ship, the young Grant noted the cut of the star's suit and width of his lapels, and adopted them for himself based on the

adage that "clothes maketh the man." In Hollywood, clothes became Grant's sophisticated and elegant uniform. Always immaculately dressed, Grant avoided fashion statements. His suits were well cut but not showy—he favored Dunhill and Aquascutum—and his shoes were highly polished. For a more casual look, he paired white T-shirts with white linen trousers. He even wore his own clothes on-screen—his gray glen-check suit in Hitchcock's 1959 film *North by Northwest* was from Savile Row's Kilgour, French and Stanbury.

Icon

Cary Grant.
b Bristol, England (UK), 1904.
d Davenport, IA (USA), 1986.

Cary Grant, 1957.

↳ ALFRED DUNHILL,
AQUASCUTUM, GABLE, J&J
CROMBIE LTD., MASTROIANNI,
DUKE OF WINDSOR

PATRICK GRANT

While studying at Oxford's Saïd Business School in 2005, Patrick Grant, a Scot with 007 good looks, stumbled upon a newspaper ad promoting the sale of Norton & Sons, an illustrious but flailing tailoring house. For Grant, who fostered more than a little love for good clothes, this was a grand opportunity. By the end of the year, he'd attained the firm and had it on its way back to suiting success on Savile Row. With Norton in order, Grant, in 2009, revitalized a once-sleepy subsidiary, E. Tautz & Sons, as an on-the-pulse runway label, with captivating broad-legged trousers, gauzy knitwear, and ample Anglo-prep flourishes. Just a year later, in 2010, he won a Menswear Designer award at the British Fashion Awards. Grant cherishes local production and in 2015 purchased Cookson & Clegg, a British wovens manufacturer. More than a suit who makes suits, Grant is a telegenic clothing celeb, thanks to stints as a judge on *The Great British Sewing Bee*.

Designer/Tailor

Patrick Grant.
b Edinburgh (UK), 1972.

Patrick Grant, London.

Photograph by Scott Schuman.

↳ ANDERSON & SHEPPARD,
NUTTER, SEXTON

CRAIG GREEN

Craig Green is a designer who can both perfectly execute a utilitarian everyday garment and put on a heart-stirring fashion show. Educated under the tutelage of the late, great Louise Wilson at Central Saint Martins College of Art and Design, Green has said that his parents' careers—his dad, a plumber, and his mom, a nurse—inspired him to toy with the idea of uniformity. That creativity led him to his signature piece: a padded four-pocket work-wear jacket that looks like a puffed-up version of photographer Bill Cunningham's famous coat. That egalitarian jacket is the backbone of Green's business, yet at his runway shows—which occasionally leave editors in tears—he parades whimsical, almost-unwearable creations that transform his models into rainbow-tinted G.I. Joes, walking yacht sails, and landscape canvases. In 2016, 2017, and 2018, he was awarded British Menswear Designer of the Year at the Fashion Awards, and recent collaborations with Adidas and Moncler show that there's still much work ahead for Green.

Designer

Craig Green.
b London (UK), 1986.

Craig Green Fall/Winter 2019 collection at London Fashion Week.

Photograph by Portia Hunt.

↳ ADIDAS, KAWAKUBO, KNIGHT, MONCLER, SPENCER

GRENSON

In 1866 William Green began making Green and Son shoes in Northamptonshire, England. Setting up his first factory in 1874, which utilized Goodyear welting, Green created a label that soon became emblematic of durable, well-crafted shoes. In 1913, following Green's death in 1901, his son CAK Green shortened the company name to a more modern portmanteau: Grenson. They supplied boots for British forces during both world wars, but Grenson gained wider recognition with its more fashionable styles, such as handmade brogues, popularized by Hollywood stars, including Cary Grant, Montgomery Clift, and Fred Astaire, often paired with Savile Row suits. In 2008 Grenson opened its first-ever shop in East London, and two years later creative director Tim Little took over the company. Revitalizing its image and expanding its styles to be design-forward with new materials and tweaked shapes, Grenson landed in high-fashion shops such as Harrods, Selfridges, and Liberty. In 2017 Little created Grenson's first sneakers, made with signature leather uppers and thick cup soles. Since then the brand has partnered with Craig Green, New Balance, Rag & Bone, Barbour, and Kith's Ronnie Fieg.

Footwear

Grenson.
est Rushden, Northamptonshire, England (UK), 1866.

Influencer Jai'me Jan wearing Grenson shoes during London Collections: Men, 2017.

Photograph by Kirstin Sinclair.

↳ ASTAIRE, BARBOUR, C. GRANT, GREEN, NEW BALANCE, RAG & BONE

GUCCI

Introduced in 1953, Gucci's horsebit loafer feels as fresh today on stars such as Harry Styles and A$AP Rocky as it did back in the day on Alain Delon and Peter Sellers. But the brand's iconic loafers hardly tell the full Gucci story. As a young man, Guccio Gucci worked at London's Savoy Hotel, where he noticed that moneyed customers were particularly cautious with their luggage. In 1921 he started his own leather goods shop in Florence—first making saddles, then bags and shoes. In the 1930s, under the stewardship of his son Aldo, Gucci introduced the interlocking G monogram—a nod to Guccio's initials. Ready-to-wear clothing arrived on the runway in 1981, and under the tutelage of Tom Ford in the '90s, Gucci was known for a sexed-up, slick style that manifested in shimmering silk shirts, slim and heavily structured suits, and luscious leather outerwear. In 2015 Alessandro Michele was appointed creative director, lending the brand a florid, gender-bending style that had a profound impact on today's menswear. The Gucci of this moment is a happily hodge-podged blend of pussy-bow blouses, checkered suits with flared '70s trousers, and slouchy mohair house cardigans.

Gucci.
est Florence (IT), 1921.

Peter Sellers in a pair of Gucci horsebit loafers, 1966.

↳ A$AP ROCKY, DELON, FORD, MICHELE, STYLES

DEMNA GVASALIA

In 2014 Demna Gvasalia and his norm-breaking brand Vetements seemed to arrive out of nowhere to take over the fashion world. Yet by that point Gvasalia had already quietly cut his teeth behind the scenes at Maison Martin Margiela and Louis Vuitton. Vetements, the label he started with his brother, Guram, subverted conventional fashion, hosting shows in a gay club and a brightly lit shopping mall. Vetements maximalist bomber jackets and trousers were often styled in a hurried, almost bricolage fashion that many reviewers noted seemed to draw heavily on Gvasalia's own experience of fleeing Georgia's civil war at the age of twelve. But they were also a hit. Celebrities such as Kanye West and Rihanna were almost immediately photographed in Vetements's marquee product: a sagging logo hoodie with elephantine sleeves. In 2015 Gvasalia was appointed creative director at Balenciaga, where he carried on with his unconventional, and unconventionally appealing, ideas such as bulbous "dad" sneakers, colossal suiting, and oversized anoraks.

Designer

Demna Gvasalia.
b Sukhumi (GE), 1981.

Model Jeremy Chetrit wearing a Vetements black hoodie during Paris Fashion Week, 2020.

Photograph by Melodie Jeng.

↳ LOUIS VUITTON, MARGIELA, RUBCHINSKIY, WEST

JEFFERSON HACK

Publisher, editor, and journalist Jefferson Hack has become
a fashion-world disrupter, changing the way the industry
operates. In 1991, as a nineteen-year-old student at the London
College of Printing, Hack launched the magazine *Dazed &
Confused* (later renamed *Dazed*) with his friend, the photographer Rankin. Entirely created on Hack's desktop computer,
the magazine took its ethos from punk-era fanzines with their
homemade, kitchen-table feel. In black and white it was the
antithesis of contemporaries that had quickly turned glossy
and mainstream. By the fourth issue David Bowie was asking
to appear on the cover. Hack's genius was interconnecting
fashion, music, art, and film and then using the magazine to
reveal the creativity of his inner circle, including friends such
as Alexander McQueen and Damien Hirst. Its men's fashion
pages were cutting-edge, venturing where few dared to go.
Foreseeing the narrowing market for magazines, Hack has
poured his efforts into digital media, starting with the video
channel Nowness in 2010, and he is currently creative director
of Dazed Media, which promotes a constant stream of
open-platform content creation.

Editor

Jefferson Hack.
b Montevideo (UY), 1971.

**Jefferson Hack at Milan Fashion Week
Fall/Winter 2014.**

Photograph by Acielle/StyleDuMonde.

↪ **BOWIE, THE FACE, i-D, RANKIN**

HACKETT

As a young Savile Row salesman for John Michael Ingram, Jeremy Hackett developed a side business selling secondhand clothes sourced from the Portobello Road market in a boutique on King's Road. When his selection of used British classics became too popular to meet the demand, he and business partner Ashley Lloyd-Jennings opened Hackett in 1983. His aim was to design modern versions of traditional Savile Row suits and upmarket outdoor British "country" clothing, but without the associated cost. Hackett sold jackets, trousers, shirts, and casualwear in a style he described as "classic but not old-fashioned." The company grew rapidly, offering its vision of updated British clothes around the world. The first international store opened in Madrid in 1989, and by 2020 there were 150 shops in more than 30 countries. In 2019 Hackett established its flagship store and bespoke operation on Savile Row, in a Georgian townhouse that was once home to designer Hardy Amies. Hackett skillfully markets its classic British credentials with partnerships and sponsorships, including the British Army Polo team, Henley Royal Regatta, and the Aston Martin Racing team.

Retailer

Hackett.
est London (UK), 1983.

Hackett Fall/Winter 2003 campaign featuring England rugby star Jonny Wilkinson.

↳ BROOKS BROTHERS, JAEGER, J.CREW, LAUREN

HALSTON

Although his history of bad business luck and disco hedonism often proceeds him, Halston was a fashion genius who created the defining look of the mid-1970s: a sleek elegance that drew on the functionality and minimalism of classic American sportswear but combined it with luxurious materials, such as cashmere and Ultrasuede. In the early 1950s Halston left his hometown of Des Moines, Iowa, to attend the School of the Art Institute of Chicago. Starting his design career as a milliner, he attained almost instant notoriety when he created the pillbox hat worn by Jackie Kennedy for John F. Kennedy's

inauguration in 1961. By the end of the decade, Halston had launched his eponymous label. In 1972 he introduced a unisex Ultrasuede line before presenting his first major menswear collection in 1975 with Ultrasuede blazers and trousers in ten colors. Like Andy Warhol, he sculpted a media-friendly image that would propel him to superstar status; his daily uniform, always in subdued shades, consisted of a black turtleneck sweater, slim-cut trousers, and a cardigan or suede jacket, a relaxed but modernizing look that influenced designers, such as Michael Kors and Tom Ford, decades later.

Designer/Icon

Halston (Roy Halston Frowick).
b Des Moines, IA (USA), 1932.
d San Francisco (USA), 1990.

Halston, 1979.

Photograph by Dustin Pittman.

↳ FORD, JAGGER, Y. SAINT
LAURENT, ST. JACQUES, STONE

KATHARINE HAMNETT

In 1983 Katharine Hamnett declared, "If you want to get the message out there, you should print it in giant letters on a T-shirt." And that's just what she did, pouring out slogan tops that read "Choose Life" (worn by George Michael), "Education Not Missiles," and "Worldwide Nuclear Ban Now." To meet Prime Minister Margaret Thatcher in 1984, Hamnett wore a hastily printed shirt reading "58% Don't Want Pershing" in protest of the housing of missiles on British soil. That T-shirt made front-page news, but Hamnett was always far more than a shirtmaker. Her lively fashion shows were full of sashaying models in densely pleated trousers, flouncy parachute silk jackets, and demure suits. In 1989 she commissioned a study examining the effects of textile production on our climate—making her among the first to acknowledge the industry's vast environmental impact. Today Hamnett remains focused on sustainability, with designs such as a recycled down puffer and organic cotton work coats. Still on offer are her signature slogan T-shirts with timely political phrases such as "Global Green New Deal Now" and "Fashion Hates Brexit."

Designer

Katharine Hamnett.
b Gravesend, Kent (UK), 1947.

George Michael and Andrew Ridgeley of Wham! performing in Katharine Hamnett T-shirts, 1984.

↳ BURTON, PARACHUTE, SUPREME, WEST, WESTWOOD

Hanes advertisement, c. 1940s.

HANES

In 1898 the US Navy issued white undergarments to its sailors serving in the Spanish-American War. Three years later, in 1901, Shamrock Knitting Mills was founded by John Wesley Hanes and was tasked with producing cotton garments for the US Marine Corps—the result was an enduring fashion staple. In 1914 the company was renamed the Hanes Hosiery Mills Company. With World War I, the company created a two-piece version of the union suit—featuring a top similar to the modern T-shirt—as underwear for US soldiers. Later popularized as casualwear by Marlon Brando and James Dean in the 1950s, and by hippies in the 1960s, the white T-shirt was a symbol of rebellion before it attained its modern ubiquity, and in the process, it helped make Hanes the world's leading apparel brand. Since the mid-twentieth century, the company's success has been boosted by innovative advertising, often for its underwear—from fashion illustrations in the 1950s to memorable TV commercials featuring Michael Jordan beginning in 1989, through the 2020 campaign "Every Bod Is Happy in Hanes."

Brand

Hanes.
est Winston, NC (USA), 1901.

Hanes advertisement, c. 1940s.

↳ JORDAN, C. KLEIN, SUNSPEL

BETHANN HARDISON

Activist/Agent

Model-turned-activist Bethann Hardison is widely acknowledged as one of the earliest and most vigorous supporters of diversity in fashion, whose efforts have made a lasting impact on the industry. While working in Manhattan's Garment District in the 1960s, she was discovered by designer Willi Smith, becoming his fit model and muse. She soon ascended to an international modeling career, gracing the pages of *Harper's Bazaar* and *Vogue* and walking numerous runways, including 1973's historic Battle of Versailles fashion show. In 1984 Hardison opened her own modeling agency, Bethann Management, focused on promoting diversity in the fashion industry and signed notable names, including Tyson Beckford, Veronica Webb, and Kimora Lee Simmons. Beckford secured a groundbreaking, career-defining exclusive contract with Ralph Lauren, becoming the first Black male model to do so. In 2020 Hardison was appointed as Gucci's executive advisor for global equity and cultural engagement. She also serves on the board of the CFDA, where she has established the Designers Hub, a mentoring group for emerging brands and designers of color.

Bethann Hardison.
b New York (USA), 1942.

Tyson Beckford and Bethann Hardison, New York, 2009.

Photograph by Jackie Snow.

↳ BECKFORD, DAPPER DAN, ENNINFUL, GUCCI, LAUREN, W. SMITH

PIERRE HARDY

Footwear Designer

One of fashion's most celebrated footwear luminaries, Paris-born Pierre Hardy got his start drawing fashion illustrations for magazines such as *Vanity Fair Italia* and *Vogue Hommes*. Born in 1956, Hardy studied plastic arts at the École Normale Supérieure in Cachan, France. In 1987 he joined the house of Christian Dior, and three years later he was appointed creative director for men's and women's shoes at Hermès. Hardy launched his own eponymous shoe line in 1999, designing innovative shoes often inspired by architecture and film. Obsessed with sketching, 3D modeling, and graphic outlines, the designer is known for his bold pops of color and geometric motifs. His versatile men's shoes include the Trek Comet sneakers, futuristic designs with neoprene and zigzag contours, while his black-and-white 112 high-tops espouse casual comfort for everyday wear. NBA stars Dwyane Wade and James Harden have been seen sporting his sneakers. Hardy was appointed Chevalier de la Légion d'Honneur in 2016 and has collaborated with Nicolas Ghesquière's Balenciaga, former NFL football player Victor Cruz, and French artist Mathias Kiss.

Pierre Hardy.
b Paris (FR), 1956.

Pierre Hardy Vibe sneakers, Paris, 2019.

↳ ADIDAS, HERMÈS, LANVIN, NIKE, WADE

HART SCHAFFNER MARX

More than a century ago, as Chicago was becoming a bustling metropolis, Max Hart, Marcus Marx, and Joseph Schaffner established a clothier in the city's busy downtown. In the early 1890s a commission to create clothes for the US military turned the trio on to the potential for mass-produced ready-to-wear. In the early 1900s their firm Hart Schaffner Marx (HSM) focused its efforts on high-end, broadly available suits in fine wools. HSM again produced uniforms during the two world wars and continued to expand by acquiring factories along the East Coast, including Hickey Freeman in

Rochester, New York. Beginning in the 1960s HSM struck gold through licensing deals that had them producing private-label suits for elite fashion houses, including Christian Dior, Perry Ellis, and Pierre Cardin, as well as for stars such as Johnny Carson and golfer Jack Nicklaus. The brand experienced a publicity boom in 2008 when Barack Obama wore their suits on the campaign trail. Nonetheless, it declared bankruptcy in the late aughts, a victim of competition from cheaper suit makers overseas and the steady casualization of American men's fashion.

Retailer

Hart Schaffner Marx.
est Chicago (USA), 1887.

Hart Schaffner Marx magazine advertisement, c. 1940s.

↳ BROOKS BROTHERS, CARDIN, ELLIS, HICKEY FREEMAN

JOSEPH HASPEL

Although American businessman Joseph Haspel did not invent seersucker, he made it the choice of Southern gentlemen and Ivy League students in the 1920s. The puckered cloth originated in colonial British India, where its uneven weave kept wearers cool; when it was later introduced in the United States, it was mainly worn by laborers. Haspel began his career at a clothing firm before joining his brother, Harry, to form Haspel Brothers in 1909 in their native New Orleans. Originally specializing in work pants and overalls, Haspel launched seersucker suits in 1922. With the now iconic blue-and-white-stripe pattern, they soon became a staple of jazz bars and cocktail parties. When Haspel patented his wash-and-wear suit in 1937, he is said to have promoted it by wearing it into the sea, hanging it up to dry, and successfully donning it again in the evening. After Haspel's death in 1959, his son Joseph continued the brand's success, including dressing Gregory Peck in a seersucker suit for the 1962 film *To Kill a Mockingbird* and Cary Grant for *Charade* in 1963. In 2002 Joseph's granddaughter Laurie joined the family business as president, reimagining Haspel for the next generation as a direct-to-consumer lifestyle brand.

Designer

Joseph Haspel.
b New Orleans (USA), 1884.
d New Orleans (USA), 1959.

Haspel advertisement, 1951.

↳ BROOKS BROTHERS, C. GRANT, LAUREN, SULKA

JAMIE HAWKESWORTH

While studying forensic science at the University of Central Lancashire in Preston, England, Jamie Hawkesworth was required to use a camera to photograph recreated crime scenes. Just like that, the camera found him, and Hawkesworth switched over to become a photography major. His early images included portraits of people passing through a bus depot, and this stripped-down, on-location approach informed his work as he crossed into fashion photography. In 2012 stylist Benjamin Bruno discovered Hawkesworth's work, which led to an introduction to British designer Jonathan Anderson. Ever since, Hawkesworth has steadily shot for Anderson. For Anderson's Loewe collection campaigns, he documented jeans-wearing models by the shore, their windswept scarves blowing up into their faces, and a pair sporting knit tunics as they scrambled up a rock face. More recently Hawkesworth's work has moved from merely documenting clothes to appearing on them. In 2020 Comme des Garçons Homme released a trio of shirts splayed with sun-drenched photographs from Hawkesworth's catalog of urban scenes.

Photographer

Jamie Hawkesworth.
b Suffolk, England (UK), 1987.

Model Brandon Becker photographed for "Le Culte de la Jeunesse," *Numero Homme*, Fall/Winter 2013.

Photograph by Jamie Hawkesworth.

↳ ANDERSON, i-D, KAWAKUBO, UNIQLO

DANIEL HECHTER

In the 1960s native Parisian Daniel Hechter saw what others couldn't. A student revolution was surging in Paris at the time, and a youthquake was brewing just below the surface, ready to pop. Hechter, a young man himself, understood that his generation craved spirited, rebellious clothes at an affordable price. The staid (and supremely expensive) couture of a previous generation wouldn't do. In 1962 he started his own label of lively separates for women. Six years later he began offering approachable dress shirts, suits, and outerwear for men as well.

With lively colors and sleek silhouettes, these budget-conscious clothes resonated with a new generation of shoppers. In the early '70s Hechter, a colossal sports fan (he would later be one of the early investors in the famed Paris Saint-Germain football club), launched some of the earliest designer collections aimed specifically at sports, such as tennis and skiing. These athletic clothes would prove to be popular decades before the term *athleisure* was bandied about by millennials.

Designer

Daniel Hechter.
b Paris (FR), 1938.

Daniel Hechter, 1977.

Photograph by Benjamin Auger.

↳ ADIDAS, CASTELBAJAC, FILA, LACOSTE, LAPIDUS

JIMI HENDRIX

Jimi Hendrix was a man who broke nearly every rule in music and fashion, and in the process, reinvented rock 'n' roll. A self-taught guitarist, Hendrix got his start performing with the Black American Chitlin' Circuit and working as a sideman for R&B acts, such as Sam Cooke and the Isley Brothers. However, Hendrix's talent was so far out, it took leaving the States and moving to London (where he formed the Jimi Hendrix Experience) for his genius to be appreciated. Despite his short career, Hendrix developed a number of style innovations, combining gypsy jewelry, fringed jackets, bell-bottoms, head scarves, boldly patterned frocks, and antique velvet Hussar military jackets with gold brocade to create a look that epitomized the late 1960s. In London style circles Hendrix marked the end of the swinging Carnaby Street look in favor of the more experimental designs from Granny Takes a Trip and I Was Lord Kitchener's Valet. His trippy glam style, unfettered by the traditional fashion rules or hang-ups, influenced generations of rock stars and fashion designers, such as Hedi Slimane and Alessandro Michele.

Icon

Jimi Hendrix
b Seattle (USA), 1942.
d London (UK), 1970.

Jimi Hendrix with his bandmates Mitch Mitchell and Noel Redding, Germany, 1967.

Photograph by Günter Zint.

↳ GRANNY TAKES A TRIP,
   I WAS LORD KITCHENER'S
   VALET, MICHELE, SLIMANE

HENRY POOLE & CO.

Henry Poole & Co. has a strong claim to have started the rise of Savile Row, dressing both Emperor Napoleon III and Charles Dickens, among others, before making Western-style clothes for the first Japanese ambassador to London in 1871. Poole's father, James, first opened his tailoring shop in 1806—where he specialized in military uniforms—before moving to Old Burlington Street in 1822, around the corner from Savile Row. In 1846 Henry inherited the business and used his contacts in the world of horse riding and field sports to attract aristocratic clients, including the Prince of Wales. It was said that Poole created the short smoking jacket, or tuxedo, for the prince in 1860 as an alternative to the dress suit. Other twentieth-century clients included Winston Churchill, Emperor Akihito of Japan, Charles de Gaulle, and Jiro Shirasu, all attracted by Henry Poole & Co.'s skilled tailoring. The company continues to hold numerous Royal Warrants and is an official supplier to the British Army. Today the tailor is based on Savile Row, where it maintains a reputation for making suits of high quality and traditional proportions.

Tailor

Henry Poole & Co.
est London (UK), 1806.

King Edward VII wearing a cape tailored by Henry Poole, Norfolk, England, 1902.

Photograph by Lafayette Photo Studios.

↳ BEEBE, FOX BROTHERS & CO, GIEVES & HAWKES

HERBERT JOHNSON HATTERS

If Herbert Johnson Hatters is known for one thing, it is without a doubt the felt hat created in 1980 for the iconic character of Indiana Jones. With a high, straight-sided crown, a narrow ribbon, and an oval brim, the Poet is based on an original Herbert Johnson design from the early 1900s and was later popular with stars such as David Bowie. The milliner's many film and TV credits also include the trilbies of Inspector Clouseau in *The Pink Panther* (1963) and the purple fedora worn by Jack Nicholson's Joker in the 1989 film *Batman*. The firm, founded in 1889, has a serendipitous origin story. Legend has it that a chance encounter between founder Herbert Johnson and the Prince of Wales led to a royal patronage for the new business, which became known for its top hats, homburgs, and bowlers—black for the city, brown for the country, gray for driving. Since World War I, virtually every regiment of the British Army has bought its hats from Herbert Johnson. Today, in a return to its roots, the company has again embraced its tradition of handmade craftsmanship, with the Poet forming the foundation of the revitalized business.

Milliner

Herbert Johnson Hatters.
est London (UK), 1889.

Harrison Ford wearing the Poet hat by Herbert Johnson Hatters in a publicity still for Paramount Pictures's *Indiana Jones and the Temple of Doom*, 1984.

↳ BORSALINO, BOWIE,
LOCK & CO. HATTERS,
DUKE OF WINDSOR

Cravates

HERMÈS

24, FAUBOURG SAINT-HONORÉ - PARIS
BIARRITZ · CANNES · DEAUVILLE · LILLE · MONTE-CARLO

Membre
du Comité Colbert

HERMÈS

A tie can be the singular point of color and expression in a man's wardrobe. And for the most discerning, that tie has often borne the mark of Hermès. Though founded as a saddlery in 1837 by the aristocrat Thierry Hermès, the company began to flourish as a fashion label beginning in 1920 under the tutelage of his grandson Émile. Ties were introduced in the 1950s, and by the late twentieth century, Hermès sold more than a million a year, in patterns ranging from stolid geometric shapes to fanciful animals. Since 1988 Véronique Nichanian has designed Hermès's men's apparel, as this quintessential Parisian label has fleshed out an increasingly robust ready-to-wear offering. In recent years, as conservative business dress has faded—and the tie along with it—Nichanian has kept Hermès relevant by inviting cashmere knits and leather jackets in surprising pastel hues. Whether it's clothing or collectible bags and accessories, Hermès attracts such sophisticated shoppers as Drake, Pharrell Williams, and David Beckham.

Designer Brand

Hermès.
est Paris (FR), 1837.

Hermès advertisement, 1962.

↳ BECKHAM, CHARVET, GOYARD,
LOUIS VUITTON, SULKA,
P. WILLIAMS

HICKEY FREEMAN

"Keep the Quality Up." That motto is carved inside the vestibule of the Temple, Hickey Freeman's Rochester, New York, suit factory. Established in 1899 by friends Jeremiah Hickey and Jacob Freeman, Hickey Freeman—alongside technology juggernauts such as Kodak and Xerox—turned Rochester into a manufacturing metropolis. From its founding, Hickey Freeman suits were some of the most elite—and expensive—on the market. Its fully canvased sport coats were assembled by hand and made from high-twist Italian wools. In the early to mid-1900s ready-to-wear suiting was rarely of a high quality—for that men had to go bespoke—but Hickey Freeman managed to offer luxury tailoring clean off the rack. At the brand's height, the Temple stretched to 225,000 square feet and Hickey Freeman employed thousands, many of whom were first-generation immigrants. As tastes tilted during the twenty-first century, the suit-obsessed company attempted to dip into casualwear with Hickey, a short-lived but influential line of rugged pea coats, burly knits, and other fetching off-the-clock clothes designed by former Abercrombie & Fitch creative director Aaron Levine.

Retailer

Hickey Freeman.
est Rochester, NY (USA), 1899.

Illustration from a Hickey Freeman catalog of men's suits, Fall 1926.

Illustration by Thomas Webb.

↳ BROOKS BROTHERS, HART SCHAFFNER MARX, J. PRESS, PAUL STUART

TOMMY HILFIGER

People's Place, Tommy Hilfiger's first shop, was located in his not-quite-bustling hometown of Elmira, New York. The upstate shop, which opened in 1969 and featured Hilfiger's first designs, became a destination for tristate style-seekers, but by the late 1970s it closed and Hilfiger relocated to New York City. In 1985 he started his eponymous Tommy Hilfiger line, specializing in sunny, preppy pieces, such as sun-yellow slickers and casual button-downs. Hilfiger evolved into an expert brander, putting his flag logo onto everything from underwear to hockey jerseys and sneakers. His logomania, and prescient embrace of hip-hop fixtures such as Aaliyah and Sean Combs, pushed Hilfiger to the fore of '90s fashion, but like many American labels, it faced an issue of oversaturation through the aughts. In recent years Hilfiger has reignited intrigue through collaborations with Zendaya and the streetwear shop Kith, as well as retro reissue collections nodding back to the brand's pre-Y2K heyday.

Designer

Tommy Hilfiger.
b Elmira, NY (USA), 1951.

Models backstage at the Tommy Hilfiger Spring 2017 Men's Tailored Collection presentation, New York, 2016.

Photograph by Neilson Barnard.

↪ BROOKS BROTHERS, COMBS, C. KLEIN, LAUREN, NAUTICA

TOSHIKIYO HIRATA

Designer

Based in Okayama, Japan, designer Toshikiyo Hirata is a denim visionary and avant-garde creative. Incorporating traditional construction with innovative techniques, his pieces, while niche, have pushed sartorial boundaries since 1984. Inspired by the Americana aesthetic after teaching karate in the United States, he opened his factory Capital Ltd. in Kojima ("the birthplace of jeans in Japan") when he returned to Japan, and a vintage store followed in 1995. After studying in the States and working as a designer for 45RPM in Japan, Toshikiyo's son Kiro joined him in 2002 to launch a new denim label called Kapital. Known for its worn-in and washed vintage aesthetic, Kapital's indigo denim garments, such as the Century Denim pants, are illustrious objets d'art. Their garments, which are often distressed, incorporate patchworking, dyeing (Kapital has its own washing and dyeing factory), and traditional Japanese craftwork, including *boro* (the art of reworking and repairing textiles) and *sashiko* (geometric, patterned embroidery). Whether it's their coveted bandanas or cult denim, Kapital is prized by A$AP Rocky, Travis Scott, John Mayer, and writer David Sedaris.

Toshikiyo Hirata.
b (JAP), (Active 1980s–).

Rugged Boss, Kapital Fall/Winter 2017 collection, Marfa, TX.

Photograph by Eric Kvatek.

↳ BODE, INOUE, LAUREN, NAKAMURA, YAMANE

DAVID HOCKNEY

David Hockney paints in lush colors and dresses in them too. The artist's sense of style was clear early on: at twenty-five he wore a gold lamé jacket to receive an award from London's Royal College of Art, where he had studied. Splashy clothing became more of an everyday choice for Hockney as he matured. A 1971 photograph shows Hockney relaxing in his studio wearing his signature brick-thick glasses, a pulsating pink-and-black rugby shirt, army fatigues, and mashed-in plimsolls. This was a typical Hockney outfit at the time, and one that would still appear quite fetching today. In his later years, he can be seen with a scarf jauntily tied around his collar in lieu of a tie or in one of his many pastel cardigans. Hockney's joyous attire continuously influenced fashion designers over the past decades: Burberry, Paul Smith, and John Galliano have designed collections drawing liberally on Hockney's striped shirts and puckish knits.

Icon

David Hockney.
b Bradford, Yorkshire (UK), 1937.

David Hockney (right) and Peter Schlesinger at Reddish Manor, Wiltshire, UK, 1970.

Photograph by Cecil Beaton.

↳ C. BAILEY, BURBERRY, GUCCI, MARNI, PICASSO, P. SMITH

DJIMON HOUNSOU

Before Djimon Hounsou became an accomplished actor, starring in blockbuster films such as *Gladiator* (2000) and *Captain Marvel* (2019), he got his start as a high-fashion model. Born in Cotonou, Benin, in 1964, Hounsou emigrated to France at thirteen. After being discovered by designer Thierry Mugler in the late 1980s, he was encouraged to pursue modeling in Paris and appeared in the designer's runway shows and advertising campaigns. By 1990 Hounsou had moved to New York; he subsequently appeared in music videos for pop singers Madonna, Janet Jackson, and Paula

Abdul and worked with photographer Herb Ritts. In a stunning 1991 editorial captured by Ritts for *Interview* magazine, Hounsou was famously featured wearing a Jean Paul Gaultier corset alongside Naomi Campbell. After breaking into film work in the mid-1990s, Hounsou was nominated for a Golden Globe for his performance in *Amistad* (1997) and two Academy Awards for his supporting roles in 2002's *In America* and 2006's *Blood Diamond*. In 2007 Hounsou returned to modeling as the face of Calvin Klein's underwear campaign, photographed by Peter Lindbergh.

Model

Djimon Hounsou.
b Cotonou (BEN), 1964.

Djimon Hounsou for Cross Colours, c. 1991.

Photograph by Michael Segal.

↳ CROSS COLOURS, C. KLEIN, LINDBERGH, RITTS

MARGARET HOWELL

Coming out of the manic 1960s the eponymous label that Margaret Howell established from her southeast London flat in 1972 was radical in its restraint. She wasn't drawing on Sgt. Pepper and his merry band of brocade-wearing dandies. Instead, she pulled from the quieter memories of her childhood. Her father's sturdy gardening Mac was an inspiration, as was a schoolteacher's corduroy sport coat. Howell gingerly revitalized countrified staples such as tweed coats, heavy wool sweaters, and weighty brogues. Her look may have pulled from the past, but it surely resonated with a contemporary customer. Jack Nicholson was such a fan of her corduroy trousers that he wore them in the 1980 film *The Shining*. In the 1980s Howell opened shops around the world, finding particular success in Japan, a country well attuned to her fabric-first simplicity. In 2004 she launched MHL, a sub-line focused on work-wear. Her polished and practical aesthetic has rarely wavered over the years and today is as comforting as ever.

Designer

Margaret Howell.
b Tadworth, Surrey (UK), 1946.

Actor George MacKay wearing Margaret Howell, 2020.

Photograph by Linda Brownlee.

↳ BARBOUR, BELSTAFF, BURBERRY, GLOVERALL, HACKETT

HUBLOT

"New watch alert," proclaimed Jay-Z and Kanye West in their 2011 chart-topping anthem "Otis," a pop cultural callout to sensational Swiss watchmaker Hublot. The brand was established by Italian businessman Carlo Crocco in 1980—a key point of inspiration being the word *hublot*, meaning "porthole" in French. Hublot's core aesthetic fuses classic craft with unexpected innovation: its original porthole-inspired bezel combined gold with a natural rubber strap—a first of its kind—and was reinforced with steel for ultralight wear. Other key styles—such as its bestselling Big Bang,

launched in 2004, or the elegant Classic Fusion—come in colored ceramic, carbon fiber, or 24-karat gold. With unique in-house movements, tweaked tourbillons, or skeletal sapphire casings and bridges, Hublot's future-forward appeal is ever-present through its collaborations, including designs by Jay-Z himself, fashion doyen Yohji Yamamoto, and artists such as Takashi Murakami, Richard Orlinski, and Shepard Fairey. As official timekeepers for FIFA and UEFA and the watch sponsor for soccer giants such as Juventus and Chelsea, Hublot's reach in sports runs the gamut.

Accessory Design

Hublot.
est Geneva (SW), 1980.

Usain Bolt wearing a Hublot watch, photographed for *GQ*, December 2016.

Photograph by Alasdair McLellan.

↳ JAY-Z, MURAKAMI, OMEGA, TAG HEUER, Y. YAMAMOTO

OLA HUDSON

Born in the United States and trained as a dancer in England, Ola Hudson's early theatrical flair informed her later work as a designer. By the time she was twenty-five years old, she had opened her own clothing boutique, Skitzo, on Los Angeles's Sunset Strip. Dressing John Lennon and Ringo Starr, she influenced the look of pop, and her David Bowie designs remain the most memorable. Shaping his role as Thomas Jerome Newton for the 1976 cult classic *The Man Who Fell to Earth*, she introduced smart suits, ruffled dress shirts, and a trademark fedora,

bringing Bowie's character to life. Bowie naturally turned to Hudson to craft his fabled persona, the Thin White Duke, for his tenth studio album, *Station to Station*, which released the same year. With an undone white shirt, cropped, gelled hair, and just the waistcoat and trousers of a three-piece suit, she transformed Bowie's thin frame and caught the public imagination. Shifting Bowie away from his colorful Ziggy Stardust persona, Hudson's mono-chrome style remains an abiding menswear reference.

Designer

Ola Hudson.
b Los Angeles (USA), 1946.
d Santa Monica, CA (USA), 2009.

David Bowie, wearing Ola Hudson, performing in Rotterdam, the Netherlands, 1976.

Photograph by Gijsbert Hanekroot.

↳ THE BEATLES, BOWIE, FISH, K. YAMAMOTO

HUGO BOSS

Best known for stylish suits associated with the yuppies of the late 1980s, Hugo Boss rebuilt itself after a troubled history of producing uniforms for the German armed forces during World War II and became one of the country's leading fashion brands. Following the death of founder Hugo Ferdinand Boss in 1948, the company passed to his son-in-law, Eugen Holy, who expanded production to make ready-to-wear men's suits in the 1950s. In 1969 Holy's sons, Jochen and Uwe, took the reins and introduced the first Boss-branded suits in 1970, establishing an international

reputation particularly for the brand's narrow-shouldered suits with single-breasted blazers. Boss expanded during the 1980s thanks to successful franchise and licensing operations—it created its first fragrance in 1984—but also because its double-breasted business suits with wide shoulder pads appealed to a new generation of conspicuously wealthy businessmen. Since the early 1990s, the company has combined the central Boss brand (which now includes business wear and leisurewear, urban sportswear, and outdoor activewear) with the more innovative Hugo line.

Designer Brand

Hugo Boss.
est Metzingen (GER), 1924.

Hugo Boss Fall/Winter 1991 campaign.

Photograph by Neil Kirk.

↳ AVEDON, COLE, JIL SANDER, VANDERLOO, WEITZ

HUNTSMAN

Established in Mayfair in 1849, Henry Huntsman's gaiter and breeches business gained a reputation for making formidable riding and hunting clothes for aristocratic clients throughout Europe, earning Royal Warrants from Queen Victoria and the future King Edward VII. Having moved to Savile Row in 1919, Huntsman dressed the then Prince of Wales and introduced bespoke men's morning suits that attracted an expanding list of clients, including Cecil Beaton, Winston Churchill, and even Marlene Dietrich. More than 130 in-house tailors and cutters made clothes for A-listers in the 1950s before

Huntsman introduced ready-to-wear during the following decade. The actor Gregory Peck enjoyed a long relationship with Huntsman: he ordered more than sixty-five of its precisely cut suits, such as the classic one-button style, which was introduced by Huntsman. The firm also dressed him for some of his most famous roles, including Atticus Finch in *To Kill a Mockingbird* (1962) and Robert Thorn in 1976's horror film *The Omen*. In 2013 Huntsman was purchased by the Belgian financier Pierre Lagrange, and in 2014 the shop was used as a location for the film *Kingsman: The Secret Service*.

Tailor

Huntsman.
est London (UK), 1849.

Gregory Peck, wearing a Huntsman suit, in London for the filming of Stanley Donen's comedy-thriller *Arabesque* (Universal Pictures), 1966.

↳ BEATON, BLASS, GABLE, NEWMAN

The ultimate in homeboy apparel is an Adidas leather tracksuit/ Too hot to dance in, too cool to run in/ This totally impractical fusion of club, sport and fetish retails at $280 from Doctor J's in Fulton Mall, Brooklyn and shops in Delancey Street, Manhattan/ Must be teamed with red Kangol beret for full effect.

PHOTOGRAPHY EDDIE MONSOON

6 : i-D THE REVOLUTION ISSUE

Public Enemy reveal militaristic red rap look/ quartz clock low-slung around neck/ gold chains and commando boots/ camouflage and shades with – wait for it – 24 Karat daisy roots/ It takes a nation of millions to lift their wardrobe/ See feature this issue.

i-D styling tip no. 20056/ Morgan Penn (no relation) second year fashion student at Harrow College of Technology and Art wears plastic kitchen hook and Yale keys/ "My kiss curls, devil horns and ponytails don't need hairspray or setting gel, and I don't have to make an appointment with Tescos when I want a new hairdo," says Morgan/ This is i-DIY going MFI.

Photography Simon Fleury

i-D NEWSFLASH

i-D

Founded in 1980 by former British *Vogue* art director Terry Jones and his wife, Tricia, the first issue of the fanzine *i-D* was created out of the Joneses' London apartment and held together with staples. Radical and raw, its pages were devoted to England's youth subcultures, including punk and street-style trends. Serving as a platform for Jones's au courant circle, a new class of vanguard talent interested in highlighting alternative narratives and lifting fashion from its traditional codes emerged. The work of up-and-coming photographers, such as Wolfgang Tillmans, Nick Knight,

and Craig McDean, and stylists, including Edward Enninful, dominated *i-D*'s pages and covers (always with one eye winking or obscured). Rich with a chaotic amalgam of lo-fi graphics, *i-D* gave way to the grunge aesthetic of later contributors, such as Juergen Teller and David Sims. Today the title retains its signature edge with former fashion director Alastair McKimm as editor in chief, and it continues to attract cutting-edge talent with photographers Gray Sorrenti, Grant Spanier, Hanna Moon, and Luis Alberto Rodriguez.

Publication

i-D.
est London (UK), 1980.

Spread from *i-D*'s The Revolution Issue, May 1988.

Photography by Simon Fleury.

↳ ENNINFUL, FOXTON, KAMARA, KNIGHT, McKIMM, SIMS, TELLER, TILLMANS

YASUMI INOUE

Identified only by a discreet letter *R* on every item, the clothes designed by Yasumi Inoue for 45R garnered a cult following (Giorgio Armani was a fan of her menswear). Founded in 1977 during Japan's craze for American popular culture, the Tokyo-based brand was originally named 45RPM, a reference to the revolutions of most seven-inch single vinyl records. With the brand, Inoue sought to bridge the gap between couture and casualwear, designing similar styles of clothes for both men and women. Turning fashion on its head, she set out to produce ready-to-wear with the exacting production methods of couture, such as a T-shirt that took a year to produce and jeans and shirts notable for their precision. Denim, an essentially American fabric, was key to the label; Inoue's design process invariably started with the material, usually dyed in indigo. This appreciation for textiles and an acute understanding of ancient Japanese methods of dyeing came from growing up in her family's kimono business. Inoue left 45R in 2018 but remained true to her belief in never chasing trends; the material should always come first.

Designer

Yasumi Inoue.
b (JAP), c. 1954.

45R Winter 2008.

Photograph by Masanori Ikeda.

↳ ARMANI, EVISU, HIRATA, NAKAMURA

ISAIA

The luxury Italian menswear brand Isaia owes its spirit to the southern city of Naples, where Enrico Isaia opened a shop in the 1920s to sell fabric to the city before he began producing clothes himself. After Enrico's death, the business passed to his sons, Enrico, Rosario, and Corrado, who relocated it to the nearby village of Casalnuovo di Napoli, where it was said that half of the population was tailors. Over the next decade, the company established its name in Italy, sourcing fine materials and supplying its wares only to high-end shops; then in the 1980s it started selling through exclusive retailers in Europe, North America, and Asia. Despite the brand's now global reach, it still manufactures its suits only in Casalnuovo. Isaia suits are worn by Hugh Jackman and Tom Cruise, among others, and their quirky detailing—such as cuffed trousers and distinctive fabrics, including checks—has made them highly desirable for the cognoscenti. Now run by a third generation of the family, Isaia remains a high-class tailor, distinguished by craftsmanship and independent spirit.

Tailor

Isaia.
est Naples (IT), c. 1920s.

Oscar Isaac wearing an Isaia suit, photographed for *GQ*, February 2018.

Photograph by Jason Nocito.

↳ BRIONI, CUCINELLI, MISSONI, RUBINACCI

I WAS LORD KITCHENER'S VALET

At the height of the Swinging Sixties, one way young Londoners expressed rejection of their elders was by co-opting the clothes of the establishment and turning them into a fashion statement, particularly Victorian military uniform, and their destination was I Was Lord Kitchener's Valet. Founded by Ian Fisk and John Paul, the store opened on Portobello Road in 1965 but started two years earlier as a stall in Portobello Market, where Fisk sold military surplus. One day Mick Jagger visited the boutique with John Lennon and bought a red Grenadier Guardsman drummer's jacket that he wore when the Rolling Stones appeared on the British rock-pop show *Ready Steady Go!*. The shop's fame skyrocketed—a hundred people turned up at the store the next day to buy the jacket—attracting patrons including Jimi Hendrix. The following year Fisk opened three more locations. The gold-frogged Victorian army tunic became a signature garment of the decade; artist Peter Blake said he got the idea for the *Sgt. Pepper's Lonely Hearts Club Band* album sleeve from walking past the shop. The Portobello Road location closed in 1967, and the last location closed in 1977.

Retailer

I Was Lord Kitchener's Valet.
est London (UK), 1965.

Jimi Hendrix wearing a vintage military jacket from I Was Lord Kitchener's Valet, 1967.

↳ THE BEATLES, GRANNY TAKES A TRIP, HENDRIX, JAGGER

KENNETH IZE

The pulse of Nigerian culture beats strongly in the work of Kenneth Ize, a Lagos-born designer raised and educated in Austria. A finalist for the esteemed LVMH Prize in 2019, Ize brings together authentic Nigerian heritage and Western tailoring. His distinctive look is a sharp menswear silhouette cut from woven fabrics of *aso-oke*—a cloth-weaving technique that is unique to the Yoruba people of southwestern Nigeria. This traditional cloth forms the basis of Ize's work, differentiating his designs with striped, checked, and rainbow-colored cotton fabrics in oranges, yellows, crimsons, purples, and greens. Supporting this tradition is Ize's experience at Edun and Asher Levine, as well as stints under Bernhard Wilhelm and Hussein Chalayan, all of which honed his eye for exacting tailoring. His skills translate dazzling fabrics into slim, contemporary cuts that nod to both a modern Western aesthetic and the sartorial smarts of Nigerian men. Ize's designs have garnered fans including star architect David Adjaye, Naomi Campbell, Beyoncé, and Donald Glover, and have been featured in leading fashion magazines, such as *i-D* and *Vogue*.

Designer

Kenneth Ize.
b Lagos (NG), 1990.

Kenneth Ize Fall/Winter 2020 collection at Paris Fashion Week.

↳ **DAILY PAPER, KAMARA, NGXOKOLO, WILLHELM**

JACOB & CO.

"I went to Jacob an hour after I got my advance, I just wanted to shine." So rapped Kanye West in his 2005 song "Touch the Sky," lyrically nodding to Jacob Arabo, the impeccably dressed jeweler who reigns as New York's King of Bling. An Uzbekistani immigrant, Jacob the Jeweler began selling his dazzling creations in Manhattan's Diamond District as a teenager in the early 1980s. Arabo's career clicked into place several years later when music-world juggernauts Slick Rick, Sean Combs, the Notorious B.I.G., Jay-Z, and Nas started flowing into his shop looking for jumbo-sized gold chains, diamonds, and rings to match their larger-than-life personas. Buying bling from Jacob the Jeweler became a rite of passage for rising rappers, and in turn, Arabo was namechecked in countless hit songs. In 2005 Jacob & Co. moved into a new flagship location on bustling 57th Street and began specializing in Swiss-made timepieces featuring rainbow jewels and intricate time-zone complications. In recent years Jacob & Co. has created extravagant watches in collaboration with Virgil Abloh and Supreme.

Accessory Design

Jacob & Co.
est New York (USA), 1986.

A$AP Rocky wearing a Jacob & Co. Five Time Zone watch, Miami, 2017.

Photograph by Kenneth Lesley.

↳ A$AP ROCKY, ABLOH, COMBS, JAY-Z, SUPREME

MARC JACOBS

During his teens and early twenties, Marc Jacobs partied at Studio 54 and studied fashion at Parsons School of Design. In 1988 the native New Yorker became the creative director at Perry Ellis, but he was fired four years later when he presented a grunge-themed collection. Jacobs unleashed his own menswear line in 1994. Its accessible grunge-meets-preppy vibe—complemented by cool knits, kitsch T-shirts, and reworked vintage classics—remains ever popular. As creative director of Louis Vuitton from 1997 to 2014, Jacobs initiated globally successful collaborations with artists such as Stephen Sprouse

and Kanye West. In more recent years Jacobs's menswear has taken a more playful approach, featuring images of Snoopy and Charlie Brown or illustrations from the artist Magda Archer, with famous faces including Harry Styles wearing his designs. Jacobs's evolving personal style is also widely discussed—from his 1990s geek-chic with large spectacles, loose pants, and sneakers to his more recent and increasingly gender-fluid image chronicled on social media. This embracing of makeup, Celine dresses, and towering Rick Owens platform boots has gained him a new generation of fans.

Designer/Icon

Marc Jacobs.
b New York (USA), 1963.

Marc Jacobs, 2019.

Photograph by Gillian Laub.

↳ ELLIS, LOUIS VUITTON, OWENS, SPROUSE, TELLER

JAEGER

The Jaeger fashion house was founded in 1884 by Lewis Tomalin, who was inspired by the writings of German reformer Gustav Jaeger—a leading advocate of wearing natural animal hair rather than plant fibers for health and sanitation. Tomalin, a London businessman, bought the rights from Jaeger to use Jaeger's name to encourage his philosophy. Early adherents of Dr. Jaeger's Sanitary Woollen System (the brand's original name) included Oscar Wilde, George Bernard Shaw, and explorer Ernest Shackleton. In the 1920s Jaeger shifted its focus to producing more fashionable clothes but

remained true to the doctrine of "healthy" materials— high-quality, fine wool-knit jersey, cashmere, and camel hair. In fact, Jaeger is credited with popularizing the camel hair coat in the UK. Such classic pieces demonstrate how the brand quickly established itself with its Regent Street flagship store as a high-street supplier of dependable clothing for work and "best" for the middle classes. Its empire eventually stretched to more than 250 shops, but declining sales beginning in the 1990s saw that number fall to around 70 before 2021, when the Jaeger name was sold to Marks & Spencer.

Designer Brand

Jaeger.
est London (UK), 1884.

Jaeger magazine advertisement, c. 1950s.

↳ D. BAILEY, GLOVERALL, J&J CROMBIE LTD., WILDE

MICK JAGGER

Icon

Mick Jagger.
b Dartford (UK), 1943.

**Mick Jagger at a press conference for the
Rolling Stones album *Goats Head Soup*,
Munich, 1973.**

Photograph by Gijsbert Hanekroot.

↳ FISH, GRANNY TAKES A TRIP,
  I WAS LORD KITCHENER'S
  VALET, NUTTER, SEXTON,
  STYLES

Having sold more than 240 million records worldwide over the past six decades, the Rolling Stones are rock-star royalty. The band's front man, Mick Jagger, has notably redefined masculine style, veering from sinewy tailoring to gender-blurring stage wear. In the late 1960s and early '70s, he wore slim lemon and green-hued suits from Savile Row's most radical tailors, Edward Sexton and Tommy Nutter, as well as androgynous styles, such as the white ruffle-sleeved "man-dress" designed by Michael Fish. In the mid-to-late '70s came a succession of slinky velvet jumpsuits designed by Ossie Clarke, pink cropped tops, embroidered waistcoats, cord jackets, shirts with huge lapels, flouncy neck scarves, and brightly colored athletic trousers by Antony Price. Before her death in 2014, Jagger's clothing onstage and off was designed by his longtime partner L'Wren Scott. Jagger's influence can be seen in the stylings of later stars, such as Steven Tyler, Bobby Gillespie, and Harry Styles, as well as designers and stylists, including Hedi Slimane and Alister Mackie. Despite the eclecticism of his sartorial choices over the years, Mick Jagger only *ever* looks like Mick Jagger—the very definition of a fashion icon.

RICHARD JAMES

It was said when British tailor Richard James moved into the largest shop on Savile Row in 2000—having had smaller premises on the street since 1992 as part of the "new bespoke" movement—that he wouldn't last five minutes. More than twenty years later, James and his business partner, Sean Dixon, have not only remained on Savile Row but have also thoroughly changed it by pioneering Saturday hours—previously unheard of on Savile Row—and introducing collaborations with brands including Marks & Spencer, as well as launching a ready-to-wear line. At the same time,

in 2004, James cofounded the Savile Row Bespoke Association, dedicated to upholding the street's traditional standards. His bespoke suits, which incorporate waisted jackets and deep side vents for a slim silhouette and feature a striking use of colors and patterns, have attracted celebrities from David Beckham to Tinie Tempah. In 2011 James designed a gold jacket encrusted with Swarovski crystals for Elton John, while his more traditional clients include Prime Minister David Cameron and Prince William. James was made an OBE for services to fashion in 2018.

Tailor

Richard James.
b (Active 1990s—).

Richard James Spring/Summer 2016 ready-to-wear collection at London Collections: Men, 2015.

Photograph by Victor Virgile.

↳ AMIES, BECKHAM, NUTTER

THE SUNAIRE — THE SPEEDAIRE

combining them all in a fashion ruggedly masculine. Typically Jantzen in its permanent perfect fit, its seasonal style and color leadership, and in the truly marvelous elasticity of the Jantzen-stitch. It really is easier to swim in a Jantzen. In addition to the Sunaire and the Speedaire, (both illustrated), there are many other smart models for men, women and children...including the popular Shouldaire, men's and boys' Diving and Speed Suits, and Twosomes for men and women. You'll find the famous red Diving Girl emblem on every genuine Jantzen. Your weight is your size. Jantzen Knitting Mills, Portland, Oregon; Vancouver, Canada; London, England; Sydney, Australia.

The suit that changed bathing to swimming

JANTZEN KNITTING MILLS, (Dept. 104), Portland, Oregon
Please send me style folder in color featuring 1931 models.
Women's ☐   Men's ☐

Name _____

Address _____

JANTZEN

"The suit that changed bathing to swimming" is how the swimwear company Jantzen described its stretch-jersey tank suit. In 1913 the founders of the Portland Knitting Company, Carl Jantzen and brothers John and Roy Zehntbauer, were asked by fellow members of their crew club to make rowing trunks from the elasticated jersey used for sweater cuffs. The successful commission led to a request for a similar garment for swimming, which was made in 1915 with fine wool knitted in a rib stitch. A year later the brand was renamed Jantzen. Although the fabric turned heavy when wet, the suit became highly popular by the 1920s and was worn by athletes, such as Johnny Weissmuller and Duke Kahanamoku, during early Olympic Games. After World War II Jantzen heavily promoted its swim shorts and trunks—now made from elasticized fabric—as sportswear. The La Quebrada Cliff Divers of Acapulco, Mexico, inspired and tested a new cut, and Sean Connery sported three different styles in *Thunderball* (1965), lending James Bond's effortless cool to the brand. From the 1970s on Jantzen turned its focus primarily to women's swimwear, eventually dropping its men's line in 1995.

Brand

Jantzen.
est Portland, OR (USA), 1910.

Jantzen advertisement, c. 1930s.

↳ CHAMPION, CONNERY, OCEAN PACIFIC, SPEEDO

JAY-Z

Jay-Z, also known as Jigga, Hova, and his legal name, Shawn Carter, is the world's most successful rapper-turned-business-mogul. Raised in Brooklyn, Carter started making records in the mid-1990s, sporting a look with big chains, oversize Knicks jerseys, and flooded Rolexes. But as Carter took his place in the center of hip-hop, his personal style leveled up from baggy jeans to luxury basics and jewel-toned suits, while still keeping his classic black New Era Yankees caps in rotation. In 1999 he launched his own clothing brand, Rocawear, with Damon Dash, doing hundreds of millions in

sales and spawning a series of hip-hop streetwear imitators. In the 2000s Carter went through a Tom Ford phase, a button-up look (from crisp white to stripes), and an all-black period, always moving his style—as his song title suggested—"On to the Next One." The billionaire rapper has name-checked an estimated sixty fashion brands in his discography—from Gucci and Hermès to Nike and Hublot. More recently his fashion sense has become increasingly adventurous, and he has begun wearing colorful tailored suits by designers such as Dries Van Noten, Givenchy, and Davidson Petit-Frère.

Icon

Jay-Z (Shawn Carter).
b Brooklyn (USA), 1969.

Jay-Z, Sean Combs, and Jim Jones attend the Roc Nation Brunch, Los Angeles, 2019.

Photograph by Kevin Mazur.

↳ AMBROSE, FORD, NEW ERA, ROCAWEAR, ROLEX, VAN NOTEN

J.CREW

Before J.Crew became one of the United States' most ubiquitous prepwear brands, it was known as Popular Club Plan—a door-to-door womenswear business founded in 1947 by Mitchell Cinader and Saul Charles. In 1983 the company relaunched as J.Crew, a more affordable catalog alternative that offered aspirational preppy classics. Six years later, in 1989, J.Crew opened its first store in New York City. Its early menswear styles boasted chambray button-downs, striped knits, and dusty chinos. The brand hit its stride in the aughts—with retail savant Mickey Drexler joining the company as CEO in 2003 and designer Jenna Lyons rising to creative director in 2008—and sold more fashion-forward products while remaining main-stream. Its men's collections offered dependable high-low styles, including the slim-fitting Ludlow suit, tuxedo and blazer jackets, and day-to-night shirts. It also launched collaborations with established menswear brands Drake's of London, New Balance, Red Wing, and Sperry. In 2021 J.Crew appointed streetwear pioneer Brendon Babenzien as creative director of its menswear.

Retailer

J.Crew.
est New York (USA), 1947.

Models at the J.Crew Spring 2014 show at New York Fashion Week, 2013.

Photograph by Brian Ach.

↳ BABENZIEN, DRAKE'S, NEW BALANCE, RED WING, SPERRY TOP-SIDER

KERBY JEAN-RAYMOND

A groundbreaking figure, designer Kerby Jean-Raymond and his Pyer Moss label have made an indelible mark on the fashion world since 2013. The Spring/Summer 2016 runway show, especially, is one that is still talked about. Before the models walked, the show began with the screening of a film that depicted police brutality and racism, and the audience was stunned. Despite this powerful political statement nearly costing him his label, Jean-Raymond continues to champion activism and challenges the underrepresentation of Black creatives in fashion. He honed his skills at Theory,

Marc Jacobs, and Kenneth Cole before founding Pyer Moss in 2013. Jean-Raymond fuses bold colors with vivid story-telling, using design to challenge social narratives and create dialogues around each collection's theme. Reworking streetwear classics, his pieces often introduce proprietary prints, seam detailing, and experimental proportions—his cropped jackets are a lauded look. Pyer Moss's incredible success has led to collaborations with heritage streetwear brands Cross Colours and FUBU, and in 2020 Jean-Raymond was named the global creative director of Reebok.

Designer

Kerby Jean-Raymond.
b New York (USA), 1986.

Kerby Jean-Raymond's "Pyer Moss Collection 3," photographed for *T: The New York Times Style Magazine*, March 2020.

Photograph by Michelle Sank.

↳ COLE, CROSS COLOURS, FUBU, JACOBS, KELLY

JEFFREY

In 1999 Jeffrey Kalinsky's boutique—simply named Jeffrey—landed with a bang in New York's Meatpacking District. The heretofore unexploited industrial neighborhood was then home to butchers and a few strip clubs. And then suddenly, there was Jeffrey, a bright shop selling Helmut Lang jackets, Jil Sander suits, and Gucci loafers. A native of South Carolina, Kalinsky opened his first boutique in Atlanta in 1990. A Palo Alto outpost followed years later, and Kalinsky made a name for himself as a swashbuckling retailer giving prime real estate to new—or just new to the States—brands such as Ann Demeulemeester, Mastermind, and Marni. Though it had only three locations, Jeffrey's reputation was so vast that the shop was even parodied (much to the annoyance of Kalinsky at the time) on *Saturday Night Live* in 2001. In 2005 Jeffrey was purchased by Nordstrom, and Kalinsky was shortly appointed the retailer's vice president of designer merchandising, elevating the mass retailer's assortment. In 2020 Jeffrey closed its stores, one of the many victims of the pandemic-era retail slowdown.

Retailer

Jeffrey.
est Atlanta (USA), 1990.

Jeffrey Fashion Cares runway show, New York, 2017.

Photograph by Gonzalo Marroquin.

↳ DEMEULEMEESTER, JIL SANDER, LANG, MARNI

CHARLES JEFFREY

Designer

If the ghost-white powder makeup that he often wears in public isn't already a dead giveaway, Charles Jeffrey is a designer who leans into theatrics. His Loverboy line, which was born out of London's Central Saint Martins College of Art and Design in 2015, is a sprawling and campy assemblage of clothes that draw on Jeffrey's club-kid sensibility. Since 2017 Jeffrey's immersive shows have been can't-miss events during London Fashion Week, and his collections have included hole-laden sweaters slumping off a model's shoulders as if they're melting,

Starry Night–esque motifs covering entire tracksuits, and jeans embellished with mushrooms right out of a Dr. Seuss book. Jeffrey slyly weaves in tartan patterns as a nod to his Scottish heritage, and his Spring 2021 collection showed garments plastered with words such as *Community*, *Health*, and *Hope*, relaying a strong, if literal, political message. In this thoughtful manner, Jeffrey is operating much like another famed designer of Scottish heritage, Alexander McQueen, a comparison that has been made by none other than fashion writer Tim Blanks.

Charles Jeffrey.
b Glasgow (UK), 1990.

Model Gulliver Whitby wearing Charles Jeffrey Loverboy, photographed for "I'll Be Your Mirror," *British GQ Style*, Fall/Winter 2018.

Photograph by Thurstan Redding.

↳ VAN BEIRENDONCK, GREEN, KAWAKUBO, PALOMO SPAIN, STYLES

JIL SANDER

Armed with her mother's sewing machine, twenty-something Jil Sander opened a small atelier in Hamburg in 1968. By 1973 it had blossomed into a full-fledged label. It took Sander until 1997 to introduce menswear, but when she did, the results were sublime. Her slender suits, in a moody palette of grays and blacks, imbued the wearer with an arresting sense of poise. The brand ushered in a trend of almost futuristic minimalism through boxy three-button suits, textural turtlenecks, and neat, straight-legged trousers. The clothes were blissfully logo-free and often monochromatic, providing a refreshing alternative to the slovenly grunge look and manic logo-mania. In 1999 Sander sold a majority stake in her label to Prada, and she decamped shortly thereafter, returning briefly in 2003 and 2012. In 2005 Raf Simons was appointed creative director, introducing innovative, modern styles, bold colors, and graphic prints while still staying true to the label's stream-lined roots. Today the brand is helmed by Lucie and Luke Meier, who have added an element of warmth, with more fluid shapes, muted color palettes, and inventive layering.

Designer Brand

Jil Sander.
est Hamburg (GER), 1968.

Model Myles Dominique for Jil Sander Spring/Summer 2019, Matsue-shi, Japan, 2018.

Photograph by Mario Sorrenti.

↪ PRADA, SIMONS, SIMS, UNIQLO

J&J CROMBIE LTD.

Initially a cloth supplier to luxury tailors, the Scottish firm of J&J Crombie Ltd. began making clothes in the mid-1800s and became known for their outerwear, particularly the Crombie, a three-quarter-length overcoat, often with a contrasting velvet collar. Much like the Chesterfield, it was based on the covert coat originally designed for horseback riding and hunting. The firm's growth in the 1800s was fueled through contracts to provide textiles for military uniforms—including for the Confederate Army during the US Civil War and British officers' uniforms in both world wars—before its own clothing gradually took precedence. In the twentieth century Crombie retained its luxury links and was worn by international figures from the Romanov family in Russia to King George VI in England, from Winston Churchill to John F. Kennedy, and from Cary Grant to the Beatles. The Crombie became the standard dress for city bankers in London—as well as a staple of youth subcultures, particularly the teddy boys and mods of the 1960s and the skinheads of the following decades—and remains an enduring classic to this day.

Designer Brand

J&J Crombie Ltd.
est Aberdeen, Scotland (UK), 1805.

Cary Grant wearing a Crombie coat, London, 1946.

↳ THE BEATLES, CORDINGS, GLOVERALL, C. GRANT, KENNEDY, DUKE OF WINDSOR

J.M. WESTON

Despite being the quintessential French shoe label, J.M. Weston is named in part for Weston, Massachusetts. The New England town is where, in the early 1900s, Eugene Blanchard studied the Goodyear welting and machine-stitching techniques perfected by American shoe manufacturers. The young Blanchard took these innovations back to Limoges, France, where his father, Edouard, had teamed up with a very dandy business partner, Jean Viard, to start a shoe company. In the decades that followed, Weston's signature styles—the 180 Moccasin, a sturdy penny loafer,

and the 677 Chasse, an understated derby shoe—became essential to the Parisian look. The 180 in particular was beloved in the 1960s by Bande du Drugstore beatniks, who congregated around the Publicis Drugstore on the Champs-Élysées. These raffish style rebels eschewed socks with their loafers, ushering in a new style trend. Rakes of a different sort, the Sapeurs of Congo, were enamored with Weston's lace-ups. The label was also beloved by more buttoned-up aristocrats, including French president François Mitterrand, who owned thirty pairs of Weston loafers.

J.M. Weston.
est Limoges (FR), 1891.

An interior display at J.M. Weston Champs-Élysées, Paris.

Photograph by Adrien Dirand.

↳ ALDEN SHOES, CHURCH'S, G.H. BASS & CO., PAPA WEMBA

STEVE JOBS

Steve Jobs was once a natty dresser, giving keynote presentations in bow ties and double-breasted suits. But in the 1980s, as reported in Walter Isaacson's exhaustive biography on the Apple visionary, Jobs visited a Sony factory in Japan and was smitten by the employees' Issey Miyake–designed uniforms. He reached out to Miyake to make some for Apple, but the individualistic employees at Jobs's California tech empire raged against the idea of company-issued clothes. But Jobs still craved uniformity, so in the early 1990s he threw on a Miyake mock neck,

washed-out jeans, and New Balance sneakers and never looked back. Jobs professed he liked the convenience, but his unwavering outfit also helped brand him. In the decades to come, wannabe tech stars, such as Facebook's Mark Zuckerberg and Twitter's Jack Dorsey, aped Jobs's sartorial consistency in their own way. In the aughts Jobs's so-basic-it's-stylish outfit made him a normcore icon, influencing the attire of on-trend urbanites.

Icon

Steve Jobs.
b San Francisco (USA), 1955.
d Palo Alto, CA (USA), 2011.

Steve Jobs, 1998.

Photograph by Michael O'Neill.

↳ LEVI'S, MIYAKE,
   NEW BALANCE

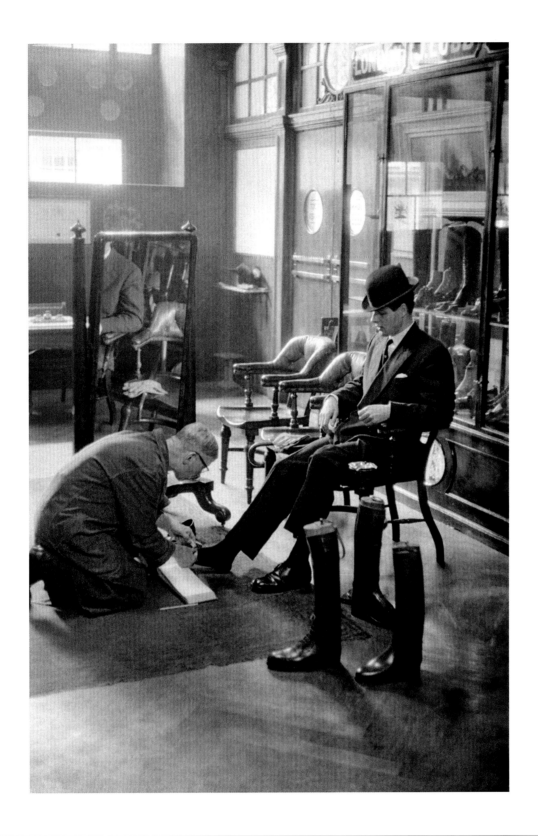

JOHN LOBB BOOTMAKER

John Lobb, the iconic family-run British bootmaker, was founded in 1849 and opened its first shop in 1866. Its namesake founder John Lobb was born in 1828 in Cornwall. Moving to London in 1851, he apprenticed as a shoemaker, later journeying to Australia to make boots for prospectors during the gold rush. In 1863 Lobb returned to London and was appointed official bootmaker to Edward, Prince of Wales, making opulent, fanciful shoes in the Edwardian style (the company still holds Royal Warrants today). In 1976 the luxury label was acquired by Hermès. Lobb's generations of master boot-makers have shaped their expertly crafted, timeless designs, such as the versatile Alder walking boot, the elegant Lopez loafer, and the William double-monkstrap shoe. John Lobb crafts shoes both by request and ready-to-wear in Northampton, England (adhering to a 190-step manufacturing process), or bespoke at its Paris atelier. In addition to the royal family, John Lobb has made shoes for politicians, business titans, and cultural icons, such as George Bernard Shaw, Cole Porter, and Frank Sinatra.

Footwear

John Lobb Bootmaker.
est Basingstoke, England (UK), 1849.

A customer at John Lobb's London shop, *Réalités*, 1959.

Photograph by Frank Horvat.

↳ CHURCH'S, HERMÈS, J.M. WESTON, R.M.WILLIAMS, SINATRA

JOHN SMEDLEY

Creators of the "World's Finest Knitwear," the family-run label was founded in 1784 by John Smedley and Peter Nightingale. One of Britain's oldest garment manufacturers, they first created cotton muslins before moving on to complex knits, including vests and long johns. In 1932 their bestselling men's Isis polo, a simple short-sleeve tennis shirt, was introduced and featured a signature fashioned collar to dress up or down. By the mid-twentieth century, John Smedley and its "Made in Britain" craft expanded to include jackets and shirts—popularized by global stars, including

Sean Connery as James Bond in 1962's *Dr. No*—and its famous roll-neck sweaters, worn by mods and celebrities, such as the Beatles. In the 1980s the brand produced high-fashion knitwear for Vivienne Westwood and Paul Smith. The label modernized the Isis in 2013, releasing the classic Adrian polo with a smaller stand collar and ribbed hem. Two years later it launched its first-ever unisex collection of wardrobe staples, joining the heritage brand's iconic repertoire built on cottons, extrafine merino wools, cashmeres, and silk blends.

Designer Brand

John Smedley.
est Matlock, Derbyshire (UK), 1784.

The Payton by John Smedley, expertly crafted in extrafine merino wool and featuring a two-button placket.

Photograph by Natasja Fourie.

↳ THE BEATLES, CONNERY, LACOSTE, PENGUIN, P. SMITH, WESTWOOD

KIM JONES

Everywhere Kim Jones goes, buzz follows. Fresh from Central Saint Martins College of Art and Design, Jones founded his eponymous label in 2003, offering neat denim, spacious pleated trousers, and sporty jackets. Jones's beguiling collections earned him plum posts at stalwarts such as Umbro and Alfred Dunhill. In 2011 LVMH came knocking. Jones helmed Louis Vuitton's menswear, delving headlong into luxury with lush sweaters, shimmering reptile jackets, and stately wool coats. In 2017 Jones and Vuitton paired with the skatewear savants at Supreme for an acclaimed collaboration—a monogrammed trunk from which fetched $125,000 at Christie's in 2019. Jones went in 2018 to Dior Homme, where his collaborative streak shone bright, notably producing collaborations with designers, such as Shawn Stussy and Yoon Ahn, and a number of artists, including Raymond Pettibon, Daniel Arsham, and KAWS. His sensual suiting and strap-happy outerwear are a favorite of celebrities such as BTS, Robert Pattinson, and Pusha T. In 2020 Jones was appointed artistic director of Fendi and received an OBE for his illustrious work.

Designer

Kim Jones.
b London (UK), 1979.

Dior Pre-Fall 2020 collection in collaboration with Stüssy, photographed for "Miami Vibes," *Dior Magazine*.

Photograph by Brett Lloyd.

↳ ALFRED DUNHILL, BLAME, BTS, LOUIS VUITTON, McLAREN, SUPREME, M. WILLIAMS

STEPHEN JONES

While studying fashion at Saint Martin's School of Art in the late 1970s, Stephen Jones discovered millinery during an internship at the couture house Lachasse. By the time he left college in 1979, he was hatmaker in chief to devotees of the New Romantic movement—including Boy George—which was fast becoming a cultural force with its playful, theatrical fashion. It was Steve Strange—the nightclub host and progenitor of the New Romantic movement—who backed Jones's first millinery salon. Jones's eponymous collections for men tended toward twists on the traditional, with exaggerated caps, berets, trilbies, and fedoras, and he became one of fashion's most prolific and enduring collaborators. In the early 1980s he created hats for Jean Paul Gaultier and Thierry Mugler and went on to work with Rei Kawakubo, creating bunny-eared leather caps for her Fall/Winter 2013 collection, and Thom Browne, who commissioned Dickensian top hats and hunting caps in frayed tweed with animal ears for his Fall/Winter 2014 show. In 1996 Jones began a working relationship with Dior that has spanned three creative directors across three decades and counting.

Milliner

Stephen Jones.
b The Wirral, Cheshire, England (UK), 1957.

Fox hat designed by Stephen Jones for the Thom Browne Fall/Winter 2014 collection.

Photograph by Marcus Tondo.

↳ BLAME, BROWNE, GAULTIER, JAGGER, KAWAKUBO

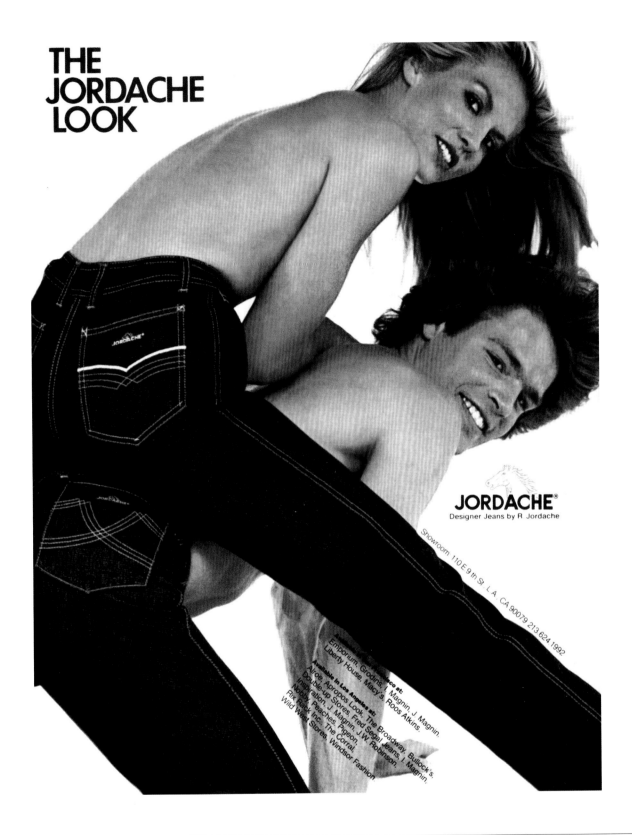

THE JORDACHE LOOK

JORDACHE®
Designer Jeans by R. Jordache

Showroom 110 E 9th St. L.A. CA 90079 213 624 1992

Available in San Francisco at:
Emporium, Grodins, I. Magnin, J. Magnin,
Liberty House, Macy's, Roos Atkins.
Available in Los Angeles at:
Airos, Apropos Look, The Broadway, Bullock's,
Double-Up Stores Fred Segal Jeans, I. Magnin,
Inspiration, J. Magnin, J.W. Robinson, J. Magnin,
Norby, Peaches, Pigeon,
Rix Mark Inc. The Corral,
Wild West Stores, Windsor Fashion.

JORDACHE

A defining 1980s staple, Jordache begins and ends with denim. After initially selling premium jeans from a Bushwick storefront in Brooklyn, in 1978—following an unfortunate storefront fire—Israeli American brothers Joseph, Ralph, and Avi Nakash decided to manufacture styles of their own design. Inspired by European fashions at the time and a more slim, skin-tight feel, the Nakash brothers entered the market of designer denim, selling a dressy style for thirty dollars that competed with Gloria Vanderbilt and Calvin Klein in the bid to make jeans form-fitting status symbols. Their jeans, which featured the Jordache horse-head logo, were made with Japanese denim that was triple-stitched for durability and included reinforced buttons and double waistbands to "hug" the waist—a trend cemented in the annals of American fashion. With the help of bold and risqué advertising campaigns—some were banned from television—including full-page ads in *New York* and *Playboy* magazines, the "Jordache Look" became widely renowned.

Brand

Jordache.
est New York (USA), 1978.

Jordache advertisement, c. 1970s.

↳ C. KLEIN, LEE JEANS, LEVI'S, WRANGLER, YAMANE

267

MICHAEL JORDAN

Michael Jordan joined the Chicago Bulls in 1984, eventually going on to win six NBA championships with the team—an achievement chronicled in 2020's docuseries *The Last Dance*. In the 1980s and '90s Jordan wore lengthy sport coats and parachute jeans, styles that befit his imposing frame but have nonetheless made him one of the most polarizing dressers of the past few decades. During his time with the Bulls, he popularized basketball around the globe, becoming a pop-culture icon and international superstar both on and off the court.

Jordan enthusiastically combined sport with fashion and business, scoring a string of trailblazing deals with brands including Nike, Oakley, and Hanes. In 1984 he signed a contract with Nike, launching the Air Jordan 1, which at the time was the most expensive basketball shoe ever made. Nike predicted sales of $3 million, but the shoes became a cult hit with $126 million in sales and kick-started the rise of the cult-sneaker phenomenon. In 2020 Dior unveiled its homage to Jordan's original shoes with the handmade Air Dior, which sold for $2,200.

Icon

Michael Jordan.
b Brooklyn (USA), 1963.

Michael Jordan, wearing Nike Air Jordans during the 1985 NBA All-Star Slam Dunk Contest.

Photograph by Andrew D. Bernstein.

↳ HANES, K. JONES, NIKE, OAKLEY

J. PRESS

Jacobi Press, a Jewish immigrant from Latvia, opened his eponymous clothing shop on the campus of Yale University just after the turn of the twentieth century. J. Press's studious styles have largely gone unchanged throughout its century-plus in business. It still offers early signatures such as its sloping three-button sack suits, brushed Shaggy Dog Shetland wool sweaters, and traddy repp ties. These designs are not only J. Press cornerstones but also are the building blocks of the Ivy League look, which shone brightest along the East Coast of the United States in the 1960s. J. Press's

Yale perch was fortuitous, allowing the label to sell its wares year after year to an endless rotation of college students. Thus J. Press, perhaps more than any other label, became most associated with a crisp, collegiate look. Students are not their only market, though. For decades J. Press's conservative styles—such as roomy pleated khakis, gold-buttoned navy blazers, and those pastel-colored Shetlands—have attracted stalwart dressers of all ages to its stores in New York City and Washington, DC.

J. Press.
est New Haven, CT (USA), 1902.

Owners Irving Press (front left) and Paul Press (front right) posing with their store clerks, New Haven, CT, 1954.

Photograph by Nina Leen.

↳ ALDEN SHOES, ANDOVER
SHOP, BROOKS BROTHERS,
PAUL STUART

BILL KAISERMAN

A Brooklynite with no formal training, just a keen eye for good clothes, Bill Kaiserman began his career on the retail floor before designing hats under the brand name Rafael. By the early 1970s he had moved into menswear (and then womenswear in 1973), with a specialty in leather and suede outerwear. In the early 1980s the fastidious Kaiserman relocated to Milan to be closer to his production. He marketed his sexy clothes not toward flighty twenty-somethings but assertive thirty- to fifty-year-olds. In Kaiserman's world, men wore turtlenecks with oily black leather coats over the top and tucked ample ties under autumnal-colored suits that brandished broad lapels. This confident look proved popular—Kaiserman's suits were even worn on the era-defining television soap opera *Dynasty*. A self-professed fitness addict, Kaiserman also helped introduce the body-hugging leisure suit to the market.

Designer

Bill Kaiserman.
b Brooklyn (USA), 1942.
d New York (USA), 2020.

Ted Dawson, wearing a Bill Kaiserman trench coat, and Pat Cleveland, photographed for *GQ*, December 1973.

Photograph by Barry McKinley.

↳ ARMANI, BANKS, DIMITRI, LAUREN, WEITZ

IBRAHIM KAMARA

Drawing upon his West African heritage and his adopted home of London, stylist and editor Ibrahim Kamara's singular vision boldly reimagines both masculinity and style. Born in Sierra Leone and raised in Gambia, Kamara moved to London at the age of sixteen. He later studied at Central Saint Martins College of Art and Design while interning with stylists Barry Kamen and Judy Blame. In 2016 a series of images styled and shot for his final college project kick-started his career. Since then his work has pulled from elements of 1970s style while casting an eye toward the future. Ever playful, he has dressed men regally in both fresh-off-the-runway creations and crowns made of dried pasta. Kamara has also consulted for brands such as Kenzo and Hermès and in 2018 was appointed fashion editor at large at *i-D*. His editorials have appeared in *Vogue Hommes*, *Love*, and *AnOther*, and he has collaborated with photographers, including Glen Luchford, Paolo Roversi, and Rafael Pavarotti. In 2021 Kamara became editor in chief of *Dazed*.

Editor/Stylist

Ibrahim Kamara.
b (SLE), 1991.

"It's a Cultural Provocation: Ib Kamara," *System*, December 2019.

Photograph by Paolo Roversi.

↳ BLAME, i-D, LUCHFORD, PETRI

KANGOL

Badged with an embroidered kangaroo, Kangol could easily be mistaken for an Australian fashion brand, but its origins lie in Cumbria, England. The brainchild of émigré Jacques Spreiregen, the brand launched in 1918 with signature felted-wool Basque berets. Twenty years later Spreiregen adopted "K-ANG-OL"—an amalgam of "knitting-angora-wool"—as the brand name, and after supplying berets to the British Army during WWII, Spreiregen saw the opportunity to grow its appeal. Collaborations with designers, such as Mary Quant and Pierre Cardin (and

modeled by the Beatles), followed. Adopting the kangaroo logo in 1983 gave rise to a transatlantic appeal of "kangaroo" hats. But it wasn't until hip-hop embraced Kangol in the 1980s and '90s that its US appeal was cemented. LL Cool J, Grandmaster Flash, and Run-DMC all sported Kangol hats; they later appeared on Wesley Snipes in the cult hit *New Jack City* (1991) and on Samuel L. Jackson in *Jackie Brown* (1997). Made in England but made famous in New York, the brand's old-school vibe continues to win fans.

Brand

Kangol.
est Cleator, Cumbria (UK), 1938.

Brooklyn Style, 1985.

Photograph by Jamel Shabazz.

↳ THE BEATLES, CARDIN, CAZAL, FILA, TIMBERLAND

KARL KANI

Growing up immersed in New York City's burgeoning hip-hop scene during the 1980s, Carl Williams lacked the skill to break out as a rapper, so he turned to fashion as a ticket to join the party. Drawing inspiration from his father's dapper style, he started Karl Kani in 1989 as his own take on streetwear. Originally produced by his father's tailor, Kani's look arrived fully fleshed out with oversized, brightly colored, easy-wearing pieces. The signature Kani logo adorned each piece—a loose scrawl that became the brand's key detail. Modeled by a young,

largely unknown Sean Combs in 1991, the brand took off. A string of celebrated hip-hop fans followed: Tupac, the Notorious B.I.G., Nas, and Snoop Dogg were often snapped with the Kani script across their chests, and allusions to Kani appear in their song lyrics. Today talents continue to champion Kani, with A$AP Rocky, Migos, and Joey Bada$$ all rocking his streetwear.

Designer

Karl Kani.
b (CR), 1968.

Tupac Shakur (left) wearing Karl Kani, Mountain View, CA, 1992.

Photograph by Tim Mosenfelder.

↳ A$AP ROCKY, COMBS, CROSS COLOURS, FUBU, SHAKUR, APRIL WALKER

REI KAWAKUBO

A woman of few words, Rei Kawakubo answers questions via her clothes. Should the sloping Abe Lincoln–esque tailcoat make a comeback? Would life be better if men wore skirts? Should dress shirts come with tattered hems? By responding in the affirmative, Kawakubo nudges men deeper down the avant-garde rabbit hole. Since she introduced menswear at Comme des Garçons in 1978, converts, such as director John Waters, writer David Sedaris, and actor Daveed Diggs, have flocked to her imaginative wares, which allude to everything from weathered fishermen to Studio 54 revelers. Kawakubo also has a keen commercial eye, and in 2002 she introduced Comme des Garçons Play, a line of mainstream-friendly tees, sweaters, and Converse sneakers affixed with a cutesy heart-eyes logo. Two years later, with her partner Adrian Joffe, she founded Dover Street Market, a clutch of experimental multibrand retail shops that have revitalized the twenty-first-century department store as a playground for fashion discovery.

Designer

Rei Kawakubo.
b Tokyo (JAP), 1942.

Comme des Garçons Shirt,
Fall/Winter 2014.

Photograph by Jerry Buttles.

↳ ABE, CONVERSE, GREEN, NIKE,
 WATANABE, Y. YAMAMOTO

WISDOM KAYE

Influencer/Model

Model, stylist, and influencer Wisdom Kaye took the fashion world by social-media storm when he served looks from his teenage bedroom in Houston, Texas. Dubbed "the best-dressed guy on TikTok" by *Vogue*, Kaye has an eclectic taste in fashion—including a love for all things 1970s—and frequently challenges gender norms. He is known in particular for his ability to remix thrifted and accessibly priced garments into outfits that feel fresh and original. With almost 6 million followers on TikTok, and another 1.6 million on Instagram (and growing),

Kaye regularly communicates with fans, mining them for content. His most popular posts are his "challenge" videos, culled from questions from followers, in which he breaks down how to pull off seemingly impossible styles. Heels and a crop top? No problem. Combining red and green separates without looking like a Christmas tree? Easy. In 2020 the fashion wunderkind was signed by IMG Models and he has since worked with Dior, Fendi, Ralph Lauren, Coach, and Revlon.

Wisdom Kaye (Wisdom Uduebor).
b (NG), 2001.

Wisdom Kaye, documented in Houston, 2021.

Photograph by Cary Fagan.

↳ MASON, OWENS, SABBAT, SAINT LAURENT, SLIMANE

PATRICK KELLY

"I want my clothes to make you smile" was, in Patrick Kelly's own words, his raison d'être and his aspiration. Full of color, energy, irreverence, and whimsy, Kelly's designs and personal style did just that. Born in Vicksburg, Mississippi, in 1954, Kelly introduced his southern roots into his designs, most famously integrating and repurposing racist iconography and racially charged images, such as the golliwog for logos, Aunt Jemima bandanna dresses, and black baby-doll brooches. After a brief stint in New York in 1979, Kelly moved to Paris, where he, as a proudly gay Black man, skyrocketed to fame.

Although he primarily designed womenswear, his trailblazing designs and his own image influenced the masses. With a quirky, glamorous yet unpretentious style, Kelly often wore playful oversized overalls and baseball caps and preferred to travel by skateboard. In 1988 he became the first Black person (and the first American) to become a member of the elite Chambre Syndicale du Prêt-à-Porter. Kelly's career was hugely influential but painfully short. After producing only ten collections, including a collaboration with Benetton, he died in 1990 of complications from AIDS.

Designer/Icon

Patrick Kelly.
b Vicksburg, MS (USA), 1954.
d Paris (FR), 1990.

Patrick Kelly, 1989.

Photograph by Keith Beaty.

↳ BASQUIAT, JEAN-RAYMOND, W. SMITH, UNITED COLORS OF BENETTON

JOHN F. KENNEDY

The second-youngest man ever elected president of the United States at forty-three years old, John F. Kennedy was assassinated three years later, becoming fixed in the world's imagination as a symbol of youth and idealism. One of the first presidents to fully use the power of television, Kennedy dressed to reflect a casual elegance typically associated with preppy Ivy Leaguers and the East Coast elite. His Oxford shirts, penny loafers, white trousers, khaki chinos, and V-neck sweaters identified him—like his two brothers—as a Brooks Brothers man. At work he matched slim-fitting suits—expensively tailored with little shoulder padding, narrow lapels, subtle patterns, a single button, and creased trousers—to ties that were thinner than those of his predecessors. He made eveningwear his own: his tuxedos might occasionally be velvet, but they were always accompanied by a crisp white shirt (often from Charvet) and a fierce trouser crease. Strikingly handsome, he formed a glittering couple with his wife, Jacqueline, herself a fashion icon of the ages.

Icon

John F. Kennedy.
b Brookline, MA (USA), 1917.
d Dallas (USA), 1963.

President John F. Kennedy, Newport, RI, 1962.

Photograph by Robert Knudsen.

↳ BROOKS BROTHERS, CARTIER, CHARVET, G.H. BASS & CO., KENNEDY JR., OMEGA

JOHN F. KENNEDY JR.

Born in 1960, shortly after his father was elected the thirty-fifth president of the United States, John F. Kennedy Jr. was America's golden child. Following his father's assassination, JFK Jr. was raised by his mother, Jacqueline Kennedy Onassis, in Manhattan's Upper East Side. Despite being surrounded by enormous privilege with an Ivy League pedigree (he studied at Brown University), his sartorial style skewed more casual than his father's preppiness. His style was dubbed "reverse elitism" by a friend. Kennedy had a penchant for wearing a beret or backward baseball cap with baggy T-shirts, button-downs,

and chinos or sweatpants with such confidence and charisma that *People* magazine declared him 1988's Sexiest Man of the Year. In 1995, after a brief law career, Kennedy launched the political and style magazine *George*. A year later he married former Calvin Klein publicist Carolyn Bessette, and together they became America's most glamorous couple, often photographed for their sophisticated, stripped-down 1990s attire, with Kennedy in a sleek tuxedo or a boxy, wide-lapeled suit. Tragically, in 1999, they were killed in a plane crash while en route to Martha's Vineyard.

Icon

John F. Kennedy Jr.
b Washington, DC (USA), 1960.
d Martha's Vineyard, MA (USA), 1999.

John F. Kennedy Jr. walks his dogs in front of his Tribeca apartment, New York, 1996.

Photograph by Dave Kotinsky.

↳ ARMANI, J.CREW, KENNEDY, C. KLEIN

FEROZ KHAN

Actor turned director and producer Feroz Khan—born Zulfikar Ali Shah Khan—was a Bollywood legend. During his forty-year career, Khan's panache and unique sense of style made him an icon in his native India, drawing affectionate comparisons to Hollywood's Steve McQueen and Clint Eastwood. After his acting debut in 1960 Khan hit gold when he switched to directing: his 1975 film *Dharmatma*, based on *The Godfather* (1972), catapulted him onto Bollywood's A-list. Throughout his career, Kahn's suave look was a part of his persona both on-screen and off, but a fascination with the West led to his signature style: tight-fitting trousers, an unbuttoned shirt (with medallions nestling in his chest hair), cowboy boots, and a leather jacket. He completed the look with his love of motorcycles and even was noted to speak with a distinct American drawl. As he aged even his open baldness became a dramatic style statement. Khan was bold, brash, and charming, and his unconventional style left an indelible mark on Bollywood fashion.

Icon

Feroz Khan.
b Bangalore (IN), 1939.
d Bangalore (IN), 2009.

Feroz Khan, Mumbai.

↳ DEAN, C. GRANT, MASTROIANNI, McQUEEN, TIN TAN

TAKEO KIKUCHI

Alongside names such as Yohji Yamamoto and Kenzo Takada, Takeo Kikuchi was part of a crop of paradigm-shifting Japanese designers that graduated from Tokyo's Bunka Fashion College in the 1960s. While many of his peers would eclipse him on the global stage, Kikuchi struck out on an impressive career spanning more than five decades. In 1970 he cofounded the Bigi Group, a now-booming Japanese fashion conglomerate. Kikuchi left that umbrella company in 1984 and established his eponymous label. His designs, such as lopped trench coats and

black bowler hats, were austere and a bit dandy. He was liable to tailor a sport coat unconventionally or lend one of his silk shirts an animated motif. Like many of his peers, he also drew upon workwear and military influences, producing workaday chore jackets and olive drab outerwear. In 2004 Kikuchi stepped away from his brand only to return eight years later. In 2015 the brand reemerged on the runway at Tokyo Fashion Week, revitalizing his breed of joyously eclectic clothes.

Designer

Takeo Kikuchi.
b Tokyo (JAP), 1939.

Takeo Kikuchi Fall/Winter 2015 collection at Tokyo Fashion Week.

Photograph by Yuriko Nakao.

↳ FRUITS, TAKADA, WATANABE, Y. YAMAMOTO

NOBUHIKO KITAMURA

Nobuhiko "Nobu" Kitamura, the founder of Japanese cult label Hysteric Glamour, built his career on cultural references both niche and mainstream from Pop art to comics, as well as his childhood passion for American punk and new wave sounds emerging from 1970s New York. These inspirations, combined with Kitamura's training at Tokyo Mode Gakuen College of Fashion and Design, resulted in designs that were street-inspired and rebellious in spirit. After Kitamura graduated in 1984, Ozone Community, a youth-driven fashion company where he worked, encouraged him to design his own line, Hysteric Glamour. Rooted in antiestablishment iconography and graphic design, Kitamura created statement denim, T-shirts, parkas, biker jackets, and workwear, pioneering a new subculture with signature slogans and Americana prints. His designs attracted clients such as the Sex Pistols, Iggy Pop, Keith Haring, and Sonic Youth. To date, Kitamura has collaborated with like-minded partners, including the Andy Warhol Foundation for the Visual Arts, Undercover, and Supreme.

Designer

Nobuhiko Kitamura.
b Tokyo (JAP), 1962.

Hysteric Glamour X Empty R__M, 2021.

Photograph by Yuta Nishiya.

↳ NIGO, PENDLETON, SUPREME, TAKAHASHI

KITON

Founded as CIPA in Naples in 1956 by fabric merchant Ciro Paone, Kiton champions Neapolitan tailoring on the world stage, rivaling its sartorial counterparts from London to Milan. Paone changed the moniker to Kiton in 1968 (a nod to *chiton* in Greek, the tunic-like garment worn by Ancient Greeks). Building on the new tailoring aesthetic born in Naples, the Neapolitan style, Paone evolved the Savile Row-inspired creations of tailors Gennaro Rubinacci and Vincenzo Attolini and designed classic, soft suits that were made with refined fabrics and attention to detail. Paone's suits promoted a distinct nonchalance. With exclusive weaves, such as micron wool and rare vicuña (from their own mill), Kiton achieves these soft shapes with signature buttonholes and *barchetta* chest pockets, and each suit is pressed with a vintage iron for utmost softness. The process takes more than twenty-five hours to complete and can carry a price tag of around ten thousand dollars. The Kiton Tailoring School also supports the Campania region, preserving techniques upheld by their factory's four hundred tailors, who strictly adhere to hand-made methods and traditional tools today.

Tailor

Kiton.
est Naples (IT), 1968.

Tailors in the Kiton workshop, Naples, 2003.

Photograph by Vittoriano Rastelli.

↳ BRIONI, CANALI, CORNELIANI, ISAIA, RUBINACCI

CALVIN KLEIN

Through the closing decades of the twentieth century, Calvin Klein made simple and sleek designer clothes men bought as gladly as they did Armani and Ralph Lauren. He left his biggest mark on the least visible part of a man's wardrobe: his underwear. In 1982, two years after Klein kick-started a nationwide controversy with sexed-up CK Jeans ads starring a fifteen-year-old Brooke Shields, he turned to men's briefs. His white shorts with Calvin Klein ringing the waistband were stark, but the seductive Bruce Weber–shot ads, which presented modern Adonises such as Olympian Tom Hintnaus in nothing but the briefs, elevated underwear from something a parent or spouse might mindlessly buy to a critical, daresay designer item— and at the same time Calvin Klein underwear became nearly a fetish in the gay world internationally. This continued into the 1990s through ads showing Marky Mark and Kate Moss in CK skivvies. In 2003 Klein sold the label at an enormous profit to Phillips-Van Heusen, and the company's designer collections were continued with the talents of Francisco Costa, Italo Zucchelli, and Raf Simons.

Designer

Calvin Klein.
b New York (USA), 1942.

Tom Hintnaus for Calvin Klein, Santorini, Greece, 1982.

Photograph by Bruce Weber.

↳ ELLIS, LAUREN, McKENNA, SIMONS, WEBER

STEVEN KLEIN

Esteemed yet elusive, the New York–based photographer Steven Klein is known for his subversive view that eschews fashion's typically glossy, airbrushed imagery. Regularly shooting for international luxury houses, such as Louis Vuitton, Chanel, Armani, Tom Ford, and Christian Dior, his influential editorials also appear on the pages of *Vogue*, *V* magazine, *i-D*, and *Interview*. A graduate of the Rhode Island School of Design, Klein's early fine art background introduced him to distorted biomorphic paintings by Pablo Picasso and Francis Bacon. These raw, confrontational,

and risqué influences can be traced in Klein's work, translated into high-fashion photography. One significant shoot, a *W* magazine editorial featuring Brad Pitt, stripped away the actor's golden face, instead showing a bruised, vulnerable, angry side—an extension of Pitt's *Fight Club* (1999) character. In another notable shoot Kanye West was photographed in black and white for Balmain with searing eyes, metal grills, and S&M references. Frequently provocative, Klein's images offer a striking and unexpected take on the world's most recognizable names in fashion.

Photographer

Steven Klein.
b Providence, RI (USA), 1965.

"Man in Mask," *Arena Homme +*, 2000.

Photograph by Steven Klein.

↳ ARMANI, DOLCE & GABBANA, FORD, i-D, C. KLEIN, LOUIS VUITTON, L'UOMO VOGUE

NICK KNIGHT

British photographer Nick Knight's career includes everything from photographs of pressed flowers in London's Natural History Museum to campaigns for brands such as Tom Ford and Calvin Klein. In 1982 Knight published his first book, *Skinhead*, which dove into the subculture and led to commissions from *i-D* and designer Yohji Yamamoto. It was the beginning of an illustrious career in fashion photography built on a surrealistic, modernist aesthetic. Determined to push the definition of beauty, his shoots for Levi's in the mid-1990s featured models in their sixties and seventies. In 2000 he launched SHOWstudio, a platform to pioneer fashion film and digital image-making, working with the industry's top creatives. One of Knight's most fruitful collaborations has been with the magazine *Another Man*, for which he created dynamic and theatrical images of clothes by Rick Owens and Craig Green, as well as a notable series showing men in lingerie. Knight himself is renowned for a stringent working uniform: black brogues, vintage black or indigo 501s with a gold silk lining, and white shirts. He was awarded the OBE in 2010 for services to the arts.

Photographer

Nick Knight.
b London (UK), 1958.

Craig Green Fall/Winter 2015 campaign.

Photograph by Nick Knight.

↳ FORD, GREEN, HACK, C. KLEIN, OWENS, RANKIN

KNIZE

The Vienna-based menswear brand Knize was founded by Czech tailor Josef Knize in 1858. Knize specialized in equestrian clothes for the gentry of the Habsburg Empire. Nearly thirty years later it rose to become the supplier to the imperial family as well as the Persian and Ottoman rulers. The brand's modern success took off in the early 1900s when Modernist architect Adolf Loos designed a flagship store based on an English gentlemen's club (Loos later designed storefronts in Berlin and Paris, among others). In the tailor's heyday, the actor Laurence Olivier wore Knize, as did the Austrian painter Oskar Kokoschka, King Juan Carlos of Spain, and even Marlene Dietrich, who favored the label's lounge suits. In 1924 Knize introduced the first fragrance for men, Knize Ten—*ten* being a nod to their equestrian past, as it's the top handicap in polo—before being taken over by the Wolff family, who fled Vienna to New York City during World War II and opened a branch there in 1941. Today, the Vienna shop is an institution, and Knize is noted for the soft shoulders and relaxed fit of its bespoke suit jackets.

Tailor

Knize.
est Vienna (AUS), 1858.

French actor Maurice Chevalier leaving Knize, Vienna, 1959.

↳ ARNYS, DEVORE, GERNREICH, LANG

JON KORTAJARENA

"I can be anyone you want me to be." With his razor-sharp cheekbones, thick eyebrows, and toned physique, Spanish model Jon Kortajarena made a career out of his ability to channel a multitude of personas in his work. In 2004, at eighteen years old, he became the face of Just Cavalli. A stratospheric career followed, with runway appearances for Armani, Versace, Bottega Veneta, and Chanel, among others, and advertising campaigns for leading fashion houses, such as Tom Ford, Lagerfeld, and Etro. Kortajarena's work with Tom Ford in 2007 led Ford to cast him as the hustler Carlos in Ford's breakout 2009 film *A Single Man*. For Kortajarena, modeling was always a sideline to acting, albeit a highly successful one—at one point he was the highest-paid male model in the world. After more than fifteen years as a model, he now concentrates on acting—he appeared as Sasha, the host, in *Eurovision Song Contest: The Story of Fire Saga* (2020)— and his humanitarian work.

Model

Jon Kortajarena.
b Bilbao (SP), 1985.

Jon Kortajarena photographed for *L'Officiel Hommes Korea*, Spring/Summer 2019.

Photograph by Matthew Brookes.

↳ ARMANI, BOTTEGA VENETA, FORD, GANDY, L. SMITH, VERSACE

DAVID LaCHAPELLE

"I love drama and outrageousness. I love crazy scenes." So says photographer David LaChapelle, summing up a career that began at *Interview* magazine in the early 1980s, with Andy Warhol as his mentor. Before his stint at *Interview*, a fifteen-year-old LaChapelle ran away from his home in Connecticut to New York City, working as a busboy at Studio 54. The club's pop aesthetic and star-studded crowd became a huge influence. By hand-painting his own negatives LaChapelle produced vivid, provocative images that documented the craze for celebrity during the 1980s and '90s. His exuberant photographs of stars, including Mark Wahlberg, Elton John, David Beckham, Leonardo DiCaprio, Michael Jackson (as Archangel Michael), and Kanye West (as Jesus), appeared in publications such as *GQ, Details, i-D, The Face, Rolling Stone, Vogue*, and *Vanity Fair*. LaChapelle has been commissioned by the more cutting-edge brands, and his advertising campaigns, particularly for Diesel—one of which in 1995, daringly for the time, showed a same-sex couple kissing in response to the US military's Don't Ask, Don't Tell policy—have reframed notions of masculinity and pushed photography as activism.

Photographer

David LaChapelle.
b Hartford, CT (USA), 1963.

David Duchovny photographed for *Details*, October 1995.

Photograph by David LaChapelle.

↳ DIESEL, GQ, SHAKUR, WEST

RENÉ LACOSTE

Known as Le Crocodile for his ability to viciously dispatch opponents on the tennis court, René Lacoste was one of the earliest and savviest sportsmen to cross over into the fashion world. Lacoste took up the game at age fifteen but learned fast and rose quickly—notching seven Grand Slam wins in the late 1920s and earning the ranking of world's best in 1926. Toward the sunset of his career in 1933, Lacoste joined André Gillier to found La Chemise Lacoste, later just Lacoste. The company's signature was a fine-tuned tennis shirt with a cuffed, stay-put sleeve, a poppable pique collar

to block the sun, and an elongated "tennis tail" that stayed tucked in during a hard-fought match. Each polo shirt carried a crocodile emblem in homage to its inventor. In time the Lacoste line blossomed into a bona fide fashion label that was particularly beloved by American prepsters through the 1970s and '80s. In the 1980 pseudo-satirical tome *The Official Preppy Handbook*, a white Lacoste polo was worn by a tennis-racket-clutching country-clubber in a section dedicated to "Men's and Women's Summer Wear." While Lacoste himself died in 1996, his label and his logo endure.

Designer

René Lacoste.
b Paris (FR), 1904.
d Saint-Jean-de-Luz (FR), 1996.

René Lacoste at a tennis match, 1927.

Photograph by George Rinhart.

↳ FILA, HECHTER, PALMER, PENGUIN, PERRY

KARL LAGERFELD

Karl Lagerfeld—the man, the myth, the legend—was one of fashion's most prolific designers. Born in Hamburg, Germany, in 1933, he moved to Paris as a teenager and in 1954 won the International Wool Secretariat's design competition. Early on he worked at Pierre Balmain, Jean Patou, Krizia, Ballantyne, Charles Jourdan, and Chloé, before becoming the creative director of Fendi in 1965 and, most notably, Chanel in 1983. In 1984 he founded his own eponymous label. As fashion's chameleon, Lagerfeld made a name for himself with his signature style.

His earlier years were characterized by an almost dandyish look with three-piece suits and silk neckties. In the 2000s he shifted to wearing slim-cut Hedi Slimane denim and a Hilditch & Key shirt with a black blazer, sunglasses, fingerless leather gloves, and Chrome Hearts rings, becoming a larger-than-life persona. Lagerfeld's presence heralded a new era of creative director as fashion personality, paving the way for Tom Ford at Gucci and John Galliano at Dior.

Designer/Icon

Karl Lagerfeld.
b Hamburg (GER), 1933.
d Paris (FR), 2019.

Karl Lagerfeld at the Chanel Spring/ Summer 2009 haute-couture show, Paris.

Photograph by Antonio de Moraes Barros Filho.

↳ CHROME HEARTS, FORD,
  Y. SAINT LAURENT, SLIMANE

HELMUT LANG

A self-taught designer, Helmut Lang steered fashion into a crisp minimalism that would define the 1990s. Lang was deft at interspersing technical fabrics, such as bonded plastic, and ingeniuous details, such as covert carrying straps, into his clothes. But his designs always shone brightly and were easy to build a wardrobe around. His men's collection, which was introduced in 1987, drew upon military staples, precise tailoring, and an almost futuristic, sci-fi vision. Over the years, he filled the line with coveted creations such as paint-splattered jeans—Lang was among the first designers to comprehend that jeans could be a luxury creation—stark, fur-trimmed parkas, and face-lifted Crombie coats. He also pioneered the digital fashion presentation when, in 1998, he canceled his in-person fashion shows and went virtual. Despite Lang exiting his label in 2005 to become a full-time artist, archivists and fans—including Nick Jonas, Justin Bieber, Travis Scott, and A$AP Rocky—continue to collect his clothes. Lang's vision was both revolutionary and relatable, and rare is the designer today who doesn't cite him as a reference.

Designer

Helmut Lang.
b Vienna (AUS), 1956.

Model Ryan Locke for Helmut Lang Spring/Summer 1998.

Photograph by Marc Hom.

↳ A$AP ROCKY, JIL SANDER, MARGIELA, SIMS, M. WARD

LANVIN

Three decades after she opened a couture house for womenswear and childrenswear, Jeanne Lanvin launched couture for men in 1926. Lanvin's influence on men's clothing was minimal throughout the twentieth century, but when Dutch designer Lucas Ossendrijver was installed as the brand's head of menswear in 2006, it became a fashion force. Working alongside creative director Alber Elbaz, Ossendrijver's designs spearheaded many trends, including combining streetwear with more formal pieces and applying sportswear materials and techniques to traditional tailoring. Even though his approach was more modern, it captured a certain Parisian elegance. Ossendrijver put sneakers on the runway long before it was de rigueur and introduced a playfulness to collections with jersey track-pant suiting or sporty cummerbunds, all of which was balanced with the romanticism that was historically part of Lanvin's DNA. Ossendrijver's suits were often cut from sumptuous terra-cotta satin or beautiful, soft taupe silk—introducing a lightness and fluidity that would traditionally be associated with womenswear—and were worn by men including Matthew McConaughey and Robert Downey Jr.

Designer Brand

Lanvin.
est Paris (FR), 1889.

Model Alex Cavell photographed for the Lanvin Men's Resort 2016 lookbook.

Photograph by But Sou Lai.

↳ CERRUTI, LOUIS VUITTON, ROUSTEING, SAINT LAURENT

TED LAPIDUS

Known as the Parisian "designer of the street," Ted Lapidus democratized a haute couture sensibility and ushered in a new age of unisex fashion. The son of a Russian-Jewish immigrant tailor, Lapidus got into the family trade in 1951, though he really soared during the free-love 1960s. In a landmark move, he sold the same epauletted, shiny-brass-buttoned, military-inspired clothes for both men and women. His sandy *saharienne* (safari) suits in particular were ubiquitous on both sexes throughout the decade. Lapidus's high-quality clothes were machine-made, and he favored workwear textiles, such as denim. These egalitarian production practices helped bring his price point down, but Lapidus's work still had high-class clout. Stars including Alain Delon and Brigitte Bardot wore his fashions, and in 1969 John Lennon tapped him to produce a scandalous leather bag called Bag One to house a collection of erotic lithographs Lennon had produced. Upon Lapidus's death, French president Nicolas Sarkozy declared him "the poet of French couture."

Designer

Ted Lapidus.
b Paris (FR), 1929.
d Cannes (FR), 2008.

Ted Lapidus with a model, 1973.

Photograph by Alain Dejean.

↳ THE BEATLES, CHARVET, DELON, GERNREICH, Y. SAINT LAURENT

RALPH LAUREN

In 1967 the man born Ralph Lifshitz began selling curiously wide Polo ties from a single drawer in the Empire State Building. From that cubbyhole, Lauren began cultivating a fashion empire that reshaped American style. After a breakthrough selling those wide ties to Bloomingdale's, he launched a full men's collection in 1969, with sensational ideas such as a white flannel suit and corded madras shirt. By 1972 he had a freestanding store on Rodeo Drive and introduced the label's legendary mesh polos. Two years later he outfitted Robert Redford in *The Great Gatsby*.

Movies captivated Lauren, and his brand simmered with cinematic flair. His sloping, wide-lapeled suits and shimmering captoe shoes molded clients in the old Hollywood suave of Fred Astaire and Cary Grant. Sublabels, including Ralph Lauren Country and RRL, transported customers west through Marlboro Man denim shirts and blanket-patterned coats. Lauren had a seismic impact on street fashion: the big-logoed, color-blocked gear of the 1990s was beloved by New York 'Lo Heads. Having celebrated fifty years in business, Lauren is American fashion's greatest success story.

Designer

Ralph Lauren.
b New York (USA), 1939.

Ralph Lauren for Polo Ralph Lauren
Fall/Winter 1985.

Photograph by Bruce Weber.

↳ BANKS, BECKFORD, BROOKS
BROTHERS, LEVI'S, SULKA

QUIL LEMONS

In 2021, at age twenty-three, Quil Lemons became the youngest photographer to shoot a *Vanity Fair* cover. Lemons started taking photographs in high school and went on to study journalism and design at the New School in New York City. In between his studies, in 2016, he started the series *Glitterboy*, photographing himself in makeup and shimmering silver stars. Inspired by Frank Ocean, Lemons's work sought to challenge notions of hypermasculinity, particularly in Black culture, a theme that has continued throughout his career. Lemons's commercial work is similarly poignant and includes close-up portraiture of men, such as Yasiin Bey (Mos Def), Evan Mock, and Thundercat, that captures a tension between their physical presence and vulnerability. Lemons's photographs have appeared in *Vogue*, *Fader*, and the *New York Times*, and he has collaborated with a number of fashion brands, including Versace Jeans Couture, Valentino (he photographed people in his hometown of Philadelphia wearing Valentino's Bounce sneakers), and Awake NY in collaboration with Levi's.

Photographer

Quil Lemons.
b Philadelphia (USA), 1997.

Quil Lemons, New York, 2018.

Photograph by Mike Coppola.

↳ CARTER, LEVI'S, VERSACE

LEVI'S

Like many nineteenth-century fortune seekers, Levi Strauss—a Jewish-Bavarian immigrant who sold dry goods—headed west. His shop in San Francisco outfitted rapacious gold rushers, but Strauss soon struck his own form of gold. In 1860 he chanced upon *serge de Nîmes*, a robust, tightly woven textile now known as denim. Around a decade later, working in tandem with Jacob Davis, he patented the first pair of riveted blue jeans. Loggers, steer herders, railroad workers—everyone bought a pair. In the early 1900s European tourists brought jeans home from dude-ranch vacations. American GIs furthered their spread into Europe during World War II. In the 1950s the fashion of blue jeans eclipsed their function. On-screen James Dean and Marlon Brando performed in crisp Levi's. Jeans were about the only thing that greasers, mods, hippies, punks, and gay men who made the 501s part of their uniform in the disco years could agree on. By the introduction of casual Friday, '90s denim had gone mainstream. Today Levi's jeans are that rarest thing in men's fashion: a solid staple with maximum style.

Brand

Levi's.
est San Francisco (USA), 1853.

Jason Priestley, Jamie Walters, Luke Perry, and Dana Ashbrook, wearing Levi's jeans, photographed for *Esquire*, May 1992.

Photograph by George Lange.

↳ CARHARTT, DEAN, DICKIES, LEE JEANS

J. C. LEYENDECKER

German-born Joseph Christian "J. C." Leyendecker was one of the leading illustrators in the United States during the first half of the twentieth century. In that time he painted four hundred covers for magazines, including the *Saturday Evening Post* and *Collier's*, and created an enduring fashion icon. The Arrow Collar Man, who Leyendecker first drew in 1905 to advertise the Arrow shirt company, became such a popular character that he received fan mail. Like Leyendecker's other male figures, the Arrow Collar Man was athletic, strong-jawed, and poised—the kind of suave American figure who is said to have helped inspire F. Scott Fitzgerald's creation of Gatsby. The success of the Arrow campaign, which ran until 1930, made Leyendecker *the* choice for menswear commissions. He also drew the chiseled men who helped sell suits for the House of Kuppenheimer and long johns for the Cooper Underwear Company. Leyendecker dominated male advertising until the 1930s and '40s, when his career went into decline both because of an economic downturn and because the artist became increasingly reclusive. He did his last cover for the *Saturday Evening Post* in early 1943.

Illustrator

J. C. Leyendecker.
b Montabaur (GER), 1874.
d New Rochelle, NY (USA), 1951.

Magazine advertisement for
Kuppenheimer, c. 1920s.

↳ ARROW, FELLOWS, PAUL
STUART, L. WARD

PETER LINDBERGH

Legendary fashion photographer Peter Lindbergh was known for his realism and award-winning, cinematic imagery. Born in 1944 in Leszno, Poland, Lindbergh studied at the Academy of Arts in Berlin, and was inspired by artists Vincent van Gogh and Joseph Kosuth. In 1973 he opened his own studio, contributing photographs to *Stern* magazine alongside other greats such as Helmut Newton and Guy Bourdin, before moving to Paris in 1978. Lindbergh's pioneering, postmodern aesthetic liberated his subjects by exalting the human spirit. His preference for naturalism sharply contrasted the heavily retouched, glossy images of the time. Primarily in black and white, his minimal photos exuded penetrating insights into diverse subject matters, whether 1990s supermodels or rugged men, as captured by his portraits of actors Brad Pitt, Adrien Brody, and Eddie Redmayne. Over his forty-six-year career, he contributed to *Vogue*, *Harper's Bazaar*, *L'Uomo Vogue*, and *Interview*. A recipient of many accolades, he received the 2005 Lucie Award for Outstanding Achievement in Fashion Photography. After influencing fashion imagery throughout his remarkable career, Lindbergh died in 2019.

Photographer

Peter Lindbergh.
b Leszno (POL), 1944.
d Paris (FR), 2019.

Alex Lundqvist, Norbert Michalke, and Mark Vanderloo, New York, 2000.

Photograph by Peter Lindbergh.

↳ AVEDON, C. KLEIN, LEIBOVITZ, L'UOMO VOGUE, MEISEL, RITTS, VANDERLOO

LITTLE RICHARD

The stage name suggests a small stature, but his larger-than-life personality, raucous music, androgynous looks, and hyperflamboyant attire made Little Richard a true rock 'n' roll icon. His first major single, "Tutti Frutti," released in 1955, was an instant success in the US and UK. Richard's boxy suits, brogues, towering pompadour, pencil mustache, and makeup thrust a radical queer sensibility into the mainstream. Richard began referring to himself as the king *and* queen of rock 'n' roll, and fans lapped it up. In the 1960s Richard's appearance became more daring, aided by the Detroit costumer Melvin

James: sequined crop tops, vividly colored jumpsuits, Cuban heels, silk scarves, pompadour wigs, turbans, and even more makeup. With innumerable Little Richard looks to mine for inspiration, the list of performers indebted to his showmanship and sartorial swagger is long—James Brown, Jimi Hendrix, David Bowie, Mick Jagger, Prince, Lil Nas X, and Bruno Mars, to name a few. Up until his death in 2020 at the age of eighty-seven, Richard always expressed self-confidence through his fierce style, proclaiming in an interview that he was the best-looking man in the business.

Icon

Little Richard (Richard Wayne Penniman).
b Macon, GA (USA), 1932.
d Tullahoma, TN (USA), 2020.

Little Richard, Copenhagen, 1975.

Photograph by Jorgen Angel.

↳ BOWIE, BROWN, CALLOWAY, HENDRIX, PRINCE

L.L.BEAN

An avid outdoorsman, Leon Leonwood Bean created his company's first product, the rubber-bottomed Maine Hunting Shoe (later renamed simply the Bean Boots) in 1911. The waterproof, ankle-high clompers were a swift mail-order success, and suddenly, the wilderness enthusiast was a clothing entrepreneur. Over the next few decades, Bean's brand rolled out beloved gear catering to outdoorsy types, such as its pocket-packed field coat, the carryall Boat and Tote, and the crunchy chamois shirt. In the latter half of the twentieth century, L.L.Bean's wares were snatched up by style-minded prepsters embracing a traditional East Coast image. The 1980s cheeky tome *The Official Preppy Handbook* classified Bean as "nothing less than Prep mecca." Though a large chunk of Bean's business remains focused on campers looking for their next fleece or galoshes, its recent higher-end line L.L.Bean Signature and a collaboration with New York designer Todd Snyder have brought the label closer to pure fashion for fashion's sake.

Retailer

L.L.Bean.
est Freeport, ME (USA), 1912.

Hunting outfit in red and black, checked hat, coat, shirt, pants, heavy socks, and boots, all from L.L.Bean, 1941.

Photograph by George Strock.

↳ CARHARTT, FILSON, PATAGONIA, PENDLETON, WOOLRICH

LOCK & CO. HATTERS

The world's oldest hatter, Lock & Co. has a predictably starry roster of clients, both past and present. Winston Churchill ordered his iconic Homburg and Cambridge hats there, and Admiral Nelson died wearing his famous Lock & Co. bicorne at the Battle of Trafalgar in 1805. Founded in 1676, Lock & Co.'s location on St. James's Street, which opened in 1765, made them perfectly placed to serve royalty, aristocracy, and the growing middle classes. The shop attracted notoriously stylish men from Beau Brummell to, more than a century later, the Duke of Windsor. Lock and Co.'s most recognizable style is arguably the bowler. Commissioned by Edward Coke as a hat for his gamekeepers at the Holkham Estate in Norfolk, the prototype was made in 1849 by Lock & Co.'s chief hatmaker, Thomas Bowler. To test its sturdiness, Coke jumped on it; the bowler passed the test. The hat has since been known as both a Bowler and a Coke, and is still worn by the gamekeepers at Holkham. Today the shop continues to make traditional trilbies, fedoras, and flat caps in British tweeds, as well as panama hats during the summer months.

Milliner

Lock & Co. Hatters.
est London (UK), 1676.

A hatmaker uses a mechanical top hat for measuring a customer's head at Lock & Co. Hatters, London, 1969.

Photograph by Norman Potter.

↳ BEATON, BRUMMELL, WILDE, DUKE OF WINDSOR

ANTONIO LOPEZ

Beginning in the early 1960s, when fashion illustration remained an influential medium, Antonio Lopez—working with his art director and onetime lover, Juan Ramos—was one of the form's most influential exponents. Lopez became an in-house illustrator at *Women's Wear Daily* in 1962 before becoming a freelancer. He went on to work for publications including *GQ*, *Vogue*, *Interview*, *Intro*, and *McCall's*. In a commission for the *New York Times* in 1963, Lopez ditched the traditional long-limbed models of fashion illustration for thicker figures inspired by the work

of Fernand Léger. His psychedelic colors, bold Cubist-inspired strokes, and sharp edges made him popular among leading designers—he had a close association with Karl Lagerfeld—as did his distinctive "street" feel drawn from break-dancers and the early 1980s Rock Steady Crew, a hip-hop group from the Bronx. Lopez's work was also popular among advertisers, who understood the power of his sketches, and he drew campaigns for Bloomingdale's and Missoni, among others.

Illustrator

Antonio Lopez.
b Utuado (PR), 1943.
d Los Angeles (USA), 1987.

"Patterns and Textures in Hand Knits," *GQ*, May 1984.

Illustration by Antonio Lopez.

↳ GQ, HALSTON, LAGERFELD, LEYENDECKER, MELENDEZ, MISSONI

JERRY LORENZO

Founder of Los Angeles–based menswear brand Fear of God, Jerry Lorenzo has been threading the needle of luxury streetwear since 2012. As a fashion neophyte with no formal training, he got his start consulting for Kanye West (via Virgil Abloh's recommendation). Over three and a half years Lorenzo helped shape the radically dark visual language of the 2013 Yeezus tour, and contributed to West's A.P.C. collaborations and the first two seasons of his eponymous line, Yeezy. Lorenzo's work for Fear of God built on the style he developed with West: elongated silhouettes, slouchy bomber jackets, and shredded jeans. These quickly became bestsellers at high-end stores, such as Barneys New York, and popular with tastemaking celebs, including Jay-Z, John Mayer, and Rihanna. Meanwhile his retro basketball sneaker silhouettes, such as the 1987 collection, have led to coveted collaborations with Adidas. Recently Lorenzo's designs have transitioned from a youthful edge to a look that's more mature, showing Italian knits and lounge suits alongside the casual clothes that first brought him to the fashion world's attention.

Designer

Jerry Lorenzo.
b Sacramento, CA (USA), 1977.

Fear of God Seventh Collection for Ssense, 2020.

Photograph by Gregory Harris.

↳ ABLOH, ADDY, ADIDAS, JAY-Z, NIGO, NIKE, WEST, P. WILLIAMS

LORO PIANA

Purveyors of discreet luxury, the generations-old textile maker Loro Piana is based in northern Italy's Piedmont region. Founded in 1924 by Pietro Loro Piana, the company was built on his family's legacy as wool traders, dating back to the early 1800s, with the desire to create noble fabrics that epitomize excellence. In 1941 Pietro's nephew Franco inherited Loro Piana, even further establishing the company as a world-class supplier of quality wool and cashmere. Over the next three decades Loro Piana expanded from providing textiles to Italian tailors to creating craft fabrics for international names, from Savile Row tailors, such as Anderson & Sheppard and Huntsman, to designers Giorgio Armani and Yves Saint Laurent. In the 1970s Franco's sons Sergio and Pier Luigi took over the business. By the mid-1990s the brand established its own ready-to-wear line with hand-stitched jackets and knits. Today Loro Piana continues to sustainably source unique fibers, whether baby cashmere from Mongolia or vicuña from the Andes, crafting elegant, fashion-forward designs.

Designer Brand

Loro Piana.
est Quarona (IT), 1924.

Loro Piana Fall/Winter 2017 campaign.

Photograph by Boo George.

↳ ANDERSON & SHEPPARD,
ARMANI, HUNTSMAN,
Y. SAINT LAURENT

LOUIS VUITTON

Louis Vuitton is the luggage brand that could. Vuitton, the man, created his eponymous company in 1854, sensing a dearth of high-quality luggage on the market. His oversized flat-top trunks became a favorite of moneyed travelers, who carted (or rather had porters cart) the cases onto transatlantic ships and trains the world over. In 1888 Vuitton's son, Georges, introduced the checkerboard monogrammed Damier canvas, further ingraining his luggage as a highly recognizable status symbol. For decades Vuitton's product line grew, encompassing everything from wallets to packable armoires and picnic sets. In 1987 Vuitton merged with Moët Hennessy to form the LVMH Group, which today is the world's most valuable luxury conglomerate. Vuitton didn't enter the clothing sphere, though, until 1997, when then–artistic director Marc Jacobs designed the brand's first ready-to-wear lines. Vuitton's menswear has flourished under Kim Jones and now Virgil Abloh, both of whom found ways to deftly marry the label's globetrotting heritage with a contemporary streetwise vision.

Designer Brand

Louis Vuitton.
est Paris (FR), 1854.

Jacques Chazot with a Louis Vuitton monogram keepall, 1965.

Photograph by Giovanni Coruzzi.

↳ ABLOH, GOYARD, JACOBS, K. JONES

GLEN LUCHFORD

British fashion photographer Glen Luchford became one of the industry's preeminent figures after coming on the scene in the 1990s. Luchford first began photographing skateboarders in his hometown of Brighton before moving in the late 1980s to London, where he was surrounded by the city's nightlife and acid house scene. Luchford is known for championing the '90s grunge aesthetic with stylist Melanie Ward and photographer David Sims during his early image-making days at *The Face* (his first commission captured the Stone Roses). Since then his remarkable

career has included working with Prada in the late '90s and masterfully reinventing Gucci's image with the Italian label's creative director Alessandro Michele beginning in 2015. Creating his signature narrative-based compositions, Luchford's disparate influences include the film artistry of Hong Kong director Wong Kar-wai and American cult sci-fi movies such as 1956's *Forbidden Planet*. He is a longtime collaborator with Rag & Bone and has photographed editorials for magazines including *Love*, *Dazed*, *Self Service*, and *i-D*.

Photographer

Glen Luchford.
b Brighton, England (UK), 1968.

"The Wedding," photographed for *Self Service Magazine*, June 2017.

Photograph by Glen Luchford.

↳ BIRD, THE FACE, MICHELE, PRADA, RAG & BONE, M. WARD

Cover of the September 1998 issue of *L'Uomo Vogue*.

L'UOMO VOGUE

Created by Flavio Lucchini in 1967, *L'Uomo Vogue* was Condé Nast's first men's edition of *Vogue*. Originally a supplement to *Vogue Italia*, *L'Uomo Vogue* became a monthly in 1975, establishing itself as one of the world's leading authorities on men's fashion, covering styles, trends, and new talent. In 1994 the pioneering doyenne Franca Sozzani was appointed editor in chief of Condé Nast Italia, and later, in 2007, editor of *L'Uomo Vogue*. Not only did she establish *L'Uomo Vogue* as a global tour de force that championed a progressive view of the modern man, published alongside stunning visuals, but

she also elevated the Italian menswear industry. The magazine featured a wide array of faces, including Prince, Daniel Day-Lewis, Iggy Pop, and Nelson Mandela, and elevated photographers such as Peter Lindbergh, Paolo Roversi, Steven Meisel, and Bruce Weber. Following Sozzani's death in 2016, Emanuele Farneti took the helm, and two years later, in 2018, the magazine was revived as a quarterly. With a new look and editorial mission to redefine manhood as more inclusive and gender-fluid, *L'Uomo Vogue* has since released covers depicting Romeo Beckham and Timothée Chalamet.

Publication

L'Uomo Vogue.
est Milan (IT), 1967.

Cover of the September 1998 issue of *L'Uomo Vogue*.

Photograph by Paolo Roversi.

↳ LINDBERGH, MEISEL, RABENSTEINER, SELIGER, WEBER

KEVIN MA

Turning a passion project devoted to a love for sneakers into a sprawling multimedia empire, entrepreneur Kevin Ma founded Hypebeast in 2005. Inspired by youth culture and niche fashion trends, Ma studied business and psychology in school before landing a job in finance. He eventually left to focus on building a temple for OG sneakerheads like himself, capitalizing on an underground niche within menswear that had previously been underserved by mainstream publications. Now based in Hong Kong, Ma has transformed Hypebeast (a neologism once used to describe trend chasers) from a sneaker blog into an international lifestyle destination for all things hype—from streetwear style to limited-edition drops. It has garnered the attention of rappers Lupe Fiasco and Jay-Z, who were early supporters of the site. In 2012 Hypebeast expanded to include a digital storefront called HBX, which sells designs from Rick Owens, Adidas, Maison Margiela, Carhartt, Comme des Garçons, and Converse. Its multimedia content includes videos that detail brand histories and features interviews with creatives, such as Lucien Smith and designer Kerby Jean-Raymond of Pyer Moss.

Editor/Influencer

Kevin Ma.
b Vancouver (CAN), c. 1982.

Kevin Ma in his New York apartment, 2018.

Photograph by Nathan Bajar.

↳ JAY-Z, JEAN-RAYMOND, PALACE, SUPREME, P. WILLIAMS

CHARLES MACINTOSH

Designer

Charles Macintosh.
b Glasgow (UK), 1766.
d Glasgow (UK), 1843.

Macintosh advertisement, 1956.

↳ AQUASCUTUM, BELSTAFF,
  BURBERRY, CORDINGS,
  HERMÈS, GUCCI, LOUIS
  VUITTON, MARGIELA

The waterproof coat that Charles Macintosh invented became such a global success story that nearly any rainproof outerwear would come to be known as a "mac." In 1824 the Scottish chemist-turned-inventor discovered the technique of sandwiching a layer of rubber between two layers of fabric, thus making it waterproof. Macintosh patented his work and a year later sold his first design. Six years later, in 1830, he began working with Thomas Hancock, a clothing company based in Manchester that specialized in rubber, and by 1843 they had developed clothes using vulcanized rubber, which made their designs much more pleasant to wear. In the following decades, the rubberized coat became a staple for the British Army.

By the 1960s the streamlined single-breasted mac became a street-fashion hit popularized by mods and actors, such as Michael Caine, who wore a similar design in *The Ipcress File* (1965). The brand, today known as Mackintosh, has undergone a twenty-first-century revival—bought out first by senior staff members and then, in 2007, by Yagi Tsusho—and has collaborated with luxury labels, including Gucci, Hermès, Balenciaga, Maison Margiela, and Louis Vuitton.

MALCOLM X

Civil rights activist Malcolm X developed a style that allowed his powerful message to be seen as well as heard. It was sartorial subversion at its finest; he wore the classic stylings of the establishment: modest black or brown plaid single-breasted suits, white tab-collar shirts, and skinny ties, often topped off with a fedora hat and his characteristic browline glasses. After a wild youth—he was jailed for larceny, stealing partly to finance his taste in expensive zoot suits—Malcolm joined the Nation of Islam. He came to understand the power of controlling his own image and

style in a way that later inspired Black activists and hip-hop artists, including the Roots and Boogie Down Productions. Malcolm's life was cut short when he was assassinated in 1965, but his family has continued his legacy, recently with a fashion-minded endeavor. In 2018 Malcolm's daughters released a clothing collection to honor their father's twelve principles. Named Malcolm X Legacy, the designs—such as T-shirts and sweatshirts—bear their father's messages, including "By any means necessary" and "A man who stands for nothing will fall for anything."

Icon

Malcolm X.
b Omaha, NE (USA), 1925.
d New York (USA), 1965.

Malcolm X, Chicago, 1962.

Photograph by Eve Arnold.

↳ ALI, AVEDON, BALDWIN,
   CALLOWAY, PARKS

MARTIN MARGIELA

Even passing fashion fans are aware of designer Martin Margiela's strict adherence to anonymity. The Belgian creative rarely granted interviews or let himself be photographed during the twenty years he ran his eponymous label. Instead Margiela let his clothes say it all. After graduating from the Royal Academy of Fine Arts in Antwerp (a year before the storied Antwerp Six) and spending two years working for Jean Paul Gaultier, he formed his label in 1988 alongside Jenny Meirens. Maison Martin Margiela, as it was known, introduced

menswear eleven years later. Dubbed Line 10, Margiela's inaugural menswear designs reverberated with slender denim, reliable leather jackets, and louche cream-colored suiting. Margiela's menswear aligned with the steely hipster look that was being propagated by bands such as the Strokes at the time. In 2009 Margiela left the brand he had built—now helmed by John Galliano—stepping away from fashion altogether. Despite this, Margiela's designs continue to remain quite collectible—often by a new generation of men who weren't yet born when he founded the label.

Designer

Martin Margiela.
b Genk (BEL), 1957.

Campaign for Maison Martin Margiela Line 10 Fall/Winter 2002 menswear collection, Paris, 2001.

Photograph by Jacques Habbah.

↳ GAULTIER, GVASILIA, LANG, OLIVER, WEST

MARITHÉ + FRANÇOIS GIRBAUD

In the 1960s Paris-based stylists Marithé Bachellerie and François Girbaud began creating casual denim wear for men and women, launching their label Marithé + François Girbaud in 1965. They quickly made a name for themselves with their innovative approach to denim, introducing stone-washing and designing baggy jeans in 1977. Their Closed denim range, launched in 1978, was technically experimental, incorporating hems that revealed a garment's precise construction. The brand expanded to the United States in the 1980s, gaining fans including Will Smith, Tupac Shakur, and Michael Jordan—it was particularly popular on the music scene. George Michael wore a pair of Closed jeans for an early Wham! television appearance. Girbaud's outsized Shuttle jeans—carpenter trousers with the baggy legs gathered by a series of Velcro straps down each leg—became linked with the emerging hip-hop scene and had a lasting influence on US urban style. The brand lost its popularity following the 1990s, but it began a resurgence in the late 2010s, with garments, both vintage and new, seen everywhere from the streets of Tokyo to San Francisco boutiques.

Designer Brand

Marithé + François Girbaud.
est Paris (FR), 1965.

Street style featuring Girbaud jeans during Tokyo Fashion Week, 2018.

Photograph by Matthew Sperzel.

↳ JORDACHE, SHAKUR, YAMANE

BOB MARLEY

A musical trailblazer, political activist, and spiritual inspiration to millions, Bob Marley brought the sounds of his native Jamaica to a world in need of sonic healing. Raised in the Kingston neighborhood of Trenchtown (at that time one of the poorest slums in the world), Marley first came to prominence in the 1960s with his band the Wailers. Their ska and rocksteady songs—and clean-cut mod style—soon gave way to the slowed-down and spaced-out feel of reggae, a genre Marley became associated with for the rest of his career. Inspired by the Pan-Africanist movement and ideas of Marcus Garvey, Marley had a penchant for revolutionary style—military surplus, denim on denim—but he was also a dedicated Rastafarian and ardent football fanatic. By the 1970s Marley had become known for his long dreadlocks, preppy sweater-vests, crocheted caps, Adidas Sambas, and signature red, green, and gold track tops, which allowed for impromptu soccer games during dull moments on tour. Marley's unique style boiled down to personal charisma and genuine feeling—a man whose clothes weren't for hiding or showing off but for expressing the way he wanted to live.

Icon

Bob Marley.
b Nine Mile (JAM), 1945.
d Miami (USA), 1981.

Bob Marley, c. 1980.

Photograph by Lynn Goldsmith.

↳ ADIDAS, CLARKS, HENDRIX, WALES BONNER

MARNI

Established in 1994 by Swiss native Consuelo Castiglioni, Marni was born as an offshoot of her family's fur business, though it certainly did not stay in the staid world of high-end pelts. Marni's collections moved nimbly, and by 2002, when Castiglioni introduced menswear, the brand was well-known for playful splashes of prints and unexpected hues. Marni's menswear maintained this spirit with arresting color-blocked sweaters, pastel-hued trousers, and easy overcoats in see-them-down-the-block patterns. Castiglioni kept a close relationship with the art world, collaborating with Richard Prince, British pop artist Sir Peter Blake, and musician/painter Kim Gordon. In 2006 Marni opened an online shop, a progressive step for a fashion label at the time. In 2012 the brand was acquired by Renzo Rosso's OTB Group, and Castiglioni left four years later. Her replacement, Francesco Risso, has favored a mischievous, almost childlike look typified by droopy, oversized knits, cartoonish patterns, and coats with raw, unfinished seams.

Designer Brand

Marni.
est Milan (IT), 1994.

Models backstage at the Marni Spring/Summer 2019 show at Milan Fashion Week, 2018.

Photograph by Martina Ferrara.

↳ COBAIN, ETRO, MISSONI, PRADA

ALTON MASON

American model Alton Mason is a poster boy for Generation Z. A backup dancer and student, Mason was scouted on Instagram in 2015—an overture he thought was a joke at first. Two years later he began an international career, becoming the first Black male model to walk for Chanel. His status was confirmed at the Models.com Awards, where he won Male Model of the Year, Social Media Star, and Best Street Style. Born to a former model and a professional basketball player, Mason traveled widely before the family settled in Arizona. His long-limbed saunter and natural athletic ability—he closed the Louis Vuitton Fall/Winter 2019 show with a backflip—have helped make him a leading social-media sensation, whose daily life seems to resemble the fantasies he creates in his fashion editorials. Now a global superstar, he has appeared in *Vogue*, *GQ*, and *Man About Town*; worked with virtually every luxury brand, including Tom Ford, Gucci, and Missoni; and been photographed by notable artists, such as Cass Bird, Luigi & Iango, and Giampaolo Sgura.

Model

Alton Mason.
b NE (USA), 1997.

Alton Mason photographed for "Air Apparent," *WSJ.* magazine, September 2017.

Photograph by Cass Bird.

↳ ABLOH, BIRD, ETRO, LOUIS VUITTON, MICHELE, MISSONI

MARCELLO MASTROIANNI

Icon

The greatest of all Italian film stars, Marcello Mastroianni embodied European, post-war masculinity: intense and cool yet delicate and discreet. The son of a carpenter, Mastroianni starred in 120 films over his career during the 1950s, '60s, and '70s, working with some of cinema's most acclaimed directors and leading ladies; he is one of only two actors to have been named Best Actor twice at the Cannes Film Festival. Mastroianni was always impeccably attired, on-screen and off. He played a playboy reporter in Federico Fellini's *La Dolce Vita* (1960), wearing sleek, tailored black suits with a white shirt—he favored a spread collar—and a tightly knotted skinny black tie. In the same movie, his white linen suit paired with a black shirt—and sunglasses day and night—represented the glamour and excess of an Italy that had finally recovered from the devastation of World War II. Mastroianni's career coincided with the growing importance of Italian ready-to-wear design, and he favored classic pieces, such as Persol sunglasses and Borsalino hats. Naturally, Il Bello Marcello's effortless elegance became a symbol of Italy's enduring appeal.

Marcello Mastroianni.
b Fontana Liri, Lazio (IT), 1924.
d Paris (FR), 1996.

Marcello Mastroianni, Milan, 1971.

Photograph by Angelo Deligio.

↳ AGNELLI, BORSALINO, DELON, KHAN, McQUEEN, PERSOL

MITSUHIRO MATSUDA

In 1964 Mitsuhiro Matsuda joined his friend and fellow graduate of the Bunka Fashion College Kenzo Takada on a journey to Paris. Though Matsuda returned to Tokyo shortly thereafter, the trip west had a profound effect on his career. In 1967 he started Nicole Ltd. (named after a model he'd spotted in an issue of *Elle* magazine while in Paris), which would rise to become a flourishing clothing empire that is still in operation today. In 1974, together with Takada and four peers in the Japanese fashion scene, Matsuda established Tokyo Designer Six, the city's first official fashion week. His collections—shown globally in New York and Paris—were a study in contrasts. His jackets and suits could be both fluid and harshly architectural. He favored lithe fabrics, such as silk taffeta, as well as hard, technically advanced materials, such as plastic. By producing everything from oversized, country club–inspired sport coats to embroidered western shirts and snap-neck sweatshirts, Matsuda was a designer who was impossible to slot into just one category or style.

Designer

Mitsuhiro Matsuda.
b Tokyo (JAP), 1934.
d Tokyo (JAP), 2008.

Matsuda Spring/Summer 1990 collection at Paris Fashion Week.

Photograph by Jacques Brinon.

↳ BEAMS, CHARIVARI, TAKADA, WATANABE, WEBER, Y. YAMAMOTO

MAXFIELD

Maxfield is the ultraposh multibrand boutique exemplifying Los Angeles's unique cultural current and cool. Founded in West Hollywood by creative director Tommy Perse, since 1969 Maxfield has pushed the all-black, punk style inspirations that have become popular throughout Los Angeles's moneyed denizens. The store was an early pioneer in bringing cutting-edge brands to California, including Giorgio Armani, Comme des Garçons, and Yohji Yamamoto. And ever since, its global, cultlike clientele has shopped the store's stock of covetable graphic hoodies, investment T-shirts, and distressed luxury denim. Vintage designs are also offered, such as collector watches, heirloom jewelry, and one-of-a-kind objects. Maxfield carries today's innovative labels, such as Virgil Abloh's Off-White, Haider Ackermann, Dries Van Noten, Rick Owens, Palm Angels, and Sacai. Los Angeles's glitterati, including Guns N' Roses, Justin Bieber, and Kanye West, are among its notable devotees.

Retailer

Maxfield.
est Los Angeles (USA), 1969.

Vidal Sassoon, shopping at Maxfield, West Hollywood, CA, 1993.

Photograph by Paul Harris.

↳ ARMANI, FRED SEGAL, JEFFREY, KAWAKUBO, WEST, Y. YAMAMOTO

JOE McKENNA

Fashion's superstylist Joe McKenna shaped era-defining Calvin Klein campaigns and minimal yet purposeful styling. Born in Glasgow, he grew up inspired by photographer Guy Bourdin and *GQ* magazine and left for London at sixteen. After a brief stint acting, McKenna began styling editorials for *The Face* magazine. In 1986 he moved to New York, working at *Vanity Fair* and *Rolling Stone*, and for Italy's *Per Lui* and *L'Uomo Vogue*, where he started his decades-long working relationship with photographer Bruce Weber. In their years of collaborating, they produced iconic campaigns for Calvin Klein and Versus by Gianni Versace. In 1992 McKenna launched his own limited-run, experimental magazine, *Joe's*, which featured interviews with figures including Miuccia Prada alongside photography by David Sims, Mario Sorrenti, Craig McDean, and Steven Klein. The former fashion director at-large at the *New York Times*'s *T* magazine, his styling has pushed boundaries, creating images that have a rawness and progressive sensibility, and have appeared in *i-D*, *Self Service*, *Love*, and *W*, as well as the campaigns of Saint Laurent, Giorgio Armani, and Jil Sander, among many other brands.

Stylist

Joe McKenna.
b Glasgow (UK), (Active 1980s–).

Valentino Men's Spring/Summer 2020 campaign.

Photograph by Hugo Comte.

↳ ARMANI, THE FACE, i-D, JIL SANDER, C. KLEIN, L'UOMO VOGUE, SAINT LAURENT, SIMS, WEBER

ALASTAIR McKIMM

Born in Belfast, Northern Ireland, Alastair McKimm is one of fashion's foremost stylists and has been a key part of the influential fashion magazine *i-D*, first as a stylist and most recently as editor in chief. His high-low styling works across the fashion spectrum. Inspired by youth and countercultures, his editorials have an irreverent, street-inspired look. After studying fashion design at Nottingham Art School, McKimm moved to London and began assisting Edward Enninful, *i-D*'s fashion director at the time. Since stepping out on his own, McKimm has worked with big-name photographers including David Sims, Craig McDean, Willy Vanderperre, Glen Luchford, Mario Sorrenti, and Inez & Vinoodh, and styled campaigns and collections for Calvin Klein, Saint Laurent, Jil Sander, and Supreme. In 2019 he was appointed *i-D*'s global editor in chief (he also served as fashion director in 2013). With McKimm at the helm, *i-D* has featured dynamic subjects, such as David Sims with son Ned, both wearing Palace, rapper Kevin Abstract, and award-winning skateboarder Tyshawn Jones. He has contributed to British *Vogue*, *Vogue Italia*, *Interview*, and *Self Service*.

Stylist

Alastair McKimm.
b Belfast, Northern Ireland (UK), 1978.

Nathan Westling photographed for *i-D*, March 2015.

Photograph by Willy Vanderperre.

↪ ENNINFUL, i-D, LUCHFORD, SIMS, VANDERPERRE

MALCOLM McLAREN

Malcolm McLaren didn't just witness a sequence of cultural recalibrations; he helped cause them. In 1971 McLaren and his then-girlfriend Vivienne Westwood opened Let It Rock on King's Road, catering to the rockabilly-loving, creeper-shoe-wearing teddy boys who were bouncing around London. In 1973, on a visit to New York, McLaren met the New York Dolls and began equipping them with their glittery glam-rock costumes. In 1974 he renamed his shop SEX, a protopunk pit stop with skin-tight bondage pants, tartan plaids, and tattered tees.

It was McLaren who convinced the Sex Pistols to form, led by front man Johnny Rotten. He managed the band and shaped their safety-pinned-together style. Post–Sex Pistols, McLaren continued to work with Westwood and emigrated to the United States to focus on his music career. Late in life he favored the genial subtlety of Prada and Dries Van Noten suits, and just before his death, McLaren released a collectible collaboration with Supreme.

Designer/Icon

Malcolm McLaren.
b London (UK), 1946.
d Bellinzona (SW), 2010.

Malcolm McLaren, 1980.

Photograph by Stuart Nicol.

↳ PRADA, SUPREME, VAN NOTEN, WESTWOOD

ALASDAIR McLELLAN

Alasdair McLellan arrived in London in 1996 after studying photography at Nottingham Trent University. He quickly began working at the ever-influential *i-D* magazine and has since shot for everyone from *WSJ* and *GQ* to Louis Vuitton and Calvin Klein. McLellan's images can be sparse and thus quite tender, relying on the clothes and the model—not complicated backdrops or camera trickery—to reel in the viewer. Through his focused lens, you can almost feel the texture of the flecked wool roll-neck sweater in one of McLellan's Margaret Howell campaign images or hear the

crinkle of the sheeny leather blazer featured in one of his shots for Berluti. McLellan has an uncanny ability to capture his subjects at their most natural—when Jake Gyllenhaal laughs at his camera, one truly believes the actor has never been happier. McLellan has also crossed over into the entertainment world, shooting the photography for Adele's album *25* and music videos for the xx. He has published four books, including *Ceremony* (2016), a witty documentation of fresh-faced British soldiers, and *The Palace* (2016), on the jocular London-based skateboarding brand.

Photographer

Alasdair McLellan.
b Doncaster (UK), 1974.

Model Tom Poppleton for Margaret Howell Spring/Summer 2018 campaign.

Photograph by Alasdair McLellan.

↳ BERLUTI, BURBERRY, GQ, HOWELL, i-D, LOUIS VUITTON, PALACE

STEVE McQUEEN

Dubbed "the King of Cool," Steve McQueen was not just the highest-paid actor in the world in the early 1970s but a fashion icon for his instinctive style and good looks. He moved effortlessly between dress codes, looking debonair in formalwear—such as his three-piece suits in *The Thomas Crown Affair* (1968)—and appearing ruggedly handsome in the battered leather jacket he wore in *The Great Escape* (1963) and his Western hat and cowboy gear from *The Magnificent Seven* (1960). McQueen's characters, often antiheroes who rejected convention but adhered to strong

values of personal honor, seemed to echo the actor himself, who after a tumultuous childhood found stability in the US Marines. McQueen's persona combined studied insolence with a cool mystique hidden behind his characteristic Persol 714 folding sunglasses. His enviable—and highly replicated—style turned many clothing items into staples for modern men, including chukka boots, Harrington jackets, Alpha Industries MA-1 bombers, and Belstaff Trialmaster jackets, as well as classics such as khaki chinos, white T-shirts, button-downs, and chunky knits.

Icon

Steve McQueen.
b Beech Grove, IN (USA), 1930.
d Ciudad Juárez (MEX), 1980.

Steve McQueen, London, 1963.

Photograph by Michel Descamps.

↳ ALPHA INDUSTRIES, BARACUTA,
  BELSTAFF, DEAN, PERSOL,
  ROLEX, TAG HEUER

STEVEN MEISEL

Photographer

Notoriously private yet hugely influential, New York–based photographer Steven Meisel calls himself the "reflection of my times." His determination to cast *just* the right face in his editorial and advertising work has led to the discovery of many of the most successful models of the modern era. Over his forty-plus-year career, Meisel has worked primarily with American and Italian *Vogue*—shooting every cover from 1988 to 2016—and *L'Uomo Vogue*. His sensitivity toward clothes stems from his early days as an illustrator for Halston and *Women's Wear Daily*, which still featured illustrations in the 1970s. Never one to shy away from controversy, Meisel has created some of fashion's most powerful artifacts, including Madonna's 1992 book *Sex* and, more recently, the 2016 *Vogue Italia* editorial "Boys & Girls," which beautifully solidified the embrace of gender fluidity in both culture and fashion today. From Calvin Klein to Prada, he has photographed a number of memorable campaigns, including Loewe's Spring/Summer 2019 men's campaign, where he wittily cast the model Oscar Kindelan as his personal clone. "What's better than one Steven Meisel? Two Steven Meisels," said *Dazed* online.

Steven Meisel.
b New York (USA), 1954.

Steven Meisel, New York, 1990.

Photograph by Ron Galella.

↳ ANDERSON, ENNINFUL,
   K. JONES, C. KLEIN,
   L'UOMO VOGUE, PRADA

DNR

Clothing:
Looks
for Lifestyles
Spring 76

Speaking Volumes

The vested suit continues as the bread-and-butter number for the clothing business. From a fashion item a season or two ago, it now makes up the backbone of the contemporary as well as mature wardrobes. For the contemporary customer the vest may be part of the ensemble concept, matching the pant or the jacket or it may be peaked, shawled or cut extremely low. For his more mature counterpart, the look for spring is much more conservative. Gone are the loud contrasting vests. They have been replaced by matching vests which give a totally sophisticated, if conservative feeling to the three-piece suit.

Left to right: Natural shoulder model in polyester/cotton poplin from Haspel Brothers. European model in polyester/wool stripe from Joseph E. Cohen & Sons. Rounded patch pockets tie together vest and coat in textured polyester woven twill from Johnny Carson by M. Wile. Shantung silk look in tan herringbone weave in textured polyester from Palm Beach Co.

ROBERT MELENDEZ

Despite the rise of digital photography overshadowing traditional fashion illustration in recent years, the work of Robert Melendez confirms the enduring authority of a hand-drawn image. Born in Florida, Melendez studied fashion illustration at Parsons School of Design. From the late 1960s onward he worked as an illustrator at *Women's Wear Daily* and Saks Fifth Avenue before changing focus to menswear at the *Daily News Record (DNR)*. During the 1970s and '80s he was privy to studio previews of collections from designers such as Calvin Klein, where he hastily produced initial sketches on-site. Melendez also regularly produced brilliant *DNR* menswear stories focused on notable names, such as Bill Blass, Emilio Pucci, Pierre Cardin, and Halston, with his palette alternating between dramatic black-and-white to full-color spectaculars. Other assignments included live-drawing outfits worn by revelers at New York's hippest fashion parties or the audience's spectacular attire at the 1974 Muhammad Ali vs Joe Frazier fight at Madison Square Garden. His drawings portray the epitome of metropolitan chic: long-limbed, broad-shouldered, and super-stylish men.

Illustrator

Robert Melendez.
b Tampa, FL (USA), 1944.

"Speaking Volumes," *DNR*, July 1975.

Illustration by Robert Melendez.

↳ BLASS, CARDIN, DNR, GELLERS, HALSTON, C. KLEIN, LOPEZ, PUCCI

MERT & MARCUS

In luxury fashion, the Mert & Marcus name is inescapable. You see it credited in jaw-dropping editorials and glowingly name-checked by designers, models, and celebrities alike. Their punchy reputation precedes them, but Mert Alas and Marcus Piggott are the high-gloss photographers behind the revered Mert & Marcus duo. After opening a joint London studio in 1997, the pair published their first work together in the British style magazine *Dazed & Confused* and have since risen to the upper echelons of high fashion. The two are responsible for dramatic campaigns by Gucci, Saint Laurent, and Givenchy, and shoot for top-tier publications, including *Vogue*, *Vanity Fair*, and *Interview*. They have also worked on projects by Madonna, Kanye West, and designer Riccardo Tisci. Mert & Marcus have helped push an artfully provocative aesthetic further mainstream, taking the torch from legendary photography auteurs Helmut Newton and Guy Bourdin. The duo has photographed the world's most famous models, musicians, and actors over the past two decades, fusing celebrity, sex, and art into fashion photography at large.

Photographers

Mert & Marcus.
Mert Alas. b Ankara (TUR), 1971.
Marcus Piggott. b Bangor, Wales (UK), 1971.

"The Forward March of Men's Fashion," styled by Ibrahim Kamara, *T: The New York Times Style Magazine*, March 2020.

Photograph by Mert & Marcus.

↳ DSQUARED2, GUCCI, KAMARA, SAINT LAURENT, TISCI

ALESSANDRO MICHELE

The fashion world waited with bated breath to witness Alessandro Michele's debut for Gucci in 2015. Stepping in to replace Frida Giannini, who had just been let go from the venerable Italian label, Michele was given but a week to pull together his first collection. In that memorable show, Michele placed men in pussy-bow blouses and women in wallpaper-floral suits. His sumptuous vintage-inspired aesthetic arrived fully formed. Though his name was not familiar to many outsiders until then, Michele had already spent more than twenty years at Gucci as an accessories designer and associate creative director. At the helm, he molded Gucci to fit his very particular vision. A scholarly designer, Michele's menswear draws upon a laundry list of influences, including postpunk musicians, such as New Order, thrift-store aficionados, and, controversially, even the attire of inmates at an insane asylum. The gender-nonconforming, splendiferous style has enticed many fans, including Harry Styles, Iggy Pop, and V of the K-pop band BTS.

Designer

Alessandro Michele.
b Rome (IT), 1972.

Alessandro Michele, overlooking Sullivan Canyon Park, Los Angeles, photographed for *Vogue*, May 2019.

Photograph by Tierney Gearon.

↪ BTS, DAPPER DAN, FORD, GUCCI, LUCHFORD, STYLES

MISSONI

Few patterns are as instantly recognizable as Missoni's rainbow-tinted chevron. Ottavio Missoni, a championship sprinter, met Rosita Jelmini at the 1948 Olympics in London. At the time, Missoni was dabbling in clothing production—he competed in tracksuits of his own design—and Jelmini came from a family of shawl makers. The pair married and established Missoni in 1953. Using machines, the ever-experimental Missonis poured out lightweight knits with multicolored zigzag motifs. They also employed flame dyeing, a process in which a yarn is only partly immersed in dye, thus leaving a white mark or allowing the color of the yarn to pierce through. The brand reached a peak during the 1970s when their splashy knits fit right in with the vibrant style of the period. In the late '90s the Missonis' daughter, Angela, took over the brand's designs, overseeing the creative direction until 2021. In recent years Missoni's menswear has evolved into pinstripe suits, tartan checks, and inky-blue tuxedos, taking the label well beyond its signature chevron.

Designer Brand

Missoni.
est Gallarate (IT), 1953.

Freddie Mercury wearing Missoni, Nagoya, Japan, 1975.

Photograph by Koh Hasebe.

↳ ARMANI, ETRO, MARNI, PRADA, PRINGLE OF SCOTLAND

ISSEY MIYAKE

A childhood survivor of Hiroshima's atomic blast, Issey Miyake left Japan for Paris in the mid-1960s. After stints at Givenchy, Geoffrey Beene, and Guy Laroche, Miyake started the Issey Miyake Design Studio in 1970. He took inspiration from the loose-fitting, utilitarian clothes of Japanese laborers but also embraced electric colors such as lemon-drop yellows and tomato reds. A breakthrough came in the 1980s when Miyake began heat-pressing garments, coating them in tiny, highly flexible accordion pleats. His ever-popular Plantation line debuted in 1981 with a collection of forty one-size-fits-all unisex designs. Throughout the '80s Miyake continued creating such fluid, genderless designs, notably the sail-sized Windcoat. In 1992 he created pleated uniforms for the Lithuania Olympic team. A year later he started Pleats Please, an ongoing line of pleated staples, and in 1998 he launched A-POC, an experimental diffusion line. A friend of Steve Jobs, Miyake made the Apple founder's trademark turtlenecks. Though he stepped away from the brand, Miyake is now a codirector at 21_21 DESIGN SIGHT, Japan's first design museum.

Designer

Issey Miyake.
b Hiroshima (JAP), 1938.

Issey Miyake.

Photograph by William Coupon.

↳ JOBS, KAWAKUBO, KIKUCHI, TAKADA, Y. YAMAMOTO

TAKAHIRO MIYASHITA

A cult designer if ever there was one, Takahiro Miyashita remains one of the more elusive and esteemed figures in the fashion industry. Born in Tokyo, he was—by his own account—a renegade youth, yet as a teenager Miyashita was already assisting on photo shoots for Japanese magazines. After working for Nepenthes, the Americana-infused clothier based in Harajuku, Miyashita started his brand Number (N)ine in 1997. The label was informed by Miyashita's own infatuation with American culture; for example, collections were inspired by the clothes of Kurt Cobain, Gus Van Sant's 1991 film *My Own Private Idaho*, and Axl Rose. A highly independent designer, Miyashita walked away from Number (N)ine in 2009, and a year later he started the aptly named brand The Soloist, a smaller operation that he could retain more control over. At The Soloist, Miyashita's work hit a new peak of craft and complexity through pieces such as angelic white floor-length pleated skirts, Wild West–inspired raw-hemmed lambskin parkas, and thousand-dollar patchwork jeans.

Designer

Takahiro Miyashita.
b Tokyo (JAP), 1973.

The Soloist Fall/Winter 2019 menswear collection at Paris Fashion Week.

↳ COBAIN, CONVERSE, FUJIWARA, NIGO, TAKAHASHI

BEPPE MODENESE

In Italy the "prime minister of fashion," as *Women's Wear Daily* dubbed Beppe Modenese in 1983, was a significant position. Modenese was instrumental in creating a ready-to-wear industry based in Milan and later became the honorary president of the National Chamber of Italian Fashion. Italy's "minister for elegance"—another unofficial title, this time from *Vogue*—was a familiar figure in the front row of fashion shows, notable for his immaculate suits brightened by signature red socks. A stalwart of the fashion industry since the early 1950s, Modenese first worked in fashion PR in Florence, then went on to launch MODIT in 1978 as a prêt-à-porter event alongside Milan Fashion Week. The event promoted local craftsmanship, and Modenese persuaded friends, such as the Missonis, to relocate their shows to the city and also discovered designers, such as Dolce & Gabbana. Giorgio Armani credited Modenese with making the "Made in Italy" campaign a global success. In 1985 Modenese was awarded the title of Cavaliere from the Italian government, and in 1994 he received the Ambrogino d'Oro from the city of Milan.

Icon

Beppe Modenese.
b Alba (IT), 1929.
d Milan (IT), 2020.

Beppe Modenese during Milan Fashion Week Spring/Summer 2016.

Photograph by Christian Vierig.

↳ AGNELLI, ARMANI, DOLCE & GABBANA, MISSONI, PRADA

MONCLER

Founded in 1952 by Alpine climber René Ramillon and Andrè Vincent, Moncler was named after the Alpine town Monestier-de-Clermont, where the coats were produced. The company's quilted jackets were popularized when French mountaineer Lionel Terray wore them on expeditions to K2 in 1954 and to Alaska in 1964 and when Moncler served as the official sponsor of the French downhill ski team at the Grenoble Winter Olympics in 1968. By the 1980s Moncler's outerwear had become a European must-have in ski resorts and cities. Around the same time, its jackets also became a streetstyle phenomenon in Italy when teen *paninari* popularized Americana, and the colorful jackets or gilets were worn with denim and belts with large cowboy buckles. But it was when Italian entrepreneur Remo Ruffini bought Moncler in 2003 that the down-filled, zip-front Maya jacket became a global hit. Ruffini diversified the brand with myriad styles and clever collaborations with designers such as Virgil Abloh, Craig Green, and Junya Watanabe. The Moncler jacket became a staple that men would wear over a suit to work, on the weekends, or on mountain getaways.

Designer Brand

Moncler.
est Monestier-de-Clermont (FR), 1952.

Lionel Terray wearing a Moncler jacket, Alaska, 1964.

↳ ABLOH, BROWNE, CANADA GOOSE, GREEN, OSTI, WATANABE

CLAUDE MONTANA

Known as the "king of the shoulder pad," French designer Claude Montana brought fresh blood to Paris fashion with oversized jackets and well-defined shapes in the 1970s. In 1981 he created his first menswear line, Montana Hommes. His men's clothes were more unstructured and casual than traditional tailoring, with an emphasis on strong colors and material rather than details and cut; he was particularly fond of leather, a byproduct of his early work at the French leather firm Mac Douglas. Montana drew inspiration from military uniforms, bikers, and cowboys—even

for his womenswear—and his clothes appealed to the young and avant-garde. He was celebrated for his highly theatrical shows and for "designer" excesses, no expense ever spared for a show or event. Poor business management led to bankruptcy in 1997 and Montana's disappearance from the fashion scene, except when his work has been referenced by other designers, such as Riccardo Tisci and Gareth Pugh.

Designer

Claude Montana.
b Paris (FR), 1947.

Claude Montana Spring/Summer 1993 collection at Paris Fashion Week, 1992.

Photograph by William Stevens.

↳ DOLCE & GABBANA, GAULTIER, TISCI, VERSACE

JIM MORRISON

The enduring appeal of Jim Morrison, the lead singer of the Doors, who died at just twenty-seven years old, went far beyond music. During his brief but influential career, Morrison became a figurehead for the youth rebelling against the establishment during the Vietnam War and the May 1968 protests in Paris. His lifestyle set a new template for rock musicians, and Morrison's appearance was equally rebellious. Inspired by both Native American designs—he wore concho belts and chunky necklaces—and a rejection of gender-specific clothing, his uniform of unisex tunics, long, dishevelled hair, and tight black leather trousers aligned with the era's hippie and bohemian styles. Morrison was an enigma, celebrating both a deep interest in the philosophy of Friedrich Nietzsche and contemporary French existentialists alongside an unbridled hedonism. Designers as influential as Alexander McQueen, Paul Smith, and Hedi Slimane all later paid homage to Morrison, underlining his enduring legacy.

Icon

Jim Morrison.
b Melbourne, FL (USA), 1943.
d Paris (FR), 1971.

Jim Morrison performing with the Doors, c. 1970.

Photograph by Michael Montfort.

↳ COBAIN, HENDRIX, PRESLEY, SLIMANE, P. SMITH

FRANCO MOSCHINO

The ability to poke fun at oneself is a quality that few in the fashion realm possess—Franco Moschino was the exception. Born to a family that owned an iron foundry in the suburbs of Milan, Moschino followed his passions for art and illustration by heading to the city, where he worked as a fashion illustrator for numerous houses, including Versace. During the 1970s Moschino designed ready-to-wear for the brand Cadette, before Gianni Versace encouraged him to launch his own namesake brand. Founded in 1983 Moschino quickly expanded from womenswear into menswear, fragrance, and jeans, and the brand developed a reputation for sharp wit and exuberant, sometimes eccentric styles. Moschino was famous for trompe l'oeil designs—suits made from material made to look like a brick wall, shirts printed with poker card symbols, or pants covered in peace or dollar signs. His brand's ad campaigns (in which he would often appear), store windows, and even the clothes themselves were to the point, featuring blunt, literal messages tinged with social activism, such as "Stop the Fashion System" or "Save Our Sea." Moschino died at the age of forty-four in 1994.

Designer

Franco Moschino.
b Abbiategrasso (IT), 1950.
d Annone di Brianza (IT), 1994.

Franco Moschino backstage at his fashion show, Milan, c. 1980s.

Photograph by Ferdinando Scianna.

↳ MISSONI, PALACE, SCOTT, VERSACE

TAKASHI MURAKAMI

Icon

Born in Tokyo in 1962, Takashi Murakami is perhaps Japan's most influential contemporary artist. A student of *nihonga*, or traditional Japanese painting, at Tokyo University of the Arts, he set up the Hiropon Factory in 1996, a studio workshop that is now known as Kaikai Kiki Co., Ltd. His radically bold and colorful pop aesthetic is equally provoking and profound, as is his celebrated personal style of clashing prints and layers, which has made him an unintentional fashion icon. A source of inspiration for Kanye West and Virgil Abloh, Murakami has attended the runway shows of Raf Simons, Off-White, and Dior. Having merged cutting-edge techniques and *otaku*, a youthful obsession with pop culture, with the high esteem of Japan's postwar artistic tradition, his public persona is almost a caricature of his own invention—bearded, bespectacled, and always grinning. Murakami has also dabbled in fashion, collaborating with Marc Jacobs's Louis Vuitton, Nigo's Billionaire Boys Club, Swiss watchmaker Hublot, artist Kaws, and Pharrell Williams.

Takashi Murakami.
b Tokyo (JAP), 1962.

Takashi Murakami after the Off-White Fall 2019 menswear show, Paris.

Photograph by Julie Sebadelha.

↳ HUBLOT, JACOBS, LOUIS VUITTON, NIGO, P. WILLIAMS

NIKE

Phil Knight, a University of Oregon middle-distance runner, and his coach, Bill Bowerman, founded Blue Ribbon Sports in 1964 to import Japan's Onitsuka Tiger shoes. But by tinkering with, of all things, a household waffle iron, the men began whipping up their own homemade trainers. In 1971 Nike (named for the Greek goddess of victory) churned out the first sneakers with the legendary Swoosh on the side. Like an Olympic sprinter, Nike took off. By 1980 it captured 50 percent of the US sneaker market. In the 1990s "Just Do It" was a household slogan, embodying the label's high-performance pitch. It didn't hurt that the shoes looked good too. Michael Jordan's signature high-tops became covetable fashion fixtures, sparking a collecting craze. Sneakerheads hoard extravagant Dunks, Air Forces, and Air Maxes by the closetful. In the twenty-first century, Nike has focused on partnerships with marquee luxury designers, such as Virgil Abloh, Chitose Abe, Riccardo Tisci, Jun Takahashi, and Rei Kawakubo, who put their own spin on limited, lusted-after Nikes.

Brand

Nike.
est Beaverton, OR (USA), 1964.

Kobe Bryant for Nike, Milan, 2016.

Photograph by Alex Majoli.

↳ ABE, ABLOH, ASICS, JORDAN, KAWAKUBO, TAKAHASHI, TISCI

TOMMY NUTTER

When the Beatles strode across Abbey Road in 1969 for their infamous album cover, three of the Fab Four were wearing Tommy Nutter suits. At the height of the Swinging Sixties, Nutter revived the fortunes of London's Savile Row, which had become synonymous with the best bespoke tailoring in the world but was languishing in the face of youthful informality. He brought a designer's sensibility to the precision of tailoring. Having worked in plumbing and architecture, Nutter undertook a seven-year apprenticeship at Donaldson, Williams & G. Ward, where he met his future

business partner, Edward Sexton, and learned the skills of traditional tailoring. In 1969 they opened Nutters, and those skills became the basis of a radical redesign of the suit: double-breasted jackets with oversize lapels and nipped-in waists to accentuate the wearer's shoulders, all in bold colors and checks. Nutter—with celebrity clients from the Beatles to Mick Jagger—made suits cool again. Nutter continued to design suits until his death in the early 1990s, although he and Sexton had parted ways after Sexton bought Nutter out of the business in 1976.

Tailor

Tommy Nutter.
b Barmouth Merioneth, Wales (UK), 1943.
d London (UK), 1992.

Tommy Nutter on Central Park West, New York, 1975.

Photograph by David Nutter.

↳ AMIES, C. BAILEY, THE BEATLES, JAGGER, SEXTON, P. SMITH

OAKLEY

In 1975 Jim Jannard created Oakley (named after his dog), selling motorcycle gear from the back seat of his car in Southern California. He eventually moved into making accessories, such as handlebar grips, before segueing into performance-based optics. His use of innovative technology to create wearable, sporty styles of sunglasses attracted the world's leading athletes during the 1980s. In 1994 the brand launched its ubiquitous O logo on Eye Jacket frames, and made its mark with campaigns featuring Michael Jordan (fellow Chicago Bulls Dennis Rodman and Scottie Pippen also sported Oakleys). The sunglasses appeared on the silver screen too, with cameos in 1999's *Fight Club*, worn by Brad Pitt, and 2000's *Mission: Impossible 2*, in which Tom Cruise dons self-destructing Oakley Romeo X-Metal shades. Having pioneered High Definition Optics in a wide array of colors and styles—from all-metal wire frames to snow goggles—Oakley transitioned naturally into fashion. The brand is beloved by Patrick Mahomes and Pharrell Williams and has produced collections with Kith and Vetements and a multifunctional apparel line with A-Cold-Wall*'s Samuel Ross.

Accessory Design

Oakley.
est Irvine, CA (USA), 1975.

Michael Jordan at the Bob Hope Chrysler Classic golf tournament, Palm Springs, CA, 1999.

Photograph by J. D. Cuban.

↳ A-COLD-WALL*, GVASALIA, JORDAN, P. WILLIAMS

GLENN O'BRIEN

Editor/Writer

New York icon, cultural influencer, and rebellious raconteur Glenn O'Brien made a name for himself as an editor and writer on art, music, and fashion. Originally from Ohio, O'Brien, after moving to New York, became part of Andy Warhol's Factory, and in 1970 Warhol hired him as editor of *Interview* magazine. Although he left the position in 1974, he returned over the following decades, contributing articles, including his "Glenn O'Brien's Beat" column, dedicated to punk and new wave music. He went on to work at publications including *Rolling Stone, High Times, Artforum,* and *Details,*

and hosted the show *TV Party* from 1978 to 1982, with guest stars including David Byrne, David Bowie, Iggy Pop, and Robert Mapplethorpe. Celebrated for his humorous wit and expansive erudition, O'Brien became *GQ*'s original Style Guy in 2000, imparting his sartorial wisdom from practical advice about custom Charvet shirts and tuxedos (his favorite dinner jacket was a peak-lapel style made by Anderson & Sheppard) to more philosophical conversations, inspired by topics such as wearing chinos to a wedding. The author of several books, O'Brien published the popular *How to Be a Man* in 2011.

Glenn O'Brien.
b Cleveland, OH (USA), 1947.
d New York (USA), 2017.

Glenn O'Brien and Andy Warhol at the Factory at 860 Broadway, New York, 1979.

Photograph by Kate Simon.

↳ BARNEYS NEW YORK, BASQUIAT, DETAILS, GQ

OCEAN PACIFIC

Brand

Ocean Pacific.
est San Diego (USA), 1972.

Ocean Pacific advertisement, c. 1980s.

↳ FRED SEGAL, OAKLEY, SPEEDO

In the 1970s shorts were short, hair was long, and Ocean Pacific was riding high. Started by Jim Jenks, a San Diego surfer, Op—as it was known—aimed to make clothes for those who spent most of their waking hours by the beach, or at least wished they did. Its ads touted "radical designs, outrageous colors, and performance," and its wares were modeled by freestyle skateboarders and shaggy-mopped surfers. The Op look was energetic, full of striped shirts in primary colors, pastel chinos, and the label's most famous design: skimpy corduroy shorts. Those thigh-flashing hot pants (made for men and women) stretched the limits of modesty at the time yet remain in demand today, with vintage dealers selling them for well over a hundred dollars. Op made coastal living aspirational, paving the way for latter-day clothing brands such as Aviator Nation, Elder Statesman, and Pilgrim Surf Supply. Op was acquired in the 2000s by the Iconix Brand Group and no longer has the sought-after sunny image it once had. But if you're patient—and daring—you can still find men's shorts from its heyday on eBay.

MOWALOLA OGUNLESI

Born and raised in Nigeria, Mowalola Ogunlesi left for England at the age of twelve to attend boarding school and later studied fashion at London's Central Saint Martins College of Art and Design. Ogunlesi's eponymous unisex label, Mowalola—which debuted with "Psychedelic," her 2017 graduate menswear collection—is rich in color, attitude, and sexiness. Inspired by Lagos car fanatics and the country's psychedelic rock scene of the 1970s, her gender-fluid design approach was translated in sleek low-cut leather pants and vibrantly hued cropped leather jackets. Subsequent Mowalola collections have triumphed on the runways during London Fashion Week. For Spring/Summer 2020 she memorably explored love's darker side—think full-length leather coats in electric colors (lime green, red, yellow, and pink), some adorned with spray-painted faces; tight pants teamed with backless halter-neck tops featuring cutouts and glossy finishes; and cropped tees printed with luscious lips. Celebrity admirers of Mowalola's work include Steve Lacy, Skepta, and Drake. Kanye West is also a massive fan—in 2020 he appointed Mowalola design director of his Yeezy partnership with Gap.

Designer

Mowalola Ogunlesi.
b Lagos (NG), 1995.

"From Lagos with Love," featuring Mowalola trousers and boots, photographed for *More or Less* magazine, Spring/Summer 2019.

Photograph by Vicki King.

↳ A$AP ROCKY, GAP, IZE, WEST

SHAYNE OLIVER

In 2017 Shayne Oliver shocked the fashion world by announcing that his haute streetwear brand Hood By Air would be going on indefinite hiatus. In less than a decade it had evolved from being something whispered about in Brooklyn's underground GHE20G0TH1K nightlife scene to becoming one of the most coveted invitations of New York Fashion Week—in 2014 it won the LVMH Special Jury Prize, followed by a CFDA Award for menswear a year later. Since its launch in 2006 club kids, celebrities, and department stores alike have clamored to get their hands on Hood

By Air, known for its bold graphics and logos, unhinged proportions, utilitarian elements, and gender-bending ethos. Oliver is responsible for creating an oversize sweatshirt (worn by names such as Kendrick Lamar, Victor Cruz, and Drake) that spawned a thousand lookalikes. While his brand was placed on hold, Oliver took his talents elsewhere, and created capsule collections for a variety of esteemed labels, including Longchamp and Helmut Lang. After four years of consulting Oliver revealed in 2021—to much fanfare—that he was relaunching the Hood By Air brand.

Designer

Shayne Oliver.
b Minnesota (USA), 1988.

Hood By Air Spring/Summer 2017 collection at New York Fashion Week.

Photograph by Kate Warren.

↳ A-COLD-WALL*, A$AP ROCKY, ABLOH, JEAN-RAYMOND, LANG, MARGIELA

OMEGA

Omega has been breaking boundaries with its horological precision since 1848, when Louis Brandt, a fledgling watchmaker, opened a workshop in the Swiss alpine village of La Chaux-de-Fonds. In 1894 sons Louis-Paul and César invented a nineteen-ligne caliber movement dubbed the Omega, as in crowning achievement. With accurate precision and interchangeable parts, this transformative innovation laid the foundation for modern watchmaking. As gatekeepers of time, Omega has clocked almost every Olympic game since the early twentieth century, even journeying to the moon in

1969's *Apollo 11* mission, when astronaut Buzz Aldrin wore the Speedmaster, now also known as the Moonwatch. The Seamaster, launched in 1948, is a brand classic, favored by Prince William and James Bond, who has worn Omega watches in every Bond film since 1995's *GoldenEye*. John F. Kennedy wore an Omega Slimline to his 1961 inauguration, and Elvis Presley owned a round-faced Omega timepiece whose bezel boasted forty-four brilliant-cut Tiffany & Co. diamonds. Today Omega's Co-Axial escapement befits stars such as actors Eddie Redmayne and George Clooney.

Accessory Design

Omega.
est La-Chaux-de-Fonds (SW), 1848.

Astronaut Edwin "Buzz" Aldrin, wearing an Omega Speedmaster Professional, in the *Apollo 11* lunar module prior to the moon landing, 1969.

Photograph by Neil Armstrong.

↳ KENNEDY, PATEK PHILIPPE, PRESLEY, ROLEX, TAG HEUER

MASSIMO OSTI

Known as the Godfather of Sportswear, Massimo Osti was responsible for a staggering number of textile innovations throughout his career, which spanned more than three decades. He began making T-shirts in the late 1970s, becoming the designer of Chester Perry—later C.P. Company. In 1982 he started Stone Island, which specialized in upscale, progressive outerwear. An avid collector of military gear, Osti, early on, invented Tela Stella, a proprietary fabric created by stone-washing military tarps. Novel ideas poured out of him, including Rosa Gommato (a rubberized coating applied to jacket lining); the Ice Jacket, which changed colors with the wearer's body temperature; and the luminous Reflective Jacket. In 2000 Osti created the ICD+ Jacket, widely known as the first piece of wearable tech. His cutting-edge coats have been coveted by everyone from Italian *paninari* to the British casual subculture. Though Osti died in 2005, Stone Island jackets haven't lost their status and remain as in demand as ever.

Designer

Massimo Osti.
b Bologna (IT), 1944.
d Bologna (IT), 2005.

Man wearing a Stone Island sweatshirt and jacket outside of Woodhouse Clothing, Notting Hill, London, 1985.

Photograph by Graham Morris.

↳ ACRONYM, CANADA GOOSE, MONCLER, PARACHUTE, PATAGONIA, WOOLRICH

OUR LEGACY

Our Legacy's trajectory has closely followed the trajectory of men's fashion since 2005. The Swedish label's early collections packaged prim prepwear, such as cozy shawl-collar sweaters, tapered chinos, and unadorned knits, at a time when men the world over were clamoring for such things. Through the aughts, as a generation of men grew more confident in their style, you could feel Our Legacy—led by friends Jockum Hallin, Cristopher Nying, and Richardos Klarén—bursting out of its shell. A decade into the business, Our Legacy's collections were steely and cool with barrel-cut trousers, investment black leather jackets, and techy turtlenecks. In more recent years Our Legacy has come to look like a child of Maison Martin Margiela, with heavily distressed collections, risqué organza bottoms, and alluring Cuban-heeled boots. Shrewdly, its commercial collections still offer the reliable staples it perfected a decade ago, because sometimes a man just needs a good sweater.

Designer Brand

Our Legacy.
est Stockholm (SWE), 2005.

Our Legacy "Draft" Spring 2017 Collection.

Photograph by Erik Wåhlström.

↳ ACNE STUDIOS, LANG, MARGIELA, RAG & BONE

RICK OWENS

To see a Rick Owens runway show in Paris is to get a glimpse into another world. Angular-faced models clomp down the catwalk in tottering high heels, with architectural leather jackets, wide trousers, and slinky, skin-hugging knits draped around their bodies. There's always ample smoke and foreboding, bass-heavy music. For all of his otherworldly atmosphere, Owens himself is a grounded, affable man who grew up far removed from France in central California. After studying at the Otis College of Art and Design and Los Angeles Trade Technical College, Owens harnessed his pattern-making prowess to start his eponymous label in 1994. His first men's collection arrived in 2003, and since, Owens has fostered a cultlike community of followers in his monumental Geobasket sneakers, drop-crotch pants, and Stooges leather jackets. Owens also designs gallery-caliber furniture and in 2019 published two books on one of his great influences: Larry LeGaspi, the late fashion designer known for dressing the band Kiss.

Designer

Rick Owens.
b Porterville, CA (USA), 1961.

Rick Owens Fall/Winter 2017 menswear collection at Paris Fashion Week.

Photograph by Victor Virgile.

↳ JACOBS, KAWAKUBO, OLIVER, Y. YAMAMOTO

PALACE

Founded by Lev Tanju, Palace is the rough-and-rowdy skate clique that transformed into a coveted label. In the late 2000s Tanju, an ex-skateboarder and self-described bum, began creating graphics for friends' skateboards. Realizing the leap to a full-fledged brand wasn't that great, he asked Fergus Purcell, the former design director at Marc by Marc Jacobs, to create Palace's now-iconic Tri-Ferg logo, which he plastered onto shirts and hoodies. Much like Supreme, as Palace grew it fashioned functional but also quite imaginative clothes, such as GORE-TEX

Puffa jackets, Vivienne Westwood–style screenprinted denim, and eclectic camp shirts. Spreading its wings, Palace has partnered with Adidas, Dover Street Market, Ralph Lauren, and the cycling label Rapha. Yet its irreverence hasn't dulled; Palace graphics often intentionally contort the brand's name (i.e., Palafel and Palasonic), and the cheeky product copy on its website—written by Tanju—is infamous. One choice entry under a shirt: "If you buy stuff, I can drink more beer."

Designer Brand

Palace.
est London (UK), 2009.

Pro-skater Lucien Clarke and stuntman wearing Palace, photographed for *i-D*, February 2019.

Photograph by David Sims.

↳ ADIDAS, KAWAKUBO, LAUREN, McLELLAN, SUPREME, WESTWOOD

ARNOLD PALMER

Icon

A seven-time major champion, Arnold Palmer was the embodiment of a very particular era in golf fashion. Decades before the sport became dominated by gym-toned athletes in skin-tight techwear, Palmer, starting in the mid-1950s, played his way across the world in pressed, pleated slacks, mod mohair cardigans, ribbed mock-neck tees, and tidy Munsingwear polo shirts with the collar brazenly unbuttoned. He was a prismatic dresser, indulging in cherry red sweaters, robin's egg blue shirts, and yolk yellow pants. Palmer became a force on the course and a cultural icon who graced the covers of *Time* and *Newsweek*. In 2011, for an issue dedicated to the "25 Coolest Athletes of All Time," *GQ* placed a classic image of Palmer on its cover, showing the hale sportsman in a striped polo and trim gray trousers, with a close-cropped haircut. Palmer did start his own eponymous apparel line, but his influence on golf fashion can really be perceived in the recent rush of upstart labels, including Bogey Boys and Metalwood Studio, which offer the sort of trim polos and smart trousers that Palmer would've putted in decades ago.

Arnold Palmer.
b Latrobe, PA (USA), 1929.
d Pittsburgh (USA), 2016.

Arnold Palmer during play at the British Open, St. Andrews, Scotland, 1960.

Photograph by Jerry Cooke.

↳ CONNERY, KENNEDY, LACOSTE, NEWMAN, PENGUIN

PALOMO SPAIN

Spanish designer Alejandro Gómez Palomo thrives in the liminal space between masculinity and femininity. Palomo graduated from the London College of Fashion and soon after established his label Palomo Spain near Córdoba in 2015. His wild and fearless approach sets his work apart—from feather boas, pussy-bow necklines, lush embroidered capes, and decadent transparent bodysuits to peplum jackets and leopard-print heels, his menswear deliberately resists conforming to gender norms. In 2016 Palomo's first complete collection, "Orlando"—inspired by the title character of Virginia Woolf's novel of the same name—set the scene for the gender-fluidity that continues to underline his work. Not surprisingly these themes have won favor with men and women alike: Beyoncé put the label on the map when she chose a gown from its 2017 menswear show to introduce her twins. Since then Palomo Spain has attracted fans, including LGBTQ advocate Olly Alexander and musician Harry Styles, known for his experimental sartorial panache.

Designer Brand

Palomo Spain.
est Posadas (SP), 2015.

Palomo Spain Fall/Winter 2018 collection at Madrid Fashion Week.

Photograph by Javier Ortega Ponce.

↳ BOWIE, CRISP, FISH, STYLES

PANERAI

Founded as G. Panerai & Figlio in 1860 by Florentine Giovanni Panerai, Officine Panerai combines Italian sprezzatura with Swiss-built precision and a love for the sea. The company was the original supplier of diving watches and underwater instruments for the Royal Italian Navy. In 1993 Panerai began issuing its designs to the public with three signature styles—the Luminor, Luminor Marina, and Mare Nostrum—all infused with history from its innovative past. Its Radiomir watch—with a glowing dial, cushion edges, and a distinct bezel—dates back to

1936, while its next of kin, the Luminor (revealed in 1949) utilizes a different luminous substance and boasts a wider, flat bezel. Mare Nostrum, Panerai's first chronograph, originally designed for deck officers in 1943, has a narrower, contemporary bezel. Continuing its maritime tradition, Panerai is the official sponsor of the Italian sailboat racing team Luna Rossa. The brand has been further popularized by actors Sylvester Stallone, Arnold Schwarzenegger, Jason Statham, and Dwayne "the Rock" Johnson, both on and off the big screen.

Accessory Design

Panerai.
est Florence (IT), 1860.

Explorer and adventurer Mike Horn wearing a custom Panerai watch, Monaco, 2016.

Photograph by Jean-Christophe Magnenet.

↳ HUBLOT, OMEGA, TAG HEUER

PAPA WEMBA

Growing up in the Congo of the 1950s and '60s, musician Papa Wemba was in the hub of Congolese rumba (or soukous), which blended African and Caribbean rhythms. Wemba's modernized sound embraced rock and soul to create rumba-rock, a new style of Afro-pop that inspired a generation of African musicians. His move to Paris in the '80s solidified his international fame (he toured with Peter Gabriel and sang with Stevie Wonder) and popularized African music globally. As influential as Papa Wemba was onstage, he was equally celebrated for his dapper sartorial choices, usually donning a beret and designer labels, favoring the likes of Armani, Versace, Gaultier, Comme des Garçons, Yohji Yamamoto, Miyake, and Watanabe. The singer was regarded as the unofficial leader of Le Sape (Society of Poseurs and Persons of Elegance), the Congolese movement of Sapeurs—young men dedicated to extravagant fashions and designer clothes. Like Papa Wemba, their selection of attire is not purely an aesthetic one—it is also an act of rebellion and of empowerment, appropriating a European visual language of gentility and abundance as their own.

Papa Wemba (Jules Shungu Wembadio Pene Kikumba).
b Lubefu (COD), 1949.
d Abidjan (CIV), 2016.

Papa Wemba performing onstage at Irving Plaza, New York, 1995.

Photograph by Jack Vartoogian.

↳ ARMANI, MIYAKE, VERSACE, WATANABE

PARACHUTE

Harry Parnass and Nicola Pelly built their brand Parachute in a hurry. Within a year after Pelly, a trained fashion designer, and Parnass, an architect, met in Montreal, the duo had established a shop in the Canadian capital city, as well as one in New York's SoHo neighborhood. Parachute's stores were known for being supremely stark—the better to spotlight the complexity of the couple's clothing designs. Parachute's steely, often gray or beige shirts, trousers, and jackets were loose and structured, with an avant-garde edge that was in line with the work of many Japanese labels during the 1980s. The brand's signature design was a cropped jacket, often worn open, with voluminous puff sleeves. Parachute's jacket was so popular during the '80s that it was often worn by the cast on the megahit television show *Miami Vice*. Indeed, Parachute's swingy, futuristic clothes were modeled by the biggest stars of the day, including Mick Jagger, Michael Jackson, and Prince.

Designer Brand

Parachute.
est Montreal (CAN), 1977.

Parachute campaign, Queens, NY, 1983.

Photograph by Bobby Sheehan.

↳ ACRONYM, CHEN, JAGGER, MIYAKE, PRINCE, Y. YAMAMOTO

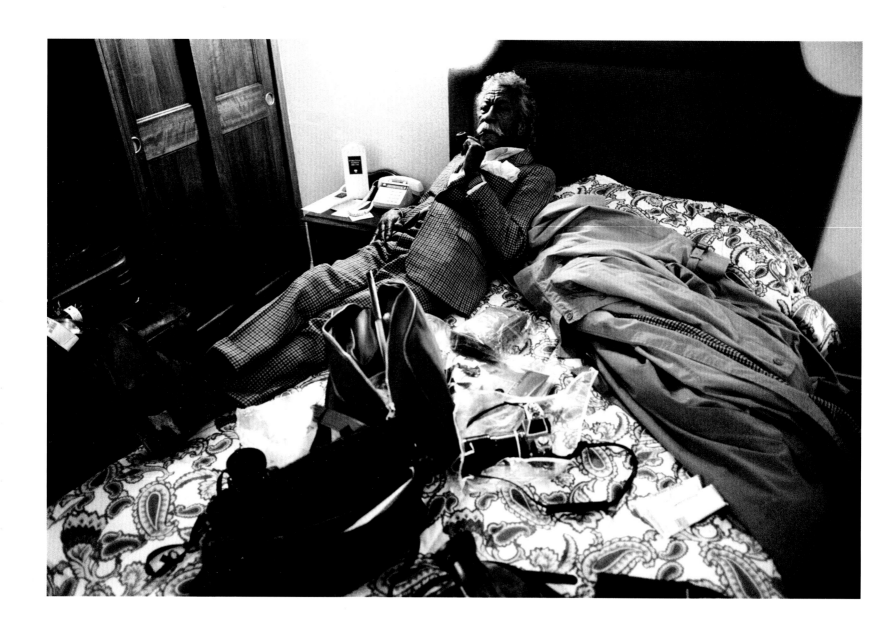

GORDON PARKS

While best known for his work as a photojournalist covering the plight of impoverished Black Americans in the 1940s, Gordon Parks was also a celebrated fashion photographer for *Vogue*, *Life*, and *Glamour* magazines—which at the time employed virtually no other Black talent. A self-taught photographer, Parks had the distinctive habit of shooting models as they moved naturally around a set, as opposed to the static poses that had previously dominated fashion photography. During his storied career, Parks became known for his personal style, with an affinity for

crisp white shirts, navy double-breasted blazers, roll-neck sweaters, Harris Tweed, and Hermès silk cravats—cool, effortless, and put together but never elitist. In 1971 Parks directed the highly fashion-forward and hit film *Shaft*, further cementing his status as an arbiter of style. With actor and former model Richard Roundtree in the titular role, Parks presented a now-iconic sensibility: leather trench coats, turtlenecks, and plaid suits with wide lapels.

Icon/Photographer

Gordon Parks.
b Fort Scott, KS (USA), 1912.
d New York (USA), 2006.

Gordon Parks, London, 1993.

Photograph by Eli Reed.

↳ ALI, BALDWIN, CONNERY, HERMÈS, SIDIBÉ

PATAGONIA

Through much of the 1950s and '60s, Yvon Chouinard, a compact, seemingly fearless Mainer, was rock climbing cliff faces across western North America. To get by (and to promote this burgeoning sport) Chouinard sold hand-forged equipment from the back of his car under the name Chouinard Equipment, Ltd. It took Chouinard more than a decade to sell his first clothes—rugby shirts imported from Scotland—but just three years later, he started Patagonia, which would rise to become America's mighti-est outdoor clothing supplier. Drawing on Chouinard's interests (climbing but also surfing, fishing, and camping), Patagonia's clothes were intended for excursions. The brand pioneered the first toasty fleece jackets in the early 1970s and squeezed bulky down insulation into lithe puffers. And with its close relationship to nature always at the fore, Patagonia was early in utilizing eco-friendly sustainable cottons and recycled polyesters. In recent years the company's vivaciously patterned fleeces have become coveted articles of fashion, with global collectors shelling out thousands for these fuzzed-out layers.

Brand

Patagonia.
est Ventura, CA (USA), 1973.

Yvon Chouinard wearing Patagonia, Taos Ski Valley, NM, 1979.

Photograph by Andy Hayt.

↳ ARC'TERYX, L.L.BEAN, MONCLER, NIKE, PENDLETON

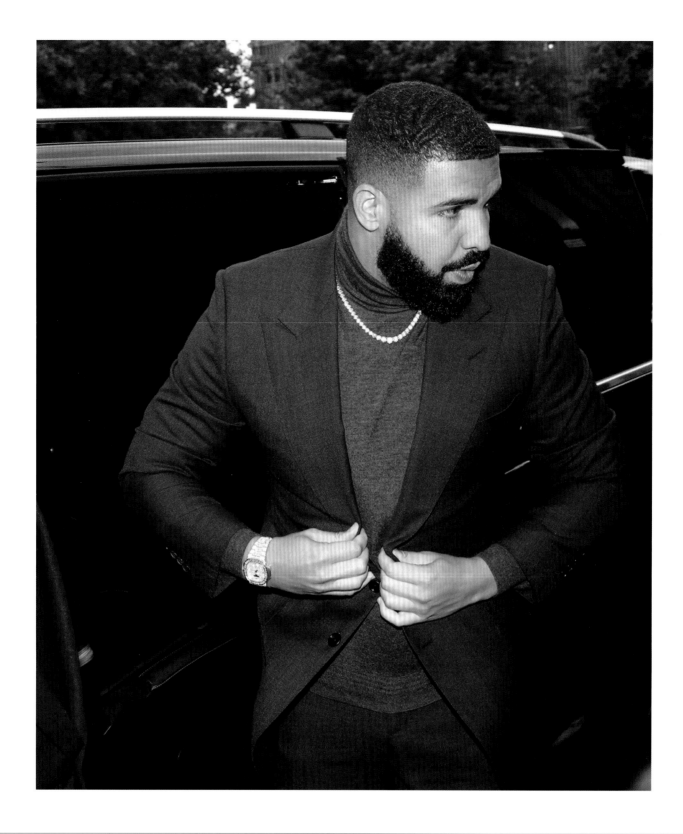

PATEK PHILIPPE

"You never actually own a Patek Philippe. You merely look after it for the next generation." This iconic line from the company's 1996 advertising campaign says all you need to know about its watches. Since its founding in 1839, Patek Philippe has firmly established itself as one of the most prestigious watch companies in the world, remaining at the forefront of innovation while never losing a sense of haute horology. Patek Philippe watches have rested on the wrists and in the pockets of both royalty and celebrities, attracting the likes of Prince Charles, Emperor Haile Selassie I of Ethiopia, King Farouk of Egypt, John F. Kennedy, Brad Pitt, and LeBron James. The company also counts among its fans Drake—who famously boasted "Virgil got that Patek on my wrist goin' nuts" about his Virgil Abloh–customized Nautilus in his song "Life Is Good." Not surprisingly, Patek Philippe's timepieces garner some of the highest price tags and longest wait times, especially for popular models such as the Nautilus, introduced in 1976 as the epitome of elegance in sports watches. Today Patek Philippe and its watches continue to be the ultimate emblems of high status and class.

Accessory Design

Patek Philippe.
est Geneva (SW), 1839.

Drake wearing a Patek Philippe Nautilus, London, 2019.

Photograph by Mike Marsland.

↳ ABLOH, CARTIER, KENNEDY, OMEGA, ROLEX

PAUL STUART

Founded by Ralph Ostrove, New York retail store Paul Stuart opened on Madison Avenue in 1938. With high-end men's "investment clothing," Ostrove rivaled its neighbor Brooks Brothers. In 1955 Ralph's son Paul Stuart Ostrove (the store's namesake) joined the company, selling shirts and ties. For the ensuing decades, the company cemented its reputation among New York's powerful elite, Wall Street bankers, and celebrities, such as Frank Sinatra, Cary Grant, and Paul Newman. Its sartorial staples delivered understated luxury—comfortable suits with soft shoulders, Italian silk shirts, traditional trousers, and elegant outerwear. In 2007 the company launched its Phineas Cole line featuring modern silhouettes. Its custom-tailored clothing, sportswear, shoes, and accessories combine Savile Row tradition with old Hollywood inspirations. What results is a distinctively New York aesthetic that embodies a classic Americana with contemporary twists. In 2020 Paul Stuart opened its first CustomLAB boutique in New York's SoHo, a concept store offering affordable made-to-measure men's fashion with highly skilled tailors and handpicked fabrics.

Retailer

Paul Stuart.
est New York (USA), 1938.

Paul Stuart magazine advertisement, c. 1970s.

↳ BROOKS BROTHERS, C. GRANT, J. PRESS, LEYENDECKER, NEWMAN

PENDLETON

Brand

Pendleton may be the only woolen manufacturer to give its name to a pop group: the Pendletones, better known as the Beach Boys. The band's original name was inspired by a late 1950s West Coast fashion trend—surfers wearing Pendleton shirts over T-shirts. The Beach Boys, donning their plaid shirts, helped popularize Pendleton among teens across the United States. Nearly a century earlier, in 1863, British weaver Thomas Kay landed in Oregon, eventually opening his own woolen mill; in 1909 his grandsons—the Bishop brothers—built on his business and opened Pendleton Woolen Mills.

The mill initially supplied trade blankets, which were used as robes or shawls, to Native Americans in the Pacific Northwest and later in the Southwest. Based on traditional designs, the blankets were made in vivid colors and bold patterns. As the company expanded, in 1924 it introduced a plaid men's wool shirt—first worn as workwear but later increasingly as casualwear. In addition to its popularity in the late 1950s, the style became a staple of the grunge movement that emerged from Seattle in the '90s. Today, thanks in part to Pendleton, the plaid shirt is a classic men's staple.

Pendleton.
est Pendleton, OR (USA), 1863.

The Beach Boys (from left to right, Carl Wilson, Mike Love, Dennis Wilson, Brian Wilson, David Marks) posing for a portrait with a vintage station wagon in Los Angeles, August 1962.

↳ COBAIN, FILSON, L.L.BEAN, PATAGONIA, WOOLRICH

PENGUIN

During the mid-twentieth century, as the United States was in the throes of a postwar suburban sprawl, Munsingwear—an underwear and military-apparel supplier—launched Penguin golf shirts. Designed for the many men taking up the country club sport, the shirts became an instant classic when they were introduced in 1955. (The Penguin name is attributed, perhaps apocryphally, to Munsingwear salesman Abbot Pederson, who purchased a taxidermic penguin on a business trip and then proceeded to drunkenly knock its head off on the flight home.) On the surface, the golf shirt appeared nearly identical to the tennis polos invented decades earlier by René Lacoste. Yet whereas a traditional polo was made in a cotton piqué knit, golf shirts commonly arrived in polyesters, the in-vogue material of the day. Penguin shirts also packed a so-called action gusset under the arm to accommodate vigorous tee shots. Technical specs aside, Penguin's sporty shirts made men—including leisure-time style icons such as Arnold Palmer, Bob Hope, and Bing Crosby—appear crisp out on the course.

Brand

Penguin.
est New York (USA), 1955.

Clint Eastwood wearing a Penguin shirt at a golf tournament in Rancho Mirage, CA, 1972.

Photograph by Martin Mills.

↳ LACOSTE, PALMER, PERRY, UMBRO

Styled to sell to the British male!

STYLES FOR '66

Fred Perry, like the British male, is getting more adventurous every year. Witness the new Fred Perry shirts . . . all in up-to-the-minute styles, in imaginative colours. (The shorts and trousers are by Fred Perry too.) Ask your representative to show you the exciting new range for 1966. Fred Perry styles keep pace with your customers' taste.
FRED PERRY SPORTSWEAR LIMITED
Showroom: 5 Vigo St., London W1. Sales Office: Bridport Rd., London N18

FRED PERRY

Fred Perry could dazzle on and off the tennis court. Arguably the best British tennis player ever, Perry sealed a staggering ten major wins during his career. But with Hollywood good looks and a raffish sense of style, Perry was also a gossip-page fixture for his dalliances with bombshells such as Marlene Dietrich and Mary Lawson. Today he's perhaps known as the inventor of the natty, wreath-logoed Fred Perry polo, which debuted at Wimbledon in 1952 and found a foothold among folks who'd never touched a tennis racket. Everyone from skinheads to Jamaican rude boys and Brit-poppers, such as Oasis, adopted Perry's slim polos. The brand crossed into higher fashion thanks to latter-day collaborations with Raf Simons and Nicholas Daley. In the 2010s Perry's polos were co-opted by the white supremacist Proud Boys, and eventually the brand took the noble stand of ceasing polo sales in North America to prevent Perry's sporty staple from being contorted into a symbol of hate.

Designer

Fred Perry.
b Portwood, Stockport (UK), 1909.
d Melbourne, Victoria (ASL), 1995.

Fred Perry advertisement, 1966.

↳ CLARKS, LACOSTE, SIMONS, UMBRO

PERSOL

Distinguished for such early innovations as folding frames and flexible stems, Persol sunglasses were developed by Giuseppe Ratti, who founded the company in 1917 after working at his family's optician business, Berry Opticians. During World War I, Ratti responded to complaints from pilots about the sun's glare by creating the Protector: smoked-glass lenses in rubber rims held in place by an elasticized headband. Later the Protector's success with pilots and racing drivers (including Juan Manuel Fangio, five-time world champion) helped Persol—a contraction of the Italian *per il sole*, or "for the sun"—become a major force. Its iconic Model 649 was originally developed in 1957 to protect tram drivers in Turin from dust but was soon being worn on-screen. Steve McQueen, already a Persol fan, popularized the 714 folding model when his character wore them throughout 1968's *The Thomas Crown Affair*. The association with cinema remains: Ryan Gosling is just one movie star rarely seen without his Persol sunglasses. With its distinctive silver sword logo, Persol became a favorite of pilots, mountaineers, and sports stars. Since 1995 the brand has been owned by eyewear conglomerate Luxottica.

Accessory Design

Persol.
est Turin (IT), 1917.

Marcello Mastroianni wearing Persol sunglasses in a publicity still for Embassy Pictures's *Divorce Italian Style*, 1961.

↳ CAZAL, MASTROIANNI, McQUEEN, OAKLEY, RAY-BAN

RAY PETRI

Though his life was cut far too short, the Buffalo style Ray Petri developed in the 1980s has left an indelible mark on men's fashion. Born in Scotland and raised in Australia, Petri left for London in 1969, hoping to make it as a soul musician. Instead he folded into London's fashion scene, and starting in 1983 Petri gave shape to the Buffalo style, a counterculture look that swirled together British and American elements. Demonstrated through editorials in influential publications, including *The Face*, *i-D*, and *Arena*, Buffalo was built around cobalt blue flight jackets and beefy paratrooper boots. Petri

stretched men's fashion into feminine pastures by styling hirsute men in oversized blazers with lengthy skirts. (Jean Paul Gaultier later credited Petri with inspiring him to do a collection of men in skirts.) The Buffalo look could be formal—pinstripe suits and dandy porkpie hats—as well as sporty, with tight Lycra leggings and tank tops. Though Petri died in 1989 as one of the industry's first AIDS victims, echoes of his work can be seen today in the gender-contorting clothes from Gucci and Molly Goddard, as well as the roguish look espoused by brands such as Palace and Noah.

Stylist

Ray Petri.
b Dundee, Scotland (UK), 1948.
d London (UK), 1989.

"Buffalo Classics," styling by Ray Petri,
The Face, November 1984.

Photograph by Jamie Morgan.

↳ BLAME, THE FACE, FOXTON,
   GAULTIER, i-D, PALACE

PABLO PICASSO

Much like his canvases, Pablo Picasso's personal style evolved from tastefully restrained to compellingly abstract during his long life. As a young man during the turn of the twentieth century, Picasso dressed in the reticent fashions of the day: club-collar shirts, dark ties, and conservative overcoats. With Cubism, Picasso's clothes grew more liberated as well. A 1927 image of Picasso shows him still clad in a conservative tie but cloaked in a sizable—and quite rakish—double-breasted, peak-lapel topcoat. By the 1950s he was toiling in his studio in Breton striped shirts,

barrel-cut trousers (often jeans, a relatively new trend in Europe), and jaunty patterned slippers. Soon thereafter Picasso swapped the artsy beret of his middle age for wilier cowboy hats. In his final years Picasso was often captured in skimpy short-shorts and billowy button-ups or no shirt at all, looking the very picture of carefree style.

Icon

Pablo Picasso.
b Málaga (SP), 1881.
d Mougins (FR), 1973.

Pablo Picasso at his home in Cannes, France, c. 1960.

Photograph by Paul Popper.

↳ BASQUIAT, GAULTIER, GOYARD, HOCKNEY, VINCE MAN'S SHOP

STEFANO PILATI

In the 1980s Stefano Pilati realized that his hometown of Milan was blossoming with a fervent fashion scene. Intuition told him his future career was in fashion; Pilati left school and started an internship at Nino Cerruti. In 1993 he signed on as a design assistant at Giorgio Armani. Two years later he went to Prada to head research and development. In 2000 Tom Ford handpicked him to be design director for Yves Saint Laurent. When Ford left in 2004, Pilati became head of design. Pilati's YSL was reverent, teeming with Parisian staples such as wide-lapeled suits, turtlenecks, and belt-waist overcoats. Over time his designs became more fluid and contemporary, an approach he continued to explore starting in 2012 as the creative director at Ermenegildo Zegna. He offered swingy double-faced cashmere overcoats, inventive hybrids of Eisenhower jackets and blazers, and confident scaled-up patterns. His runway collections rarely went into production, and in 2016 he left Zegna. After a hiatus, Pilati launched Random Identities, a relatively affordable label, in 2018 from his new home base of Berlin.

Designer

Stefano Pilati.
b Milan (IT), 1965.

Stefano Pilati, Paris, 2007.

Photograph by Alec Soth.

↳ ARMANI, ERMENEGILDO ZEGNA, FORD, PRADA, SAINT LAURENT

CAROL CHRISTIAN POELL

Carol Christian Poell's Milan-based brand could best be described as an anti-fashion label. His theatrical wares—such as ankle-high zippered Tornado boots and lengthy overcoats with pronounced shoulders—do not appear in the pages of *Vogue* or *GQ*. Since he founded the brand in 1994, he has eschewed mass production, releasing his extravagantly expensive clothes in small batches. He does not show during any traditional fashion week, choosing instead to debut collections only when they are "ready." Not that his eventual presentations skimp on the drama—for his Spring 2004

collection, "Mainstream-Downstream," he sent models floating down Milan's Naviglio Grande canal. Poell has a reputation for painstakingly researching his designs, as he revels in rarefied materials that other labels wouldn't consider. His signature pieces include kangaroo leather sneakers that are hand-dipped in rubber to give them a "drip" effect, and skin-tight bison leather jackets with curvaceous, articulated sleeves that bend at the elbow. Despite his atypical approach, Poell's superlative clothes have garnered notice from fashion obsessives including Jude Law and the late Karl Lagerfeld.

Designer

Carol Christian Poell.
b Linz (AUS), 1966.

Carol Christian Poell U-Jack Prosthetic sneaker, In Between Male 2010 collection.

Photograph by Hamid Bagherzadeh.

↳ ACKERMANN, ACRONYM, GVASALIA, LAGERFELD, OWENS

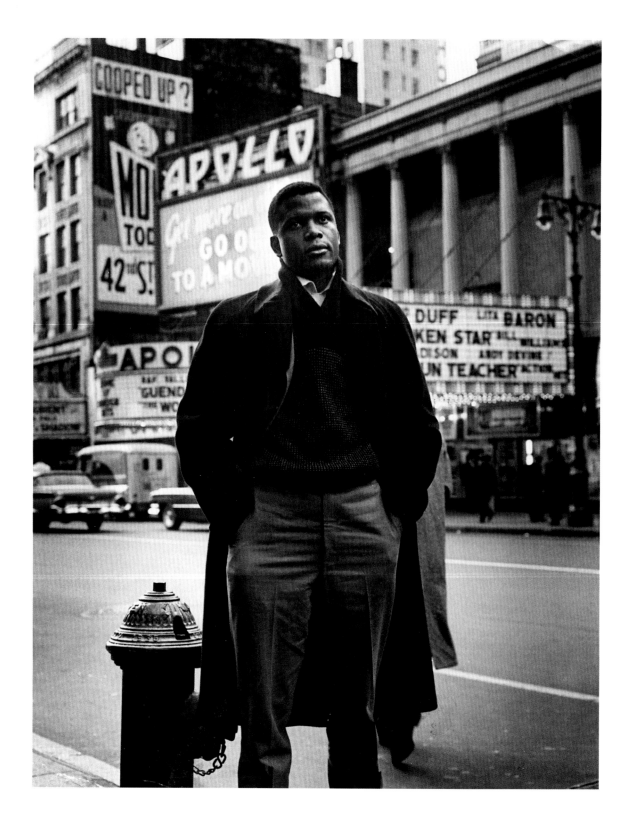

SIDNEY POITIER

Cool, calm, and collected, Sidney Poitier broke stereotypes and box-office records as one of Hollywood's first Black leading men. In 1964 he became the first Black man to win an Academy Award for Best Actor (for 1963's *Lilies of the Field*), and received continued acclaim for his performances in such films as *Guess Who's Coming to Dinner* (1967), as a doctor visiting his white fiancée's family, and *In the Heat of the Night* (1967), playing a Philadelphia detective investigating a murder in Mississippi. In both these roles and his life off-screen, Poitier wore Ivy Style: black cap-toe derbies, gray worsted and flannel suits, tweed sport coats, and narrow knit and striped repp ties. His button-down oxford cloth shirts were made by custom shirtmaker Frank Foster (also worn by Cary Grant, Frank Sinatra, and three of the actors to play James Bond). Poitier's polished look and smooth manners were sometimes criticized as caving to the politics of respectability, but throughout his life the actor and director remained faithful to his vision of simple, elegant dressing, projecting an image of dignity in the face of prejudice.

Icon

Sidney Poitier.
b Miami (USA), 1927.

Sidney Poitier standing on 125th Street, New York, January 1959.

Photograph by Sam Falk.

↳ M. DAVIS, C. GRANT, PARKS

MIUCCIA PRADA

A cerebral creative, Miuccia Prada has steered her family's leather-goods company since the 1970s, building it into a fashion behemoth. In 1993 she introduced menswear. Each collection marches to its own beat, but over the years Prada staples have emerged, such as slender polo shirts, suiting in muted pastels, and over-the-elbow bowling shirts. Sporty, swishy zip-up jackets popped up in Prada's early men's collections and were separated into a dedicated line called Linea Rosa in 1997. Prada also introduced simple nylon designs for bags, track pants, and parkas,

which proved financially prudent for the brand and helped blaze a trail for later iterations of designer sportswear. Prada was also one of the first brands to experiment with luxury sneakers, in 1996. The label has long dressed leading men and featured stars in its shows and campaigns, including Adrien Brody, Gary Oldham, and Willem Dafoe for the Fall 2012 collection. Prada continues to operate as co-CEO with her husband, Patrizio Bertelli. In 2019 it was announced that Raf Simons would join Prada as the label's co-creative director.

Designer

Miuccia Prada.
b Milan (IT), 1949

Models backstage at the Prada Fall/Winter 2020 menswear show at Milan Fashion Week.

Photograph by Tullio M. Puglia.

↳ GUCCI, JIL SANDER, LOUIS VUITTON, LUCHFORD, MARNI, SIMONS

ELVIS PRESLEY

To many, Elvis Presley remains the King of Rock 'n' Roll and a symbol of barely concealed sexual energy. Whether that air was exciting or dangerous, largely depended on one's age in July 1954, when he released his first single, "That's All Right." Strikingly handsome, Elvis created his own antiestablishment style. With a knowing sneer and quiffed hair, the young Elvis wore everything with panache, from drape jackets with bowling shirts and tight trousers to a leather Perfecto, Hawaiian shirts, and black Levi's jeans. While most men spent the 1950s in their Brooks Brothers–esque suits, Elvis wore bubble gum–pink clothing onstage and high-waisted trousers with Cuban-collar shirts and Harrington jackets offstage. With body-skimming jumpsuits, often designed by Bill Belew, Elvis predated David Bowie's look by decades. He wore a ten-thousand-dollar gold lamé suit by celebrated tailor Nudie Cohn on a 1959 album cover, and at his comeback in 1968, he donned head-to-toe black leather. As he grew older his iconic bejeweled high-collared jumpsuits became a staple of the Las Vegas experience—and opened the way for later generations of stage performers to embrace a love of all things bling.

Elvis Presley.
b Tupelo, MS (USA), 1935.
d Memphis (USA), 1977.

Elvis Presley, 1956.

↳ THE BEATLES, BOWIE, COHN, CUEVAS

380

PRINCE

Icon

Over his nearly forty-year career, Prince rarely gave interviews, but his style always spoke volumes. Since signing his first recording contract at nineteen, Prince's inventive funk-R&B-rock-jazz-pop fusions were mirrored by a genre-defying image. He posed on the 1980 *Dirty Mind* album cover in bikini briefs, thigh-high boots, a trench coat, and neckerchief. Many more sensational looks—created by costume designers including Louis Wells and Stacia Lang—duly draped his lithe frame as did the occasional subtle stylistic nod to icons Jimi Hendrix and Little Richard. Frilly shirts, polka-dot suits, sequined paisley jackets, lace gloves, and stack-heeled boots were accessorized with eyeliner, a mustache, and elaborately curled hair. Purple was a common choice, which he believed conveyed royalty—his 1984 film *Purple Rain* and the cover of its accompanying album saw him resplendent in a purple coat. Prince's mix of sexed-up pop glamour and gender nonconformity was future-facing and unforgettable, and the Grammy Award–winning pop star has been referenced by designers, such as Jean Paul Gaultier, and hailed as an inspiration by Frank Ocean, Lenny Kravitz, and Beck.

Prince Rogers Nelson.
b Minneapolis (USA), 1958.
d Chanhassen, MN (USA), 2016.

Prince, c. 1985.

↳ GAULTIER, HENDRIX, LITTLE
  RICHARD, STONE

PRINGLE OF SCOTLAND

In 1815 Robert Pringle launched his eponymous firm, producing knitted long johns and other underwear, in Hawick, the knitting capital of the Scotland. While certainly practical, the brand didn't become truly fashionable until after World War II, when their wool sweaters became a hot commodity. The trend-setting Duke of Windsor wore Pringle's distinctive argyle knits with plus fours (often with matching long argyle socks) to play golf, forever associating this design—and similar ones—with the sport. The brand's intarsia pattern with a repeat diamond and stripe motif in contrasting colors was derived from the traditional patterns on the kilts and socks of Clan Campbell of Argyll. Pringle was also the preferred brand of the casuals—a youth culture in England during the late 1970s and 1980s that inherited the mods' sharp, cultish dress sense. In 2016 designer Fran Stringer joined the company, becoming creative director two years later, and she has reimagined and patchworked designs from the 1980s for a new generation using deadstock knits—including Aran, Fair Isle, and Argyle—to make one-off pieces.

Designer Brand

Pringle of Scotland.
est Hawick, Scotland (UK), 1815.

Pringle Fall/Winter 2015 collection at London Collections Men.

Photograph by Matt Crossick.

↳ JAEGER, JOHN SMEDLEY,
LORO PIANA, SAVILLE,
DUKE OF WINDSOR

PUBLIC SCHOOL

New York designers Dao-Yi Chow and Maxwell Osborne launched Public School in 2008 and were soon heralded by *Vogue* as "the new princes of cool." After growing up in New York City and attending public schools (the brand's titular inspiration), the fashion prodigies met in the early aughts working at Sean John, the streetwear line created by hip-hop mogul Sean Combs. In 2005 they left Sean John and started their own brand three years later. Their inaugural collection of street-inspired joggers and T-shirts was launched with Barneys New York. In 2010 Chow and

Osborne joined the CFDA's Fashion Incubator program, later garnering industry-wide acclaim for their sporty suiting with a stripped-down and uncompromising feel. The label's preference for black jackets and drool-worthy sneakers carried through a distinctly New York image. The brand became known for its swishy nylon bombers, sharp shirts, and overcoats paired with shorts or cargo pants in monochromatic hues, as well as its collaborations with brands such as New Balance and Nike.

Designer Brand

Public School.
est New York (USA), 2008.

Public School Spring/Summer 2016 presentation during New York Fashion Week, 2015.

Photograph by JP Yim.

↳ BARNEYS NEW YORK, COMBS, NEW BALANCE, NIKE

EMILIO PUCCI

Emilio Pucci's prismatic, graphic swirls and patterns are as influential as they are widely mimicked. The vibrant prints became a jet-set must-have in the 1950s and '60s after the former Olympic skier Emilio Pucci, the Marchese di Barsento, introduced his skiwear designs in the '40s. His first collection included innovative stretchy ski pants and all-in-one suits. In 1949 Pucci opened a shop in Capri, Italy, where he sold his swimwear and accessory designs, and a boutique in Rome followed the next year. He created many technical fabrics with Italian textile firms, and during the 1950s he developed his

iconic prints inspired by nature, art, architecture, and culture, with each one featuring his signature *Emilio*. His dazzling patterns were popularized just as psychedelic print was becoming a key part of the peacock revolution in the 1960s, and his vivid shirts and ties, with their swirling graphics, fit seamlessly into the aesthetic. After the designer's death in 1992, his daughter, Laudomia Pucci, continued to design under the Pucci name; in 2000 LVMH acquired a stake in the firm and installed a succession of creative directors, including Christian Lacroix, Matthew Williamson, and Peter Dundas.

Designer

Emilio Pucci.
b Naples (IT), 1914.
d Florence (IT), 1992.

Emilio Pucci with his wife, Cristina, Capri, Italy, 1959.

Photograph by David Lees.

↳ AGNELLI, ELKANN, GUCCI, TOD'S, VERSACE

ROBERT RABENSTEINER

Milan-based Robert Rabensteiner is one of menswear's most prominent stylists—and a street-style icon himself. As the former fashion editor at large of the influential *L'Uomo Vogue*, where he worked under editor Franca Sozzani, Rabensteiner was responsible for styling editorials featuring such names as Jeremy Irons, Duran Duran, Pedro Almodóvar, Pelé, and Daft Punk. Inspired by his childhood growing up in nature, surrounded by the Italian Dolomites in South Tyrol, as well as classic films, including the work of award-winning filmmaker Luchino Visconti, Rabensteiner's images carry a cinematic,

dreamlike quality that communicates a signature eclecticism and elegant style for the modern gentleman. Over his career he has collaborated with photographers, such as Norman Jean Roy, Deborah Turbeville, Jean-Baptiste Mondino, Michel Comte, and Peter Lindbergh; contributed to *Vogue Italia* and *Purple* magazine; and consulted for brands, including Bally, Roberto Cavalli, Moncler, and Trussardi. Rabensteiner is a regular subject of street-style blogs, such as *Tommy Ton* and Scott Schuman's *The Sartorialist*, often seen wearing custom Charvet and dapper, tailored designs.

Editor/Stylist

Robert Rabensteiner.
b Meran, South Tyrol (IT), 1965.

Prince Konstantin of Bavaria styled by Robert Rabensteiner for "The Romantic Prince," *L'Uomo Vogue*, January 2012.

Photograph by Dylan Don.

↳ BALLY, CHARVET, LINDBERGH, L'UOMO VOGUE, MONCLER, SCHUMAN, TON

RAG & BONE

Rag & Bone founder Marcus Wainwright built an American fashion brand inspired by the world he inhabited in downtown New York. Creating modern classics predominately made in the United States, the label's ready-to-wear line is punctuated by British tailoring and American workwear sensibilities. When he started Rag & Bone in 2002, Wainwright was in pursuit of perfecting jeans and produced them with skilled local manufacturers based in Kentucky and North Carolina. (More recently manufacturing has expanded to Los Angeles as well.) Iconic styles,

such as an all-purpose bomber, the five-pocket jean, and the classic T-shirt, helped Rag & Bone reimagine men's contemporary fashion as heritage workwear began to become mainstream. In 2007 the first of many awards came when Wainwright received the CFDA Swarovski Award for Emerging Talent in menswear. Rag & Bone has collaborated with Radiohead's Thom Yorke (he composed music for their runway shows), photographer Glen Luchford, actors Michael Pitt, John Turturro, Mark Hamill, and rapper Wiz Khalifa.

Designer Brand

Rag & Bone.
est New York (USA), 2002.

Mikhail Baryshnikov for Rag & Bone's Fall/Winter 2015 campaign.

Photograph by Andreas Laszlo Konrath.

↳ ACNE STUDIOS, COLE, HILFIGER, C. KLEIN, LUCHFORD

ANDREW M. RAMROOP

For more than thirty years, Andrew M. Ramroop has been the owner and creative director of Maurice Sedwell, Savile Row's ultrabespoke tailor that dates back to 1938. Born in Trinidad and Tobago, Madan Ramroop left for the UK in 1970, and shortly after arriving he secured a job sewing at Huntsman on Savile Row. He left the position to attend the London College of Fashion, and upon graduation in 1974 he began a one-month trial at Maurice Sedwell. (At the time, the firm told him to change his name to something more anglicized, hence Andrew.) Over the years, Ramroop

has built a roster of clients—including heads of state, cricket stars, and actors Tony Curtis and Samuel L. Jackson, among other appreciators of his signature soft-structured tailoring. In 1988, when founder Maurice Sedwell retired, Ramroop acquired ownership of the company, which made him the first Black bespoke tailor who owned a shop on Savile Row. In 2008 he was awarded an OBE for his services to Bespoke Tailoring and Training, and that same year he set up the Savile Row Academy to inspire the next, more diverse generation of tailors.

Tailor

Andrew Madan Ramroop.
b Maingot Village (TT), 1952.

Andrew Ramroop, London.

Photograph by Andreas Hofer.

↳ BOATENG, HUNTSMAN, NUTTER

RANKIN

After dropping his accounting studies and changing to photography, Rankin—born John Rankin Waddell—cofounded the highly influential magazine *Dazed & Confused* with Jefferson Hack in 1991. Together, Rankin—still a student at the London School of Printing—and Hack forged provocative links between art, fashion, film, and music. During this time Rankin began to build a remarkable photographic portfolio, covering everything from fashion editorials to Oxfam campaigns. In his thirty-plus-year career, Rankin has embraced a characteristically wide range of subjects and worked in every visual medium from photography to books and films, and in 2011 he founded *Hunger*, a magazine aimed at bringing together collaborators from a range of backgrounds. A fan of the British menswear brand Oliver Spencer, Rankin has shot its ad campaigns using Spandau Ballet's Gary Kemp, skateboarder Tom Harrison, and actor Allen Leech, among others. Despite his intimate, playful, and democratic approach, by his own admission, there is no Rankin style; rather, he says, there is a search for truth and honesty.

Photographer

Rankin (John Rankin Waddell).
b Paisley, Scotland (UK), 1966.

Models Almantus Petkunas and Tim Schuhmacher photographed for "Eight Persons (Max)," *Hunger*, January 2013.

Photograph by Rankin.

↳ BOWIE, HACK, i-D, KNIGHT

RAY-BAN

For sunglasses that are now synonymous with Hollywood glamour, Ray-Ban had purely practical roots in the 1930s, when the optical company Bausch & Lomb designed anti-glare glasses in response to complaints about the sun by US Air Force pilots. Dubbed the Ray-Ban Aviator, the glasses were released to the public in 1937 and grew in popularity during and after World War II, at a time when military clothing had a profound influence on civilian fashion. Nearly two decades later, in 1952, the Wayfarer model was introduced, and it was soon adopted by movie stars, such as James Dean in *Rebel Without a Cause* (1955), and future president John F. Kennedy. Ray-Ban continued to innovate both in glass technology and frame design, but its reputation rested in large part on the enduring popularity of the Aviator and Wayfarer. Those models' prominent appearances both on-screen—*The Blues Brothers* (1980), *Top Gun* (1986), *Men in Black* (1997)—and onstage, where they were worn by a wide range of musicians, such as Bob Dylan, John Lennon, and DJs the Martinez Brothers, certainly helped make them iconic.

Accessory Design

Ray-Ban.
est Rochester, NY (USA), 1937.

Robert Redford wearing Ray-Ban Aviators, Washington, DC, 1974.

Photograph by Ron Galella.

↳ THE BEATLES, CAZAL, DEAN, KENNEDY, PERSOL

RED WING

An iconic American workwear boot, Red Wing was established in 1905 in Red Wing, Minnesota, by shoe merchant Charles Beckman. Known as the Red Wing Shoe Company, the family-run factory provided functional, lasting work boots with "pegged-and-nailed construction" for miners, farmers, and loggers in the Midwest. In 1909 they introduced an innovative production technique using modern welt construction, making the shoes more durable; this durability later led Red Wing to become an integral bootmaker for soldiers during both world wars. Crafted with quality, its Style 234,

launched in 1934, was among the first shoes to feature a protective steel toe. Other Red Wing signatures include its 877 Moc (1952) and the SuperSole (1977), which became a new work boot standard. As cult favorites of Japan's street-style craze in the 1980s, Red Wing began to collaborate with fashion brands in the 2000s, including J.Crew, Hiroshi Fujiwara's Fragment Design (they revamped the 4679 Moc Toe), Brooks Brothers, and Beams. In 2007 the brand introduced its premium Red Wing Heritage line with high-quality leather, traditional construction, and lifestyle-driven designs.

Footwear

Red Wing.
est Red Wing, MN (USA), 1905.

Red Wing Classic Moc boot.

Photograph by Horst Friedrichs.

↳ BEAMS, BLUNDSTONE, BROOKS BROTHERS, FUJIWARA, J.CREW

JASON REMBERT

A Queens native, Jason Rembert started his career working on photo shoots for major magazines, including *Harper's Bazaar* and *W.* As a celebrity stylist Rembert has brought that same editorial, high-fashion point of view to his clients. That's not to say Rembert is not well-versed in the traditional codes of menswear, having dressed actors, such as John Boyega and Michael B. Jordan, in elegant camel coats, tobacco turtleneck sweaters, and slim Burberry pinstripe suits. But he is also completely unafraid to challenge those traditional notions. Rembert is behind

many of Odell Beckham Jr.'s scene-stealing pregame outfits from brands such as Louis Vuitton, and he has also incorporated aspects of gender fluidity and futurism into his work. Rembert put Zayn Malik in a Versace tux with robot arms for the 2016 Met Gala; Ezra Miller in a couture Valentino puffer gown in 2018; and Lil Baby in a bullet-proof vest covered in crystals for the 2021 Grammys. Whether styling his male clients or designing for his luxury womenswear label Aliétte, Rembert is an absolute master of knowing when—and when not—to take risks.

Designer/Stylist

Jason Rembert.
b Queens, NY (USA), 1988.

Lil Baby, styled by Jason Rembert, performs onstage for the American Music Awards, Los Angeles, 2020.

Photograph by Kevin Winter.

↳ AMBROSE, BURBERRY, LOUIS VUITTON, WELCH, YANG

HERB RITTS

British critic Bryan Appleyard once said of the photographer Herb Ritts, "It's difficult to say who came first—Ritts or the gym cult—but they're the same thing." Ritts's career was largely built on the depiction of the toned body—a cultural obsession of the 1980s—using light to create clean lines and bold forms in which flesh resembled statuary in his photographs. Born and raised in Los Angeles, Ritts studied economics and art history before making his name as a photographer in 1977 with pictures of his friend and aspiring actor Richard Gere. At ease with any kind of celebrity, the prolific Ritts specialized in intimate black-and-white portraiture but also explored unconventional ideas about race and gender. His portraits and fashion editorials appeared in *Vanity Fair, Rolling Stone, Vogue*, and *Interview* magazines, among others. He created successful ad campaigns for fashion brands, from Gap and Levi's to luxury labels including Armani, Versace, Valentino, and Polo Ralph Lauren. Ritts's graphic simplicity revolutionized American photography in the same way as greats, such as Richard Avedon, Robert Mapplethorpe, and Irving Penn.

Photographer

Herb Ritts.
b Los Angeles (USA), 1952.
d Los Angeles (USA), 2002.

Mark Findlay 1, Los Angeles, 1990.

Photograph by Herb Ritts.

↳ ARMANI, AVEDON, C. KLEIN, M. WARD

ROLEX

A Rolex watch is a symbol of success (it was worn by Malcolm Campbell when he broke the world speed record in 1935, Edmund Hillary when he climbed Everest in 1953, and Tiger Woods as he won fifteen golf majors) and of glamour (John F. Kennedy was given his Rolex by Marilyn Monroe). The five-pronged gold crown logo is instantly recognizable—and desirable—making Rolex one of the world's most copied brands. The watch's creator, German-born Hans Wilsdorf, worked with a Swiss watchmaker to achieve a precision movement that made Rolex's reliable wristwatches as accurate, beautiful, and functional as the fast-moving twentieth century required. In 1926 he created the Rolex Oyster, which was water- and dustproof, and began a tradition of promoting Rolex watches through celebrity endorsement, and later sports sponsorship. Rolex's differing models satisfy various approaches to men's style: the neat, all-metal Datejust as worn by Winston Churchill and Roger Federer; the subtle leather-strapped Cellini favored by Barack Obama; the Submariner, originally created for adventurous divers; and the eye-catching Daytona, made famous by Paul Newman and worn by Jay-Z.

Accessory Design

Rolex.
est London (UK), 1905.

Dizzy Gillespie wearing a Rolex during his British tour, 1960.

↳ CARTIER, JAY-Z, KENNEDY, OMEGA, NEWMAN, PATEK PHILIPPE

MARTINE ROSE

"Probably the best designer in the world." That cheeky declaration appeared on Martine Rose's website and T-shirts by her eponymous London-based label, which she established in 2007. As with any good joke, there's some truth to it. In the aughts, men's fashion steered toward high-low contrasts, and Rose deserves credit for lifting that seesawing style to the runway. Born of Jamaican-British heritage, she pulls from "melting-pot cultures of London," including 1990s reggae and the rave scene. A friendly local, she's held shows in open, accessible spaces such as a neighborhood cul-de-sac in Camden. Her collections can tip toward normcore—dress shirts arrive in standard-issue stripes; denim jackets are unremarkable blue—yet the construction of her wares sends them into a different sphere. In particular, Rose toys with proportions, layering piles of pleats into trousers and creating ankle-kissing leather coats. Her merry creativity has not gone unnoticed: Rose consulted on Balenciaga's menswear and has collaborated with Nike and Napapijri.

Designer

Martine Rose.
b London (UK), 1980.

Models backstage at the Martine Rose Spring/Summer 2019 menswear show at London Fashion Week, 2018.

Photograph by Tabatha Fireman.

↳ DAPPER DAN, GVASILIA, NIKE, PALACE, WALES BONNER

OLIVIER ROUSTEING

It was a bold choice to appoint an unknown twenty-five-year-old fashion-school dropout to the top job at one of Paris's most storied couture houses, but since 2011 Olivier Rousteing has led Balmain into an exciting new chapter. After a stint at Roberto Cavalli he joined Balmain in 2009, working under its previous creative director, Christophe Decarnin, for two years before taking the helm. Menswear now accounts for nearly half of Balmain's revenue—a feat in itself for a house whose roots are in the feminine world of haute couture. Rousteing has earned fans the world over for his quintessentially Parisian menswear, instantly recognizable for its precise tailoring, couture-level ornamentation, decadent fabrics, and military inflections. And perhaps better than any other creative lead of a major French fashion house, Rousteing bridges the gap between couture tradition and celebrity culture, leveraging relationships with celebrities, such as Justin Bieber, Swae Lee, Kanye West, and the K-pop band BTS, to spread the gospel of Balmain. It is no coincidence that Balmain is the first French *maison* to surpass one million followers on Instagram.

Designer

Olivier Rousteing.
b Bordeaux (FR), 1986.

Balmain Fall/Winter 2016 menswear collection at Paris Fashion Week.

Photograph by François Guillot.

↳ BTS, JEAN-RAYMOND, S. KLEIN, TISCI, WEST

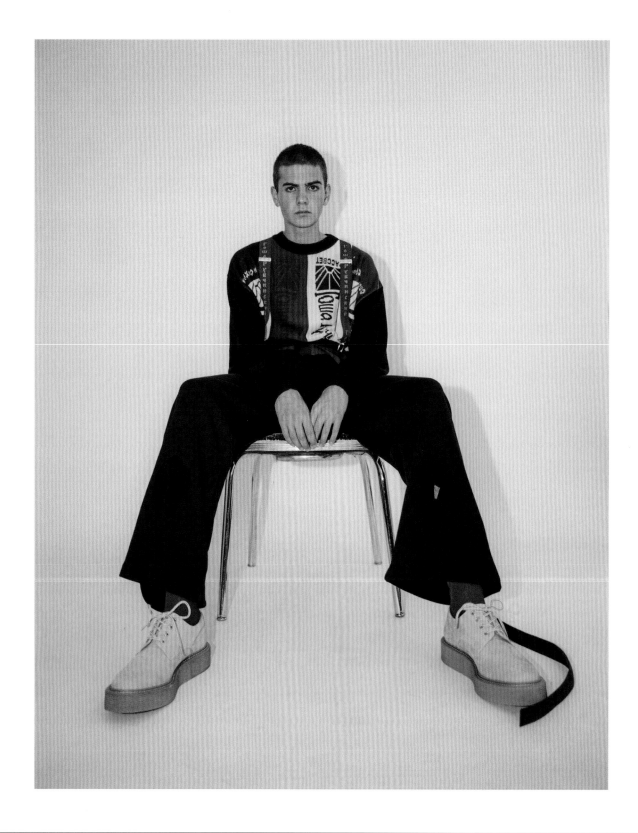

GOSHA RUBCHINSKIY

Since founding his label in 2008, Moscow-born Gosha
Rubchinskiy has helped usher in a new era of streetwear
inspired by skateboarding, Russian raves, and subcultures
spanning Saint Petersburg to London. Launching his
eponymous men's line after studying at Moscow College of
Technology and Design, Rubchinskiy quickly amassed a loyal
cult following with his Cyrillic slogans and retro, graphic
fashions. Once industry insiders took notice of Rubchinskiy's
viral impact and sartorial sensations, he was invited to show
at London Fashion Week. In 2012 his reach expanded when

he was invited to show at Paris Fashion Week and Florence's
Pitti Uomo, and later when he partnered with Comme des
Garçons's label head Adrian Joffe—who also stocks Gosha
Rubchinskiy at the multiconcept Dover Street Market. His
roguish designs, which include signature motif-laden
T-shirts, shorts, track pants, oversized boxy blazers, and
printed puffer jackets, have made the post-Soviet aesthetic
mainstream, serving as a fresh counterpoint to today's high
fashion. Since launching his label, he has collaborated with
Burberry, Dr. Martens, Adidas, FILA, Kappa, and Levi's.

Designer

Gosha Rubchinskiy.
b Moscow (RUS), 1984.

Gosha Rubchinskiy Fall/Winter 2016.

Photograph by Melchizedek Chan.

↳ ADIDAS, BURBERRY,
DR. MARTENS, FILA,
GVASALIA, S. JONES

RUBINACCI

The storied house of Rubinacci was founded in 1932 by cavalry officer and dandy Gennaro Rubinacci after he decided he could make a business as the go-to tailoring consultant for his friends. Despite being based in Naples, Rubinacci named the business the London House, echoing the English dominance of high-quality menswear, but sold unstructured and unlined jackets that were far less formal than British suits at that time. In 1961 the business passed to his son, Mariano, who renamed the company Rubinacci. The antithesis of the Savile Row cut, with its stiff padding and layers, Rubinacci instead pioneered the Neapolitan style with jackets so soft and light they can be folded up to eight times. Mariano opened branches in Milan and London and founded a museum dedicated to preserving the skills of Neapolitan tailoring. Today, with Mariano's son Luca as creative director—he trained as a tailor on Savile Row and is a street-style star himself—the firm produces up to one thousand bespoke suits a year, including an option to enjoy six nights at the family's hotel, Casa Rubinacci, while the suit is being made.

Tailor

Rubinacci.
est Naples (IT), 1932.

Luca Rubinacci, Naples, 2019.

Photograph by Abraham Engelmark.

↳ CANALI, CORNELIANI, ISAIA

MORDECHAI RUBINSTEIN

Mordechai Rubinstein's reverent snaps of average well-dressed passersby have made him the Bill Cunningham of the Instagram age. Born to an Orthodox family in Rhode Island, Rubinstein became a garment-industry veteran who spent time at Levi's, Kate Spade, and Marc Jacobs. An appreciator of great style, no matter the person, Rubinstein began taking images of beguilingly attired urbanites in the mid-2000s, posting them to his Flickr page. A blog—*Mister Mort*—soon followed. In more recent years taking photographs primarily for his madcap Instagram page @MisterMort has been

Rubinstein's main focus. He's captured an elderly man in a clementine puffer and a fanny pack, a doorman in a double-breasted suit with a gold-buttoned topcoat, and a UPS man with an umbrella hat on his head with one of Rubinstein's signature hashtags, #BeautyIntheEverydayUniform. Rubinstein has also been a prolific documentarian of the joyous style of Grateful Dead fans. He's photographed Deadheads (including celebrities such as Jonah Hill) outside shows and on the street, capturing the idiosyncrasies of this subculture wherever he can find it.

Photographer

Mordechai Rubinstein.
b Providence, RI (USA), 1976.

Jonah Hill, New York, 2019.

Photograph by Mordechai Rubinstein.

↳ CUNNINGHAM, GENTRY, JACOBS, SCHUMAN, TON

RUPAUL

As the world's most famous drag queen, RuPaul has spurred men to open their minds and fearlessly experiment with the possibilities of self-image. In 1987 RuPaul moved from Atlanta to New York, where he made a modest living by singing and dancing within the city's queer nightlife scene. Propelled into the mainstream by his 1993 international hit single "Supermodel (You Better Work)," he then broke new ground as the gender-blurring face of MAC cosmetics in 1994. The ensuing years saw RuPaul unleash albums, singles, and books, appear in films, such as *To Wong*

Foo (1995), and launch a unisex fragrance called Glamazon. As the host and judge of the globally successful *RuPaul's Drag Race* franchise since 2009, he has alternately appeared on the show in stunning gowns designed by Zaldy and colorful made-to-measure men's suits from Klein Epstein & Parker. From his 1990s style of blond wigs, stiletto heels, and skin-tight dresses to his sharp, tailored look in eye-popping colors and patterns today, RuPaul has proudly shown that dressing on your own terms ultimately creates the most authentic style statement of all.

Icon

RuPaul Andre Charles.
b San Diego (USA), 1960.

RuPaul, Los Angeles, photographed for *ES Magazine*, July 2014.

Photograph by Steve Schofield.

↳ JACOBS, MEISEL, SCOTT

LUKA SABBAT

Before Luka Sabbat turned eighteen years old, he had already established himself as one of the most stylish teenagers on the internet. (Not many high schoolers can say their prom suit was personally provided by Tom Ford.) A city kid, Sabbat was raised between Paris and New York, the son of two jet-setting creative parents. At the age of fifteen he was discovered by a modeling agency and has since bloomed into a Gen-Z renaissance man: model, influencer, stylist, actor, and multidimensional creative. Sabbat has strutted the runway for Calvin Klein and Yeezy and fronted billboards for Adidas sneakers and Evian spring water. He's a front-row mainstay at fashion weeks across the globe, and his personal style—an effortless blend of head-turning streetwear, razor-sharp tailoring, and next-level footwear—lands him front and center in more street-style roundups than you can count. Sabbat has established himself as a different kind of influencer, as new wave and New York as it gets, with the attitude, talent, and next-level style to back it up.

Influencer/Model

Luka Sabbat.
b New York (USA), 1997.

Luka Sabbat, Paris, 2016.

Photograph by Alexandre Gaudin.

↳ ABLOH, FORD, KAYE, WEST

SAINT LAURENT

The legendary brand, started by its namesake, Yves Saint Laurent, has defined French luxury since 1961. Saint Laurent was a pioneer in bridging couture and ready-to-wear and bringing men's tailoring over to womenswear, most notably with his 1966 women's tuxedo, Le Smoking. In the 2000s Saint Laurent was purchased by the Gucci Group and revived by Tom Ford, who injected a new sexy appeal into the brand, but the true heir to the founder was Hedi Slimane, appointed creative director in 2012. Dropping the *Yves*, the brand was revitalized by a rock 'n' roll chic and a renewed emphasis on menswear. Skinny suits, leather jackets and pants, and pointy boots brought an edgy, devil-may-care attitude to the storied French house. Saint Laurent quickly became a favorite among a new generation of clients, from Lenny Kravitz to 2 Chainz. In 2016 Anthony Vaccarello replaced Slimane, bringing the brand—then largely based in Los Angeles—back to Paris.

Designer Brand

Saint Laurent.
est Paris (FR), 1961.

Saint Laurent Spring/Summer 2020 menswear collection, Malibu, CA, 2019.

Photograph by Etienne Laurent.

↳ FORD, Y. SAINT LAURENT, SLIMANE

YVES SAINT LAURENT

Yves Saint Laurent was a modernizing force in twentieth-century fashion and certainly one of its most influential designers. He celebrated elegant and functional style, and many of these timeless pieces came straight out of his own wardrobe: tailored blazers, velvet tuxedos, and exotic safari suits. Saint Laurent's bohemian style—developed after he bought a home with his partner, Pierre Bergé, in Marrakech in 1966—popularized kaftans and vivid shirts. And Saint Laurent's potency as a cultural force was summed up in 1971 when he appeared nude in an ad for his men's cologne photographed by Jeanloup Sieff. Saint Laurent grew up in Algeria but moved to Paris in 1954 to study fashion, and after winning the International Wool Secretariat design competition, he was hired as an assistant to Christian Dior in 1955. When Dior died two years later, his young protégé was installed as head designer at just twenty-one years old. In 1961 Saint Laurent founded his eponymous house with Bergé, and the designer's signature close-fitting tailoring was reintroduced at the house under Hedi Slimane, creative director between 2012 and 2016, who was succeeded by designer Anthony Vaccarello.

Designer/Icon

Yves Saint Laurent.
b Oran (ALG), 1936.
d Paris (FR), 2008.

Yves Saint Laurent in his Paris home, photographed for *Vogue*, November 1971.

Photograph by Horst P. Horst.

↳ CARTIER, FORD, LAGERFELD, SAINT LAURENT

SALVATORE FERRAGAMO

As a child in Bonito, Italy, Salvatore Ferragamo crafted shoes for his sisters and studied shoemaking in nearby Naples. He moved to Boston when he was just sixteen, and then to California, where he opened a shop in Santa Barbara, making made-to-measure shoes, developing his business, and building connections with film studios and directors, such as Cecil B. DeMille. His clients also included silver-screen stars Rudolph Valentino—who favored calfskin riding boots and black Oxfords—and Charlie Chaplin. In 1927 Ferragamo moved his business

back to Florence, and by the 1950s he employed 700 artisans who made 350 pairs of handmade shoes each day. While the brand has focused on timeless classics, most famously the horsebit Gancini loafers (and the bestselling Gancini belt, among other accessories), the twenty-first century has seen a swift modernization in their menswear. Recently the company presented a more fashion-forward aesthetic with Nappa leather tees, workwear-inspired cargo pants, and boilersuits.

Designer Brand

Salvatore Ferragamo.
est Florence (IT), 1927.

Johannes Huebl for Salvatore Ferragamo's "Escape" campaign for the Made-to-Order Driver shoe, Spring/ Summer 2015.

Photograph by Alberto Colombo.

↳ BERLUTI, CHURCH'S, JOHN LOBB BOOTMAKER, TOD'S

PETER SAVILLE

In 1978 graphic designer and art director Peter Saville cofounded Factory Records and would go on to create some of the most iconic album covers of the era. His idiosyncratic style combines a nostalgia for the past with a fascination with the digital age, often appropriating images from art history and repurposing them as part of his designs. For Joy Division's 1980 album *Closer*, he used a Bernard Pierre Wolff photograph of the Appiani family tomb in Genoa. Three years later he took the blousy 1890 floral still life *A Basket of Roses* by Henri Fantin-Latour and put it on the cover of New Order's *Power, Corruption & Lies*. Saville crossed over into fashion, cofounding SHOWStudio in 2000 with photographer Nick Knight and working with brands, including Jil Sander, Yohji Yamamoto, and Christian Dior. One of his most notable collaborations has been with Raf Simons, who has used Saville's archival work in his own collections (in 2003 he created classic parkas featuring album-cover artwork). Saville has also redesigned logos for fashion houses, working with Simons at Calvin Klein and Riccardo Tisci at Burberry.

Art Director

Peter Saville.
b Manchester, England (UK), 1955.

Parkas from the Raf Simons Fall/Winter 2003 collection, featuring artwork by Peter Saville.

↳ BURBERRY, JIL SANDER, C. KLEIN, KNIGHT, SIMONS, TISCI, Y. YAMAMOTO

MARCUS SCHENKENBERG

The Swedish model Marcus Schenkenberg grabbed the world's attention in 1991, appearing in a Calvin Klein advertising campaign wearing nothing but a pair of jeans to display his supremely chiseled abs. Discovered two years earlier while roller-skating on Venice Beach in California, the Swede's physicality and supreme self-confidence put him on a path toward becoming a top male supermodel. He soon had global name recognition and was greeted by screaming crowds at public appearances. Over his career Schenkenberg set many trends in men's fashion,

including inspiring men to grow out their hair. Admired by photographers and designers alike, Schenkenberg understood intuitively how to perform for the camera, working with Richard Avedon for Versace and Bruce Weber for Calvin Klein, as well as for Armani, Donna Karan, and Iceberg, among others. Fashion show producer Kevin Krier has called him a chameleon; Gianni Versace also commented on his versatility, saying, "He knows his body, how to move it, and how to use his energy to give life to the pictures."

Model

Marcus Schenkenberg.
b Stockholm (SWE), 1968.

Kate Moss and Marcus Schenkenberg, New York, photographed for *Harper's Bazaar Uomo*, 1992.

Photograph by Stephanie Pfriender Stylander.

↳ ARMANI, AVEDON, C. KLEIN, VERSACE, WEBER

409

FREDERICK SCHOLTE

Dutch tailor Frederick Scholte is famed as the inventor of the London drape, the cut of suit jacket that came to dominate Savile Row between the world wars—with its classic V shape tapered down from the roomy shoulders to a narrow waist. Softer than earlier suits and generous in the chest and shoulder blades, the cloth hung in gentle ripples, giving off an easy drape. Scholte's influence was enduring, partly because his most famous client was the Duke of Windsor, then recognized as one of the most elegant men in the world. From 1919 to 1959 Scholte

dressed the duke in perfectly tailored jackets, exhibiting a "soft look" that granted more freedom of movement. Scholte had previously shared his technique with a younger colleague, Peter Gustav Anderson, who in 1906 cofounded Anderson & Sheppard. Anderson's business adopted the London drape during its rise to become *the* tailor not only to establishment gentlemen but also to show-business stars, such as Noël Coward and Fred Astaire.

Tailor

Frederick Scholte.
b (NL), (Active 1900s—1950s).
d c. 1959.

The Duke of Windsor wearing a drape suit, the Bahamas, 1943.

Photograph by Peter Stackpole.

↳ ANDERSON & SHEPPARD,
  ASTAIRE, COWARD,
  DUKE OF WINDSOR

COLLIER SCHORR

Upon graduating from New York's School of Visual Arts in 1985, photographer Collier Schorr began an artistic career that came to life in the city's exhilarating art scene of the 1980s and '90s. Part photojournalism and part portraiture, her body of work revolves around the central theme of identity and how we use concepts such as gender, nationality, and fashion to construct who we are. Her subjects are as disparate as high school wrestlers in New Jersey and young cowboys on the threshold of adulthood. In 1995 Schorr shot her first fashion editorial for Olivier Zahm's *Purple* magazine. She has since contributed fashion photography to numerous magazines, such as *Fantastic Man*, *Document Journal*, *i-D*, and *AnOther* magazine, and has photographed campaigns for Louis Vuitton, Comme des Garçons, and Dior. Her work is instantly recognizable for its straightforward aesthetic, often in black and white. She captured a pared-back, androgynous Lady Gaga for *T: The New York Times Style Magazine* in 2016, and also a young (equally androgynous) Timothée Chalamet for a 2018 cover of *V* magazine.

Photographer

Collier Schorr.
b New York (USA), 1963.

"Touched By Youth," *Dazed & Confused*,
June 2010.

Photograph by Collier Schorr.

↳ ABLOH, BIRD, FANTASTIC
MAN, i-D, KAWAKUBO, LANG,
LANVIN

SCHOTT NYC

Initially making raincoats in a basement on Manhattan's Lower East Side and selling them door-to-door around the city, brothers Jack and Irving Schott went on to create one of the most iconic American garments: the black leather motorcycle jacket. Schott NYC was founded in 1913, but it wasn't until 1928, when Irving Schott was approached by a motorcycle distributor to design a jacket for his customers, that the company took off. In response Irving created one of the first zippered jackets, the Perfecto, combining ruggedness and durability with practical pockets, snap fasteners, and

small chains that allowed zippers to be opened while wearing gloves. As a symbol of freedom, adventure, and rebellion, the Perfecto remains the template for all leather jackets—worn by motorcycle couriers before World War II, by Marlon Brando in 1953's *The Wild One*, and by punks, such as the Ramones and Joan Jett. In addition to this iconic piece, Schott NYC has a long history of creating outerwear, having produced leather bomber jackets and naval pea coats for the US government in World War II. Today it remains a family-run business appealing to the rebel spirit of the United States.

Designer Brand

Schott NYC.
est New York (USA), 1913.

Marlon Brando in a publicity still for Columbia Pictures's *The Wild One*, 1953.

Photograph by Michel Dufour.

↳ BARBOUR, BELSTAFF, CARHARTT, DEAN, GOLDEN BEAR, RED WING

SCOTT SCHUMAN

The Sartorialist, the blog founded by fashion industry veteran Scott Schuman in 2005, changed the way people saw fashion. Inspired by noted street-style photographers such as Bill Cunningham and by *National Geographic*'s Steve McCurry, Schuman began roaming New York City with a digital camera. He photographed anyone whose originality he admired and published a single portrait for each subject on his blog with a location and the occasional brief caption. His images captured real everyday people—albeit stylish ones—going about their daily lives, and in

turn caught the eye of the fashion industry. Photographing men from Mumbai to Florence on the street or in cafés, Schuman—whose own fashion guru is Giorgio Armani and who often works in a simple, elegant suit—has an eye for what's stylish, be it white jeans worn in winter or a printed or leopard-pattern shirt layered under a plain jacket. Schuman has published five books of his photographs and has shot fashion editorials for *GQ*, *Esquire*, and *Interview* magazines, as well as campaigns for brands including Burberry and Gap.

Photographer

Scott Schuman.
b Indianapolis (USA), 1968.

Street style photographed for
The Sartorialist in Seoul, South Korea.

Photograph by Scott Schuman.

↳ BURBERRY, CUNNINGHAM, GAP, GQ, RUBINSTEIN

JEREMY SCOTT

Before Jeremy Scott became one of fashion's brightest stars, he studied fashion at the Pratt Institute, interned at Moschino, and was a wildly dressed club kid on New York's nightlife scene in the early 1990s. He moved to Paris in 1996 and launched his eponymous label the following year. Experimental early collections that used repurposed flea-market fabrics gave way to a kitschy 1980s pop-culture enthusiasm. Scott has since harnessed inspiration from the McDonald's logo, cigarette cartons, and 1990s internet graphics. Such gloriously brash-trashy mash-ups characterize his ever-popular designs at Moschino, where he was appointed creative director in 2013. His own menswear line has showcased everything from fluffy mohair sweaters and PVC trousers to biker-style jackets in retina-popping colors and graphic tees adorned with nostalgic cartoons or ironic slogans. Scott's collaborations with Adidas from 2002 onward have been similarly well received, in particular the winged high-tops of 2008. Karl Lagerfeld was one of Scott's earliest high-profile fans, joined in more recent years by Justin Bieber, Kanye West, and A$AP Rocky.

Designer

Jeremy Scott.
b Kansas City, MO (USA), 1975.

Moschino Spring/Summer 2015 collection at London Collections: Men, 2014.

Photograph by Leon Neal.

↳ A$AP ROCKY, ADIDAS, LAGERFELD, MOSCHINO

MARK SELIGER

For decades Mark Seliger has been taking intimate pictures of ultrafamous rock stars and heartthrob Hollywood stars. The acclaimed photographer grew up in Houston and graduated from East Texas State University before moving to New York City in 1984. A few years later he started working for *Rolling Stone* and became the magazine's chief photographer from 1992 to 2002, snapping more than 175 covers during his tenure. Seliger has shot iconic portraits of a stone-faced Kurt Cobain and photographed the always-stylish Lenny Kravitz for *L'Officiel Hommes Italia*.

Seliger has been documenting Kravitz throughout his career, creating a massive catalog of the charismatic musician's outrageously stylish clothes in the process. He has also been responsible for many memorable advertising campaigns by Ralph Lauren, Levi's, and Ray-Ban. Seliger's specialty is showing a different side of well-known celebrities in a manner that highlights their soul and style. And it is these striking, often unexpected, images of larger-than-life personalities that have made Seliger a luminary in his own right.

Photographer

Mark Seliger.
b Amarillo, TX (USA), 1959.

Lenny Kravitz, 2020.

Photograph by Mark Seliger.

↳ COBAIN, GQ, JAGGER, LAUREN, LEVI'S, L'UOMO VOGUE, RAY-BAN

EDWARD SEXTON

Throughout his half-century career, Edward Sexton's clothes have never skimped on flair. A native Londoner, Sexton spent years apprenticing at illustrious tailoring firms, such as Cyril A. Castle and Kilgour, French and Stanley. In 1967, while working as a cutter at Donaldson, Williams & G. Ward, Sexton met Tommy Nutter, and the pair decided to start their own shop together. Nutters of Savile Row opened in 1969 with Sexton's cut—a flared jacket with towering roped shoulders and oversized lapels—instantly pulling stars in. Three of the Beatles (John Lennon, Paul McCartney, and

Ringo Starr) wore Nutter pieces on the cover of *Abbey Road*. Starr would later pose in a Nutter advertisement wearing a beguiling outfit of a glen-plaid jacket with a contrasting gingham vest and trousers. Nutter himself left the shop in 1976, and Sexton forged on, forming partnerships with Saks Fifth Avenue and Wilkes Bashford. In 1990 Sexton set up a studio under his name in Knightsbridge, where he continues to produce vivacious clothes—often for celebrities—including a pink getup for Harry Styles and a white wedding suit for Mark Ronson.

Tailor

Edward Sexton.
b London (UK), 1942.

Tommy Nutter advertisement featuring Ringo Starr, 1974.

Photograph by Bob Gothard.

↳ THE BEATLES, JAGGER,
   NUTTER, STYLES

TUPAC SHAKUR

Tupac Shakur, recording under the name 2Pac, was one of the most influential rappers in the 1990s, and continues to be a cultural touchstone to this day. Born the son of Black Panthers in New York and relocating to California in 1988, Shakur's music career began with the genre-bending, Oakland-based group Digital Underground. As a solo artist, he blended socially conscious lyrics with brutally honest accounts of life in the American ghettos. Infamous for a "Thug Life" tattoo across his stomach and a bandanna tied in a bunny-ears knot on his head, Shakur's persona blended violence with vulnerability,

especially in his breakout film role in *Juice* (1992) and in 1993's *Poetic Justice*. His celebrity made him a fashion trendsetter; baggy overalls, snapbacks, Carhartt denim, and Timberlands were all popularized by the rapper. He was regularly seen in designs by streetwear pioneers, such as Cross Colours, Karl Kani, and Walker Wear. Gianni Versace even invited Shakur to walk the runway for his Fall/Winter 1996 collection dressed in a gold velvet suit designed for Shakur's "California Love" music video. Though he was killed in a drive-by shooting shortly after, Shakur defined 1990s style and remains an inspiration.

Tupac Shakur.
b New York (USA), 1971.
d Las Vegas (USA), 1996.

Tupac Shakur, c. 1990s.

↳ CARHARTT, CROSS COLOURS, KANI, TIMBERLAND, VERSACE, APRIL WALKER

SHANGHAI TANG

Designer Brand

One of the most recognizable Chinese luxury brands, Shanghai Tang got its start in 1994, the brainchild of the late, legendary Hong Kong businessman and bon vivant Sir David Tang. As a notable cultural and sartorial East-meets-West attaché, who held court with the global elite from Prince Charles and Mick Jagger to supermodel Kate Moss, Tang made bold, upscale *tangzhuang*, or Tang jackets, fashionable for the uninitiated, if not de rigueur. A traditional men's style from the late Qing dynasty (1644–1911), Tang jackets were worn by ruling Manchu horsemen.

Shanghai Tang modernized them in bright, trippy velvets, silks, and jacquard, while retaining the Mandarin collar and distinct frog-button details. In 2019 David's daughter Victoria Tang-Owen was appointed Shanghai Tang's creative director, further promoting the possibilities of luxury "Made in China." She returned the company "back to the roots" with more lifestyle-oriented designs, even launching a collaboration with Chinese contemporary artist Xu Bing before leaving the position in 2020.

Shanghai Tang.
est Hong Kong (CHN), 1994.

Shanghai Tang Spring/Summer 2019 menswear campaign.

Photograph by Kwannam Chu.

↳ ALFRED DUNHILL, CHANG, CHARVET, JAGGER

MALICK SIDIBÉ

Working during the renaissance that followed Mali's independence from French rule in 1960, photographer Malick Sidibé captured young revelers on the streets, beaches, and dance halls. His subjects were fiercely dressed, posing in hip bell-bottoms, oversize hats, stylish suits, and occasionally traditional African clothing. Born in 1935 in Soloba, Mali, Sidibé started as an illustrator but later worked with French photographer Gérard Guillat-Guignard and found his true calling. Soon after, he opened Studio Malick, where he produced his iconic images of the 1960s and '70s—often in black and white and always awash with style and vitality. In the studio Sidibé created graphic juxtapositions using his sitters and lush backdrops, such as a young man wearing a plaid suit against multipatterned textiles. Sidibé's bold images not only influenced local designers of the time, such as Amadou Ballo, but have also had an impact on contemporary names, including Gucci, Stella McCartney, and Duro Olowu. In 2007 Sidibé became the first African and the first photographer to be awarded the Golden Lion Award for Lifetime Achievement at the Venice Biennale.

Photographer

Malick Sidibé.
b Soloba (ML), 1936.
d Bamako (ML), 2016.

Un Jeune Gentleman, 1978.

Photograph by Malick Sidibé.

↳ A. SAUVAGE, MICHELE, PARKS

SID MASHBURN

Ralph Lauren, J.Crew, Land's End—Sid Mashburn clocked time at these great American retailers before relocating to Atlanta in 2007 to erect a sartorial empire of his own. Mashburn's vision was a classically appointed men's clothier not unlike the ones that once sat in small towns across the United States. It's the utopian ideal of a men's shop: racks of elegant suits, alluring knit ties, a custom tailor on-site, and polished shoes glimmering in their displays. But what sets Mashburn apart is his bravura quirks. The man rarely wears socks, lets his double-monkstrapped shoes fly

unbuckled, and never secures the tail of his tie. When customers shop with Sid, they're buying into this look (call it Italian sprezzatura by way of the US southeast) as much as they are buying a belt or a new raincoat. With recently opened locations in Los Angeles, Houston, and Washington, DC, the Mashburn style is marching its way around the United States.

Retailer

Sid Mashburn.
est Atlanta (USA), 2007.

Sid Mashburn (right) with his tailors and shopkeepers, Atlanta, 2009.

Photograph by F. E. Castleberry.

↳ ALDEN SHOES, ANDOVER SHOP, J.CREW, LAUREN, PAUL STUART, POITIER

RAF SIMONS

A student of industrial design, Raf Simons entered fashion with his eponymous label in 1995, drawing on the puckish sensibility of his young peers. In his early runway shows, fresh-faced models wore slouchy, oversized fishtail parkas, crunchy knits, shrunken suits, and flowy, skateboard-inspired trousers. His clothes were often sprinkled with references to new wave bands, such as New Order and Kraftwerk. In recent years, his highly collectible early designs have become particularly coveted, with fans, including Kanye West and A$AP Rocky, paying top dollar for them—in 2018 a camo bomber from Simons's 2001 collection resold for a staggering $47,000. Yet Simons also has an eye for elegance, something he increasingly relies on, lacing satin opera coats and crisp work shirts into his label. This fusion has made him a prime candidate to steer several high-end fashion houses since the mid-2000s, including Jil Sander, Dior, Calvin Klein, and now Prada alongside Miuccia Prada.

Designer

Raf Simons.
b Neerpelt (BEL), 1968.

Fernando Cabral models Raf Simons x Sterling Ruby Fall 2014 collection for *GQ Style* Germany, September 2014.

Photograph by Julia Noni.

↪ A$AP ROCKY, JIL SANDER, C. KLEIN, PRADA, RIZZO, VANDERPERRE

DAVID SIMS

A pioneering minimalist who defined a new graphic standard in fashion photography, David Sims got his start in 1985 shooting editorials for niche style magazine *i-D*. In the 1990s he captured unkempt youth and a subversive, underground men's aesthetic, including Nirvana's grunge icon Kurt Cobain wearing a dress for the cover of *The Face*, or the menswear designs of Raf Simons in the portrait series Isolated Heroes. Throughout his career, Sims has also contributed to *L'Uomo Vogue*, *Arena Homme +*, and *AnOther* magazine and collaborated with iconic stylists, including

Joe McKenna, Katy England, and Melanie Ward. His early campaign imagery for Calvin Klein is among his standouts, as are later advertisements for Yohji Yamamoto, Prada, Helmut Lang, Jil Sander, Supreme, Acne Studios, and Alexander McQueen. Sims has also photographed notable celebrities, such as David Bowie, Michael Pitt, Frank Ocean, and Travis Scott. His refined, modern images have entered the permanent collections of London's Victoria and Albert Museum and the Tate Modern, and he has exhibited at the Museum of Contemporary Art Tokyo.

Photographer

David Sims.
b Sheffield (UK), 1966.

Travis Scott photographed for Saint Laurent's Spring/Summer 2019 campaign.

Photograph by David Sims.

↳ THE FACE, i-D, C. KLEIN, McKENNA, M. WARD

ANTHONY SINCLAIR

When tailor Anthony Sinclair created the Conduit Cut in the 1950s at his showroom on Conduit Street, just around the corner from Savile Row, he found a new take on the classic British suit. Originally developed for Sinclair's clientele of British Army officers, the design featured slim trousers and a single-breasted jacket with a generous chest, soft shoulders, and a nipped waist. At a time when most suits were heavy and double-breasted, the lightweight, hourglass cut highlighted athleticism and youth, and its construction from worsted, mohair, or flannel cloth in such patterns as

glen plaid created a stately look. Among Sinclair's military customers was Terence Young, who would later enter the film industry and direct the first James Bond movie, *Dr. No*, in 1962. Young's familiarity with Sinclair's tailoring made the latter a natural fit to dress Scottish actor Sean Connery for a suit. Connery wore the now-iconic Sinclair suit in six Bond movies. It did become a little tighter over time, but Sinclair observed, "The only comment I want about my suits is that they are elegant. I've given Connery the same cut I've given every customer all my working life."

Tailor

Anthony Sinclair.
(Active 1950s–1980s).

Anthony Sinclair fitting Sean Connery for a suit in a publicity still for United Artists's *From Russia with Love*, London, 1963.

↳ BRIONI, CONNERY, HUNTSMAN, NUTTER

HEDI SLIMANE

Hedi Slimane's skin-tight, heavily rock star–infused look had a cataclysmic impact on men's fashion in the late 1990s and early 2000s. Though he considered becoming a journalist, Slimane was handpicked by Pierre Bergé in 1996 to steer Yves Saint Laurent's menswear, revitalizing a sensual 1970s aesthetic with kick-flare trousers, leather slickers, and sheeny suits. In 2001 he went to Dior Homme, perfecting an uber-tight suit-and-jean silhouette—Karl Lagerfeld very famously went on a diet to squeeze into Slimane's jeans. During this period, Slimane helped kick off a trend for slim suiting that trickled down to mass-market shops. He reigned as a celebrity favorite, dressing stars such as David Bowie and Brad Pitt. In 2012 he bounced back to Saint Laurent and landed at Celine in 2018, introducing menswear at the beloved French house. In the years that followed, a well-documented love affair with Los Angeles inspired Slimane's designs, which are resplendent with loud ponchos, bleached-out denim jackets, and slouching track pants.

Designer

Hedi Slimane.
b Paris (FR), 1968.

Hedi Slimane, 2012.

↳ **BOWIE, BROWNE, JAGGER, LAGERFELD, SAINT LAURENT, STYLES**

LUCKY BLUE SMITH

Scouted at just ten years old, Lucky Blue Smith grew up to be a teenage sensation who amassed 2.7 million followers on Instagram by his early twenties, making him one of the most popular male models in the world. With his striking pale blue eyes—described as the "iciest sapphire"—sharp jawline, and rockabilly style, Smith already had two international campaigns under his belt in 2015, when his agency advised him to revamp his look: become a little less homey and add a little more edge. His career took off the same year, with catwalk appearances and campaigns for fashion houses, including Tom Ford, Armani, Dunhill, Bottega Veneta, and Fendi, and appearances in magazines, such as *Vogue*, *V Man*, *GQ*, and *Harper's Bazaar*. Smith continues to book high-profile campaigns, appearing in ads for John Varvatos and Trussardi in 2020. That same year, he debuted an even further departure from his classic looks—a bleached, sleek buzz cut—sporting the style on two covers for *Man About Town*.

Model

Lucky Blue Smith.
b Spanish Fork, UT (USA), 1998.

Lucky Blue Smith outside the Maison Margiela Spring/Summer 2020 show, Paris, 2019.

Photograph by Hanna Lassen.

↳ ALFRED DUNHILL, ARMANI, BOTTEGA VENETA, FORD

PAUL SMITH

Paul Smith transformed British tailoring by combining traditional techniques and materials, such as houndstooth or tweeds, with whimsical flourishes, including colorful suit linings and eye-popping ties. After leaving school at fifteen, Smith took evening classes in tailoring and then went to work on Savile Row at Lincroft Kilgour, where he made clothes for high-profile men, including soccer star George Best. In 1970 he opened his own tiny shop, Paul Smith Vêtements Pour Homme, in his hometown of Nottingham with his girlfriend Pauline Denyer, who later became his wife. Smith showed his first collection in Paris in 1976 and three years later opened his much-loved shop on London's Floral Street. He was key, along with Giorgio Armani, in softening men's suiting during the 1980s, becoming a favorite of David Bowie, Bill Nighy, and Manolo Blahnik, who all wore his colorful socks. In 1995 London's Design Museum honored Smith with a retrospective, and he was knighted in 2000. Smith is admired for his lighthearted approach to clothing and applies this to his stores as well, such as the hot pink Luis Barragán–inspired Los Angeles location.

Designer

Paul Smith.
b Nottingham, England (UK), 1946.

Paul Smith in his London office.

Photograph by Tom Cockram.

↳ ARMANI, BEST, BOWIE, JOHN SMEDLEY, WESTWOOD

WILLI SMITH

In his all-too-short career, Willi Smith's exhilarating yet comparably affordable designs lent a jolt to American fashion. Smith specialized in easy-wearing, accommodating separates—for men and women—cut from natural fabrics that hung flatteringly on the wearer. In 1983, the year after Smith introduced menswear to his brand, WilliWear, he won the Coty American Fashion Critics' Award. A diligent patron of the arts, Smith lent his buoyant touch to costumes for the stage and screen, including for Spike Lee's 1988 film *School Daze*. WilliWear tees carried the work of

New York artists, such as Keith Haring, Barbara Kruger, and Jenny Holzer. In 1983 Smith created staff uniforms for Christo and Jeanne-Claude when the artists wrapped an island archipelago in Miami in pink fabric. Sadly, Smith died of AIDS in 1987 at the prime of his career. In 2020 the Cooper Hewitt, Smithsonian Design Museum in New York exhibited the first career retrospective of Smith's work.

Designer

Willi Smith.
b Philadelphia (USA), 1948.
d New York (USA), 1987.

Willi Smith, 1984.

Photograph by Jack Mitchell.

↳ BARTLETT, HARDISON,
   JEAN-RAYMOND, KELLY,
   ST. JACQUES

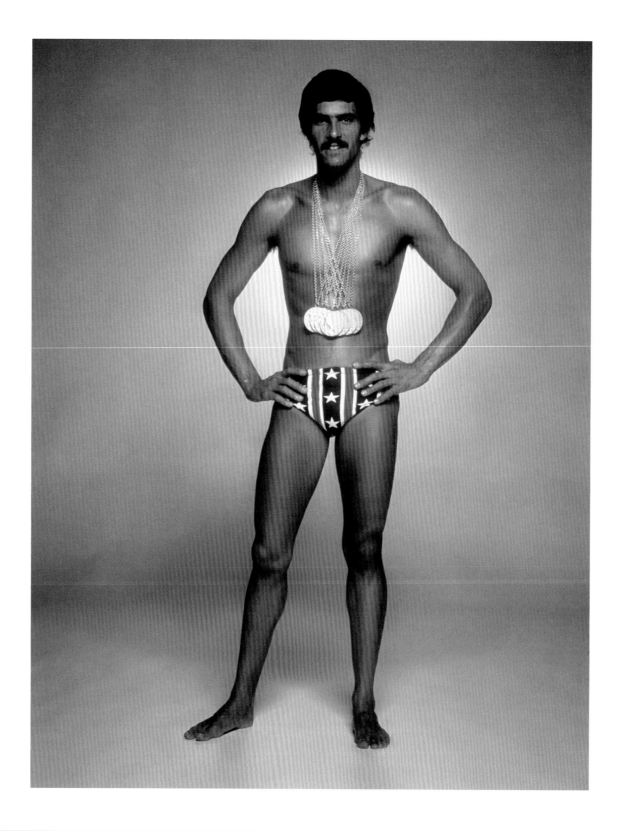

SPEEDO

Although its name has been used generically for skimpy swimming trunks, Speedo is a distinct brand with more than a century of innovative swimwear and closely linked to the Olympic Games: twenty-one of the twenty-two new world records at the 1972 games in Munich were set in Speedo swimwear. The success of American swimmer Mark Spitz, who won seven gold medals in his Speedo, established the brand as men's swimwear of choice for the next two decades. Speedo's founder, Alexander MacRae, a Scot who emigrated to Australia in 1910 and opened a knitwear factory,

anticipated the popularity of competitive swimming. In 1928 he began to produce the figure-hugging Racerback, a one-piece, non-wool women's bathing suit. The sleekness of the Racerback inspired employee Captain Parsons to invent the slogan "Speed on in your Speedos," and Speedo was born. Speedo's appeal to both Olympians and recreational swimmers has been reinforced by constant innovation, including introducing new textiles—such as nylon in 1957; Fastskin, based on sharkskin, in 2000; and most recently Hydralign, which helps maintain proper body alignment in the water.

Brand

Speedo.
est Sydney (ASL), 1914.

American swimmer Mark Spitz sporting a Speedo and the seven gold medals he won at the 1972 Munich Olympic Games, c. 1973.

Photograph by Terry O'Neill.

↳ GERNREICH, JANTZEN, OAKLEY, OCEAN PACIFIC, PENDLETON

ROBBIE SPENCER

Working at *Dazed* magazine since 2004, and eventually serving as the publication's creative director and executive fashion director, Robbie Spencer has helped mold contemporary British fashion. He has styled some of the magazine's most striking covers, including Ashton Sanders, Frank Ocean, Finn Wolfhard, and Young Thug. Spencer studied at the London College of Fashion, and in 2004, while still in school, he started an internship as a fashion assistant at *Dazed*, where he was mentored by the fashion director Nicola Formichetti. Spencer worked his way up,

getting involved in styling editorials, which drew on both his art background and his ability to find beauty in the unexpected. He often builds a shoot around a setting—rather than the clothes themselves—giving his work a directness reminiscent of street style. At *Dazed* he helped form the magazine's distinct identity while championing a new generation of photographers, such as Harley Weir, Tyler Mitchell, and Daniel Shea. Spencer has also styled shows and consulted for brands including Craig Green, A-Cold-Wall*, and Y/Project.

Stylist

Robbie Spencer.
b Swindon, England (UK), c. 1984.

Craig Green Fall/Winter 2020, styled by Robbie Spencer for *Dazed* China.

Photograph by Tom Johnson.

↳ A-COLD-WALL*, GREEN, HACK, SCHORR

SPERRY TOP-SIDER

"A wet deck was such a damn dangerous thing," exclaimed Paul Sperry, the Connecticut-born founder of Sperry and visionary behind America's preppy boat shoes. After falling from his sailboat deck in 1934 in the Long Island Sound, he devised a nonslip solution for slippery decks. By cutting herringbone-patterned grooves into natural rubber soles, paired with lined canvas uppers, his first 1935 prototype, the Circular Vamp Oxford, or CVO, was born. In 1937 Sperry evolved his original design to include a new upper crafted from specially tanned, water-resistant leather.

Using a classic stitched moccasin toe and unique saddle lacing, he created today's iconic Top-Sider, also called the Authentic Original, or A/O. It has become a defining staple of the Ivy League prep style and has been further popularized by sponsorships of America's Cup and the US Olympic sailing team. Its Sperry Cloud collaborations have creatively reimagined its materials and designs, partnering with contemporary men's labels including Beams, Noah, Band of Outsiders, A Bathing Ape, and Rowing Blazers.

Footwear

Sperry Top-Sider.
est New Haven, CT (USA), 1935.

John Legend wearing the Gold Cup Authentic Original Camden Boat Shoe, 2020.

↳ **ANDOVER SHOP, BABENZIEN, BEAMS, KENNEDY, NIGO, STERNBERG**

STEPHEN SPROUSE

Pioneering and irreverent, American fashion designer and artist Stephen Sprouse made a name for himself by mixing uptown polish with downtown punk. Sprouse began making clothes at nine years old, and by twelve he had met fashion greats such as Bill Blass and Geoffrey Beene. At fourteen the creative prodigy was sketching for Blass during the summer. Sprouse attended the Rhode Island School of Design but dropped out to work with Halston for three years. In 1983 he launched his own line of radical, couture-quality fashion. His collection ranged from men's fluorescent-colored spandex

tights with oversized blazers to retro-futuristic suiting in Day-Glo neons mixed with a handcrafted sensibility that captured the high-low spirit of the times. Sprouse established himself as part of New York's cultural guard, with friends including Jean-Michel Basquiat, Andy Warhol, and Keith Haring, all of whom he collaborated with on clothing designs. In 2001 he partnered with Marc Jacobs at Louis Vuitton, who featured Sprouse's graphic painting and graffiti-like lettering in his signature neons on the runway and applied them to men's T-shirts, sneakers, and leather accessories.

Designer

Stephen Sprouse.
b Dayton, Ohio (USA), 1953.
d New York (USA), 2004.

Models wearing Stephen Sprouse, 1984.

↳ BASQUIAT, BLASS, HALSTON, JACOBS, LOUIS VUITTON

GEORGE STAVRINOS

In his short life, George Stavrinos applied his meticulous, heavily detailed drawing style to depict women in ornate designer fashions and men at their most handsome. After graduating from the Rhode Island School of Design in 1969, Stavrinos started working with the design firm Push Pin Studios, leading him to commissions for Bonwit Teller and *GQ*. A few years later, he began to illustrate for Barneys New York, which was moving its image away from being a discount emporium and into high fashion, and eventually he worked for Bergdorf Goodman. He was also

creating covers for groundbreaking gay men's magazines, such as *Christopher Street*, *Blueboy*, and *Gay Source: A Catalog for Men*. Much like the work of his friend and peer Mel Odom, Stavrinos's loving depictions of muscular men in bicep-squeezing sweaters, taut trousers, high-collared dress shirts, and thigh-flashing shorts accentuated the beauty of the male body. In 2013, several decades after Stavrinos died of an AIDS-related illness, the Museum of American Illustration hosted an exhibition of his work, *The Vision of George Stavrinos*.

Illustrator

George Stavrinos.
b Somerville, MA (USA), 1948.
d New York (USA), 1990.

The Duke of Windsor, *GQ*, 1976.

Illustration by George Stavrinos.

↳ BARNEYS NEW YORK, FELLOWS, GQ, LOPEZ, L. WARD

EDWARD STEICHEN

Photographer

Born in Luxembourg in 1879, Edward Steichen was one of the twentieth century's most iconic photographers, contributing to the medium's development as high art with his signature soft focus. In 1881 Steichen arrived in the United States, and he took up photography in 1896, later capturing the attention of Alfred Stieglitz. In 1902 he cofounded Photo-Secession with Stieglitz, set up the Little Galleries of the Photo-Secession in New York, and contributed to legendary photo quarterly *Camera Work*. After working in Paris in the early 1900s, Steichen became the chief photographer for Condé Nast, a position he held from

1923 to 1938, and delved into his standout portraiture of iconic men, such as Charlie Chaplin, George Gershwin, Mei Lanfang, and Fred Astaire. Using a crisp, modernist style to capture the glamour of the times for *Vogue* and *Vanity Fair*, his oeuvre predated the field of men's fashion photography, further influencing later greats, including Richard Avedon and Bruce Weber. From 1947 to 1962 he was the Museum of Modern Art's director of photography, curating the momentous 1955 exhibition *The Family of Man*. His awards span France's Legion of Honor and the Presidential Medal of Freedom.

Edward Steichen.
b Bivange (LUX), 1879.
d West Redding, CT (USA), 1973.

William Haines wearing a three-piece flannel suit, photographed for *Vanity Fair*, c. 1930s.

Photograph by Edward Steichen.

↳ ASTAIRE, AVEDON, BEATON, LINDBERGH, WEBER

JOHN STEPHEN

Retailer John Stephen turned Carnaby Street, a small London backstreet, into the epicenter of the Swinging Sixties. Moving to London as a young man, the Scot worked at Moss Brothers and Vince Man's Shop. In 1957 Stephen and his partner, Bill Franks, opened their first boutique on Carnaby Street with young staff, loud music, and affordable clothes—including colorful jeans, unlined three-button jackets, and matelot shirts. Within a decade, Stephen— known as the King of Carnaby Street—owned fifteen different stores on the street, each selling its own barely perceptible variation on the look, making the thoroughfare a destination for fashion followers from around the world. A master of PR, he collaborated with pop stars (the Who, the Kinks, and the Rolling Stones all wore his designs), photographed his own clothes on models, and parked his Rolls-Royce outside his shops. After Carnaby Street lost its vibe, Stephen moved to Mayfair in 1973, selling luxury fashion, but the company closed by 1975. He once said, "Carnaby is my creation. I feel about it the same way Michelangelo felt about the beautiful statues he created."

Retailer

John Stephen.
b Glasgow (UK), 1934.
d London (UK), 2004.

John Stephen (second from the right) with three models outside of his shop on Carnaby Street, London, 1966.

Photograph by Terence Spencer.

↳ BEST, GRANNY TAKES A TRIP, I WAS LORD KITCHENER'S VALET, JAGGER, VINCE MAN'S SHOP

SCOTT STERNBERG

After a stint as a Hollywood agent, Scott Sternberg took a hard left turn into the world of fashion. In 2003 Sternberg launched Band of Outsiders, a throwback prep label with a hefty splash of modern wit. With Band of Outsiders, it was as if Sternberg had taken the clothes seen in 1965's revered photo book *Take Ivy* and spun them through the washer. His ties and oxford shirts—unadorned yet considerably slimmed down—became must-have items. In time Sternberg's slender corduroy blazers, tasteful ombré trucker jackets, and nautical-like knitwear were sold at more than two hundred stores worldwide. Band of Outsiders campaigns were as smile-inducing as the clothes, with stars such as Frank Ocean, Josh Brolin, Ed Ruscha, and Jason Schwartzman captured in pseudo-candid scenes. Sternberg's time at Band of Outsiders ended in 2015, but he soon started Entireworld, a sprightly direct-to-consumer label whose comfy sweatpants—in a Pantone-ian range of colors—became beloved in the COVID-quarantine moment.

Designer

Scott Sternberg.
b Dayton, OH (USA).

Band of Outsiders Fall/Winter 2019 collection at London Fashion Week Men's.

Photograph by Mitchell Sams.

↳ BABENZIEN, BROOKS BROTHERS, J.CREW, OUR LEGACY, SPERRY TOP-SIDER

STETSON HATS

STETSON

Born to a hatmaker in New Jersey in 1830, John B. Stetson headed west in search of gold as a young man, but instead his journey led him to create an American icon. In the late 1800s the broad-brimmed hat dubbed the Boss of the Plains became a symbol of the American West. While out West, Stetson realized that traditional fur-felt hats would make a more durable alternative to the impractical headwear of his fellow prospectors. In 1865, unsuccessful at finding gold, he borrowed sixty dollars from his sister and began making his "cowboy hats" in Philadelphia. The hat's high crown kept the wearer's head cool or warm, while the brim protected from the sun or rain. The light felt meant the hat could be worn easily. By 1899 the company was selling fifty thousand hats a year and was notable for its beneficial working conditions. The Stetson has been worn by everyone from Hollywood stars—including John Wayne, Matthew McConaughey, and Bradley Cooper, among others—to Texas oilmen and US presidents, whom the company still presents with personalized hats.

Milliner

Stetson.
est Philadelphia (USA), 1865.

Stetson advertisement, c. 1920s.

↳ DEAN, HERBERT JOHNSON HATTERS, LEE JEANS, LEVI'S, RED WING, ROCKMOUNT RANCH WEAR, WRANGLER

STERLING ST. JACQUES

During the hedonistic days of the late 1970s and '80s, model Sterling St. Jacques was a household name who ruled both the fashion runways and the dance floor of the infamous Studio 54. Along with good friend and fellow supermodel Pat Cleveland—as well as Bianca Jagger, Liza Minnelli, and even Caroline Kennedy—St. Jacques showed off his dancing skills at the hot spots of New York City nightlife. With breathtaking good looks and mesmerizing gray eyes, St. Jacques was arguably the first Black male supermodel. He walked for prestigious labels, such as

Givenchy, Willi Smith, and Halston, and modeled for both elite magazines (*Vogue*) and lowbrow publications (*Playmen*). The model also participated in the ground-breaking Battle of Versailles in 1973, which pitted five American fashion designers against five French designers considered the best in the world—including Yves Saint Laurent and Hubert de Givenchy. Although St. Jacques died from AIDS in 1984, at age twenty-six, he left an enduring legacy for future Black male models.

Model

Sterling St. Jacques.
b Salt Lake City, UT (USA), 1957.
d New York (USA), 1984.

Sterling St. Jacques dancing down the runway with model Pat Cleveland during a fashion show, 1977.

Photograph by Robin Platzer.

↳ BECKFORD, HALSTON, W. SMITH

SLY STONE

To many disco fans in the late 1960s and early '70s, Sly and the Family Stone was *the* band and Sly Stone (born Sylvester Stewart) was *the* man. With his extravagant Afro, mutton-chop sideburns, tight jumpsuits, flashy vests, and chunky gold chains, Stone not only invented a new fusion of funk and soul but also set the style for a generation of Black performers. Stone carefully controlled the clothes worn by the band, from appliquéd overalls to go-go dresses. As bassist Larry Graham recalls, "It was very deliberate: men and women, different races, dressing different." A natural

showman, Stone was wearing an eye-catching Halston outfit covered head-to-toe with gold sequins when he got married onstage before a concert crowd at Madison Square Garden in 1974. He also favored colorful suits in unexpected materials, such as a black velvet design with metallic stripes from the mod hotspot Granny Takes a Trip. The band's musical career peaked with a celebrated set at Woodstock in 1969 before the band gradually withdrew from public view—interrupted by a memorable Grammy appearance in 2006, when Stone sported a gold lamé trench coat and blond Mohawk.

Icon

Sly Stone (Sylvester Stewart).
b Denton, TX (USA), 1943.

Sly Stone of Sly and the Family Stone, London, 1973.

Photograph by Michael Putland.

↳ DAPPER DAN, M. DAVIS, GRANNY TAKES A TRIP, HALSTON

STÜSSY

In 1980 surfboard shaper Shawn Stussy was selling shirts promoting his New Wave Designs brand from his car along the California coastline. Stussy's hand-scrawled typography—inspired in part by his uncle, abstract painter Jan Stussy—made the shirts more than primitive promos. In 1984 Stussy took on Frank Sinatra Jr. (no relation to the performer) as a partner, and the line blossomed with chunky-logoed varsity jackets, all-over-print tees, and patterned button-ups that often riffed on monograms of haute institutions, such as Chanel. Stussy's profile was raised by the International Stussy Tribe, a loose consortium of stylish folks who cut across cultural lines. Keith Haring, hip-hop producer Dante Ross, Hiroshi Fujiwara, and The Clash's Mick Jones were all affiliated with the IST. In 1996 Shawn Stussy walked away from the brand, but the Sinatras continue to run the company. Today Stüssy is the rare label to be carried by both Urban Outfitters and Dover Street Market, reflecting its world-conquering scale.

Designer Brand

Stüssy.
est Laguna Beach, CA (USA), c. 1980.

A man wearing a Stüssy sweatshirt, c. 2000.

↳ FUJIWARA, KAWAKUBO, PALACE, SUPREME

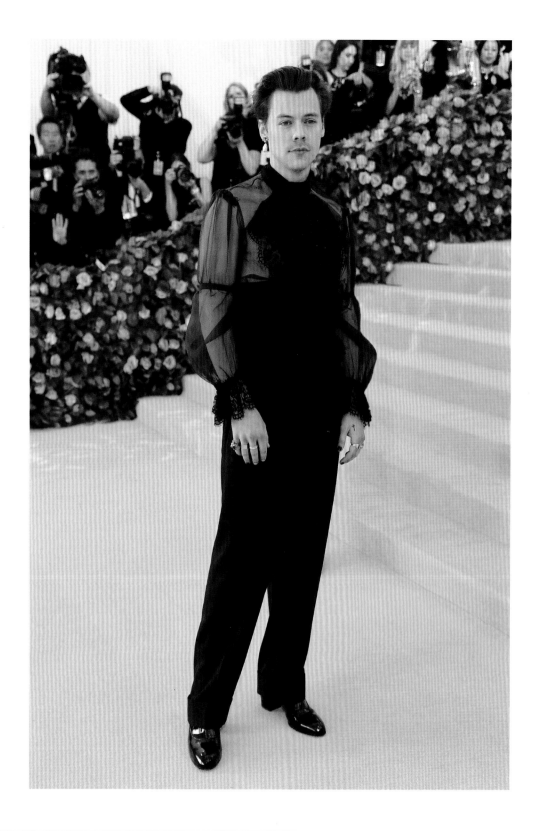

HARRY STYLES

Harry Styles was introduced to the world at just sixteen as a member of the British pop band One Direction. The group sold seventy million records, released five albums, and rebooted the concept of the boy band globally before taking a hiatus in 2015. Always the most flamboyant dresser in the band, Styles received a British Fashion Award in 2013 for his personal style. When he launched his solo career in 2017, he debuted a campy, colorful, and theatrical look with the help of British stylist Harry Lambert. Onstage or on the red carpet (Styles made his film debut in 2017's *Dunkirk*), he is regularly spotted in velvet, lamé, or floral suits that reference British glam rock, and he favors designers such as Charles Jeffrey, Harris Reed, and Jonathan Anderson. In 2018 Styles became the face of a Gucci campaign, kicking off a long and fruitful collaboration with designer Alessandro Michele. Styles regularly dresses in gender-bending clothing: in 2020 he wore a brown Gucci suit with a broderie anglaise shirt, a pearl necklace, and Mary Jane shoes to the BRIT Awards and appeared on the cover of *Vogue* in a tiered pale blue Gucci gown.

Icon

Harry Styles.
b Worcestershire, England (UK), 1994.

Harry Styles, wearing Gucci at the 2019 Met Gala celebrating the exhibition *Camp: Notes on Fashion* at the Metropolitan Museum of Art, New York.

Photograph by Jamie McCarthy.

↳ ANDERSON, GUCCI, JAGGER, C. JEFFREY, MICHELE

Sulka sang-froid

a pure silk robe

by

A. Sulka & Company Ltd

160 NEW BOND STREET, LONDON, W1Y 0LP.

SULKA

In the mid-1980s the *New York Times* confidently declared, "Nothing from Sulka will ever go out of style." By that point, the Manhattan haberdashery was nearing its one-hundredth year in business and had seen the likes of Winston Churchill, Henry Ford, and Clark Gable knot up its sumptuous silk neckties. Amos Sulka, a traveling salesman, and custom shirtmaker Leon Wormser established Sulka as a humble, compact shop in the waning nineteenth century. Located on lower Broadway, the shop's early clientele consisted of working-class Manhattanites,

such as police officers and butlers seeking custom-made shirts, yet soon a more upper-crust customer wandered in to buy the label's wares. By 1904 Sulka had a shop in Paris and its name was ringing out worldwide. What Sulka offered was high-caliber conservative dress clothes. Around the 1960s Sulka began to veer to its luxury side with more gusto through over-the-top vicuña wool dressing gowns and leopard skin gloves. Though its shops have closed in recent years, Sulka's reputation lives on: its ornate silk smoking jackets are still treasured vintage finds.

Designer Brand

Sulka.
est New York (USA), 1895.

Advertisement for Sulka silk robes, c. 1970s.

Photograph by Huxley.

↳ ARNYS, CHARVET, GABLE, HERMÈS

SUNSPEL

Though Nottingham would eventually become the heart of England's lace industry, in 1860 Thomas Hill established the Sunspel undergarment factory in the region. Sunspel's creamy, tender-to-the-touch cotton tops were among the first rudimentary T-shirts ever produced. As the British Empire sprawled in the early twentieth century, Sunspel acquired uber-plush Sea Island cotton from the West Indies, upping the luxury quotient of its posh underwear. In 1947 Sunspel introduced the men's boxer short to the British. The short's popularity took off in 1985 when Levi's

rolled out an ad campaign called "Laundrette," in which a handsome young man clad in nothing but a set of Sunspel boxers (you can tell they're Sunspel by the distinctive back panel) loads his jeans into the wash as onlookers ogle. The ad converted men to boxers, and Sunspel's sales soared. Sunspel again enjoyed a marketing boom in 2006 when James Bond (played by Daniel Craig) wore the label's specifically designed snug polos in *Casino Royale*.

Designer Brand

Sunspel.
est Nottingham, England (UK), 1860.

Model Nick Kamen in the Levi's "Laundrette" advertisement wearing Sunspel boxer shorts, 1985.

↳ CONNERY, HANES, C. KLEIN, LEVI'S

SUPREME

Though founded by James Jebbia as a traditional skate shop in 1994, Supreme simmered with larger ambitions from the start. Just a year into its existence, *Vogue* compared Supreme's magnetic appeal to a certain breed of in-the-know downtown denizen to that of haute-couture favorite Chanel. In the following years Supreme nimbly navigated the fashion industry, collaborating with brands both mainstream (Levi's, Timberland, Nike) and high-fashion (Undercover, Louis Vuitton, Comme des Garçons), without shedding its outsider status. Traditions be damned, its wares arrive in weekly "drops" that still garner around-the-block lines at its twelve stores worldwide. In 2018, when Jebbia won the CFDA Menswear Designer of the Year award, he said, "I never considered Supreme to be a fashion brand." His description has merit. By partnering with artists such as Damien Hirst and Nan Goldin and minting curious objects—including BMX bikes and punching bags—which sell at auction for small fortunes, Supreme has become not just a clothing label but an unstoppable cultural force.

Designer Brand

Supreme.
est New York (USA), 1994.

Photographer Antonio Griffith wearing a Supreme shirt during New York Fashion Week, 2017.

Photograph by Matthew Sperzel.

↪ BABENZIEN, LOUIS VUITTON, NIKE, PALACE, STÜSSY

DAIKI SUZUKI

Growing up in northern Japan in the 1970s, Daiki Suzuki pored over magazines documenting American fashion, such as *Popeye* and *Made in U.S.A. Catalog.* Suzuki studied at Vantan Design Institute in Tokyo, a city that was then (and often still is) fascinated by American fashion. He met Keizo Shimizu, owner of Union Square, an Americana-drenched clothing shop, who convinced Suzuki to relocate to the States to dredge up gear to resell back in Japan. By the late 1990s the men stopped selling clothes and started making their own. Shimizu established Nepenthes and

Suzuki founded Engineered Garments, where he has continuously refreshed his assorted Americana references, such as fishing gear, army uniforms, and workaday tailoring. EG is blissfully broad; its spring 2021 collection offered a saturated ikat poncho and a shimmering lounge singer–ready jacquard suit alongside staid button-downs and proper khaki shorts. In 2006 Woolrich appointed Suzuki head of its higher-end Woolen Mills line, and in 2008 *GQ* (belatedly) awarded Engineered Garments the label of Best New Menswear Designers in America.

Designer

Daiki Suzuki.
b Hirosaki City (JAP), 1962.

Daiki Suzuki, Nepenthes New York City office, 2011.

Photograph by Akira Yamada.

↳ ALDEN SHOES, BEAMS, BROOKS BROTHERS, MIYASHITA, WOOLRICH

SWATCH

With its colorful, playful, and pop aesthetic, Swatch transformed the wristwatch into a fashion accessory that was tailor-made for the disposable and fun sensibilities of the 1980s. Developed by Ernst Thomke, Elmar Mock, and Jacques Müller to counter the dominance of the digital watch, the analog Swiss-made design used a new injection-molding technique, creating a standard case that could be produced in endless iterations with different-colored parts, features, and prints, many of which were inspired by artists. This automated production also meant the Swatch could

be mass-produced and sold at just thirty-five dollars apiece. Sales of the watch increased from $3 million dollars in 1984 to $105 million in 1985, and collaborations turbocharged the brand's popularity. Kiki Picasso, Keith Haring, Vivienne Westwood, and Damien Hirst were brought in to create limited editions, which made many of the watches collector's items. The most covetable pieces have reached dizzying prices at auction; in the late 1990s, an original Kiki Picasso design sold for more than sixty thousand dollars. In 2015 Sotheby's sold a collection of 5,800 watches for six million dollars.

Accessory Design

Swatch.
est Zurich (SW), 1983.

Swatch founder and designer Jacques Müller showing off some of his creations, 1984.

Photograph by Ralph Crane.

↳ CASIO, NIGO, SCOTT, WESTWOOD

TAG HEUER

Founded in 1860 by twenty-year-old Edouard Heuer—who initially perfected silver pocket watches in Saint-Imier—the Swiss watch brand TAG Heuer has become a global phenomenon with a rich legacy in motorsport. This famously manifested on-screen when Steve McQueen wore the TAG Heuer Monaco while driving a Porsche 917 in the 1971 film *Le Mans*. In real life, the brand has a long-standing alliance with Formula 1 racing, including collaborative designs with the legendary F1 champion Ayrton Senna and the Aston Martin Red Bull Racing team. TAG Heuer's instruments are crafted for movement and precision, reaching an accuracy of 5/10,000 of a second. Over its 150-plus-year history, TAG Heuer's innovations include perfecting the stopwatch and inventing a self-winding crown. The brand also introduced series such as the Carrera, which was born in 1963 with a sports chronograph, along with the 1969 Monaco with its square case and automatic Calibre 11. Further championing the brand are its contemporary notable devotees, such as former US president Barack Obama (TAG Heuer 1500) and actor Matt Damon (Link Chronograph).

Accessory Design

TAG Heuer.
est Saint-Imier (SW), 1860.

Race car driver Mario Andretti before the USAC Champ Car race at Michigan International Speedway, 1970.

Photograph by Alvis Upitis.

↳ HUBLOT, McQUEEN, OMEGA,
    PANERAI, ROLEX

"THE TAILOR & CUTTER," JUNE 16, 1939
(Registered at the G.P.O. as a Newspaper)

PRICE FOURPENCE WEEKLY
ANNUAL SUBSCRIPTION 25/6 POST FREE

THE TAILOR & CUTTER
AND OUTFITTING NEWS
VOLUME 74   NUMBER 3791

Ascot Attire

HEREWITH two kits correct for Ascot, smart weddings and garden parties. On left, black morning coat with notched lapels, cream waistcoat, boldly striped trousers. Wing collar and grey cravat. Black top hat or, as alternative, grey.

On right, an all-grey pinhead outfit. Morning coat has double-breasted revers. Waistcoat double-breasted. Grey hat with black band. Double collar and narrow loose-end silk tie; grey gloves.

Morning coats as depicted are notable for graceful run of fronts, full chest and square shoulders. Both are cut short - waisted and have long tapering skirts. White buttonholes for weddings, coloured carnations at Ascot.

A. 7

THE TAILOR & CUTTER

For more than a century the *Tailor & Cutter* was *the* trade publication for tailors, transmitting the latest men's styles throughout the United Kingdom and the world. It was founded as the *Tailor* by John Williamson in Scotland in early 1866, but later that year he relocated to London, famed as the global center of men's tailoring, and merged his publication with another magazine, the *Cutter*. The weekly featured detailed illustrations and patterns that other tailors could reproduce—both promoting and benefiting from London's preeminence in bespoke menswear. At its height in the 1930s and '40s, the *Tailor & Cutter* proclaimed that it had "the largest circulation of any trade journal in the world issued for the tailoring, clothing, and allied trades." The *Tailor & Cutter*'s commercial empire also included a London academy for training tailors and worldwide correspondence courses; its annual awards were described as the Oscars of the industry. In the mid-twentieth century, the *Tailor & Cutter* lost its audience with the rise of ready-to-wear and the subsequent fall in the number of tailors, and it ceased publication in 1972.

Publication

The Tailor & Cutter.
est London (UK), 1866.

Cover of the *Tailor & Cutter*, June 1939.

↳ APPAREL ARTS, DNR, GENTRY

KENZO TAKADA

Kenzo Takada was one of fashion's great designers, whose dalliances with color and print caused a riotous stir over his thirty-five-year career. Among his peers, such as Karl Lagerfeld and Yves Saint Laurent, Takada stood out with his Japanese-inspired, avant-garde creations, paving the way for designers such as Rei Kawakubo and Yohji Yamamoto. Born in Himeji, Japan, Takada traveled to Paris after graduating from Tokyo's Bunka Fashion College in 1964. Six years later, in 1970, Takada opened a small boutique called Jungle Jap to sell his designs, which played with liberating proportions and gender-nonconforming aesthetics. After renaming his company Kenzo, the designer introduced menswear in 1983, furthering his cross-cultural codes and theatrical expressions, with bold-hued patterns, striped knits, voluminous overcoats, and tailored flair. In 1984 he was awarded the Chevalier de l'Ordre des Arts et des Lettres. After selling Kenzo to LVMH in 1993, Takada retired in 1999 and died in 2020. His energizing spirit endures and has been carried on by the label's successive creative directors, including Humberto Leon and Carol Lim (co–creative directors) and Felipe Oliveira Baptista.

Designer

Kenzo Takada.
b Himeji (JAP), 1939.
d Paris (FR), 2020.

Kenzo Takada in his Jungle Jap boutique in Galerie Vivienne, Paris, 1970.

Photograph by Hiroyuki Iwata.

↳ KAWAKUBO, LAGERFELD,
Y. SAINT LAURENT,
Y. YAMAMOTO

JUN TAKAHASHI

"We Make Noise, Not Clothes" is a slogan that appears often on clothes from Undercover, the label Jun Takahashi founded in 1990. It's an apt summation of Undercover's men's designs, which tend to startle and surprise. Winter caps brandish devilish horns, jackets are printed with stills from *A Clockwork Orange* (1971), and pleated skirts flow to the floor. Takahashi is apt to transform his clothes into billboards for the work of creatives whom he admires, such as the artist Cindy Sherman. He has a special love for musical acts (in the early 1990s, Takahashi played in a Sex Pistols cover band), including the Talking Heads and Television, both of which have appeared on Undercover pieces. Takahashi is also a savvy businessman—Undercover stores stock a heap of easy-to-wear graphic tees—and since 2010 has designed the Gyakusou running collection for Nike (*gyakusou* is Japanese for "running in reverse"). In 2012 he created the brisk-selling UU collection for the Japanese mass retailer Uniqlo.

Designer

Jun Takahashi.
b Kiryu (JAP), 1969.

Undercover's UNDERMAN collection,
Spring/Summer 2011.

Photograph by Peter White.

↳ ABLOH, NIGO, NIKE,
SIMONS, UNIQLO

ANDRÉ LEON TALLEY

André Leon Talley discovered *Vogue* as a child in Durham, North Carolina, in the late 1950s, sparking a desire to explore the world of fashion. Receiving a scholarship to Brown University, he graduated in 1972, eventually relocating to New York. There he assisted Diana Vreeland at the Costume Institute at the Metropolitan Museum of Art, opening the door for later jobs for Andy Warhol at *Interview* magazine, *Women's Wear Daily*'s Paris bureau, and *W* magazine. Talley joined *Vogue* in 1983 and over the next three decades ascended as a writer, editor, and influencer. Whether it was tailored

shorts, fine suits, or bespoke shirts given to him by Karl Lagerfeld, his clothing choices were celebrated, earning him a permanent place in *Vanity Fair*'s International Best-Dressed Hall of Fame in 1994. In recent years he has worn magnificent kaftans custom-made by Tom Ford, Valentino, and Ralph Rucci. He has also made a statement in daywear with velour tracksuits and Uggs, even appearing in the brand's ads. Talley is the author of several books, including his memoir *The Chiffon Trenches,* published in 2020, the same year he was awarded France's Chevalier de l'Ordre des Arts et des Lettres.

Icon/Writer

André Leon Talley.
b Washington, DC (USA), 1948.

André Leon Talley wearing a coat and tie by Tom Ford, smoking suit by Ralph Lauren, shirt by Charvet, and shoes by Roger Vivier, Paris, photographed for *Vanity Fair*, 2013.

Photograph by Jonathan Becker.

↳ CHARVET, FORD, LAGERFELD

JUERGEN TELLER

With his offbeat, gritty aesthetic and a readiness for self-parody, German photographer Juergen Teller is firmly established in the fashion world. Fearless, Teller moved to London in 1986 not speaking a word of English and worked in the music industry shooting album covers, creating portraiture with stark, overexposed images. His entry into the world of fashion was explosive: the 1996 photograph of a naked Kristen McMenamy with *VERSACE* in a heart scrawled in red lipstick across her chest made major headlines. Since then he has collaborated with fashion royalty, including Yves Saint Laurent and Celine, although the clothes often play only one part in the complex images he creates. Despite that, Teller shot every Marc Jacobs campaign between 1998 and 2014—including photographing the band Sonic Youth wearing the clothes onstage—and the Missoni family invited him to their home in 2010 to shoot three generations of the family. All were drawn by Teller's uncompromising, distinctive vision, his refusal to sugarcoat his images, and his sardonic sense of humor.

Photographer

Juergen Teller.
b Erlangen (GER), 1964.

Cole Mohr and Shane Gambill, Marc Jacobs Men's Spring/Summer 2013 for *AnOther* magazine.

Photograph by Juergen Teller.

↳ JACOBS, MISSONI, PALACE, STÜSSY

KARL TEMPLER

A British-born stylist and the former creative director of *Interview* magazine, Karl Templer's love of fashion started early. For his first job he worked at Woodhouse, a menswear store in London, and it was there that Templer caught wind of the city's dynamic nightlife scene and style magazines, including *i-D* and *The Face*, the latter of which he contributed to early in his career. After moving to New York in the 1990s, he worked alongside photographer Richard Avedon for a Hugo Boss men's campaign. But soon Templer built his own clientele, styling for DKNY and

Costume National with his signature aesthetic, portraying men as polished yet youthful, irreverent, and cool. He cemented longstanding partnerships with photographer Steven Meisel, often shooting together for *Vogue Italia*, and art director and photographer Fabien Baron. In addition to being the former creative director of *Arena Homme +*, Templer has contributed to *Pop*, *V*, and *W* magazines. He has also consulted for Sacai and styled campaigns and collections for Dior, Coach, Moncler, Valentino, and Tommy Hilfiger.

Stylist

Karl Templer.
b London (UK), (Active 1990s—).

Idris Elba styled by Karl Templer for *Interview* magazine, August 2016.

Photograph by Craig McDean.

↳ ABE, AVEDON, BARON, THE FACE, HUGO BOSS, MEISEL

THE TEMPTATIONS

The Temptations were perhaps the original boy band, whose costumes—though sometimes a bit kitsch—became synonymous with a certain kind of brilliant showmanship. From 1960 onward the Motown quintet spent more than a decade at the top of the charts, with each member adding his voice to songs that have become American classics, such as "Ain't Too Proud to Beg" and "My Girl." Their vocal harmonies and tightly choreographed dance moves were echoed by the group's uniform attire. These stage costumes were widely imitated: matching sharply cut tuxedos or jewel-tone suits and, later, fringed and floppy disco frippery that looked over-the-top even then but proved hugely influential on other musical acts. The style lesson of the Temptations wasn't so much in what they wore but how they wore it—as a team. Despite a rotating cast of singers, the matching outfits created a sense of visual unity that has become the template for boy bands from the Jackson 5 and the Backstreet Boys to BTS.

Icons

The Temptations (1973). Dennis Edwards. b Fairfield, AL (USA), 1943. d Chicago (USA), 2018. Melvin Franklin. b Montgomery, AL (USA), 1942. d Los Angeles (USA), 1995. Damon Harris. b Baltimore (USA), 1950. d Baltimore (USA), 2013. Richard Street. b Detroit (USA), 1942. d Las Vegas (USA), 2013. Otis Williams. b Texarkana, TX (USA), 1941.

The Temptations at the Hammersmith Odeon, London, 1973.

↪ THE BEATLES, STONE, WHITTEN

OUIGI THEODORE

Through his New York City–based menswear boutique and label, The Brooklyn Circus—or BKc—designer Ouigi Theodore meticulously curates haberdashery and tailored casual designs. Born in Port-au-Prince, Haiti, Theodore moved to Brooklyn when he was eight. Growing up in Crown Heights, his fashion influences were Fred Astaire, James Brown, and Liberace. Theodore is an alumnus of the State University of New York at Stony Brook and later studied graphic design at the Fashion Institute of Technology. In 2006 he opened BKc in the Boerum Hill neighborhood of Brooklyn.

Once dubbed the Bearded Dandy of Brooklyn by the *New York Times*, Theodore elevates streetwear style to an artform, creating clothing and accessories that are retro yet modern, including varsity jackets, sweatshirts, graphic T-shirts, bow ties, and straw boaters. The Brooklyn Circus's Culture editorial platform celebrates Black creatives, including celebrity men's stylist Marcus Paul and Guinean shoe designer Armando Cabral. With fans from Japan to Johannesburg, The Brooklyn Circus has collaborated with brands, including Mark McNairy, Todd Snyder, Champion, and Casio.

Designer

Ouigi Theodore.
b Port-au-Prince (HT), (Active 2000s—).

Sam Lambert and Shaka Maidoh of Art Comes First, styled by BKc, c. 2015.

Photograph by John Midgley.

↳ CASIO, CHAMPION, GOLDEN
   BEAR, J.CREW, LAUREN

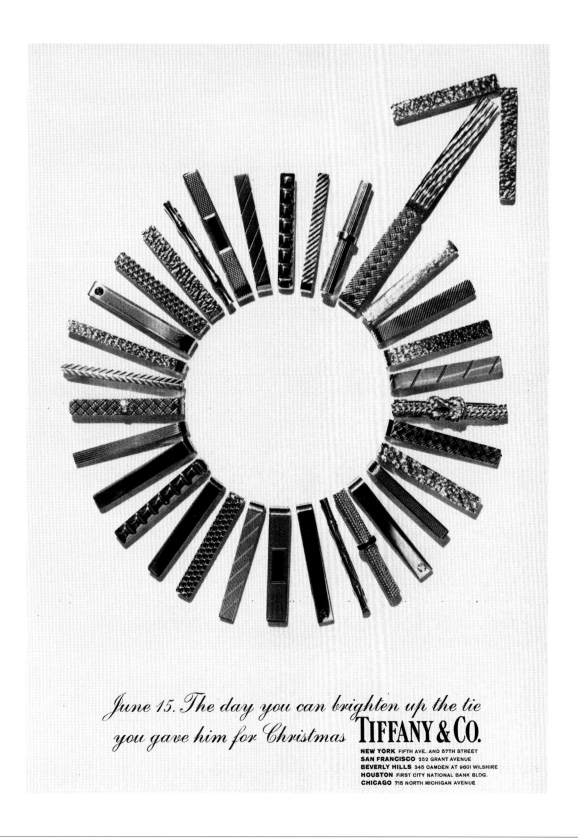

June 15. The day you can brighten up the tie you gave him for Christmas **TIFFANY & CO.**

NEW YORK FIFTH AVE. AND 57TH STREET
SAN FRANCISCO 252 GRANT AVENUE
BEVERLY HILLS 345 CAMDEN AT 9601 WILSHIRE
HOUSTON FIRST CITY NATIONAL BANK BLDG.
CHICAGO 715 NORTH MICHIGAN AVENUE

TIFFANY & CO.

What began in 1837 as Charles Lewis Tiffany's "stationery and fancy goods emporium" has become a global leader in the jewelry industry—and one of the most enduring purveyors of American style. In its nearly two-centuries-long history, Tiffany & Co. has influenced American culture in a multitude of ways, from publishing the country's first mail-order catalog—the *Blue Book*—in 1845 to producing the US's first stopwatch in 1866. By the turn of the twentieth century there was such demand for Tiffany & Co. gold pocket watches that the company built its own factory in Geneva. Through the mid-twentieth century, Tiffany watches were an all-American status symbol—President Franklin D. Roosevelt received one for his birthday in 1945. While men's wedding bands, cuff links, and luxury leather goods have long been part of Tiffany's repertoire, the company introduced its first dedicated men's collection in 2019, offering a range of elegant yet unpretentious pieces, including styles such as calfskin cuffs, signet rings, and chain necklaces—the sort of items that seem only to get better with time.

Accessory Design

Tiffany & Co.
est New York (USA), 1837.

Tiffany & Co. advertisement, 1969.

↳ CARTIER, JACOB & CO.,
  LINDBERGH, PATEK PHILIPPE

WOLFGANG TILLMANS

German artist and photographer Wolfgang Tillmans had a leading role in documenting London's club scene of the 1990s. Working for contemporary magazines such as *Purple* and *i-D* after graduating from art school in Bournemouth, England, he approached photojournalism with the same attitude he employed in his fashion work. Always dressed casually in T-shirts, sneakers, and jeans or sweatpants, Tillmans captured the flamboyance, excitement, and sexuality of fashionable young Londoners listening to electropop in clubs; his editorials featured fashion models who were more likely to appear in baggy old T-shirts and army-surplus kit than the latest high fashion. Tillmans, who took his first photographs at ten years old, creates images that capture an alternate reality in which the environment— be it a park bench or a tree—plays as important a role as the model and the clothes they wear. He has also explored extensively the nature of gender and sexuality, with images of female and male friends naked from the waist up and down, respectively. In 2000 he won the Turner Prize for "challenging the boundaries between art and photography."

Photographer

Wolfgang Tillmans.
b Remscheid (GER), 1968.

Actor Félix Maritaud, 2019.

Photograph by Wolfgang Tillmans.

↳ FANTASTIC MAN, i-D, SCHORR, TELLER

TIMBERLAND

Founded in New England, Timberland has achieved a universal appeal, worn by sharply dressed creatives and construction workers alike. But back in 1952 the company was born as a small shoemaker known as the Abington Shoe Company, which produced unlabeled hand-stitched leather shoes. Everything changed two decades later when a first-of-its-kind molding technique resulted in the brand's now-iconic six-inch nubuck leather boot. Dubbed the Timberland, the waterproof shoe quickly became a megaseller in army-surplus stores across the region.

A global revolution soon followed when the company was rebranded as Timberland in 1978 and the label expanded to upscale retailers, such as Bloomingdale's. In the early 1990s Timberland footwear became a street-fashion staple, reportedly popularized by New York drug dealers, and sales skyrocketed. Notorious B.I.G. and Tupac Shakur wore the boots on magazine covers and name-checked them in lyrics. Timberland initially tried to distance itself from the hype, but has since fully embraced this fan base, who have solidified the shoe as an emblem of hip-hop style.

Footwear

Timberland.
est Boston (USA), 1952.

Jay-Z attending the 1st Annual Roc City Classic, New York, 2015.

Photograph by Prince Williams.

↳ CARHARTT, CLARKS, CONVERSE, DR. MARTENS, JAY-Z, RED WING, SHAKUR

TIN TAN

Born Germán Valdés, Tin Tan was a scene-stealing Mexican comedian and actor, who appeared in more than one hundred films over his prolific career. On-screen Tin Tan was an avatar for the Pachuco style. Originated by proud Mexican American youths in border towns in the 1930s, this subculture wore lengthy zoot suits with tilted fedoras and listened to swinging jazz music. Its reach expanded to Los Angeles and the American Southwest, and the style was eventually imported to Mexico City around the 1940s by local comics—most prominently Tin

Tan. In movies—in which he first appeared in 1944—Tin Tan wore prime Pachuco fashions, such as sport coats that were nearly as long as most topcoats, towering wide-brimmed hats, and patterned pocket squares that flowed from his jacket pocket like waterfalls. He, of course, added his own signature details, most notably his petite, almost drawn-on mustache. Tin Tan also could pare back his style, and in many films he wore pristine tuxedos and white bow ties that further revealed just how raffish this comedian really could be.

Icon

Tin Tan (Germán Valdés).
b Mexico City (MEX), 1915.
d Mexico City (MEX), 1973.

Tin Tan, Mexico City, c. 1954.

Photograph by Simón Flechine.

↪ ASTAIRE, BRUMMELL, CALLOWAY, CHAVARRIA, GABLE

RICCARDO TISCI

A graduate of Central Saint Martins College of Art and Design, Riccardo Tisci soared quickly through the fashion world. In 2005, just a year after debuting his own collection at Milan Fashion Week, Tisci was appointed creative director of womenswear at Givenchy. In 2008 he took over men's design for the posh Parisian label, tilting in a decidedly gothic and graphic-rich direction. The Givenchy men's look was defined by voluminous checked shirts, leather skirts, and boxy shorts worn intriguingly over tights. Tisci's ornate, almost severe style was said to be inspired by his Catholic upbringing, but he also keenly brought streetwear codes into runway fashion. His high-priced T-shirts, which were coated in mammoth prints, such as a snarling rottweiler, were inescapable for a time. In 2011 he made Kanye West a conversation-stirring leather kilt for the *Watch the Throne* tour and dressed him and Kim Kardashian for their wedding in 2014. Tisci left Givenchy in 2017 but soon joined Burberry as its chief creative.

Designer

Riccardo Tisci.
b Taranto (IT), 1974.

Riccardo Tisci, Oxford, 2018.

Photograph by Mikhael Subotzky.

↳ BURBERRY, JAY-Z, NIKE, WEST, WESTWOOD

TOD'S

The Gommino, an Italian-made soft moccasin constructed using thirty-five pieces of leather, is the most instantly recognizable design from luxury empire Tod's. Named after the 133 rubber pebbles on its soles, this functional and stylish shoe became a commercial hit after it was worn by Italian industrialist and menswear icon Gianni Agnelli in the late 1970s. Started by Filippo della Valle in the 1920s as a small shoemaking business, Tod's later transformed when his grandson Diego dropped out of law school to join the family business. In 1978 Diego introduced what would become Tod's iconic driving shoe, and after the official launch of the brand in 1983, it began to build its international profile, eventually collaborating with designers including Calvin Klein and Geoffrey Beene. In its forty-plus-year history, the basic structure of the Gommino has not changed, but it has been produced in endless iterations, with styles available in dozens of leathers, suedes, and exotic skins, as well as hand-painted editions. Diego continues to produce Tod's products in Italy, as the style and heritage of the country remain central to the brand.

Footwear

Tod's.
est Cassett d'Ete, Marche (IT), 1983.

Sotheby's France president Alexander Kraft wearing Tod's Gommino loafers during Milan Fashion Week, 2014.

Photograph by Vanni Bassetti.

↳ AGNELLI, BEENE, BELGIAN SHOES, ELKANN, GUCCI, C. KLEIN

TOMMY TON

In the early 2010s there was no greater status symbol in fashion than having your street style captured by Tommy Ton. Thanks to his work, what was happening on the streets felt just as relevant as what was happening on the runway. Hailing from the suburbs of Toronto, Tommy Ton began his career in the buying office at Canada's luxury department store Holt Renfrew, and in 2005 created *Jak and Jil*, a blog about stylish Torontonians going about their daily lives. Ton had no formal photography training, yet his images, noted for their personality and authenticity, quickly gained momentum and popularity on a global scale. Ton preferred candid, in-motion images, as well as close-up detail shots: Nick Wooster flashing an unbuttoned collar suddenly sparked a must-follow trend; and men everywhere started ditching their socks when Ton photographed European editors wearing dress shoes without them. As his blog grew in popularity, Ton became a fixture at fashion weeks around the world, shooting street style for the likes of *GQ* and *Style.com*. Changing from his photography career, Ton was appointed creative director of the contemporary fashion label Deveaux New York in 2017.

Photographer

Tommy Ton.
b Oakville, Ontario (CAN), 1984.

Street style during Pitti Uomo 86, Florence, 2014.

Photograph by Tommy Ton.

↳ CORTINA, CUNNINGHAM, GQ, RUBINSTEIN, SCHUMAN, TALLEY, WOOSTER

JEAN TOUITOU

Jean Touitou entered the fashion world in the late 1970s as an office assistant for Kenzo Takada. Following a brief and unsuccessful foray into the music business, Touitou established A.P.C. (Atelier de Production et de Création) in Paris in 1987. The label presented an uncomplicated French style with camel-colored cargo trousers, reliable raglan-sleeved coats, and crisp T-shirts. Within its first decade, A.P.C. opened shops in Tokyo and New York, as well as a catalog business and an online shop. Seriously stiff raw jeans became its signature product, which customers would diligently break in over years. A keen collaborator, Touitou tapped Kanye West for a capsule collection in 2014 and more recently worked on clothes with Kid Cudi and Catherine Deneuve. In the early 2010s, A.P.C. introduced the Butler Program, through which customers can trade in their masterfully worn-in A.P.C. indigo jeans for a new pair at half price, and then A.P.C. resells the used pair at a premium—an early example of upcycling.

Designer

Jean Touitou.
b Tunis (TUN), 1951.

Luke Jenner for A.P.C. Fall/Winter 2004.

Photograph by Pierre Bailly.

↳ ACNE STUDIOS, LEVI'S, TAKADA, TROUBLÉ, YAMANE

TRICKER'S

The oldest continuous footwear firm in England, Tricker's was established in 1829 in Northampton, the country's central cradle of shoe manufacturing. It's said that by 1840 there were as many as 1,821 shoemakers that called Northampton home, yet Tricker's was distinguished by its smart, country-oriented boots. Farmers and other rural denizens cherished these solid, Goodyear-welted stompers, which were markedly weatherproof. Through the 1900s Tricker's fabricated dressy brogued lace-ups and derby walking shoes, bringing its sturdy style into towns across England. A favorite of Prince Charles, Tricker's received a Royal Warrant in 1989. Around this period the company's rugged, almost chunky boots and shoes became appreciated as objects of pure style, particularly in Japan. In recent years Tricker's has collaborated with British boutiques, such as End, and runway designers, such as Junya Watanabe. In 2019, the same year it opened a shop in Tokyo, Tricker's reported that 80 percent of its shoes are now sold overseas.

Footwear

Tricker's.
est Northampton, England (UK), 1829.

Tricker's Stow Country Boot.

Photograph by Charles Ward.

↳ CHURCH'S, JOHN LOBB BOOTMAKER, R.M.WILLIAMS, UNITED ARROWS, WATANABE

AGNÈS TROUBLÉ

Agnès Troublé perfected the art of simple Parisian chic. A single mother of two at only twenty years old, Troublé spent time at *Elle* magazine and as a stylist before deciding in the early 1970s that she was more interested in design. In 1975 she opened her first agnès b. shop, drawing on the look of Left Bank Beats to offer unpretentious staples that cut a graceful silhouette without ever getting in the way. For women she became renowned for the simplest of garments: a peasant-ish snap cardigan that she put onto her store racks in 1979. Her menswear—which she introduced in 1981—exuded a confident restraint. There were Breton striped shirts, workwear-ish navy sport coats, trim khakis, and scarves to tie the whole subdued look together. Troublé is a functional designer, not one preoccupied with fantasy. Despite her stint at *Elle*, she has never taken out an advertisement in a magazine—a fact she is quite proud of. As Troublé told the *Guardian* in 2006, reflecting back on her three-decade career: "Fashion does not interest me, only style."

Designer

Agnès Troublé.
b Versailles (FR), 1941.

agnès b. Spring/Summer 2018.

↳ HOWELL, JIL SANDER, PICASSO, TOUITOU

TURNBULL & ASSER

If you can judge a clothier by its clients, then Turnbull & Asser earns exceptionally high marks. The 135-year-old atelier—which has sat in the same location on London's Jermyn Street since 1903—has fashioned clothes for a deep well of discerning gents, such as Ronald Reagan, Pablo Picasso, and Charlie Chaplin. In 1941 Winston Churchill commissioned Turnbull to make a "siren suit," a pull-on tailored set for maximum wartime efficiency. In the 1962 film *Dr. No*, Turnbull & Asser outfitted Sean Connery in shirts with curious turnback cuffs that would be dubbed

the "James Bond cuff." Around this period, the youthquake that rocked London shook Turnbull & Asser out of its safe conservatism. The label got hip to a modish style with riotous spotted shirts and slick silk turtlenecks. A bolder edge still permeates Turnbull's wares today, particularly in the brand's regal tapestry-weave robes. Yet Turnbull's bread and butter remain its immaculate thirty-three-piece dress shirts, the perfect example of why the label has held a Royal Warrant since 1980.

Designer Brand

Turnbull & Asser.
est London (UK), 1885.

Robert Clark, head pattern cutter at Turnbull & Asser, 1955.

Photograph by Slim Aarons.

↳ BROOKS BROTHERS, CHARVET, CONNERY, PICASSO, SULKA

UMBRO

Founded by brothers Harold and Wallace Humphreys in 1920, Umbro, during the first many decades of its existence as a soccer supplier, focused on the pitch. And there it thrived. In 1958 the Brazil national team won its first World Cup while draped in Umbro uniforms. By 1966 nearly every team competing in the World Cup wore signature Umbro kits. Yet as "casuals" culture swept through soccer hooliganism beginning in the mid-to-late 1970s, and rowdy fans wore luxury labels such as Stone Island, C.P. Company, Lacoste, and Sergio Tacchini

to camouflage themselves, soccer outfitters began aligning with broader fashion. The lively, colorful jerseys Umbro trotted out in the waning twentieth century could be worn as easily with jeans off the field as with nylon shorts on it. To this day, Umbro's aquamarine and geometric jerseys inspire streetwear brands such as Supreme and Palace. In the 2010s Umbro collided with high fashion as never before by collaborating with Off-White and Gosha Rubchinskiy.

Brand

Umbro.
est Wilmslow, Cheshire (UK), 1924.

Umbro Pro Training x The Rig Out
Spring/Summer 2015.

Photograph by Glenn Kitson.

↳ ABLOH, PALACE, RUBCHINSKIY,
   SUPREME

Wool Cashmere Chesterfield Coat £129.90

Ultra Light Down Jacket £59.90

Ultra Light Down Parka £69

Outerwear is you. Show your inner self on the outside.

LifeWear

UNIQLO

Japanese entrepreneur Tadashi Yanai likes to say that Uniqlo is not a fashion company but a technology company. The fast-fashion brand known globally for its well-designed and well-priced basics made its name by combining stylish clothes with technical prowess. Since opening his first Unique Clothing Company store in Hiroshima in 1984, Yanai has followed the principles of American brands such as Gap, producing everything that is sold in his stores. To create these products, Uniqlo works with textile masters, or *takumi*, who develop cutting-edge materials such as

HEATTECH, LifeWear, and AIRism, which have become defining elements of the brand, and also collaborates with designers, including Jil Sander, Jonathan Anderson, and Christophe Lemaire. Since 2016 Lemaire has been the artistic director of Uniqlo U, creating everyday basics, such as blazers, T-shirts, and chinos, in his signature muted palette. Despite its global reach, Uniqlo remains committed to giving back to society through sustainable practices, and in 2004 they signed a Global Quality Declaration pledging to stop making low-priced, low-quality clothing.

Retailer

Uniqlo.
est Yamaguchi (JAP), 1949.

Uniqlo Fall/Winter 2015 advertisement featuring designers Joe and Charlie Casely-Hayford, choreographer Wayne McGregor, and dancer Louis McMiller.

Photograph by Sebastian Kim.

↳ ANDERSON, GAP, J.CREW, JIL SANDER, LEMAIRE, UNITED ARROWS

UNITED ARROWS

Founded in 1989, United Arrows's next-generation retail concept gave birth to Japan's legendary select shops. Created by alums of multiconcept store Beams, cofounders Osamu Shigematsu, Yasuto Kamoshita, and Hirofumi Kurino decided to invent their own sartorial stamp, beginning with a storefront in Tokyo's Shibuya district that both offered stylish clothes and promoted a fashionable way of life. With a highly curated edit of tailored clothing and elevated fashions—the founders were initially inspired by the 1980s fashion photography of Bruce Weber and styling by Joe McKenna—United Arrows evolved the notion of men's dress, taking modern classics and adding a highly honed Japanese twist. They continue to stock designers from across the world, such as Dries Van Noten, Haider Ackermann, and Chitose Abe's Sacai, and also sell their own sublabels, such as Kamoshita's eponymous brand Camoshita and current creative director Motofumi Kogi's United Arrows & Sons. Their bestselling suits and ties are also paired with limited-edition collaborations with Adidas, Nigo, The North Face Purple Label, Kith, Dr. Martens, and Rimowa.

Retailer

United Arrows.
est Tokyo (JAP), 1989.

Motofumi "Poggy" Kogi, Hirofumi Kurino, and Yasuto Kamoshita, photographed for *GQ Japan*, October 2017.

Photograph by Ryosuke Maezawa.

↳ ABE, BARNEYS NEW YORK, BEAMS, BROOKS BROTHERS, McKENNA, WEBER

UNITED COLORS
OF BENETTON.

UNITED COLORS OF BENETTON

Before United Colors of Benetton became globally renowned for both its rainbow-colored knits and attention-grabbing, progressive advertisements, the brand was the seed of an idea of Italian businessman Luciano Benetton. Established in 1965 with his three siblings, Benetton espoused an easy, casual wearability with Italian flair. The brand came to prominence in the 1980s designing affordable, comfortable separates, such as polo shirts and windbreakers, in bright, candied hues. However, it wasn't until 1982, when Benetton joined forces with photographer Oliviero Toscani on campaigns that raised

awareness of issues of inequality, social injustice, and the AIDS epidemic, that the brand proved the power of socially conscious marketing—something that has become inseparable from its identity. After years of the brand's steady decline, Luciano Benetton returned to the company in 2017, hoping to revive the label as "Benetton." In 2019 he appointed designer Jean-Charles de Castelbajac artistic director to elevate the label's look, reviving house codes with new, contemporary men's silhouettes, such as quilted tactical vests and velcro puffers in clashing colorways.

Brand

United Colors of Benetton.
est Ponzano Veneto (IT), 1965.

United Colors of Benetton advertisement, c. 2000s.

Photograph by Oliviero Toscani.

↪ CASTELBAJAC, GAP, HILFIGER, MISSONI, UNIQLO

ELLEN VON UNWERTH

Discovered at twenty years old while passing by a scout on the street, Ellen von Unwerth, an orphan who had grown up in Frankfurt's foster-care system, left her native Germany for Paris in 1974 to model. About a decade into her career, a boyfriend gave her a camera before she embarked on a trip to Kenya, where she would stage her first impromptu photo shoot. Her career behind the viewfinder took off in 1989 after she captured Claudia Schiffer in a Guess campaign. Unwerth's images, which have been published in high-fashion magazines, such as

Vanity Fair and *L'Uomo Vogue*, as well as on album covers, are provocative and playful. The subjects of her work are frequently women who are unapologetically in control and men who appear remarkably sultry. She's portrayed a dark-eyed Christian Bale lounging in bed while wearing a silk robe, a henley-wearing Brad Pitt contemplatively staring off into the distance, and, more recently, Gen Z star Cole Sprouse in a leather jacket with swoopy Elvis-inspired hair. In 2018 she published the first issue of her own magazine, *VON*.

Photographer

Ellen von Unwerth.
b Frankfurt (GER), 1954.

Hugh Grant, *W* magazine, October 2016.

Photograph by Ellen von Unwerth.

↳ BIRD, HAWKESWORTH,
L'UOMO VOGUE, MEISEL

ILARIA URBINATI

For more than a decade, the Los Angeles–based stylist Ilaria Urbinati has been dressing some of the most high-profile men in entertainment. Born in Rome and raised in Paris, Urbinati entered the fashion world as a writer, penning articles for style and culture publications, and a buyer before becoming a stylist. Urbinati's past and present clients are truly A-list—Dwayne Johnson, Chris Evans, Rami Malek, Bradley Cooper, Tom Hiddleston, and Donald Glover, to name a few—and their red-carpet looks frequently land them on best-dressed lists. Her success is due in part to her adeptness at dressing men in clothing that aligns with their personal style—the clothes don't wear them—and working closely with designers to create looks that fit her clients' physiques. Urbinati also made a name for herself as a designer when she collaborated on a line of richly colored, impeccably tailored suits—including a forest green design worn by Ryan Gosling's character in 2011's *Crazy, Stupid, Love*. Urbinati's continued dominance in Hollywood has landed her on the *Hollywood Reporter*'s "Most Powerful Stylists" list for six consecutive years.

Stylist

Ilaria Urbinati.
b Rome (IT), 1979.

Josh Duhamel styled by Ilaria Urbinati for *August Man*, April 2013.

Photograph by Bleacher + Everard.

↳ ACNE STUDIOS, GUCCI,
 C. KLEIN, REMBERT,
 WELCH, YANG

MARK VANDERLOO

Dutchman Mark Vanderloo remains a supermodel well into his fifties, disproving the idea that fashion is all about youth (he once joked that he tried to retire in 1996 but missed his stop). Vanderloo stumbled into modeling in 1990 when he accompanied his girlfriend to a shoot for a milk commercial and the photographer asked him to join in. His first fashion campaign was for Banana Republic, but he made his name when he became the face of Calvin Klein's Obsession alongside Christy Turlington in 1994. With his career taking off, Vanderloo moved to New York, where he was said to have appeared in some fifty shows every fashion week and was hailed by VH1 as Model of the Year in 1995; in 1996 he became one of the first male cover models for *Marie Claire*. Throughout the 1990s Vanderloo was the face of DKNY, H&M, and, most famously, Hugo Boss, with one of his Boss campaigns photographed by Richard Avedon. Vanderloo's combination of charm and style, likened to Cary Grant, has led to a long, prosperous career, and he recently appeared in ad campaigns for Brunello Cucinelli and Etro.

Model

Mark Vanderloo.
b Waddinxveen (NL), 1968.

Mark Vanderloo, 2013.

↳ AVEDON, CUCINELLI, HUGO BOSS, C. KLEIN

WILLY VANDERPERRE

The prolific Belgian fashion photographer Willy Vanderperre came to prominence documenting the avant-garde Antwerp Six while studying at the prestigious Royal Academy of Fine Arts in Antwerp. Working with his close friends and collaborators, designer Raf Simons and stylist Olivier Rizzo, Vanderperre frequently contributed to Terry Jones's *i-D* magazine, and his photographs have also been featured in *Love, Another Man, W,* and *Vogue Hommes International.* Inspired by youth culture, isolation, and the influence of Pop, his images are directly expressive of human impulses. His

work is dark, beautiful, and transcendent. He has created visually arresting and visceral campaigns for Jil Sander, Prada, Christian Dior, and Dior Homme and captured notable icons, such as Willem Dafoe, Frank Ocean, and A$AP Rocky. In 2014 Vanderperre turned his lens to Jan Fabre's dance company for the book *The Power of Theatrical Madness II,* and he published *635* in 2015, which chronicles Vanderperre's ephemeral Instagram posts. In 2016 he debuted his first film, *Naked Heartland,* at the Institute of Contemporary Arts in London and in 2018 had his first solo photography exhibition.

Photographer

Willy Vanderperre.
b Flanders (BEL), 1971.

From *10 Works for Raf Simons,*
IDEA Books, 2016.

Photograph by Willy Vanderperre.

↳ i-D, JIL SANDER, PRADA,
  RIZZO, SIMONS

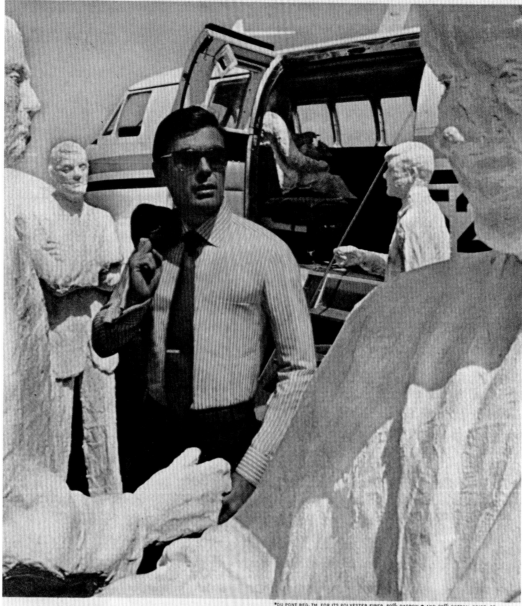

When you come on in a Van Heusen® shirt

*DU PONT REG. TM FOR ITS POLYESTER FIBER. 80% DACRON ® AND 20% COTTON. PRICE: $8.

the rest come off like a bunch of stiffs.

with Dacron*

The people who unstuffed the shirt

VAN HEUSEN

Known as "the people who unstuffed the shirt," Van Heusen pioneered an early twentieth-century invention in men's shirtmaking: the soft, structured collar. The company's story began in 1881 when Moses Phillips and his son Isaac sold shirts handmade by Endel, Moses's wife, and their daughters to local coal miners in Pottsville, Pennsylvania. By 1919 their business had expanded to New York City, where they met John Manning Van Heusen, a Dutch immigrant who invented a revolutionary technique that attached soft-folding collars to shirts, rendering removable collars obsolete. Isaac purchased

the patent, and in 1921 signature Van Heusen shirts were born, boasting the "World's Smartest Collar." A breakthrough in men's attire, the shirts caused a customer rush that allegedly led to a riot at a Fifth Avenue store. Over the decades the styles evolved, and they introduced wrinkle-free Century shirts, Como chambray, oxford button-downs in superfine white and prints, and Vanuana sports shirts with short sleeves. To sell these shirts, the company used recognizable faces—including the "King of Comedy" Jerry Lewis, Charlton Heston, and a young Ronald Reagan—in their ad campaigns.

Designer Brand

Van Heusen.
est New York (USA), 1921.

Van Heusen advertisement, 1968.

↳ ARROW, C.F. HATHAWAY
COMPANY, CHANG, CHARVET

DRIES VAN NOTEN

At the end of his runway shows, when Belgian designer Dries Van Noten steps out to take his bow, he is often dressed conservatively in a navy sweater and earth-toned chinos. This personal uniform belies the rampant creativity that can be found in his collections. After studying at Antwerp's Royal Academy of Fine Arts, Van Noten erupted onto the scene with his first menswear collection in 1986. His regal clothes drip with joyous colors and romantic patterns, drawing on everything from the ornate emblems of military uniforms to the pouty visage of Marilyn Monroe and the flowers found in his own sprawling Antwerp garden. Yet, crucially, Van Noten can still cut a stalwart day-in-day-out suit. Perhaps it's in his genes: his grandfather worked as a tailor and his father ran a menswear shop. As Van Noten enters the third decade of his career, his ability to balance flair and formality remains on full display. Models in his Fall/Winter 2020 runway show walked in ensembles that were either stately—double-breasted navy blazers and classic Chesterfield coats—or downright fanciful—faux-fur stoles and patterned silk trousers—covering all the bases for Van Noten's wide-ranging customers.

Designer

Dries Van Noten.
b Antwerp (BEL), 1958.

Model Finnlay Davis wearing a Dries Van Noten quilted coat, 2019.

Photograph by Umit Savaci.

↳ VAN BEIRENDONCK, BIKKEMBERGS, BURTON, DEMEULEMEESTER, MARGIELA, SIMONS

VANS

In the beginning Vans, the sneaker company founded in part by brothers Paul and Jim Van Doren as the Van Doren Rubber Company, operated more like a fast-food restaurant than a whirring shoe factory. Customers stopped by the factory to order plimsolls, which were made on-site and available for pick up in a few hours. Skateboarders—who were then spreading across all corners of Southern California—adored Vans's robust construction and rubber sole. By the late 1970s venerated pros, such as Tony Alva and Stacy Peralta, were brandishing the low-top Era and

high-top Old Skool. The footwear firm got a jolt in 1982 when the lovable Jeff Spicoli (played by Sean Penn) wore its checkerboard slip-ons in *Fast Times at Ridgemont High*. Despite Vans's massive scale (in 2004 VF Corp bought it for $396 million), the brand's cultural clout is as potent as ever. The elite fashion set still clings to their Vans, and the company has lately collaborated with everyone from renowned Chicago retailer Notre Shop to Italian luxury label Alyx and the Japanese fashion emporium Beams.

Footwear

Vans.
est Anaheim, CA (USA), 1966.

A skateboarder wearing Vans at Upland Skate Park, California, 1984.

Photograph by Doug Pensinger.

↳ BEAMS, KAWAKUBO, SUPREME, M. WILLIAMS

JOHN VARVATOS

A prodigious talent, Detroit native John Varvatos started his career in fashion working for two iconic American brands. After stints designing menswear for Calvin Klein, where he helped launch cK, and Polo Ralph Lauren, where he created RLL and Polo Jeans, Varvatos broke out with his eponymous label for the Fall/Winter 2000 season. Inspired by modern tailoring and a lifelong passion for rock 'n' roll, Varvatos's black leather jackets, flannel shirts, textured knits, and sturdy boots embody an inherent cool. His rocker sensibility has even appealed to the world's top acts, including Bruce Springsteen, Bob Dylan, Iggy Pop, ZZ Top, and Alice Cooper, with a number of them having appeared in his advertising campaigns. In addition to his lifestyle range of men's belts, bags, eyewear, fragrance, and watches, Varvatos has had a longtime collaboration with Converse, designing Chuck Taylors (including the popular slip-on style). In 2008 Varvatos opened a flagship store at the former site of CBGB, New York's East Village punk music club.

Designer

John Varvatos.
b Detroit, MI (USA), 1955.

John Varvatos and Iggy Pop, New York, 2006.

Photograph by Danny Clinch.

↳ COLE, CONVERSE, C. KLEIN, LAUREN

GIANNI VERSACE

Gianni Versace did not make clothes for shrinking violets. His menswear was not only a spotlight, a neon sign, a flashing red beacon shouting "Look at me!" but it also referenced classical Italian art and architecture. And men—especially the fitness focused—ate it up. Versace founded his eponymous label in 1978, and throughout the 1980s and '90s he dressed men the world over in painterly silk shirts, Saran Wrap–tight leather pants, and punchy printed blazers. His clothes hugged the body, accentuating all parts of the male anatomy. In ad campaigns men

often didn't wear shirts at all—their sculpted muscles were just part of the outfit. Versace's clothes pulled in flamboyant dressers of all backgrounds. He frequently collaborated with Elton John, who wore Versace's ornate creations on album covers and at concerts, and he dressed Sylvester Stallone in the early 1990s. The steely rapper Tupac Shakur also wore Versace, as did *Malcolm X* producer Marvin Worth.

Designer

Gianni Versace.
b Reggio Calabria (IT), 1946.
d Miami (USA), 1997.

Versace South Beach Stories campaign, 1993.

Photograph by Doug Ordway.

↳ AVEDON, SCHENKENBERG, SHAKUR, WEBER

VINCE MAN'S SHOP

Located in a small store at 5 Newburgh Street in London's Soho district, Vince Man's Shop began a menswear revolution in the 1950s. Launched by Bill Green, or "Vince"—a photographer who specialized in homoerotic portraits of athletes at a time when homosexuality was still a crime—it started as a mail-order business for Green to sell his "posing" clothes. In 1954 he opened the shop to sell wholesale clothing adapted by local tailors for a predominantly gay market while also designing some items himself. The garments soon attracted a variety of well-known customers, including Sean Connery, Peter Sellers, and Pablo Picasso. Vince largely created the idea of "leisurewear," enabling all men to wear more colorful and less formal styles, including velvet hipster trousers, faded denim, and garish shirts. Green also introduced the beatnik look of black jeans and black sweaters to Britain. The store was eventually overshadowed by the growing popularity of Carnaby Street, where one of Green's former employees, John Stephen, opened a boutique. Green tried moving his store but ultimately closed it in 1969.

Retailer

Vince Man's Shop.
est London (UK), 1954.

Sean Connery modeling clothing in an advertisement for Vince Man's Shop, 1957.

↳ CONNERY, I WAS LORD KITCHENER'S VALET, PICASSO, STEPHEN

TONY VIRAMONTES

The heyday of fashion illustration was largely over by the late 1970s when Tony Viramontes started his career, yet his tough, sexually charged style, inspired by punk and new wave, made him influential in shaping the fashion image of the 1980s. Viramontes studied at FIT and Parsons in New York before drawing lookbooks in Paris. In 1983 he was hired for an advertising campaign by the Genius Group in Italy and began to combine illustrations with Polaroids and photographs. This led to work for designers including Karl Lagerfeld and Yves Saint Laurent (he reinvigorated fashion by drawing with punchy colors and strong jagged lines), magazines such as *i-D* and *The Face* (he regularly added his illustrations to Ray Petri–styled fashion editorials), and album covers for Duran Duran and Janet Jackson. Following in the footsteps of illustrator Antonio Lopez, Viramontes used faces in his work—for example, Paul Hendrix, a studio manager and model, Nick Kamen, and the transgender model Teri Toye— saying, "It is essential to capture the image; not a detail, not a garment, or an expression, but an impression." Viramontes died from an AIDS-related illness at the age of thirty-one.

Illustrator

Tony Viramontes.
b Los Angeles (USA), 1956.
d Santa Monica, CA (USA), 1988.

Ottobre '84, 1984.

Illustration by Tony Viramontes.

↳ THE FACE, i-D, LOPEZ,
    MELENDEZ, PETRI

MATTHIAS VRIENS

Amsterdam-born Matthias Vriens made his name in magazines before progressing to fashion photography and eventually interior design. He earned his reputation in the 1990s working on the fashion magazine *Dutch*—originally launched in the Netherlands but by then published from Paris—where he rose to become creative director and editor in chief. Vriens quickly received international recognition through coups such as an issue featuring only naked models, each credited to a fashion brand despite no clothes being visible. In 1999 Vriens held senior creative roles for Giorgio

Armani and Gucci before moving to New York City and starting to photograph fashion for publications, including *Vogue Hommes*, *Fantastic Man*, and *Butt*. His images were notable for their lively personality and frank sexuality. Vriens moved to Los Angeles in 2003, where he set up Atelier MVM to showcase interior designers and furniture makers while continuing to shoot editorials for *Wallpaper** and *Numéro Homme*, among others, and advertising campaigns for labels including Etro and BL33N, a project cocurated by Donovan McGrath.

Editor/Photographer

Matthias Vriens.
b Amsterdam (NL), (Active 1990s—).

Model Josh Upshaw photographed for "Zoomwear," *Style Magazine* (*Corriera Della Sera*), February/March 2021.

Photograph by Matthias Vriens.

↳ ARMANI, ETRO, FANTASTIC MAN, GUCCI

481

DWYANE WADE

Dwyane Wade is one of the few NBA players who have been as celebrated for their fashion choices as for their basketball career. A three-time champion with the Miami Heat, twelve-time All-Star, and Olympic gold medalist, Wade is both a basketball legend and a fashion icon. Wade's risk-taking love of pattern and color (see his all-green velour tracksuit worn courtside to the 2017 NBA Finals) makes headlines but has also opened up the possibilities for athletes interested in using fashion as a mode of self-expression. When Wade began his basketball career,

NBA fashion was a monoculture of baggy suits and baggier jeans—now each game is practically a catwalk. While leading the NBA in scoring and flexing, he palled around with teammate LeBron James and fellow Miami boss Rick Ross, whose love of fashion surely made a mark on this basketball star. Wade's style is as versatile as his playing on the court, mixing designer gear from the likes of Tom Ford and Balmain, sportswear from Li-Ning, and sharply tailored suits from A. Sauvage and Waraire Boswell.

Icon

Dwyane Wade.
b Chicago (USA), 1982.

Dwyane Wade, wearing a tuxedo by DZOJCHEN, and Gabrielle Union, 2019.

Photograph by Gillian Laub.

↳ A. SAUVAGE, BOSWELL, FORD, FRAZIER, NGXOKOLO, WESTBROOK

GRACE WALES BONNER

In a manner that so many bookish designers fail to achieve, Grace Wales Bonner deftly balances the commercial with the cerebral. Born in South London to an English mother and a Jamaican father, Wales Bonner studied at Central Saint Martins College of Art and Design, showed her first collection in 2015, and swiftly earned notice from the British Fashion Awards and the LVMH Prize. Her collections have potently drawn from and refocused attention on Cuban mambo culture, Black intellectuals at Howard University, and the Jamaican diaspora of 1970s London.

In 2019 the contemporary art–focused Serpentine Sackler Gallery in London held her debut exhibition, *A Time for New Dreams*. But her clothes are also highly wearable and have been worn by everyone from NBA player Nick Young to the Duchess of Sussex and Gen Z influencer Luka Sabbat. Her carefully patchworked suits, refreshed Fair Isle sweaters, and functional duffle coats would complement any man's wardrobe. In 2020 Wales Bonner partnered with Adidas on tracksuits and earthy sneakers, propelling her blossoming business into a new spotlight.

Designer

Grace Wales Bonner.
b London (UK), 1992.

Model George Hard in Wales Bonner Fall/Winter 2015, photographed for *Dazed* magazine, Spring/Summer 2015.

Photograph by Brett Lloyd.

↳ ADIDAS, GREEN, ROSE, SABBAT

ANDRE WALKER

London-born, New York–raised Andre Walker saw his future mapped out at nine years old when his mother subscribed to *W* magazine in the early 1970s. As a teenager Walker traveled into the city to buy fashion magazines and window-shop at Henri Bendel. When he was just fifteen, he staged his first fashion show at a Brooklyn nightclub, going on to make his name in the 1980s and '90s with original clothing such as coats fashioned in the shape of oven mitts and trousers that looked like wraparound skirts long before Jean Paul Gaultier put them on the runway. Walker also designed for Patrick Kelly

and Willi Smith, becoming the lead designer for WilliWear in 1989 following Smith's death. Always innovative—he has consulted for Marc Jacobs and Kim Jones—Walker released an exclusive collection for Dover Street Market in 2014 that was designed to be unisex. In 2021 he collaborated with Virgil Abloh's Off-White to produce a capsule wardrobe with pieces including a hoodie with an extended pocket, a T-shirt with pleats and a belt, and a black leather knapsack with elastic straps (he wears one while roller-skating). It is a collection that perfectly embodies Walker's aesthetic: practical with a twist.

Designer

Andre Walker.
b London (UK), c. 1965.

Models Kaya Holl and Serge Sergeev, styled by Vincent Levy for *10 Men* magazine, February 2018.

Photograph by Dham Srifuengfung.

↳ ABLOH, GAULTIER, JACOBS, K. JONES, KELLY, W. SMITH

APRIL WALKER

Sometimes called the godmother of hip-hop fashion, April Walker has a sensibility that flowed organically out of the energy of rap and New York City in the late 1980s. In demand as a stylist for music shoots and videos, Walker established Fashion in Effect, an independent boutique in Brooklyn, in 1987, at just nineteen years old. Alongside one-off pieces, the shop won favor for its customized approach—lowering jean crotches, enlarging pockets, and recutting hems to fit Timberland boots, as well as designing bespoke pieces for hip-hop artists. Word spread and orders increased, providing the proof Walker needed to create Walker Wear, badged *WW* in a classic graffiti scrawl. Launched in the late 1990s, her label catered to the hip-hop crowd's preference for baggy styles that allowed easy movement, infused with a crazy, cool edge. Walker Wear fans included the Notorious B.I.G., Tupac Shakur, and Run-DMC's Jam Master Jay. Ahead of her time, Walker gave men the street style they wanted in the shapes they loved.

Designer

April Walker.
b Los Angeles (USA), 1968.

Tupac Shakur, wearing Walker Wear, and actor Jaye Davidson, New York, 1994.

Photograph by Lawrence Schwartzwald.

↳ COOGI, DAPPER DAN, JAY-Z, KANI, SHAKUR, TIMBERLAND

FENG CHEN WANG

Feng Chen Wang has become a standout fixture at London Fashion Week, designing functional, sculptural menswear with her signature deconstruction and 3D draping. With studios in London and Shanghai, Wang harnesses ancient craft techniques to create a futuristic, multidimensional style. For inspiration she often draws from her cross-cultural identity and heritage and her childhood growing up in China's southern countryside by the sea. In 2015 Wang graduated from London's prestigious Royal College of Art and debuted her first collection at New York Fashion Week for the Spring/Summer 2016 season. While her collections have evolved to include more unisex designs, their prevailing aesthetic remains youthful and emotional with touches of high-concept craft. This holds true whether she is utilizing *lanyinhuabu* dyeing with a native, natural-resist pigment created in collaboration with local Fujianese artisans or conjuring up asymmetrical overcoats and innovative layers, such as cutaway sweaters and oversized denim jackets. Wang has also collaborated with Converse, Nike, and Levi's to create inventive capsule collections.

Designer

Feng Chen Wang.
b Fujian (CHN), (Active 2010s—).

Feng Chen Wang Spring/Summer 2020 campaign.

Photograph by Sarah Piantadosi.

↳ CONVERSE, LEVI'S, NIKE

SIR LESLIE MATTHEW "SPY" WARD

Spy was an apt nom de plume for Sir Leslie Matthew Ward, who over his four-decade career painted 1,325 exaggerated portraits of England's aristocrats. Long before street-style photography became the most accessible way to take in fashion trends, starting in 1873 readers of *Vanity Fair* could rely on Ward's caricatures to provide a glimpse at what notable names were wearing. Doodling from memory, the Eton College graduate captured the swooping, curved shirt collar on slender Italian inventor Guglielmo Marconi, the fluffy top hat of British businessman Sir Charles Cayzer, and the bouffant breeches on golfer Robert Maxwell, to name a few. His watercolors were not quite biting—Ward was known for capturing only the best angles of the royalty, nobility, and women he painted—but they were, and still are, a reliable record of how fashion choices ebbed and flowed through the nineteenth century and into the twentieth.

Illustrator

Sir Leslie Matthew "Spy" Ward.
b London (UK), 1851.
d London (UK), 1922.

Grand Duke Michael Mikhailovich of Russia, *Vanity Fair*, c. 1900.

Illustration by Leslie "Spy" Ward.

↳ FELLOWS, GENTRY, LEYENDECKER

MELANIE WARD

In the late 1980s and early '90s, Melanie Ward's raw and gritty aesthetic came to dominate fashion. With more than thirty years spent as a stylist, muse, fashion editor, and occasional designer, Ward has permeated fashion from haute couture to the high street. By her own admission none of this was planned. Working alongside photographers Corinne Day and David Sims, Ward transformed a then-unknown Kate Moss into a global superstar with her cover for the July 1990 edition of *The Face*. Her groundbreaking mixture of vintage and army surplus with

designer and high street pieces combined to create an effortless, real look and easily translated to men's fashion. Ward's unique take on fashion led to a thirteen-year collaboration with Helmut Lang (both shared a love of sexy minimalism) and styling for Jil Sander, Calvin Klein, and Karl Lagerfeld, among others. She also had a fourteen-year stint at *Harper's Bazaar*, hired by the late Liz Tilberis, the editor in chief from 1992 to 1999. Ward continues to have a hand in shaping men's fashion: in 2021 she styled both advertising campaigns and runway looks for Dior Men.

Stylist

Melanie Ward.
b London (UK), (Active 1980s—).

Anthony, Leslie, and Melanie Ward for Helmut Lang Spring/Summer 2002.

Photograph by Anthony Ward.

↳ THE FACE, JIL SANDER, K. JONES, C. KLEIN, LANG, SIMS

TONY WARD

Tony Ward, born Anthony Borden, disliked having his picture taken as a child but would end up spending more than four decades in front of the camera as a model, being photographed by talents such as Herb Ritts and Bruce Weber—collaborations that helped shape the contemporary male image. For more than twenty years he was an important muse for Ritts, whose image *Tony in White, Hollywood* (1988) hangs in the Getty Museum today. Rugged and with a distinctive Roman nose—he was once advised to have plastic surgery—Ward was discovered following his high school

graduation, when he was a body builder modeling for gay erotica. Ward's first fashion photo shoot, in 1985, was with Weber for *SoHo Weekly News*, and soon after Ritts photographed him for a Calvin Klein campaign. Ward went on to become the face of brands such as Chanel, Dolce & Gabbana, Fendi, and Hugo Boss. In the early 1990s he appeared in music videos for his then-girlfriend Madonna and in her notorious 1992 book *Sex*. An early agent insisted that Ward train in acting and dance, and, with support from Madonna, he broke into the movie industry with 1996's *Hustler White*.

Model

Tony Ward (Anthony Borden).
b Santa Cruz, CA (USA), 1963.

Tony in White, Hollywood, 1988.

Photograph by Herb Ritts.

↳ ARMANI, DOLCE & GABBANA, HUGO BOSS, C. KLEIN, RITTS, WEBER

JUNYA WATANABE

Just three years after graduating from Tokyo's Bunka Fashion College in 1984, Junya Watanabe found himself in charge of the Tricot line for the illustrious Comme des Garçons. In 2001 Watanabe introduced his menswear collection under the Comme des Garçons label. A protégé of Rei Kawakubo, Watanabe has adopted a similar reticence to speaking with the press and forges his own path, operating his own stores and eschewing traditional advertising. Known for using atypical, often gray-haired models on the runway, Watanabe has carved out his signature pieces over the years, such as compact three-button suits (often in Anglo-like plaids and tweeds) and punk-inspired patchwork jeans. In more recent years, he has become an ardent collaborator, lacing as many as ten-plus partners into a single collection. The Spring 2020 collection was filled with pieces created in partnership with the likes of Carhartt, Gieves & Hawkes, Levi's, New Balance, and even St. John, a farm-to-table restaurant in London.

Designer

Junya Watanabe.
b Fukushima (JAP), 1961.

Junya Watanabe Man Fall/Winter 2020 collection at Paris Fashion Week.

Photograph by Anne-Christine Poujoulat.

↳ CARHARTT, GIEVES & HAWKES, KAWAKUBO, LEVI'S, NEW BALANCE

BRUCE WEBER

In the summer of 1982 traffic screeched to a halt in Times Square thanks to a towering billboard showing Brazilian pole vaulter Tom Hintnaus in the nude, save for his white Calvin Klein briefs. Hintnaus's portrait—dubbed by *American Photographer* magazine as one of the "Ten Photographs That Changed America"—was shot by Bruce Weber and was a quintessential image by the American photographer: athletic, sexual, and aspirational. As the photography critic Vince Aletti said, Weber's lengthy career was built on "turning jocks into demigods," which is evident in his work for brands such as Abercrombie & Fitch, Versace, and his many campaigns for Ralph Lauren, selling not just the clothes but a desirable lifestyle. Ever since his first *GQ* shoot in 1974, Weber's photography—often shot in black and white—has celebrated the male form in groundbreaking imagery. For the rest of the decade and into the 1980s, Weber's editorials for *GQ*, which featured models such as Jeff Aquilon—a chiseled, lean former water polo player—not only created a new ideal of the American man but also shaped men's fashion photography.

Photographer

Bruce Weber.
b Greensburg, PA (USA), 1946.

Andrew Wyeth, Penobscot Bay, ME, 1981.

Photograph by Bruce Weber.

↳ ABERCROMBIE & FITCH, AQUILON, GQ, C. KLEIN, LAUREN

JOHN WEITZ

John Weitz was a licensing genius who understood that his name was gold. A German immigrant who came to the United States at an early age, Weitz entered the women's garment industry in the 1940s and established his eponymous brand in 1954. A decade later he added menswear and proved to be his own best model. A trim man blessed with rugged good looks, Weitz dressed in his brand's narrow European-cut dress shirts and sleek navy suits—a look that appealed to executive types wanting high-end conservative wear. More significantly, Weitz was one of the earliest designers to embrace licensing by stamping his name on everything from socks to fragrances and sweaters. (He later said he drew the line at police uniforms and cigarettes.) This put-my-name-on-it strategy led Weitz to grand success but radically shifted the fashion industry by opening the door for licensing mania. Later in life, after he turned his focus to writing novels and histories about Nazi-era Germany, Weitz readily accepted the blame for creating a climate in which a designer's name perhaps mattered more than the clothes they made.

Designer

John Weitz.
b Berlin (GER), 1923.
d Bridgehampton, NY (USA), 2002.

John Weitz wearing his own designs for the cover of a promotional brochure, *Men's Multi-Fashion*, c. 1974.

⤷ BEENE, CARDIN, KAISERMAN, C. KLEIN, LAUREN

KARLA WELCH

Karla Welch has reshaped what it means to be a Hollywood stylist, positioning herself as an image architect and a multifaceted partner to her superfamous clientele. She has had a strong impact on street (non–red carpet) fashion, thanks to her guiding hand in the surprising off-duty style of pop star Justin Bieber. Welch was exposed to menswear at an early age—her father owned a small haberdashery—and after moving to Los Angeles, her styling career took off, first with commercials, then with dressing A-listers after signing with the Wall Group in 2006. Welch possesses the lofty ability to dress both men and women with off-kilter touches—a shoestring belt to secure a pair of opulent trousers, a fluorescent beanie to top off an otherwise inconspicuous outfit—yet does it so tactfully as not to overshadow the celebrity. She has also designed collections for brands such as Levi's, Hanes (inspired by an attempt with Bieber to create the perfect tee), and Dockers, where she introduced an inclusive, unisex line of clothing. Welch remains one of the most commanding celebrity stylists today, communicating a style that is both aspirational and authentic.

Stylist

Karla Welch.
b Powell River, British Columbia (CAN), 1975.

Justin Bieber styled by Karla Welch for *L'Uomo Vogue*, July 2015.

Photograph by Francesco Carrozzini.

↳ AMBROSE, DOCKERS, HANES, LEVI'S, REMBERT, URBINATI, YANG

KANYE WEST

From Kanye West's first record in 2004, as he nimbly rapped about Air Force Ones and diamond rings, the Chicago-bred MC/businessman/provocateur was direct about his obsession with all things fashion and style. Ever the fashion chameleon, West's career could be divided by his outfits: popped Polo Kanye, Celine blouse Kanye, Givenchy kilt Kanye, Vetements hoodie Kanye, and on and on. More than an icon, though, West has forged a successful design career. In 2005 he started Pastelle, a sprightly yet short-lived sportswear label, and then in 2009 he interned at Fendi (alongside Virgil Abloh). Collaborations with Nike and A.P.C. created a stir but didn't endure. But then in 2013 West began a long-term relationship with Adidas on his Yeezy label. His tubular-soled, socklike sneakers shifted the course of sneaker design and became mind-bogglingly sought-after. Yeezy's apparel—such as doughy cropped sweatshirts, enveloping camo parkas, and sagging logoed sweatpants—was not always as successful as his sneakers, but the dusty, puttylike palette West favored had a strong influence on trends during the mid-aughts. In 2020 West announced a ten-year apparel partnership with the Gap.

Designer/Icon

Kanye West.
b Atlanta (USA), 1977.

Kanye West at his studio, Calabasas, CA, 2020.

Photograph by Paolo Pellegrin.

↳ ABLOH, ADIDAS, GAP, NIKE, OGUNLESI

RUSSELL WESTBROOK

In the early 2010s a sartorial-inclined group of NBA players became known not merely for their theatrics on the court but for their tantalizing fashion choices when out of their jerseys. This fashion-forward pack included some of the game's latter-day greats, such as LeBron James, Dwyane Wade, Amar'e Stoudemire, and Russell Westbrook. Even in a league where players were beginning to view their entrances into their games as their own personal catwalk, Westbrook always stood out. Today, his outré fashion sense—oversized patchwork tees, swiss-cheesed shirts, calf-clenching capris, denim overalls—is impossible to miss, and he mixes everyday pieces with high-end designer wear. Though some of his choices are brow-raising, Westbrook's risk-taking has earned him ample praise and press. Recognizing his influence, the fashion industry brought Westbrook into the fold: he became a front-row fixture at runway shows for brands such as Louis Vuitton and Dior, and in 2014 he launched a collaborative clothing collection with Barneys New York.

Icon

Russell Westbrook.
b Long Beach, CA (USA), 1988.

Russell Westbrook arriving at the Bankers Life Fieldhouse in Indianapolis, 2017.

Photograph by Jeff Haynes.

↳ ACNE STUDIOS, BARNEYS NEW YORK, FRAZIER, REMBERT, WADE

VIVIENNE WESTWOOD

Vivienne Westwood's design career began humbly in the late 1970s as she crafted teddy-boy clothes for her then-boyfriend, Malcolm McLaren. The drape jackets and prim Edwardian shirting the couple favored were a retro antidote to the hippie-dippiness of the 1960s. In 1971 the pair opened Let It Rock, a trend-setting boutique on London's King's Road. Just a year later, Westwood's tastes started to tip toward punk. Soon the shop—rebranded SEX—was pumping out tattered, pinned-together threads that would define the ragged look of '70s London. By the early '80s Westwood

grew disenchanted by punk's mainstream movement. She split with McLaren in 1983 and, after a brief stint designing for Fiorucci in 1984, Westwood leaned on her many talents to become a full-fledged runway designer. Her esteemed collections through the '80s and beyond were eclectic (to say the least), with heaps of pirate-esque trousers, sky-high Buffalo hats, droopy asymmetrical shirts, Anglo-plaid suiting, and patchwork leather coats. During her later career, Westwood has focused on environmental initiatives, such as her Save the Arctic campaign.

Designer

Vivienne Westwood.
b Glossop, Derbyshire (UK), 1941.

Boy George wearing Vivienne Westwood, 1980.

Photograph by Laura Levine.

↳ BURTON, COX, DR. MARTENS, HAMNETT, McLAREN, PALACE

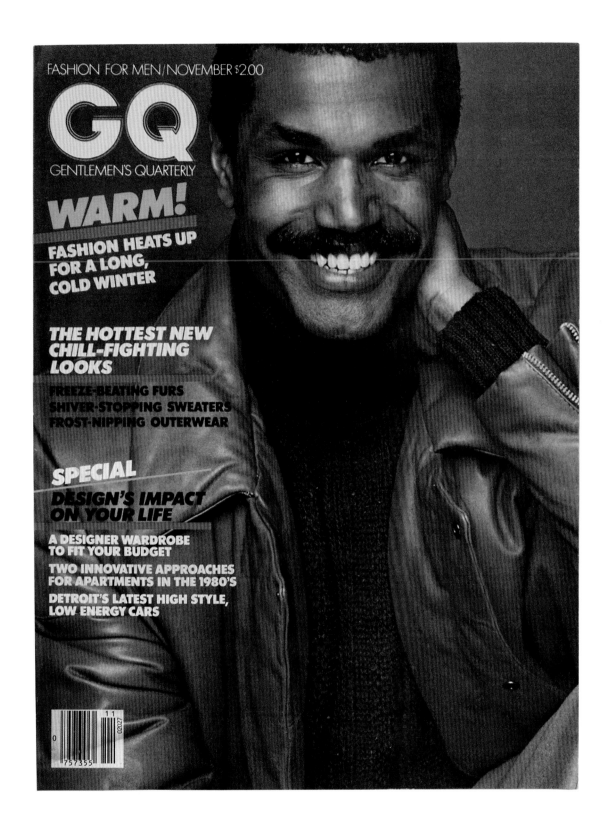

FASHION FOR MEN/NOVEMBER $2.00

GQ
GENTLEMEN'S QUARTERLY

WARM!

FASHION HEATS UP FOR A LONG, COLD WINTER

THE HOTTEST NEW CHILL-FIGHTING LOOKS

FREEZE-BEATING FURS
SHIVER-STOPPING SWEATERS
FROST-NIPPING OUTERWEAR

SPECIAL
DESIGN'S IMPACT ON YOUR LIFE

A DESIGNER WARDROBE TO FIT YOUR BUDGET

TWO INNOVATIVE APPROACHES FOR APARTMENTS IN THE 1980'S

DETROIT'S LATEST HIGH STYLE, LOW ENERGY CARS

RENAULD WHITE

When Renauld White appeared on the cover of the November 1979 issue of *GQ* magazine, he became the first Black American model to grace the publication's cover. That was not the only barrier he broke in the world of modeling: he was also the first Black male model to work for American designers Bill Blass, Calvin Klein, Ralph Lauren, Jeffrey Banks, and Donna Karan. With classic, chiseled good looks and an irresistible smile, he was one of fashion's top male models in the 1970s and '80s. White was originally from Newark, New Jersey, and modeling was not something he had considered until—while taking night classes at Rutgers University—he befriended model Jeff Blynn and designer Stephen Burrows, who nudged him onto the path of fashion. In addition to his groundbreaking *GQ* cover, White was also featured on the pages of *Ebony, Essence,* and *Jet* magazines. During his thirty-plus-year career, White appeared in more than twenty issues of *GQ* and walked runways for names including Valentino, Armani, Yves Saint Laurent, and Versace, inspiring generations of models who followed in his footsteps.

Model

Renauld White.
b Newark, NJ (USA), 1944.

Renauld White on the cover of the November 1979 issue of *GQ*.

Photograph by Bob Krieger.

↳ BANKS, BLASS, EBONY, GQ

BILL WHITTEN

Think of Elton John's sweeping capes or Neil Diamond's sparkling shirt yokes, and you're picturing the work of Los Angeles designer Bill Whitten. His extravagant sense of style married well with pop and rock royalty, introducing details such as beading, rhinestones, high-shine lamé fabric, and over-the-top embroidery, to embellish the onstage personas of many Grammy-winning artists. From his humble atelier Workroom 27, Whitten gradually found success alongside his starry clients, beginning with a commission from Neil Diamond for a bespoke outfit. Diamond's recommendations led to a litany of clients, including the Commodores, Chicago, Lionel Richie, and Earth, Wind & Fire. But Whitten's most famous designs were for Michael Jackson—from the striped, sequined ensemble worn in the "Rock with You" music video to his *Off the Wall* look. Whitten's genius created MJ's single white glove, cropped black pants, and glittering white socks that made visible the singer's dazzling moonwalk moves. Despite his high-profile clients and now-iconic ensembles, Whitten flew under the radar and was largely unrecognized outside the music industry during his lifetime.

Designer

Bill Whitten.
b Bessemer, AL (USA), 1944.
d Los Angeles (USA), 2006.

In his West Hollywood atelier Bill Whitten adjusts a custom tuxedo for Eddie Kendricks, lead singer of the Temptations, 1975.

Photograph by Bruce W. Talamon.

↳ COHN, CUEVAS, DEVORE, THE TEMPTATIONS

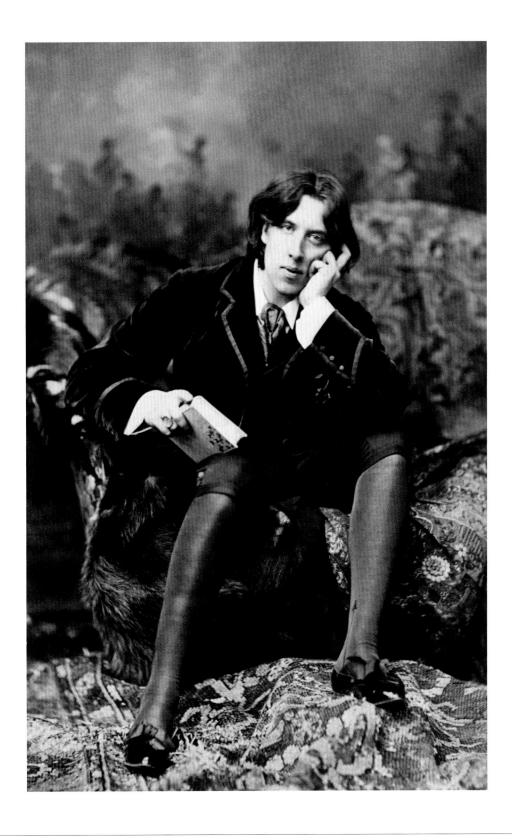

OSCAR WILDE

"One should either be a work of art or wear a work of art." Witty and revolutionary, the Irish writer Oscar Wilde, an early adherent of self-promotion, is as well-known for his style and dandyism as for his witticisms. Drawn to the contemporary aesthetic movement, which championed "art for art's sake," Wilde arrived in London in the late 1870s dressed to signal his commitment to the "artistic"— with knee breeches, a velvet Norfolk jacket, a flat, wide-brimmed hat, a turned-down collar, a flowing tie, and foppish hair. Deliberately affecting the antithesis of

respectable Victorian starched collars and stiff suiting, Wilde was ahead of his time in understanding the power of men's clothes. He believed fashion was ephemeral but should be joyful—the last thing Victorian men associated with what they wore. For Wilde that joy lay in the sky-blue cravats that matched his eyes, the natural fibers he championed, and the sunflower he sported in his buttonhole, among his many other stylings prescient in so much of today's neo-dandyism.

Icon

Oscar Wilde.
b Dublin (IRE), 1854.
d Paris (FR), 1900.

Oscar Wilde, 1882.

Photograph by Napoleon Sarony.

↳ AHLUWALIA, BRUMMELL, COWARD, CRISP

BERNHARD WILLHELM

Over his twenty-plus-year career, German designer Bernhard Willhelm has come to be known for his experimental outfits—think graphic, oversize T-shirts or tailored separates with colorful, provocative prints. As a student at the Royal Academy of Fine Arts in Antwerp, Willhelm studied under an equally avant-garde designer, his mentor Walter Van Beirendonck, and went on to assist Alexander McQueen, Vivienne Westwood, and Dirk Bikkembergs. In 1998 he founded his eponymous line with business partner Jutta Kraus, launching womenswear at Paris Fashion Week. Two years later he started designing menswear. Willhelm's Los Angeles–based label treats fashion as art and utilizes a transgressive approach that regularly nods to queer culture and critiques mainstream consumption—he is known for unisex kimono-style jackets, dramatically proportioned shirtdresses, velour jumpsuits, and hooded sweatshirts. Willhelm has collaborated with brands such as Camper and Mykita, as well as singer Björk and photographer Nick Knight.

Designer

Bernhard Willhelm.
b Ulm (GER), 1972.

Bernhard Willhelm Fall/Winter 2016 collection.

Photograph by Josh Paul Thomas.

↳ VAN BEIRENDONCK,
  BIKKEMBERGS, KNIGHT,
  WESTWOOD

MATTHEW WILLIAMS

By the time Matthew Williams had reached the age of thirty, he had already left quite an imprint on pop fashion. Williams, an admitted "club kid" with no formal fashion training, linked up with fixtures of the New York music world in his early twenties, placing him in the orbit of both Lady Gaga and Kanye West. He worked on famed outfits for each star, including a mesmerizing LED-light jacket West wore during the 2008 Grammys. While working with West, Williams partnered with Virgil Abloh, Justin Saunders, and Heron Preston to start Been Trill, a roving DJ collective that released hoodies and tees. In 2015 Williams formally entered the high-fashion realm with the Italian-based label 1017 ALYX 9SM. The brand's glossy reptile leather jackets, shimmering leather blazers, and chunky, utilitarian bags looked like *Blade Runner* mashed with California skate culture. Shortly after, in 2019, Kim Jones asked Williams to bring his hardware-heavy accessories to the Dior Homme line. In 2020 Williams was hired as the creative director of Givenchy, becoming one of a number of contemporary streetwear designers tasked with injecting vitality into stalwart French fashion labels.

Designer

Matthew Williams.
b Evanston, IL (USA), 1985.

Givenchy Spring/Summer 2021 menswear collection.

Photograph by Alain Gil-Gonzalez.

↳ ABLOH, GVASALIA, K. JONES, SLIMANE, WEST

PHARRELL WILLIAMS

From coastal Virginia, the maestro known simply as
Pharrell became a musical titan with many number-one
hits. Simultaneously Pharrell conquered the fashion
industry by nimbly navigating across labels and trends
from Harajuku to the haute runways. In 2005 Pharrell and
Nigo of A Bathing Ape started the boisterous skatewear
labels Billionaire Boys Club and ICECREAM, known for
hectic, all-over-print hoodies and candy-colored sneakers.
Soon after, Pharrell was collaborating with fashion labels,
such as Louis Vuitton and Moncler. The singer is an
undeniable clothing aficionado and never shy about
wearing the latest fashions, such as soaring Vivienne
Westwood hats, a patchwork Comme des Garçons coat,
and a Lanvin tuxedo with shorts, among other memorable
looks. Pharrell has also worked with Adidas since 2010 and
before Karl Lagerfeld's death in 2019, he collaborated with
the couturier on a cobranded collection. Pharrell has
enjoyed the distinction of being one of the rare men to
have ever walked the runway for Chanel.

Designer/Icon

Pharrell Williams.
b Virginia Beach, VA (USA), 1973.

Pharrell Williams, 2014.

Photograph by Brian Bowen Smith.

↳ **ADIDAS, LAGERFELD, LOUIS
VUITTON, MONCLER, NIGO**

DUKE OF WINDSOR

Edward VIII was crowned king of the United Kingdom in 1936, but less than a year later he abdicated, becoming known as the Duke of Windsor. Although his reign was short, he had incredible influence on menswear. During the 1920s, before he ascended the throne, he became known for his impeccable sense of style. He sought out comfort and practicality in his clothing, popularizing more relaxed tailoring—his jackets in the "full English drape" style were made by Frederick Scholte of Savile Row—and his unique sporting look of bright argyle or Fair Isle sweaters and loose plus fours. He helped modernize eveningwear, publicly condemning stiff-fronted "boiled shirts" in 1928; he instead wore softer dinner shirts with Hawes & Curtis–designed turndown collars to accommodate his ties and the Windsor knot he popularized. With a keen eye to his image, the duke introduced a midnight blue evening suit that showcased his tailoring better in photographs; he also made cuffed trousers fashionable. His style was a forerunner of the soft suiting of Giorgio Armani and Ralph Lauren, and he was widely emulated by other distinctive dressers, including Fred Astaire.

Icon

Duke of Windsor.
b Richmond, London (UK), 1894.
d Paris (FR), 1972.

Edward VIII, Duke of Windsor, at his residence in Paris, photographed for *Vogue*, April 1964.

Photograph by Horst P. Horst.

↳ ARMANI, ASTAIRE, CORDINGS, LAUREN, PRINGLE OF SCOTLAND, SCHOLTE

WOOLRICH

The United States' oldest outfitter, Woolrich was established in 1830 when founder John Rich built a wool mill in Plum Run, Pennsylvania. The son of a wool weaver from Liverpool, England, Rich continued the family tradition in the States, creating fabrics, blankets, and socks for local outdoorsmen. In 1850 Woolrich introduced its iconic Buffalo Check flannel; the red-and-black motif has since become an integral part of classic Americana. Over the next century the label expanded its apparel range, providing outdoor apparel for cold-weather climates, fit for everyone from Arctic engineers to the US military. Woolrich stood apart by making stylish, recreational clothes, and its Railroad Vest, Alaskan Twill Overshirt, and Mountain Jacket had an impact on modern men's workwear. The company's time-honored slogan, "We keep America warm," lives on through updated designs, such as woolen bombers, check puffers, and soft-brushed flannel shirts. Espousing a lumberjack style for the more modern city dweller, Woolrich's premium parkas and products include collaborations with Aimé Leon Dore, Stüssy, Converse, Supreme, nanamica, Engineered Garments, and Beams.

Brand

Woolrich.
est Plum Run, PA (USA), 1830.

Woolrich advertisement, 1962.

↳ BEAMS, CONVERSE, FILSON, L.L.BEAN, PATAGONIA, STÜSSY, SUPREME

NICK WOOSTER

The mighty Woost God, as Nick Wooster is known to his legion of followers, is one of the internet age's most unexpected style icons. In his twenties Wooster traded his sleepy Kansas hometown for the frenzy of New York, winding his way into the buying departments at Barneys New York and Bergdorf Goodman. Behind-the-scenes posts at Calvin Klein, Ralph Lauren, and John Bartlett followed. In the early 2010s he became the men's fashion director at Neiman Marcus and then a senior vice president of JCPenney. The rise of street-style photography took Wooster down an unanticipated path. Ever an outré dresser who favored vivacious floral trousers, camo blazers, and hefty brogues (always worn sans socks), photographs of Wooster outside fashion shows turned him into a viral internet star. Thom Browne suits with shorts instead of trousers remain a Wooster favorite—the better to show off his inked-up calves. Wooster has lately parlayed this meme-ified fame into a new career as an influencer. He now has more than eight hundred thousand followers on Instagram and has lent his name and design sense to collaborations with Lardini, Paul & Shark, and United Arrows.

Influencer

Nick Wooster.
b Salina, KS (USA), 1960.

Nick Wooster during Paris Fashion Week, 2015.

Photograph by Tommy Ton.

↳ BARNEYS NEW YORK, BARTLETT, BROWNE, UNITED ARROWS

WORKERS FOR FREEDOM

In 1985 Richard Nott and Graham Fraser opened their menswear store in London's Soho with a mission to create reliable men's clothing with a worldly sensibility. Their provocative name, Workers for Freedom, signaled their liberation from the "corporate" design underlying the era's ubiquitous and preppy fashions. The *Glasgow Herald* summed up their work as having "a stylishness based on subtlety and fine construction which stands remote from fashion's general glitzkrieg"—as shown notably in their hallmark piece, the appliqué shirt. Working with linen,

silk, and cotton in a black-on-white or white-on-black palette, the duo had such success with their first men's collection that they expanded into womenswear the following season. In 1990 they were named Designer of the Year at the British Fashion Awards. Ahead of the curve, Workers for Freedom promoted slow, rather than fast, fashion—each season added to the previous season rather than replacing it. The label went through several incarnations—the colors expanded to include muted tones of brown, ivory, and indigo blue, and Lycra was introduced—before it was sold in 1998.

Designer Brand

Workers for Freedom.
est London (UK), 1985.

Workers for Freedom campaign, 1989.

Photograph by Trevor Leighton.

↳ BODYMAP, CASELY-HAYFORD,
  GRANNY TAKES A TRIP, ROSE

WRANGLER

The iconic jeans for cowboys, Wranglers were developed in 1947 by tailor Bernard Lichtenstein, also known as Rodeo Ben, for Blue Bell Overall Company. Founded by C. C. Hudson and his brother Homer in Greensboro, North Carolina, Blue Bell prototyped thirteen pairs of denim jeans, which Rodeo Ben then tested on professional cowboys, including world bull-riding champion Jim Shoulders, Bill Linderman, and Freckles Brown. They landed on Wrangler's original 11MWZ style. The jeans featured felled seams and repositioned rear pockets for horse riding, and they lacked rivets to avoid

scratching leather saddlery. Nearly two decades later, in 1963, Wrangler incorporated Sanforized fabric, a novel treatment to help reduce shrinking; applied to denim, the process creates a heavy-duty look and feel, perfect for retaining structure. By 1974 these authentic Western jeans became the official partners of the Professional Rodeo Cowboys Association. Worn across the US, Wranglers have been beloved by cowboys, race-car drivers—including Dale Earnhardt and his son Dale Earnhardt Jr.—and music stars, such as "King of Country" George Strait, Jason Aldean, and rapper Lil Nas X.

Brand

Wrangler.
est Greensboro, NC (USA), 1947.

Wrangler advertisement, 1947.

↳ LEE JEANS, LEVI'S, ROCKMOUNT RANCH WEAR, STETSON

KANSAI YAMAMOTO

A full decade before Rei Kawakubo and Yohji Yamamoto made their revolutionary debuts in Paris, Kansai Yamamoto presented his collection in London in 1971, making him one of the first Japanese designers to enter the Western fashion world. His voluminous, vibrant clothes caused a stir—*Harpers & Queen* magazine billed his collection the "Explosion from Tokyo"—and Yamamoto soon caught the attention of David Bowie, Elton John, and Stevie Wonder. It was Bowie with whom he would have the most fruitful partnership, creating scads of tantalizing, Technicolor showpieces for the British star. "I approached Bowie's clothes as if I was designing for a female," Yamamoto said at a talk for a Brooklyn Museum show on Bowie in 2018. For the *Ziggy Stardust* and *Aladdin Sane* tours, Yamamoto placed Bowie in a glimmering striped jumpsuit with gigantic ovular legs, skimpy bodysuits, and streaming kimonos, costumes that were a vital part of his other-worldly look.

Designer

Kansai Yamamoto.
b Yokohama (JAP), 1944.
d Tokyo (JAP), 2020.

Kansai Yamamoto fits David Bowie in one of his designs, 1973.

Photograph by Masayoshi Sukita.

↳ BOWIE, KAWAKUBO, TAKADA, Y. YAMAMOTO

YOHJI YAMAMOTO

With his ever-present fedora perched on his head, Yohji Yamamoto has been the fashion world's smirking man in black since his debut on the Tokyo runway in 1977. As a young man, Yamamoto pursued becoming a lawyer, but in the late 1960s he left law to aid his mother with her dressmaking business. After earning a degree in fashion design from Bunka Fashion College, Yamamoto began his own line. In 1984 he introduced Yohji Yamamoto Menswear, an extension of the sly, shadowy clothes he had been offering for women. Yamamoto has spent his career honing key silhouettes such as fluid pleated trousers, deconstructed shirts, cocooning wool overcoats, and stocky sweaters with impactful, centralized graphics. In 2003 he struck a groundbreaking partnership with Adidas to start Y-3, fusing Yamamoto's studied, avant-garde aesthetic with an everyday sportiness. Yamamoto's artful but highly wearable pieces have rarely fallen out of fashion and today inspire designers such as Evan Kinori, Jan Jan Van Essche, and Nicholas Daley.

Designer

Yohji Yamamoto.
b Tokyo (JAP), 1943.

Model Tony Ward for the Yohji Yamamoto Senses campaign, 2013.

Photograph by Ross Kirton.

↳ ADIDAS, KAWAKUBO, KNIGHT, MIYAKE, MIYASHITA, OWENS

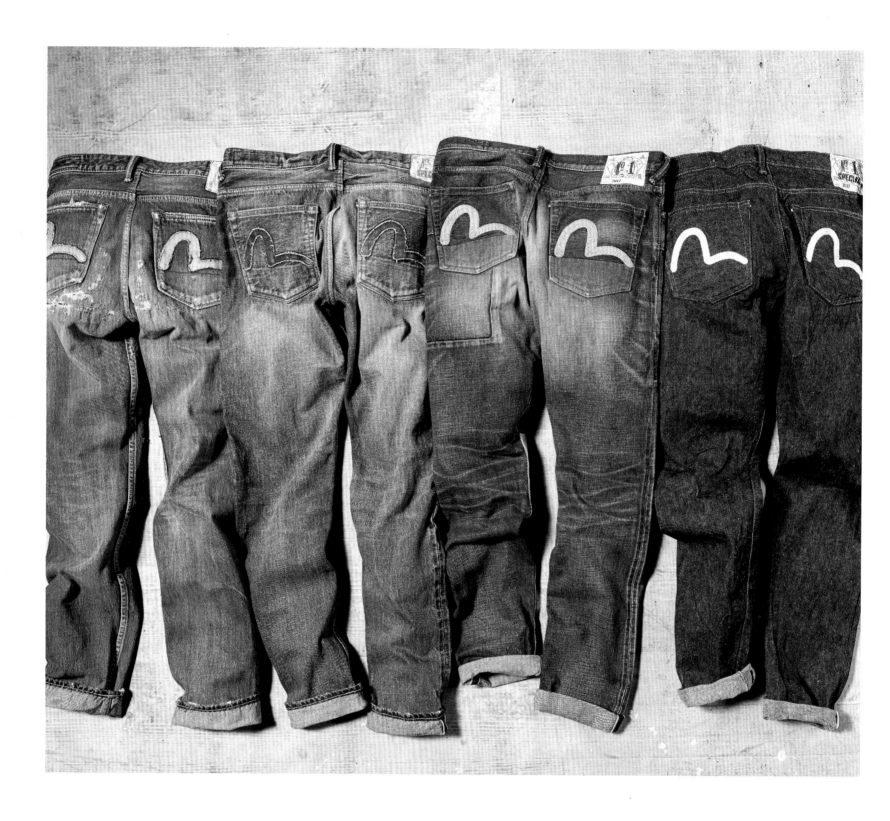

HIDEHIKO YAMANE

With his Evisu label in the 1990s, Hidehiko Yamane helped transform jeans from a humble fashion statement into an artisanal craft. An ardent lover of retro American denim, Yamane named his brand after both Ebisu (the Japanese folk god of fishermen and luck) and Levi's—he dropped the *L* and later added a *u* to avoid any potential lawsuits. Initially Yamane was able to produce just fourteen pairs of the stiff, raw denim jeans per day, each one hand-painted with the brand's signature white "seagulls" on the back pockets. Evisu's popularity skyrocketed in Japan—by the late 1990s it had sixty-five stores there alone—and it eventually found a following in England, where the jeans were picked up by acid house–loving club kids and celebrities such as David Beckham. Moving into the 2000s the jeans dominated American hip-hop, showing up in Hype Williams's film *Belly* (1998) and on stars including Jay-Z, Lil Wayne, and Beyoncé. Yamane left the label in the mid-2000s, but the brand has surged again, with its jeans appearing on rapper Travis Scott and in a collaboration with London streetwear label Palace.

Designer

Hidehiko Yamane.
b Osaka (JAP), 1959.

A collection of Evisu jeans.

↳ BECKHAM, HIRATA, INOUE, JAY-Z, PALACE, TOUITOU

JEANNE YANG

Celebrity stylist Jeanne Yang has been dressing Hollywood's leading men for decades. Born and raised in Los Angeles, she has worked with many longtime clients, including Keanu Reeves, Christian Bale, and Robert Downey Jr. After starting out as an intern at a fashion magazine, she eventually became the associate publisher and managing editor of *Detour* magazine. She discovered her love of styling there and in the early aughts began working on music videos for 311, Blink-182, and Weezer; she also managed to secure her first Hollywood client—styling Reeves for *The Matrix*'s (1999)

promotional tour. Over time Yang developed a keen mastery of men's dressing, customizing fashion to suit her clients' highly distinctive tastes and personalities. She was responsible for Jason Momoa's pink velvet Fendi suit with matching scrunchie at the 2019 Oscars, as well as John Cho's tailored gray Zegna joggers at the 2019 Film Independent Spirit Awards. Yang remains in demand, having styled for A-listers including Taika Waititi, Anthony Mackie, and Kumail Nanjiani, and also contributing to *Vanity Fair*, *GQ*, *Esquire*, and the *Hollywood Reporter*.

Stylist

Jeanne Yang.
b Los Angeles (USA), (Active 1990s—).

Jason Momoa styled by Jeanne Yang for *InStyle*, December 2020.

Photograph by Carter Smith.

↳ AMBROSE, ERMENEGILDO ZEGNA, GQ, REMBERT, URBINATI, WELCH

1500s Tailors' guilds control the production of garments from at least the thirteenth century. Aspiring tailors work their way up the guild system from apprentice to journeyman, then master tailor. Cutting skills are the most desirable, whereas sewing is often hired out to lower-skilled workers.

1509 Henry VIII (1491–1547) of England ascends the throne. His attire during his reign demonstrates the boxy, square-cut silhouettes and codpieces of the early sixteenth century.

Henry VIII marries the Spanish princess Catherine of Aragon (1485–1536). Her presence in the English court helps spread the influence of Spanish tailoring throughout Europe.

1510 Henry VIII passes a sumptuary law against the wearing of fur by anyone ranked lower than a gentleman.

1519 Upon hearing that King Francis I (1494–1547) of France had grown a beard, Henry VIII lets his beard grow out.

1520 Henry VIII and Francis I meet diplomatically in the famous Field of the Cloth of Gold, an event so named because of the large amount of golden cloth seen in both camps.

German accountant Matthäus Schwarz commissions a *Klaidungsbüchlein*, or Book of Fashion, documenting the best outfits he wore throughout his life. The project is completed in 1560.

1525 The Battle of Pavia pits Francis I against the Habsburg emperor Charles V (1500–1558). Swiss Landsknecht soldiers, known for their elaborate slashed clothing, prove decisive for the victory, and their slashed aesthetic spreads through all the courts in western Europe.

Captured at the Battle of Pavia, Francis I is only freed when his mother, Louise de Savoy (1476–1531), writes the Ottoman sultan Suleiman the Magnificent (1494–1566) for help. This leads to the development of the Franco-Ottoman Alliance in 1536, which directs Turkish trade goods, such as carpets, coffee, and textiles, into Europe through France. The alliance lasts until the late eighteenth century.

1528 Baldassare Castiglione (1478–1529) publishes *Il libro del cortegiano* (The Book of the Courtier) in Venice. The book discusses the proper etiquette of a gentleman at court, including manners, wit, and dress.

1533 Henry VIII's government issues five apparel orders under his regime, and a generation later, Elizabeth I (1533–1603) issues twelve. These regulations often aimed to limit the luxurious dress of young men, even though contemporary cultural polemics targeted women as luxury consumers.

1540s The codpiece, a bulky decorative appendage attached to men's hose over the genitals, reaches a peak in popularity, size, and decoration. It goes out of style by the 1580s.

Francis I grants the city of Lyon in southern France a monopoly on French silk production. It remains the chief French silk production center until the nineteenth century.

1547 English courtier Henry Howard, the Earl of Surrey (1517–1547), is beheaded for treason, with a major complaint being that he wore "foreign dress."

1554 King Philip II (1527–1598) of Spain visits London to marry Princess Mary Tudor (1516–1558), thus strengthening the popularity of Spanish garments throughout Europe.

1555 Textile manufacturer Chiso opens in Kyoto, Japan. Today, it still produces high-quality silk for kimonos.

1564 Mistress Dinghen van der Plasse sets up her starch-making business in London. The starch is used to stiffen fashionable ruffs higher and wider.

1570s Doublets begin to appear with added padding around the belly to mimic a well-fed silhouette. Called a peascod belly, this fashion falls out of favor by the 1590s.

1571 Elizabeth I opens the Royal Exchange in London as a place to purchase luxury goods, such as textiles, wigs, feathers, and even some early ready-to-wear garments.

1582 The Piana family founds Piana Clerico in Biella, Italy, to make high-quality woolen garments. Today, the family is famous for its 24-karat gold thread.

1588 The multiple guilds for French tailors are united under one group, the Maitres Tailleurs d'Habits.

1589 Englishman William Lee (1563–1614) invents a stocking-frame knitting machine. When Queen Elizabeth refuses his request for a patent, Lee travels to France, where his machine-knit stockings quickly become popular as a faster alternative to woven or hand-knit stockings.

Juan de Alcega's *Libro de Geometria Practica y Traca*, the first surviving tailor's manual of patterns, is published in Madrid.

1590 Cesare Vecellio's *De gli habiti antichi et moderni di diversi parti del mundo*, part travel book, part costume parade, is published in Venice to great acclaim. Vecellio's book pairs costume illustrations with vivid descriptions of different groups of people from around the world.

1597 King Henry III (1551–1589) of France's favorite courtiers are reported to wear makeup, single earrings, lovelock hairstyles, and feathered fans.

1600 The East India Trading Company is founded in London as a trading conglomerate working in the East Indies, Southeast Asia, and China. It brings large quantities of Indian cotton textiles and textile technology to Europe.

1604 The Dutch engine loom allows twelve ribbons to be woven at once, increasing the production and availability of ribbons and narrow fabrics. The following decades see a boom of fashionable ribbons on doublets, petticoat breeches, garters, and accessories.

1630s The French court under Louis XIII (1601–1643) adopts a Croatian military scarf called the cravat, which ties around the neck. This new trend probably came from Croat soldiers fighting in the Thirty Years' War (1618–1648).

Long hair, especially draped over the shoulder on one side, becomes fashionable in northern European courts.

1633 Louis XIII goes bald and starts wearing a wig. By the end of the eighteenth century, the popularity of wigs spreads to men and women from many social backgrounds.

1645 The New Model Army raised by Charles I (1600–1649) of England is the first to establish a more standardized military uniform—based on civilian dress—with ornamental or colored facings. Colored scarves and sashes also help determine friend or foe.

1655 Firmin & Sons begins producing buttons. Today, it supplies uniforms, liveries, parade and ceremonial insignias, and armor to the British military. It has worked with every British monarch since Charles II.

1660s As the East India Company brings foreign goods into Europe, dressing gowns and robes become a fashionable style of home dress. Many are made of a painted or printed cotton material called calico.

1662 Louis XIV (1638–1715) of France allows a small number of his inner circle to wear a blue justaucorps jacket. Some scholars chart the development of the justaucorps from the military influence of the Thirty Years' War.

1664 The Compagnie des Indes Orientales forms in France as a response to the British East India Company and the Dutch Vereenigde Oostindische Compagnie. Louis XIV gives the company a trading monopoly in the East Indies.

1666 Charles II (1630–1685) of England, along with his brother the Duke of York, appears at court in a new collarless long coat called a waistcoat. The waistcoat, along with the justaucorps and breeches, make up the first iteration of the three-piece suit.

1669 Louis XIV adds a new position to his payroll: *le grand maitre de la garde-robe du roi*, or the Grand Master of the King's Wardrobe. In this role, the master supervises all people and things relating to Louis XIV's clothing and even keeps Louis's three-room closet organized.

1670 Between 1670 and 1760, the East India Company imports as much as three yards of cotton textiles per person, per year, into Britain.

1671 Le Sieur Benist Boullay publishes *Le Tailleur Sincère*, the oldest known French tailoring manual, in Paris.

1672 Louis XIV follows in his father's footsteps and goes bald, leading to wigs becoming fashionable at the French court. These wigs are often made of horse, goat, or even human hair.

Jean Donneau de Visé (1638–1710) publishes the first edition of the *Mercure Galante*, a French periodical dedicated to reporting on the drama, culture, and fashion of Louis XIV's France. The *Mercure* is the first print publication to include fashion-plate illustrations, and continues in various forms until 1832.

1673 King Louis XIV of France popularizes high heels with red bottoms at court.

1680s The European "calico craze" for printed cottons imported from southwest Asia reaches its peak.

The three-piece suit—made up of justaucorps, waistcoat, and breeches—is firmly established at the French court.

Louis XIV's patronage of French luxury industries requires a biannual presentation of new designs and materials. This sets the pace for the development of seasonal luxury collections.

1682 Louis XIV moves his court to the Palace of Versailles.

1689 Ede & Ravenscroft opens for business in London. Today, it is known as the oldest continuous tailoring business, making graduation gowns, legal and church robes, and menswear and womenswear.

1692 The Battle of Steinkirk prompts a new style of cravat, one in which the linen wraps around the neck and the ends are pushed through the buttonhole on the coat.

1698 After touring western Europe, Czar Peter the Great (1672–1725) of Russia bans traditional Russian dress at his court in favor of western-style breeches, hose, coats, and wigs.

1700s   The Calico Acts of 1700 and 1721 ban the importation of Indian calico cloth into England. Despite creating these laws to boost domestic textile production, England is unable to prevent smuggling, which still allows Indian textiles to circulate in English markets.

Cotton becomes the first global commodity, feeding the Industrial Revolution in England and western Europe by 1800.

In the early decades of the eighteenth century, 40 percent of Parisian workers are employed in garment and textile trades.

1709   Giovanni Maria Farina (1685–1766) creates the first eau de cologne and names it after his hometown of Cologne, Germany.

1714   Jean-Baptiste Vanmour's *Receuil des cent estampes représentant différentes nations du Levant* is published in Paris as a collection of Ottoman costume plates. The book is so popular that second and third editions are printed in 1750 and 1769, respectively.

1720   Most European armies are outfitted in uniforms, with soldiers receiving new ones, on average, every two years.

1721   Mehmed Çelebi Efendi (1670–1732) travels to France as the first Ottoman ambassador. His diplomatic presence in Paris popularizes elements of Ottoman culture, such as turbans and loose kaftan coats.

1730   Parisian jeweler Georges Frédéric Strass (1701–1773) creates imitation gemstones called paste jewels that can be worn on shoe buckles, hats, and other accessories.

1731   *The Gentleman's Magazine* is first published, featuring articles on politics, gossip, and dress. Publication continues until 1922, with the magazine remaining one of the few menswear-dedicated periodicals available throughout this time.

In 1664 the third Earl of Burlington, Richard Boyle (1694–1753), moved to a mansion in Piccadilly named Burlington House. A generation later, Boyle's son renovates and builds on the surrounding property, including a throughway called Savile Street, known today as Savile Row, the custom-made tailoring capital of the UK.

1756   Chevalier d'Éon (1728–1810) begins working for King Louis XV's (1710–1774) spy network the *Secret du Roi*. It is thought that d'Éon's spying activities were aided by his androgynous appearance; one popular account claims he traveled to Russia dressed as a woman. He presents as a woman for the last thirty-three years of his life.

1765   James and Mary Locke establish Locke & Co. Hatters at No. 6 St. James's Street, London. Over the years they design hats for notable names, including Admiral Lord Nelson, Beau Brummell, Oscar Wilde, Winston Churchill, and Charlie Chaplin.

1770s   Anglomania begins in France. The popularity of English goods and culture includes horses, hunting, male aristocratic culture, clubs and pubs, and fashion.

With the exception of France, many European rulers begin to reject wearing traditional court costumes in favor of military uniforms at court.

1771   Richard Arkwright (1732–1792) opens the first water-powered cotton mill at Cromford Mill, Derbyshire, in England.

1772   The caricaturists Mary and Matthew Darly publish "The Miniature Macaroni," a caricature of the portrait miniaturist Richard Cosway (1742–1821). His tight-fitting French silk suit, large wig, sword, and affected mannerisms identify him as a member of the Macaroni subculture.

Thomas Fox founds the cloth mill Fox Brothers & Co in West England. The mill continues to produce cloth today and is credited as the official inventors of flannel.

1774   Johann Adam Birkenstock (1687–1733) founds Birkenstock Orthopädie GmbH & Co. Today, Birkenstock shoes are famous for their cork footbed that contours to the foot.

1785   *Le Cabinet des modes*, the first true fashion magazine, is published in Paris by François Buisson.

1786   The first European patent is approved on an umbrella. However, umbrellas were present up to three thousand years earlier at different moments in Egypt, China, and India.

1789   Louis XVI (1754–1793) calls together the Estates General for the first time in one hundred years to discuss France's economic situation. The three estates abide by a clear dress code: the clergy must wear their robes, the aristocrats must wear silk and swords, and the third estate must wear black.

In the wake of the French Revolution, fashionable court society breaks down, luxury markets leave France, and greater austerity of dress and manners reigns supreme.

1790s   The advent of neoclassical art in the 1780s revives an interest in classical statuary and sparks a trend for tight, buff-colored pantaloons that appear nude from a distance.

French royalists and revolutionaries alike demonstrate their political allegiance by wearing a cockade, which is a knot of ribbons, often in distinctive colors, affixed to a hat.

1790   British inventor Harvey Kennedy patents a new type of shoelace with aglets, the plastic or metal covering at each end of the lace.

1791   Goldsmith Jean-François Bautte (1772–1837) begins designing watches in Geneva. The company left to his successors is eventually renamed Girard-Perregaux in 1856.

1793– 1794   French artist Jacques-Louis David (1748–1825) is invited to design new civilian dress that reflects the republican conventions and represents the revolution, but his designs never catch on beyond his students.

1795   The Incroyables strut around Paris in high-collared tailcoats and tight breeches. Their female counterparts, the Merveilleuses, exaggerate female fashion by going without a corset or chemise.

1796   The first English-language tailoring publication, *The Taylor's Complete Guide*, is launched.

1799 –1801   After the Coup de Brumaire, Napoleon Bonaparte (1769–1821) legislates for lavish, embroidered uniforms at every level of his regime.

1800s   The modern tailor's tape measure is invented. Prior to this, tailors used paper strips with cut notches to measure each client individually.

1804   Napoleon crowns himself emperor of France and brings back the luxury and sophistication of the French court, as well as the court costumes.

Joseph-Marie Jacquard (1752–1834) invents the Jacquard loom.

Napoleon requires that all those present at his court dress in French textiles.

The Napoleonic Wars (1803–1815) further popularize the military uniform.

1810   George Bryan "Beau" Brummell (1778–1840), the first dandy, exerts enormous influence over George, Prince of Wales (1762–1830), later George IV. His dandified ensemble of a navy blue or black tailcoat and tan breeches or pantaloons, with impeccable fine linen shirting, represents the simplicity and austerity of nineteenth-century menswear. Dandyism takes European menswear by storm.

A renunciation of ornament, color, and variety in menswear in favor of precise tailoring, simplicity of silhouette, and collective identity occurs. This is later termed the Great Masculine Renunciation, by the psychoanalyst John Carl Flügel (1884–1955).

1812   The first ready-to-wear uniforms are used for the War of 1812.

The War of 1812 also encourages the development of more standardized sizing systems for menswear based on chest circumference. This measurement is later used to develop standardized womenswear sizing but, unfortunately, with much less success.

Aaron Benedict (1785–1873) founds Waterbury Buttons in Waterbury, Connecticut, and supplies metal buttons for the War of 1812. In recent decades the company has produced buttons for top designers, such as Ralph Lauren and Brooks Brothers.

1815   Robert Pringle founds Pringle of Scotland as an underwear and hosiery company. Their most popular argyle pattern was worn by the Duke of Windsor, and in 2019 they collaborated with the retail clothing company H&M.

The Duke of Wellington, who defeats Napoleon at the Battle of Waterloo, gives his name to the Wellington boot.

1818   Henry Sands Brooks (1772–1833) opens H. & D. H. Brooks & Co. in New York City. In 1850 his four sons rename the company Brooks Brothers, and future presidents, including Abraham Lincoln and Barack Obama, go on to wear Brooks Brothers suits for their inaugural addresses.

L'art de la toilette is published with seventy-two different instructions for tying a cravat.

1820s Trousers finally take over from pantaloons and breeches as the standard daywear option.

The male corset becomes a popular way to achieve the pigeon-breasted silhouette of the 1820s and 1830s. It is also fashionable to layer multiple waistcoats to achieve a bigger chest.

1822 George IV popularizes the stock, which is a stiffened black or white band fastened at the back of the neck and covered with velvet and satin.

1825 Hannah Lord Montague invents detachable, reusable collars in Troy, New York.

1830s English company Liverpool Rubber makes sand shoes by bonding canvas to rubber.

1830 A fashionable dandy, Alfred, the Count d'Orsay (1801–1852), attempts to reinvigorate male fashion with the vivid colors it lost after the French Revolution. He is ultimately unsuccessful.

1837 Thierry Hermès (1801–1878) establishes Hermès as a leather-goods store in Paris.

When Queen Victoria (1819–1901) visits HMS *Blazer*, the sailors wear loose, double-breasted jackets made especially for the occasion. These jackets, given the name "blazer," become part of their regular uniforms.

1839 A machine known as the Delas's somatometer is used to calculate a client's body measurements by fitting them in an adjustable metal cage.

1840s The majority of trousers are now made with center flies instead of fall fronts.

The sack suit, or lounge suit, is introduced, in the form of a loose suit, small lapels, three or four buttons, and no waist seam.

1840 Antoine Gibus invents the collapsible top hat.

Beau Brummell dies in Caen, France, penniless after falling out with George IV.

1846 Henry Poole becomes the first Savile Row tailor, enlarging his father James's 1806 storefront on Old Burlington Street to open on Savile Row.

The British military adopts khaki-colored uniforms in India. In later conflicts, khaki is painted in patterns to add camouflage.

1849 Lock & Co. invents the bowler hat for Edward Coke after he requests that they make a hat for his estate gamekeepers.

1850s The tie appears as part of sportswear.

1851 Isaac Merritt Singer (1811–1875) invents the sewing machine.

1852 The Bon Marché—the world's first department store—opens in Paris, establishing shopping as a new kind of leisure activity.

1853 Charles Frederick Worth (1825–1895) is introduced to Empress Eugénie de Montijo (1826–1920), the wife of Emperor Louis-Napoleon III (1808–1873). Her patronage sets Worth up as the first couturier, and his innovations include using mannequins to display his clothing, selling his designs wholesale, and attaching labels to his designs.

Levi Strauss (1829–1902) heads to California and starts making sturdy pants from tent canvas for miners. He opens a dry goods store in San Francisco.

James Thomas Brudenell (1797–1868), the seventh Lord Cardigan, dresses his officers in the Crimean War (1853–1856) in fashionable new uniforms—short knitted wool jackets and vests. The former eventually become known as cardigans.

1854 Louis Vuitton (1821–1892) establishes his luggage company. In 1888 his son George designs the famous company monogram.

1856 British chemist William Perkin (1838–1907) extracts the first synthetic dyes from coal tar to create brilliant colors, such as purple. Previous dyes were all derived from nature.

1858 Rowland H. Macy (1847–1878) opens the department store R. H. Macy & Co. in New York City. In 1902 the store moves to Herald Square, where it becomes the largest store in the world in 1924.

1861 The American Civil War (1861–1865) demonstrates the enormous demand for mass-manufactured garments when the Northern Army wears out 1.5 million uniforms in a single year.

1862 Albert, Prince of Wales (1841–1910), later Edward VII, travels to Jerusalem and gets a Jerusalem cross tattooed on his arm to honor the event.

1865 John B. Stetson (1830–1906) creates the Stetson hat, known as the "Boss of the Plains."

1868 Charles Frederick Worth establishes the Chambre Syndicale de la Couture, des Confectionneurs et des Tailleurs pour Dame, known today as Chambre Syndicale de la Haute Couture, the regulating body for haute-couture houses.

The Cincinnati Red Stockings are the first sports team to adopt a uniform.

1870 Celluloid is invented and becomes a popular material choice for detachable collars.

1871 Brown, Davis & Co. makes the first button-down men's shirt.

1872 Lyman (1841–1905) and Joseph Bloomingdale (1842–1904) open Bloomingdale Brothers, Inc. in New York City.

1873 Levi Strauss and the tailor Jacob Davis (1831–1908) patent denim jeans with metal rivets at certain stress points.

1879 Thomas Burberry (1835–1926) invents gabardine, a lightweight waterproof material.

1880s The ready-to-wear sack suit becomes the most popular businesswear option for men.

American inventor Whitcomb Judson (1846–1909) designs a clasping lock, a precursor to the zipper, for shoes.

1882 Oscar Wilde (1854–1900) travels to the United States on a lecture tour to talk about aestheticism, a movement of which he is both a spokesperson and visual example, dressed in a velvet suit with a big tie.

1884 Dr. Gustav Jaeger (1832–1917) founds Jaeger as part of the dress-reform movement. His clothing advocates for wearing wool against the skin to facilitate healthy living.

1885 William Hickson and Sons market their Renshaw shoe, named after the popular lawn tennis-playing twins William (1861–1904) and Ernest Renshaw (1861–1899). The shoes are made with rubber soles to prevent slipping and sliding in the grass.

1886 The Tuxedo Club's annual Autumn Ball is a huge social event in suburban New York. Hosted by the Lorillard family, they design their own version of the tuxedo (dinner jacket) for the ball after the Prince of Wales introduced them to it a year earlier.

1889 Hamilton Carhartt (1855–1937) founds Carhartt in Detroit, Michigan, and begins production of overalls.

1890s Thomas Burberry sells his first gabardine raincoat.

1891 Tattoo artist Samuel O'Reilly (1854–1909) patents the first electric tattooing device.

1892 *Vogue* begins publication.

1893 Sears, Roebuck and Company launches its mail-order catalog service.

1895 The Prince of Wales cuffs his trousers to avoid mud at the horse track. By 1900 the style is ubiquitous.

Oscar Wilde is tried and convicted for gross indecency. He serves two years in jail.

1896 The first modern Olympic Games are held in Athens, Greece, and demonstrate a growing interest in sport, physical activity, and sportswear.

Siegel-Cooper Company opens their store on Sixth Avenue in New York City. At 750,000 square feet, the store has up to 120,000 visitors a day.

The American Impressionist painter William Merritt Chase (1849–1916) founds Parsons School of Design in New York City.

1899 Soldiers in the Boer War (1899–1902) wrap pocket watches around their wrists to coordinate military operations.

1904 Cartier designs a men's wristwatch called the Santos, named after the famous aviator Alberto Santos-Dumont (1873–1932), which features a flat face and square bezel.

1905 Cluett Peabody & Company releases the first Arrow Collar Man campaign. Illustrated by J. C. Leyendecker (1874–1951), Arrow's men's ads help Cluett Peabody sell more than four million detachable shirt collars per week by the 1920s.

Wilsdorf and Davis is founded with the goal of creating an accurate wristwatch. The company becomes Rolex Watch Co. Ltd. in 1915.

1906 Van Cleef & Arpels opens at 22 Place Vendôme in Paris, where it has remained ever since.

William J. Riley founds New Balance Arch Support Company in Boston.

1907 Carhartt debuts their Carhartt Chore Coat, which remains virtually unchanged today.

1909 Harry Gordon Selfridge (1858–1947) opens Selfridges & Co. on Oxford Street in London.

1910 Edward VII inherits the English throne at the age of sixty; by this time he is already a major force in menswear, especially by popularizing dressing with "practical elegance."

American Viscose Company starts producing rayon as a synthetic alternative to silk.

Ermenegildo Zegna (1892–1966) founds his woolen textile company in Trivero, Italy.

Lady Duff Gordon (1863–1935) uses professional models, known as mannequins, to show off her designs at her Lucile Ltd. boutiques.

1911 Paul Poiret (1879–1944), the King of Fashion, develops the concept of "total lifestyle" for his label by marketing a perfume called Parfums de Rosine.

1913 Carl Jantzen (1883–1939) and his brothers create the world's first elasticized swimming suit when the Portland Rowing Club in Oregon asks them to design trunks for cold morning rows.

The US Navy adopts the white cotton T-shirt as underwear. The US Army later embraces the garment in 1942.

Gideon Sundback (1880–1954) improves on earlier zipper designs, but his hookless fastener design only appears on clothing beginning in the 1930s.

1914– Thomas Burberry invents the trench coat during
1918 World War I.

1915 The Triangle Shirtwaist Factory Fire in New York City kills 146 workers. The tragedy sparks an interest in garment worker rights and protections.

The United Garment Workers' Union forms in the UK.

1916 British *Vogue* begins publication.

1917 The Converse Rubber Shoe Company debuts their indoor gym shoe, the All Star. In 1932 basketball coach and design advisor Chuck Taylor adds his name to the All Star.

Henry Nelson McKinney, an ad agent for N. W. Ayer & Son, coins the term "sneakers," because the rubber sole lets the wearer be sneaky.

The US Rubber Company markets Keds as the first mass-market sneaker brand in the United States.

1920s As more people participate in sports, having a suntan gains social acceptance.

Army Air Corps flyer John Macready (1887–1979) works with Bausch & Lomb to engineer antiglare pilot's goggles. By 1937 these goggles are patented as Ray-Ban Aviators.

Edward, Prince of Wales (1894–1972), starts wearing midnight blue evening suits instead of the traditional black.

Jazz music takes mainstream American culture by storm. As part of their stage performances, Duke Ellington (1899–1974) and Louis Armstrong (1901–1971) are among the musicians that wear dandy-style sack suits and tuxedos, as well as the groups Zach Whyte's Chocolate Beau Brummels and Buster Bailey & His Seven Chocolate Dandies.

Sweaters become popular as an alternative to the stiffness and formality of the men's suit coat.

Enrico Isaia opens Isaia as a textile store in Naples. By the late 1950s Isaia has become a prominent Italian tailoring company.

1920 Garment Center Realty Co. moves to Seventh Avenue between 36th Street and 38th Street in New York City. This area becomes the twenty-first-century Garment District.

Dada artist Marcel Duchamp (1887–1968) first appears as Rrose Sélavy, his female alter ego.

Vogue Paris begins publication.

1921 Guccio Gucci (1881–1953) launches the House of Gucci in Florence, Italy.

1922 Dickies is founded by C. N. Williamson and E. E. "Colonel" Dickie in Texas.

Golden Bear Sportswear begins manufacturing dockworker coats in San Francisco. They continue to create high-quality, long-lasting jackets today.

1923 John Powers (1892–1977) opens the first US modeling agency, the John Robert Powers Agency, in New York City.

1924 Henry Gerber (1892–1972) founds the Society for Human Rights, the first gay rights organization, in Chicago.

Jesse Langsdorf's company Resilio patents a three-piece tie construction that remains the standard necktie today.

1925 Oxford University students wear loose trousers called "oxford bags" over plus fours, or knickerbockers—a way to avoid Oxford's rules against sports clothing in college—helping to popularize the style for men generally.

1926 Jeanne Lanvin (1867–1946) begins production of her first menswear line.

1927 Cecil Beaton (1904–1980) begins working at *Vogue* as a cartoonist before changing to photography for the magazine and for *Harper's Bazaar* and *Vanity Fair*.

1928 The Australian swimwear company Speedo introduces the racerback swimsuit.

1929 The growing influence of casual dressing leads to the development of the Men's Dress Reform Party. The group formed with the goal of making menswear looser and, therefore, healthier and more interesting. The sociologist and writer John Carl Flügel (1884–1955), famous for developing the idea of the "Great Masculine Renunciation," was a member.

1930s Frederick Scholte (died c. 1959), a Dutch tailor on London's Savile Row, develops the English "drape" cut in imitation of the officers of the Royal British Guards. The cut's wide shoulders, slim waist, and loose armholes create a classically athletic male silhouette.

Menswear simplifies even further and becomes less formal. Accessories, such as spats, canes, stiff collars, and gloves, are cast aside for soft sweaters and loose trousers.

Duffle coats become a fashionable style in interwar Europe and are adopted by the Royal Navy.

Male movie stars are often expected to provide their own filming costumes. Cary Grant (1904–1986), one of the best-dressed stars, shops on Savile Row for his suits.

1931 *Apparel Arts* begins publication as an industry-specific magazine. In 1958 the magazine becomes *Gentleman's Quarterly* and then simply *GQ* in 1983.

1932 Henry "Bunny" Austin (1906–2000) causes a stir by wearing shorts to the US National Tennis Championship.

1933 René Lacoste (1904–1996), a well-known tennis player, develops a sports shirt based on a traditional polo shirt with a longer tail that will not come untucked when playing tennis.

Esquire begins publication.

Jankel Grimbert establishes the high-end, made-to-measure menswear boutique Arnys in Paris. Orson Welles and Jean Cocteau are frequent clients.

1934 Clark Gable's shirtless appearance in the film *It Happened One Night* reportedly leads to the slump of undershirt sales following its release.

Paul Sperry (1895–1982) falls overboard from his sailboat, the *Sirocco*. As he struggles to get back on board, the idea for the Sperry Top-Siders boat shoe is born, and he develops the shoe in 1937.

As part of the "dress soft" revolution, promoted by Edward, Prince of Wales, he and his cousin Lord Louis Mountbatten wear pants with zippers instead of button flies.

Ernest Daltroff (1867–1941) of Parfums Caron creates Pour un Homme, the first perfume for men.

Jantzen's topper-style swimsuit features a zipper around the waist for easy removal of the shirt portion of the suit, demonstrating how changing social codes increasingly allow men to swim topless.

1935 Originally named Cooper's, the brand introduces Jockey underwear with the Y-front opening and an elastic waistband.

1936 Olympian Jesse Owens (1913–1980) tests Adolf "Adi" Dassler's (1900–1978) running shoes at the Berlin Olympic Games. Dassler founds Adidas in 1949 and designs shoes with his signature three stripes.

Ellery Chun (1909–2000) is the first to trademark the Aloha, or Hawaiian, shirt, and produce it in bulk. Chun's shirts are short-sleeved and block-printed versions of traditional Hawaiian palaka shirts, and he hires local artisans to design the prints.

Inspired by a traditional Norwegian slipper-type moccasin, G.H. Bass and Co. designs the Weejun, which is to become better known as the penny loafer, getting its name from the popular practice of hiding a penny in the vamp slot.

1939 DuPont markets nylon at the New York World's Fair as the first chemically created textile fiber. Other synthetic fibers soon follow, such as acrylic in 1950 and polyester in 1953.

1940s World War II restricts the production and consumption of fashion in Europe. Many designers leave Paris, resulting in the rising influence of American designers in New York City.

1941 The UK introduces the Consumer Rationing Order, which limits textile and garment consumption for UK citizens.

1942 Following the UK, the US War Production Board issues General Limitation Order L-85, which also limits textile and garment consumption in the United States.

1943 Oversize zoot suits are popular among young Mexican and Black American men. The heavy drape of the suits is viewed as unpatriotic and violence erupts against those wearing the suits.

Jazz musician Cab Calloway (1907–1994) wears a zoot suit in the film *Stormy Weather*.

Publicist Eleanor Lambert (1903–2003) establishes New York Fashion Week by launching Press Week. Later developments include the organization of Ruth Finley's (1920–2018) Fashion Calendar in 1945.

1944 Mortimer C. Ritter and Max Meyer found the Fashion Institute of Technology in New York City.

1945 Richard Avedon (1923–2004) begins working at *Harper's Bazaar* as a staff photographer.

John H. Johnson (1918–2005) founds *Ebony* magazine in Chicago.

Nazareno Fonticoli (1906–1981) and Gaetano Savini (1909–1987) set up Brioni in Rome as an Italian alternative to the hegemony of Savile Row. Brioni goes on to dress well-known men, including John Wayne, Gary Cooper, and Sidney Poitier.

Dr. Klaus Maertens and Dr. Herbert Funk team up to create an air-cushioned shoe. Although Dr. Martens today are favored for their punk and grunge aesthetic, their first decade of business predominately caters to older women.

1946 Eileen and Gerald W. Ford establish the Ford Modeling Agency in New York City.

1947 Saul Charles and Mitchell Cinader found Popular Merchandise, Inc. The company changes its name to J.Crew in 1983.

1948 Charlie Davidson's Andover Shop opens in Harvard Square, Cambridge, Massachusetts, and sells Ivy League–style clothes to college students and notable names, including Miles Davis and Chet Baker. Eleanor Lambert establishes the Met Gala at the Metropolitan Museum of Art.

Esquire publishes a spread dedicated to the Bold Look, which encourages men to be less conservative and experiment with wide borders, big patterns, and plenty of color in their clothing.

1949 Onitsuka Shokai founds Onitsuka Tiger (later known as Asics) in Kobe, Japan. Both Bill Bowerman (1911–1999) and Phil Knight (1938–), the founders of Nike, begin their footwear careers working with Asics.

1950s As postwar haute-couture markets decline, fashion houses expand their labels to include perfumes, makeup, and even home goods.

1952 Brioni hosts the first men's fashion show, at the Palazzo Pitti in Florence.

Working-class teenagers in London, known as the teddy boys, adopt the new Edwardian look popularized on Savile Row after World War II.

1954 Bill Green opens Vince's Man's Shop on Newburgh Street, London, and sells modish garments, such as bum-freezer jackets, narrow trousers, and his signature "ultra-briefs."

1955 James Dean's appearance in the film *Rebel Without a Cause* bottles teenage angst in the form of a red Harrington bomber jacket, a white T-shirt, and jeans. Although Dean dies in 1955 at only twenty-four years old, he represents the growing youth culture taken up by other leading men, such as Marlon Brando in *A Streetcar Named Desire* (1951) and Elvis Presley in *Jailhouse Rock* (1957).

Mary Quant (1930–) opens her boutique Bazaar on King's Road in Chelsea, London.

Sloan Wilson's (1920–2003) novel *The Man in the Gray Flannel Suit* and subsequent 1956 film starring Gregory Peck (1916–2003) present the gray suit as the symbol of 1950s-era conformity.

Bill Haley's (1925–1981) "Rock Around the Clock" introduces the world to rock 'n' roll.

1957 John Stephen (1934–2004) opens his boutique on Carnaby Street in London. This location becomes the center of mod fashion and the Peacock Revolution, and by 1966 seventeen other menswear shops are on the street.

Pierre Cardin's (1922–2020) first menswear shop, Adam, opens in Paris.

Jack Kerouac's (1922–1969) novel *On the Road* inspires a generation of beatniks.

1959 Pierre Cardin is expelled from the Chambre Syndicale de la Couture Parisienne. He shows his first womenswear line this same year.

"Mainly for Men," a fifteen-minute TV spot, advertises Cecil Gee's menswear on British television.

1960s The Peacock Revolution releases any remaining nineteenth-century formality from menswear and embraces color, texture, and variety. Secondhand shopping, military-inspired looks, and youthful subcultures diversify menswear.

Illustrator Antonio Lopez (1943–1987) and art director Juan Ramos (1942–1995) provide the groovy fashion imagery of the 1960s.

1960 Pierre Cardin shows his first menswear collection.

1961 In frigid winter weather, a vigorous John F. Kennedy goes without an overcoat and top hat for his inauguration speech, unintentionally influencing younger men to dress more youthfully than their elders, and causing shock waves in the coat and hat industries.

Elvis Presley (1935–1977) appears in a rayon Hawaiian shirt in a promo ad for the film *Blue Hawaii*.

Yves Saint Laurent (1936–2008) designs his first collection.

1962 Eleanor Lambert launches the Council of Fashion Designers of America to promote American design.

1963 During more than half of the film *From Russia with Love*, Sean Connery (1930–2020) wears either a dinner jacket or a suit while playing James Bond. Connery's other performances as Bond in *Dr. No* (1962) and *Diamonds Are Forever* (1971) connect Bond forever to the tuxedo.

1964 André Courrèges (1923–2016) presents his Space Age collection, which experiments wildly with materials.

1965 *Vogue* editor Diana Vreeland (1903–1989) uses the term "youthquake" to describe Carnaby Street's youthful influence.

Ian Fisk and John Paul open I Was Lord Kitchener's Valet just off Carnaby Street, London.

1966 Granny Takes a Trip opens on King's Road, London. A vintage store famous as a swinging psychedelic hot spot, it paves the way for other shops, such as Vivienne Westwood's Let It Rock.

Paul (1930–2021) and Jim Van Doren (1939–2011) open the Van Doren Rubber Company in Anaheim, California, which later becomes Vans.

Richard Avedon leaves *Harper's Bazaar* for *Vogue*.

1967 Gilbert Féruch's (1924–) Nehru-style jacket with a low-standing collar is named for Jawaharlal Nehru (1889–1964), who became prime minister of a newly independent India in 1947.

Ralph Lauren (1939–) designs a collection of wide ties he labels Polo.

1968 Calvin Klein (1942–) creates his eponymous label in a small showroom in New York City.

Ralph Lauren establishes his preppy menswear label Polo Ralph Lauren.

1969 Festival goers at the Woodstock Music Festival in New York wear secondhand, anti-fashion garments.

Tommy Nutter (1943–1992) and Edward Sexton (1942–) open Nutters on Savile Row in London.

Riots break out at the Stonewall Inn in New York City's Greenwich Village in response to a police raid.

The Boston Celtics wear Adidas Supergrip to win the 1969 NBA Championship. One year later Adidas changes the shoe's name to Superstar.

1970s   Jeans and a T-shirt become a ubiquitous unisex uniform that has yet to go out of fashion.

1970   Bill Blass (1922–2002) creates Bill Blass Ltd. in New York.

Japanese designer Kenzo Takada (1939–2020) opens his first boutique in Paris. His menswear ready-to-wear collection debuts in 1984.

Paul Smith (1946–) opens his first shop in Nottingham, England, selling designer clothes as well as his own designs.

The first gay pride parades are held in the United States.

Marsha P. Johnson (1945–1992) and Sylvia Rivera (1951–2002) launch the Street Transvestite Action Revolutionaries.

1971   Malcolm McLaren (1946–2010) and Vivienne Westwood (1941–) open Let It Rock in King's Road, London. The store is rebranded multiple times as Too Fast To Live Too Young To Die, SEX, Seditionaries, and Worlds End.

Willi Smith (1948–1987) of WilliWear becomes the youngest designer nominated for a Coty Award.

The first Pitti Uomo fashion industry event is held in Florence. Today, it is one of the leading menswear events of the year.

1972   David Bowie (1947–2016) releases his album *The Rise and Fall of Ziggy Stardust and the Spiders from Mars*; Bowie's Ziggy Stardust persona dresses in jumpsuits designed by Kansai Yamamoto.

Bill Bowerman and Phil Knight revolutionize running by creating Nike's waffle-soled running shoe.

Ralph Lauren debuts his iconic polo shirt that incorporates the polo pony logo from the cuff of his womenswear shirt line released a year earlier.

1973   Chambre Syndicale du Prêt-à-Porter des Couturiers et des Créateurs de Mode is founded and the Chambre Syndicale de la Mode Masculine is established in France.

The Battle of Versailles fashion show pits American and French designers against each other and includes talented designers such as Stephen Burrows (1943–), Halston (1932–1990), and Oscar de la Renta (1932–2014).

Stephen Burrows becomes the first Black designer to win a Coty Award.

1974   Ralph Lauren designs the costumes for the film *The Great Gatsby*, starring Robert Redford and Mia Farrow.

1975   Giorgio Armani's (1934–) first independent collection loosens the traditional silhouette of the suit by elongating the lapels and pushing the buttons low.

Amancio Ortega (1936–) opens the first Zara in Spain.

Issey Miyake (1938–) opens his boutique in Paris.

1976   Jean Paul Gaultier's (1952–) first collection earns him the title enfant terrible of the Paris fashion world.

Jonathan Ned Katz's (1938–) book *Gay American History: Lesbians and Gay Men in the U.S.A.* is the first to document gay US history.

One of the earliest propagators of contemporary sportswear, Willi Smith blends this style with high fashion in his first WilliWear collection.

1977   Punk fashion and music reach peak influence.

1978   Calvin Klein launches his denim line, with his underwear line following in 1982. Both are hugely successful.

1980s   The Hugo Boss suit becomes the standard for a rising generation of young urban professionals known as yuppies.

Womenswear designers, such as Karl Lagerfeld, Jean Paul Gaultier, and Thierry Mugler (1948–), expand into menswear.

The growing importance of street style spreads innovation from the bottom up instead of from the top down.

Apple cofounder Steve Jobs (1955–2011) hires Issey Miyake to create his signature black turtleneck.

1980   Giorgio Armani dresses Richard Gere (1949–) in the film *American Gigolo*.

i-D magazine, founded by British *Vogue* art director Terry Jones, launches and celebrates London street style.

Lisa Birnbach (1957–) publishes *The Official Preppy Handbook* to catalog the polos, khakis, and loafers associated with preppy style.

1981   Acquired Immune Deficiency Syndrome, known as AIDS, becomes a global epidemic.

Rei Kawakubo (1942–) and Yohji Yamamoto (1943–) debut their collections during a show in Paris. Along with Issey Miyake, these designers make up a new Japanese avant-garde.

Music Television (MTV) begins.

The premiere of the television show *Dynasty* on NBC popularizes power dressing, with suits featuring wide lapels, padded shoulders, and a double-breasted design.

1982   Bruce Feirstein's (1956–) book *Real Men Don't Eat Quiche* is a *New York Times* bestseller for more than a year. The book is part of a conservative turn following the liberalism of the 1970s.

Dapper Dan (1944–) opens his boutique in Harlem, New York.

Bruce Weber (1946–) photographs the iconic Calvin Klein campaign with model and pole-vaulter Tom Hintnaus (1958–).

1983   Jean Paul Gaultier's first menswear collection, Boy Toy, solidifies the Breton striped shirt as a fashion staple.

Karl Lagerfeld (1933–2019) is appointed creative director of Chanel.

1984   John Galliano (1960–) presents his graduate collection at Central Saint Martin's School of Art and Design, titled Les Incroyables. He then launches his own label.

London Fashion Week begins.

Run-DMC's debut album, *Run-D.M.C.*, is the first rap album to receive gold status. Their style—which includes black jeans and leather, gold chains, and Adidas without laces—becomes synonymous with their music.

Nike releases the first Air Jordans, the shoe designed for basketball phenom Michael Jordan (1963–).

Jean Paul Gaultier's Fall/Winter collection features men in kilts, sarongs, and harem pants, prompting the *New York Times* fashion critic Bernadine Morris to write, "If it's all right for women to wear fully tailored clothing, why isn't it all right for men to wear skirts?"

Six years after debuting Comme des Garçons's menswear line, Comme des Garçons Homme, Rei Kawakubo launches Comme des Garçons Homme Plus, which offers more experimental designs.

1985   Tommy Hilfiger (1951–) launches his eponymous brand, combining classic Americana with influences from streetwear and hip-hop.

Leigh Bowery (1961–1994) founds the nightclub Taboo in London. His outfits, song selections, and extreme makeup designs transform him into a cult figure.

1986   Run-DMC's song "My Adidas" turns Adidas into an emblem of street style.

A group of students at the Royal Academy of Fine Arts in Antwerp, Belgium, travel by truck with their collections to London Fashion Week. They become known as the Antwerp Six.

The artist Jean-Michel Basquiat (1960–1988) walks in the Comme des Garçons Spring/Summer 1987 show.

1987   Bruce Weber's Calvin Klein campaign Obsession for Men debuts.

Nirvana forms. Lead singer Kurt Cobain (1967–1994) helps create the grunge look of the 1990s.

The French multinational corporation LVMH is created when Louis Vuitton merges with Moët Hennessy.

1988   Patrick Kelly (1954–1990) is the first American to be accepted into the Chambre Syndicale du Prêt-a-Porter des Couturiers et des Créateurs de Mode.

André Leon Talley (1948–) becomes creative director at *Vogue*. Known for his luxurious kaftans, Talley is editor at large from 1998 through 2013.

1989   Central Saint Martins College of Art and Design is created from Central School of Art and Design and Saint Martin's School of Art. Alumni include Sarah Burton, Alexander McQueen, Mowalola Ogunlesi, and Riccardo Tisci.

1990s   Influences such as grunge rock help create a more casual, distressed look in men's fashion.

1990   Photographer Corinne Day (1965–2010) publishes her first fashion editorial of Kate Moss in *The Face* magazine. Her approach to styling soon takes on the label "grunge."

Dolce & Gabbana launch their menswear line.

1991   Hu Bing (1971–) becomes the first Chinese model to work internationally.

Ermenegildo Zegna opens its first store in Beijing, becoming the first western luxury menswear brand to open in China.

1992   Isabella Blow (1958–2007) of *Tatler* magazine buys Alexander McQueen's (1969–2010) graduation collection.

Marc Jacobs (1963–) debuts his Perry Ellis grunge collection in New York City.

1993   Issey Miyake's acclaimed collection Pleats Please is released.

1994   Tom Ford (1961–) becomes creative director at Gucci.

James Jebbia (1963–) launches Supreme.

Journalist Mark Simpson coins the term "metrosexual" in his essay "Here Come the Mirror Men," published in *The Independent*.

Franco Moschino (1950–1994) dies. His creative director Rosella Jardini takes his place until 2013, when Jeremy Scott is hired to head the label.

1995   Raf Simons (1968–) launches his menswear label.

The Union of Needletrades, Industrial and Textile Employees forms in the United States.

1996   Tupac Shakur (1971–1996) walks the Versace runway, cementing his relationship with the brand and demonstrating the growing high-fashion influence of hip-hop. Tupac's influential style includes bandanas, overalls, and Timberlands.

David LaChapelle's makes his iconic "Becoming Clean" photo shoot of Tupac Shakur.

1997   Marc Jacobs is named creative director at Louis Vuitton.

Gianni Versace (1946–1997) is murdered in Florida. His sister Donatella (1955–) takes over his empire.

1998   Maison Martin Margiela's first menswear collection, Line 10, premieres.

David Beckham (1975–) receives negative press for wearing a Jean Paul Gaultier sarong in public.

2000s   Brands such as Zara, Topshop, and H&M take part in the development of fast fashion, which prioritizes rapidly shifting trends and a quick turnover of merchandise.

Menswear becomes increasingly casual as tech entrepreneurs, such as Apple's Steve Jobs and Facebook's Mark Zuckerberg, wear turtlenecks and crew-neck T-shirts and jeans.

A greater culture of inclusive masculinity and acceptance leads to more makeup options for men, including foundation and "guyliner."

2000   Junya Watanabe (1961–) designs his first menswear collection under his own name for Comme des Garçons.

Shaun Cole publishes his book *Don We Now Our Gay Apparel*, which describes the limits and varieties of gay men's dress.

H&M opens its first North American location, in New York City.

2001   Christopher Bailey (1971–) joins Burberry.

Hedi Slimane (1968–) is named creative director for Dior Homme.

2002   Crocs shoe company is founded in Boulder, Colorado. Since then, the company has sold more than 600 million shoes.

2003   Yohji Yamamoto collaborates with Adidas on Y-3, demonstrating the blurring lines between high fashion and sportswear.

Takashi Murakami (1962–) collaborates with Louis Vuitton to rework the company's classic LV monogram on a bestselling collection of handbags.

The television show *Queer Eye for the Straight Guy* appears on Bravo.

2004   Massachusetts is the first state to legalize same-sex marriage.

The design-competition television show *Project Runway* premieres on Bravo.

Thom Browne (1965–) launches his ready-to-wear menswear collection.

2005   Kevin Ma launches the website Hypebeast, which tracks sneaker culture and streetwear; the print magazine launches in 2012.

Raf Simons is named creative director at Jil Sander.

Scott Schuman (1968–) begins photographing street style for his blog, *The Sartorialist*.

David Beckham debuts his Instinct fragrance.

2006   Christopher Kane (1982–) launches his eponymous label.

Target debuts its Go International brand, which facilitates collaborations with designers that include Richard Chai (1974–), Jean Paul Gaultier, and Alexander McQueen.

2007   *Monocle* magazine launches.

2008   Riccardo Tisci (1974–) becomes menswear and accessories designer of Givenchy.

Jeremy Scott (1975–) collaborates with Adidas on his JS Wings and JS Bears sneakers.

Lucky Blue Smith (1998–) is scouted in Utah at ten years old.

André 3000 (1975–) unveils his Benjamin Bixby clothing line.

L'Oréal introduces a professional salon hair dye for men.

2009   The television show *RuPaul's Drag Race* first airs on the Logo network.

Eric Anderson's (1968–) book *Inclusive Masculinity* evaluates the development of a softer form of masculinity in the US and UK, and points to a new twenty-first-century version of masculinity that is less concerned about behaving in a hypermasculine way, recoding and embracing behaviors once deemed feminine.

Luis Venegas (1979–) launches *C*NDY* magazine as the first publication dedicated to the transgender community.

2010s   Fast-fashion retailers, such as H&M and Zara, replace their in-store merchandise on average every fourteen days.

Fashion continues to diversify and becomes more about personal style than dressing to match trends.

Sportswear brands, such as Supreme, Nike, and Adidas, increasingly collaborate with designers.

The turnover of high-profile designers increases at brands. There is also an increase in brand and designer collaborations.

Models are increasingly diverse in ethnicity, size, and gender expression in runway shows and marketing campaigns.

The rise of athleisure brands, such as Lululemon, makes sportswear acceptable outside of the gym.

2010   Alexander McQueen dies. His assistant Sarah Burton (1974–) succeeds him.

2011   The Metropolitan Museum of Art in New York City opens the *Alexander McQueen: Savage Beauty* exhibition, which stays open until midnight on the show's final days to accommodate demand.

GQ names Miles Davis (1926–1991) the most stylish musician of all time.

Rapper Kanye West's (1977–) first Yeezy show opens as part of New York Fashion Week.

2012   Raf Simons is named creative director of Dior.

Hedi Slimane is named creative director of Yves Saint Laurent.

London Collections: Men is launched by London Fashion Week to highlight British menswear designers. The event is renamed London Fashion Week's Men in 2017.

Nike unveils their Flyknit shoe, which is made with significantly less production waste.

LVMH purchases the made-to-measure Parisian brand Arnys and incorporates it into a branch of the high-end menswear and leather-goods maker Berluti.

2013   Nicolas Ghesquière (1971–) is named creative director of Louis Vuitton.

Jeremy Scott is named creative director of Moschino.

Kanye West and Adidas collaborate on Adidas Yeezy Boost 750.

More than one thousand garment workers are killed when the Rana Plaza garment-manufacturing building collapses in Bangladesh.

Thomas Pink Limited sues Victoria's Secret for marketing its Pink lingerie label.

2014   Riccardo Tisci collaborates with Nike on Air Force 1 shoes, then Nikelab x RT: Training Redefined in 2016.

Artist and model Sang Woo Kim (1994–) becomes the first Korean model to walk for Burberry.

2015   The Metropolitan Museum of Art opens the *China: Through the Looking Glass* exhibition, which sells more than 815,000 tickets.

Harold Koda (1950–) retires as chief costume curator at the Costume Institute, the Metropolitan Museum of Art. Andrew Bolton (1966–) steps in as his successor.

The US Supreme Court decision on Obergefell v. Hodges proclaims marriage equality for all.

The Council of Fashion Designers of America's (CFDA) New York Fashion Week: Men's launches, opening up more opportunities for menswear designers to show in New York City.

Alessandro Michele (1972–) is named creative director at Gucci.

Actors Ben Stiller (1965–) and Owen Wilson (1968–) close Valentino's Fall/Winter 2015 show in their roles as Derek Zoolander and Hansel to promote *Zoolander 2*.

2016 Designers, such as Tom Ford and Ralph Lauren, develop a see-now, buy-now style of runway show.

Raf Simons is named creative director at Calvin Klein.

A$AP Rocky (1988–) becomes the new face of Dior Homme, while also collaborating with JW Anderson on a menswear capsule collection. *Forbes* calls him the "Fashion Prince of Hip-Hop."

Fashion brands, including Tommy Hilfiger, Burberry, and Gucci, begin showing their menswear and womenswear collections together. While this consolidation is cited as a cost-saving measure, menswear-specific calendars, such as New York Fashion Week: Men's and London Collections: Men, slowly empty in response.

Vogue Man is launched as part of Condé Nast's *Vogue Arabia* publication.

Jaden Smith (1998–) appears in a skirt in Louis Vuitton's Series 4 womenswear campaign.

Street-style photographer Bill Cunningham dies.

2017 The CFDA announces it will combine its menswear and womenswear calendars for the Fall/Winter 2018 season at New York Fashion Week, with plans to maintain a menswear-specific week scheduled each year in July.

L'Uomo Vogue folds as part of a streamlining effort by Condé Nast Italia. The magazine relaunches in 2018 as a quarterly publication.

Models and designers wear a white bandana during fashion week as part of the #TiedTogether campaign, which celebrates unity and common humanity in the aftermath of the divisive 2016 American political election cycle.

Riccardo Tisci leaves Givenchy.

Edward Enninful (1972–) becomes the first Black editor in chief at British *Vogue*.

J.Crew restructures following the departure of creative director Jenna Lyons (1969–) and CEO Mickey Drexler (1944–).

Hugh Hefner (1926–2017), the founder of *Playboy* magazine, dies.

2018 Hedi Slimane is named creative director at Celine.

Riccardo Tisci is named chief creative officer of Burberry.

Dwyane Wade (1982–) signs a lifetime contract with the Chinese company Li-Ning Apparel.

Queer Eye for the Straight Guy is rebooted as *Queer Eye* on Netflix.

The Metropolitan Museum's *Heavenly Bodies: Fashion and the Catholic Imagination* exhibition becomes the most visited show ever, with more than 1.6 million tickets sold.

TikTok launches in the United States as a short-form video app. Influencers, such as Wisdom Kaye (2001–) and Everett Williams (1992–), amass millions of followers by posting outfit and style-related content.

Burberry burns 37.8 million dollars worth of unsold clothing, sparking a conversation about sustainable practices in the fashion industry.

Alton Mason (1997–) becomes the first Black male model to walk for Chanel.

Virgil Abloh (1980–) is named creative director of Louis Vuitton menswear, becoming the first Black designer to hold this position.

Marc Jacobs reissues his Perry Ellis Spring/Summer 1993 grunge collection.

Dapper Dan and Gucci collaborate on a collection based on Dan's 1980s creations. Gucci also helps him reopen his original Harlem boutique, which closed in 1992 after accusations of copyright infringement.

Colin Kaepernick (1987–) joins Nike's "Just Do It" campaign.

2019 Karl Lagerfeld dies.

Rihanna launches her Fenty brand with LVMH.

Tom Ford becomes chairman of the Council of Fashion Designers of America.

Kering, the parent company of Balenciaga, Gucci, Saint Laurent, and Bottega Veneta, makes plans to go carbon neutral by planting trees, casting local models, and sourcing more sustainable materials. Other companies, including Target, H&M, and Nike, have now joined Kering by pledging to be carbon neutral by 2050.

Actor Billy Porter (1969–) wears a tuxedo dress designed by Christian Siriano (1985–) to the Academy Awards.

Rent the Runway receives a billion-dollar valuation, demonstrating the development of a new market for rentable fashion.

Model Oslo Grace (1997–), who is nonbinary and transgender, wears both men's and women's looks in Kenzo's Fall/Winter show.

Aperture publishes the monograph *Kwame Brathwaite: Black Is Beautiful* dedicated to Brathwaite's photography, his founding of the African Jazz Arts Society and Studio (AJASS), and his use of the phrase "Black is beautiful" in the 1960s to advocate for Black beauty standards in US media.

2020s The COVID-19 pandemic creates a new market for virtual fashion shows by fashion brands such as Chanel, Saint Laurent, Balmain, Prada, and Maison Margiela.

The Korean boy band BTS is the most popular musical group of the moment.

Beauty influencers, such as Jeffree Star (1985–), James Charles (1999–), and Manny Mua (1991–), demonstrate that makeup for men is here to stay.

2020 Raf Simons is named cocreative director at Prada, sharing equal creative responsibilities with Miuccia Prada.

London Fashion Week opts for a combined presentation of fashion by incorporating menswear and nonbinary collections into the womenswear calendar.

Nigerian-British designer Mowalola Ogunlesi (1995–) is tapped to lead Kanye West's Yeezy Gap collaboration.

Barneys New York files for bankruptcy.

Black Lives Matter protests lead to a reevaluation of the fashion industry and its role in perpetuating systemic racism. The protests also spark a renewed interest in protest dressing, with many seeing the power in clothes as a tool for communication.

André 3000 releases a collection of T-shirts in support of the Black Lives Matter movement.

Gucci's Alessandro Michele introduces Gucci Mx, a genderless/nonbinary category on their website.

Harry Styles (1994–) becomes *Vogue*'s first solo male cover model, for the December issue.

The Chinese sportswear brand Li-Ning celebrates its thirtieth anniversary by teaming up with the Centre Pompidou in Paris for a three-year design partnership.

2021 Actor Timothée Chalamet (1995–) cochairs the 2021 Met Gala with tennis star Naomi Osaka (1997–), singer Billie Eilish (2001–), and poet Amanda Gorman (1998–).

As a response to the COVID-19 pandemic, Jonathan Anderson (1984–) and Jeremy Scott use paper doll faces and doll models, respectively, to show their Spring/Summer 2021 collections.

Brendon Babenzien (1972–), founder of the streetwear label Noah, is named creative director of the J.Crew men's collection.

CREDITS & ACKNOWLEDGMENTS

A project of this size requires the commitment and expertise of many people. We are particularly indebted to our consultant editor Jacob Gallagher for his vital contribution to the shaping of this book and his exhaustive knowledge.

Special thanks are also due to: Tom Beebe, Sarah Bell, Tonya Blazio-Licorish, Ed Burstell, Dr. Shaun Cole, Clare Coulson, Simon Doonan, Jenny Faithfull, Lucie Greene, Brontë Hebdon, Linda Lee, Laine Morreau, Natalie Nudell, Rosie Pickles, Marcellas Reynolds, Stefan Sagmeister, Jerry Stafford, André Leon Talley, Sarah Tucker, Jen Veall, and Elizabeth Way.

Finally, we would like to thank all the brands, designers, photographers, illustrators, collectors, and institutions who have given us permission to include their images.

TEXT CREDITS

James Anderson: 23, 130, 171, 199, 249, 251, 271, 303, 329, 354, 381, 403, 414, 450

Tim Cooke: 17, 22, 25, 29, 44, 48, 50–54, 65, 67, 69–70, 72, 78, 84, 86, 91, 108, 111, 114, 117–18, 120, 127, 135–36, 139, 141, 143, 152, 158, 160, 173–74, 177, 179, 186, 189–90, 203, 207, 210–12, 218–19, 222, 226, 230–31, 241–42, 244–46, 250, 252–53, 260, 277, 279, 285–88, 295–97, 299, 301, 306, 314, 316, 319–20, 327–28, 335, 337–38, 343, 350, 370, 373, 380, 388–89, 392, 394, 397, 401, 409–10, 412–13, 423, 425, 428–29, 434, 436, 438, 447, 451, 456, 472, 479–81, 484, 488–89, 491, 499, 506

Clare Coulson: 39, 58, 61, 63, 66, 68, 73, 83, 90, 100, 113, 129, 165, 180, 188, 209, 220, 266, 268, 292, 305, 313, 336, 382, 384, 406–8, 426, 440, 445, 460, 467, 503

Jacob Gallagher: 5–10, 13–16, 18–19, 21, 27, 32, 34, 36–38, 40, 42–43, 49, 56–57, 59, 62, 74, 76, 79, 87–89, 92, 94, 97, 99, 103–4, 109–10, 116, 119, 122, 131–32, 134, 142, 145–47, 149, 154, 157, 161, 168, 172, 178, 182–85, 187, 191, 193–94, 196, 202, 204, 206, 208, 213–14, 216–17, 221, 225, 227–28, 232–34, 236, 238, 248, 257–59, 261–62, 265, 269–70, 274, 280, 283, 289, 291, 293–94, 298, 300, 304, 309, 315, 318, 321, 325–26, 331–34, 341, 348–49, 353, 357–61, 365, 367, 371–72, 374–77, 379, 398, 402, 416, 420–21, 424, 427, 432, 435, 439, 441–44, 449, 458–59, 462–66, 470, 475–76, 478, 483, 487, 490, 492, 494–96, 501–2, 505, 508–10

Brontë Hebdon: 512–19

Linda Lee: 30, 95, 144, 167, 276, 364, 368, 419, 437, 497

Elizabeth Peng: 20, 24, 28, 33, 35, 41, 45–47, 55, 64, 71, 75, 77, 80–81, 85, 96, 102, 106–7, 115, 121, 123, 125–26, 128, 133, 138, 155–56, 159, 162, 164, 170, 175–76, 195, 197, 200–1, 205, 215, 224, 234, 237, 239, 243, 255, 263–64, 267, 278, 281–82, 290, 302, 308, 310–12, 322–24, 340, 342, 347, 351–52, 356, 363, 369, 383, 385–87, 390, 396, 400, 418, 422, 430–31, 433, 446, 448, 452, 454, 468–69, 473–74, 477, 486, 500, 504, 507, 511

Daniel Penny: 60, 93, 98, 105, 112, 150–51, 166, 169, 192, 198, 229, 254, 275, 307, 317, 378, 405, 417, 453, 482

Todd Plummer: 26, 31, 101, 140, 223, 339, 355, 366, 391, 399, 411, 455, 461

Rebecca Roke: 82, 137, 148, 153, 163, 181, 240, 247, 256, 272–73, 284, 344, 346, 362, 395, 485, 498

Tyler Watamanuk: 12, 124, 330, 345, 393, 404, 415, 457, 493

PICTURE CREDITS

Every effort has been made to trace the copyright holders and obtain permission to reproduce this material. The publisher apologizes for any errors or omissions in the below list and would be grateful if notified of any corrections that should be incorporated in future reprints or editions of this book.

Slim Aarons/Getty Images: 69, 96, 465; Slim Aarons/Hulton Archive/Getty Images: 153; Brian Ach/Getty Images for Mercedes-Benz Fashion Week Spring 2014: 255; © Acielle/ Styledumonde.com: 175, 218; Campbell Addy/Trunk Archive: 23; Courtesy The Advertising Archives/Levi Strauss & Co. Archives: 442; © agnès b.: 464; © Mert Alas and Marcus Piggott/Art Partner: 330; American Movie Classics (AMC)/Radical Media/ Album: 97; © Andover Center for History and Culture, Massachusetts: 35; www.Andreas-Hofer-Photography.at: 387; Jorgen Angel/Redferns/Getty Images: 303; Photography: David Nana Opoku Ansah, Art Direction: Florian Joahn (@Florian Joahn), Styling: Edem Dossou (@edemdl), Make Up: Elizabeth Boateng (@elizabethboateng.mua): 148; Shoichi Aoki/FRUiTS: 193; Don Arnold/WireImage/Getty Images: 502; © Eve Arnold/ Magnum Photos: 170, 314; Courtesy A. Sauvage: 14; Benjamin Auger/Paris Match via Getty Images: 228; Avalon.Red: 417, 472; AVCO Embassy Pictures/John Springer Collection/CORBIS/ Corbis via Getty Images: 207; Hamid Bagherzadeh/Samsa G. Tuchwaren: 377; © David Bailey: 52; © Lachlan Bailey/Art Partner: 140; Photograph: Pierre Bailly, Styling: Camille Bidault-Waddington, Makeup: Christine Corbel, Hair: Sébastien Richard: 462; Nathan Bajar/The New York Times/Redux: 312; Marc Baptiste/Corbis via Getty Images: 37; © Gian Paolo Barbieri: 179; Photo Anthony Barboza: 56; Neilson Barnard/ Getty Images for Tommy Hilfiger: 234; Courtesy Fabien Baron: 61; Vanni Bassetti/Getty Images: 460; Sophie Bassouls/Sygma via Getty Images: 53; © The Cecil Beaton Studio Archive: 66; © The Cecil Beaton Studio Archive at Sotheby's: 236; Keith Beaty/Toronto Star via Getty Images: 276; Jonathan Becker: 450; © Janette Beckman: 165; Janette Beckman/Getty Images: 181; The Geoffrey Beene mark is used Courtesy PVH Corp: 70; General Collection, Beinecke Rare Book and Manuscript Library, Yale University/© DACS 2021: 54; Peter Berlin: 76; Bettmann/ Getty Images: 47; Bettmann Archive/Getty Images: 169; Bikkembergs: 80; Ben Birchall/WPA Pool via Getty Images Entertainment: 41; Cass Bird: 82, 319; Bleacher + Everard/Corbis via Contour by Getty Images: 471; BodyMap Archive: 90; Gregory Bojorquez/Getty Images: 348; Jean-Pierre Bonnotte/ Gamma-Rapho via Getty Images: 154; Bottega Veneta Fall/ Winter 2010 Ad Campaign, photographed by Robert Longo: 93; Victor Boyko/Getty Images: 163; Samuel Bradley: 49; Courtesy The Kwame Brathwaite Archive and Philip Martin Gallery: 95; Bridgeman Images: 100, 219, 309, 356; Jacques Brinon/AP/ Shutterstock: 321; Matthew Brookes/Trunk Archive: 287; Hamish Brown/Avalon.Red: 395; © Linda Brownlee/Guardian/ eyevine: 238; Courtesy Galerie Buchholz, Berlin/Cologne, Maureen Paley, London, David Zwirner, New York: 456; Courtesy the Burton Historical Collection, Detroit Public Library: 233; Jerry Buttles: 274; Courtesy the Carhartt Archive: 110; Francesco Carrozzini/Trunk Archive: 111, 493; © Micaiah Carter/AUGUST: 112; The Cary Collection: 50; F. E. Castleberry: 420; Catwalking.com/Image from Raf Simons Autumn/Winter 2003 collection (on Parka imagery by Peter Saville): 408; Catwalking/Getty Images: 104, 107; Alo Ceballos/FilmMagic/ Getty Images: 341; Melchizedek Chan: 400; charlesward.com: 463; © Brent Chua: 124; Ricky Chung/South China Morning Post via Getty Images: 126; William Claxton/Courtesy Demont Photo Management, LLC: 203; Danny Clinch/By kind permission of Iggy Pop: 477; © Tom Cockram: 426; Courtesy Kenneth Cole: 133; © Alberto Colombo/Karen Film: 407; Columbia Pictures/ Michel Dufour/Getty Images: 412; Hugo Comte: 323; Jerry Cooke/Sports Illustrated via Getty Images: 361; Mike Coppola/ Getty Images for Instagram: 299; Cordings of Piccadilly: 138; Laura Jane Coulson: 128; © Wyatt Counts: 149; William Coupon/ Trunk Archive: 333; Ralph Crane/The LIFE Images Collection via Getty Images: 445; Matt Crossick/Alamy Stock Photo: 382; J. D. Cuban/Sports Illustrated via Getty Images: 351; Lachlan Cunningham/Getty Images: 99; Fabrice Dall'Anese/Corbis via Getty Images: 88; Darling Creative: 385; Loomis Dean/The LIFE Picture Collection via Getty Images: 141; Alain Dejean/Sygma via Getty Images: 293; Angelo Deligio/Mondadori via Getty Images: 320; Michel Descamps/Paris Match via Getty Images: 327; DETAILS/Stephan Lupino/Courtesy Galerija Fotografija Gallery: 156; James Devaney/GC Images/Getty Images: 68; Dickies: 158; Digital Catwalk: 195; © Henry Diltz: 396; Dinodia Photos/Alamy Stock Photo: 279; © Adrien Dirand: 261; John Dominis/The LIFE Premium Collection via Getty Images via Getty Images: 73; © Dufoto/ArchiviFarabola: 216; François Durand/Getty Images: 71; Alfred Eisenstaedt/The LIFE Picture Collection via Getty Images: 48; Embassy Pictures/ Courtesy Everett Collection: 373; Empty R_ _M/Yuta Nishiya: 281; Abraham Englemark: 401; Published in Esquire magazine, June 1965. Photography by Timothy Galfas: 173; Estrop/Getty Images: 247; Evisu Group Limited: 510; © The Face/Photography by Sheila Rock: 176; Courtesy Cary Fagan: 275; Sam Falk/The New York Times/ Redux: 378; Courtesy Fanatics: 345; Lam Yik Fei/Bloomberg via Getty Images: 121; Kay-Paris Fernandes/Getty Images: 74, 89; © Martina Ferrara/Courtesy Marni: 318; © Pierpaolo Ferrari: 26; Tristan Fewings/Getty Images for Woolmark/Stringer: 85; Filson: 182; Tabatha Fireman/BFC/Getty Images: 398; © firstVIEW/IMAXtree: 62; © Fondo SEMO, Fototeca Nacional, Pachuca, Hidalgo, Mexico (329514 CONACULTA. INAH-SINAFO-FN-Mexico): 458; Natasja Fourie/Courtesy John Smedley: 264; © Horst Friedrichs: 205, Horst Friedrichs/Alamy Stock Photo: 390; The Estate of David Gahr/Getty Images: 94; Ron Galella/Ron Galella Collection via Getty Images: 389; Ron Galella, Ltd./Ron Galella Collection via Getty Images: 199, 328; Advertisement provided by Gap Inc. Heritage Lab/With permission from the Hans Malmberg Estate: 198; Jack Garofalo/ Paris Match via Getty Images: 184; Jesse D. Garrabrant/NBAE via Getty Images. Styling: Wesmore Perriott of Defending Champs, LLC. @padrewesmore: 208; © Alexandre Gaudin: 404; Tierney Gearon: 331; Stan Gellers/Robert Melendez/Courtesy Fairchild Archive. Copyright © by Fairchild Publishing, LLC. All Rights Reserved. Used by Permission.: 161, 201; Boo George: 308; Alain Gil-Gonzalez/Abacapress.com: 501; Lynn Goldsmith/ Corbis/VCG via Getty Images: 317; Bob Gothard: 416; Goyard: 209; Tim Graham Photo Library via Getty Images: 58; Sergio Del Grande/Mondadori via Getty Images: 118; Granger Historical Picture Archive/Alamy Stock Photo/The Arrow mark is used Courtesy PVH Corp: 44; Richard Grassie: 33; Milton Greene/ Condé Nast/Shutterstock: 151; François Guillot/AFP via Getty Images: 200, 298, 399; Jacques Habbah: 315; Emme Gene Hall/ Condé Nast/Shutterstock: 210; Gijsbert Hanekroot/Redferns via Getty Images: 240, 251; Gregory Harris/Trunk Archive: 307; Paul Harris/Getty Images: 322; Frazer Harrison/Getty Images: 188; Paul Hartnett/PYMCA/Universal Images Group via Getty Images: 84; Koh Hasebe/Shinko Music/Getty Images: 332; Haspel Photo Archives: 226; Jamie Hawkesworth: 227; Jamie Hawkesworth/Courtesy Loewe: 34; Andy Hayt/Sports Illustrated via Getty Images: 367; Hemingway Copyright Owners: 198; Thearon W. Henderson/Getty Images: 115; Hermès advertisement for ties, 1962. Draeger. Archives Hermès © Hermès 2021.: 232; © Lizzie Himmel: 63; Kin Ho/Camera Press/Redux: 142; © Thomas Hoepker/Magnum Photos: 29; Marc Hom/Trunk Archive: 291; Dale Hope: 127; Horst P. Horst/Condé Nast/ Shutterstock: 406; Horst P. Horst, Vogue © Condé Nast: 503; Frank Horvat: 263; Hulton Archive/Getty Images: 242, 346, 487; Hulton-Deutsch/Hulton-Deutsch Collection/Corbis via Getty Images: 212; © Hulton-Deutsch Collection/CORBIS/Corbis via Getty Images: 397; Portia Hunt: 214; Courtesy i-D Magazine: 190, 243; Masanori Ikeda: 244; Imagno/Getty Images: 113, 286; ITV/ Shutterstock: 221; Hiroyuki Iwata: 448; Colin Jacob/Waraire Boswell/wb@wbi.me: 92; Paul Jasmin: 59; Melodie Jeng/Getty Images: 13; Melodie Jeng/Getty Images Entertainment Video: 217; Photographer: Tom Johnson, Stylist: Robbie Spencer: 429; Johnson Publishing Company Archive. Courtesy Ford Foundation, J. Paul Getty Trust, John D. and Catherine T. MacArthur Foundation, Andrew W. Mellon Foundation and Smithsonian Institution: 160, 167; © Colin Jones/TopFoto: 211; Keystone Pictures USA/ZUMA Press/Alamy Stock Photo: 174; Keystone/Getty Images: 39; Keystone/Hulton Archive/Getty Images: 260; © King Collection/Retna/Photoshot: 246; Vicki King: 354; Neil Kirk: 241; Douglas Kirkland/Corbis via Getty Images: 79; Ross Kirton: 509; Glenn Kitson on behalf of Umbro: 466; © Steven Klein: 284; Nick Knight/Trunk Archive: 285; Robert Knudsen/White House Photographs/John F. Kennedy Presidential Library and Museum, Boston: 277; Kobal/ Shutterstock: 380; Dave Kotinsky/Getty Images: 278; © Bob Krieger, GQ/Condé Nast: 497; K & K Ulf Kruger OHG/Getty Images: 229; Photography: Maciej Kucia, Fashion Director: Grant Pierce, Styling: Jason Lee, Hair & Make-up: KEN, Model: Hu

Phaidon Press Limited
2 Cooperage Yard
London E15 2QR

Phaidon Press Inc.
65 Bleecker Street
New York, NY 10012

phaidon.com

First published 2021
© 2021 Phaidon Press Limited

ISBN 978 1 83866 247 9

A CIP catalogue record for this book is available from the
British Library and the Library of Congress.

Commissioning Editor: William Norwich
Project Editors: Lynne Ciccaglione and Sarah Massey
Production Controller: Lily Rodgers
Design: Hans Stofregen
Layout: Luísa Martelo

Cover design by Julia Hasting
Cover artwork by Christoph Niemann

Printed in China

Abbreviations

		JAM	Jamaica
		JAP	Japan
AG	Antigua and Barbuda	KOR	Korea
ALG	Algeria	LUX	Luxembourg
ASL	Australia	MEX	Mexico
AUS	Austria	ML	Mali
BEL	Belgium	MOR	Morocco
BEN	Benin	NG	Nigeria
BHS	Bahamas	NL	Netherlands
CAN	Canada	NZ	New Zealand
CHN	China	PH	Philippines
CIV	Ivory Coast	POL	Poland
COD	Democratic Republic	PR	Puerto Rico
	of the Congo	RUS	Russia
COL	Colombia	SA	South Africa
CR	Costa Rica	SLE	Sierra Leone
DOM	Dominican Republic	SP	Spain
FR	France	SW	Switzerland
GE	Georgia	SWE	Sweden
GER	Germany	TT	Trinidad and Tobago
GHA	Ghana	TUN	Tunisia
HT	Haiti	TUR	Turkey
IN	India	UK	United Kingdom
IRE	Ireland	USA	United States
IT	Italy	UY	Uruguay